HOSPITALITY Information Technology

LEARNING HOW TO USE IT

Galen R. Collins, Ph.D.
Northern Arizona University
galen.collins@nau.edu

Cihan Cobanoglu, Ph.D., CHTP
University of South Florida, Sarasota–Manatee
cihan@udel.edu

Anil Bilgihan, Ph.D.
Florida Atlantic University

Kendall Hunt
publishing company

Cover image © Shutterstock, Inc.

Kendall Hunt
publishing company

www.kendallhunt.com
Send all inquiries to:
4050 Westmark Drive
Dubuque, IA 52004-1840

ISBN 978-1-4652-2407-1

Printed in the United States of America

10 9 8 7 6 5 4 3 2 1

Imagination

In a 1996 study, college students were given a set of data and were asked to see if they could come up with a mathematical relation. Almost a third did. What they did not know was that they had just solved one of the most famous scientific equations in history: the Third Law of Planetary Motion, an equation that Johannes Kepler came up with in 1618...Kepler's genius was not so much in solving a mathematical challenge. It was thinking about the numbers in a unique way—applying his mathematical knowledge to his observations of planetary motion. It was his boldness that set him apart.

Michael Ryan, "Who Is Great,"
The Arizona Republic, June 16, 1996

Contents

A Special Message from Galen Collins...

The hospitality industry is quickly becoming automated. Because hospitality information technologies are evolving rapidly and becoming more complex, it is imperative that a person wishing to enter the hospitality business be trained to deal with a pioneering and ever-changing industry.

As in other types of industry, manpower is being replaced daily by machine power and the only people who will survive in an automated society are those who are familiar with the technology propelling it forward. Actually, a computerized and automated world presses the population to be better educated and more highly skilled even as it seemingly cruelly reduces the workforce.

It is wise to remember that, as useful as sophisticated computer systems are, the hospitality industry is first and foremost a people business. A computer cannot replace the warmth and personal attention from a well-trained employee nor can it embody the spirit of this Hospitality Creed:

The Hospitality Creed

Galen Robert Collins
Ann Averitt Collins

Help us to serve
Our guests with
Sensitivity and concern
Providing for their requests
Inspired by their needs
Transmitted through their words
Always looking for better ways to
Lighten their burdens and to
Improve conditions for them as they
Travel through life and
Yearn for the best...

Acknowledgments

I think and think for months and years.
Ninety-nine times, the conclusion is false.
The hundredth time I am right

Albert Einstein

We wish to acknowledge the following individuals for their contributions to the book:

Barry Biegler, President, Resort Data Processing, Inc.
Todd Davis, CIO, Choice Hotels International
Michael Fodor, Vice President of Marketing and Sales, F&B Management
Jon Inge, President, Jon Inge and Associates
Rick Munson, President and CEO of Multi-Systems, Inc.
Andrew Nataf, Senior Business Development Manager, Menusoft Systems
John Nessel, President, Restaurant Resource Group, Inc.
Lenore O'Meara, Publisher, Hospitality Technology
Bill Schwartz, CEO, Systems Concepts, Inc.
Richard Siegel, President and Publisher, Hospitality Upgrade

CHAPTER 1

Information Systems & Technology

"The most valuable commodity I know of is information. Wouldn't you agree?"

Gordon Gekko, the character played by Michael Douglas in the film Wall Street

CHAPTER OUTLINE

Source: © Adchariyaphoto, 2013. Used under license from Shutterestock, Inc.

> *"How do you create influential content that creates absolute focused engagement and a relationship with you? The answer is through using massive amounts of raw data, referred to as "big data" that has been transformed into relevant, personalized, localized, and interactive content and delivered to your ubiquitous device on demand."*
>
> Todd Davis,
> CIO, Choice Hotels International

Information Processing

Input Phase

Information is a finished product. It is data or raw material that has been processed to give it meaning and usefulness. The transformation process can be viewed as the **information system**. The information system consists of four phases:

1. **Input Phase.** During this phase, data is collected and converted into a form suitable for processing. Data is generated when a comment card is completed, a food order is placed, a wake-up call is requested, or a beverage invoice is received.

Processing Phase

2. **Processing Phase.** Processing is the work performed on the data. This includes calculating, classifying, sorting, and summarizing.

Calculating

a. *Calculating.* This is the manipulation of data using the arithmetic functions of addition, division, multiplication, and subtraction. Some common hospitality calculations include average guest check, average daily rate, and occupancy rate. Since the majority of work is performed during this phase, it is the most crucial.

Classifying

b. *Classifying.* This involves the grouping and categorizing of data according to some criteria. For example, a restaurant operator may request average wage rates by job position or a hotel operator may request an occupancy summary by market segment.

Sorting

c. *Sorting.* Once data is classified, it can be arranged alphabetically or numerically. For example, an employee list can be sorted by last names or by identification numbers.

Summarizing

d. *Summarizing.* This involves condensing data into a precise and meaningful form. An example of a summary report would be an income statement.

Output Phase

3. **Output Phase.** This phase involves the preparation of processed information into a form acceptable for analysis. The most common form of output is a report. A report is of little value unless it reaches the person who can act upon it. Communication is a critical link. For example, a report indicating an acute linen shortage must be promptly communicated to the executive housekeeper.

An effective information system will inform management when results deviate from predetermined goals. This **FEEDBACK** is necessary for operational control so that management knows when corrective action is necessary. For example, a guest comment card analysis indicates 60 percent of guests will return to the hotel, far below the management's projected goal of 90 percent. The problem must be precisely defined before making any operational changes. Consequently, questions are added to the guest comment card. The next guest comment card analysis reveals that the room rates are perceived as a poor value. Management decides to reduce the room rates. The next guest comment card analysis reports that the percentage of guests returning to the hotel exceeds the 90 percent goal. Management decides that no further action is necessary.

Feedback makes the information system responsive and focused on producing meaningful management information.

An information system may be composed of many subsystems (see Figure 1-1), each with a distinct purpose but where the output of one subsystem often becomes the input to another. For example, a front desk clerk cannot assign a room unless it is unoccupied and clean. Housekeeping provides this information. Likewise, housekeeping needs to know

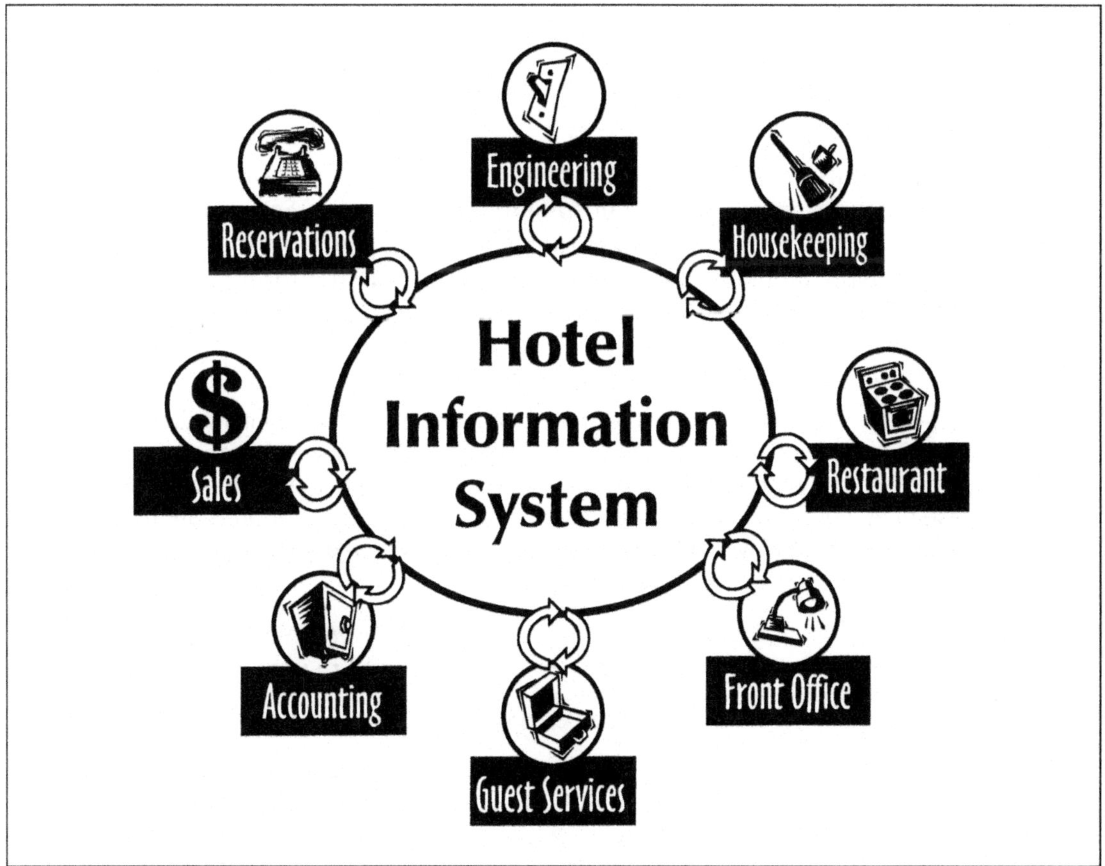

FIGURE 1-1. INFORMATION SYSTEM.

what rooms are occupied to make cleaning assignments each morning. The front office provides this information. This **INTERDEPENDENCY** or mutual dependence forces subsystems such as housekeeping and the front office to be linked together to function properly. If this interaction is not well-coordinated, it can cause serious problems such as guests being checked into dirty rooms.

Storage Phase

4. **Storage Phase.** After data has been processed, it is commonly stored for later use. There are many instances where historical information is required. Operations need to accumulate year-to-date statistics and financial totals for accounting purposes and to frequently compare these totals to previous periods to gauge performance. An example would be a five-year sales summary (shown in Figure 1-2). Information can be kept in the form of handwritten guest records in a reservation book or stored in a computerized reservation system. Computers have had a dramatic impact

on information processing. Data is collected, processed, stored, retrieved, and communicated more easily as a result of computers.

Computer-Based Information System

Information systems and technology are key enablers of information management and successful operations in competitive hospitality environments. Selecting appropriate technology solutions, however, requires careful research and planning and alignment with business strategies, which remains a top priority for business and information technology (IT) professionals (1).

> A computer—any computer, even a slow one—is fast because it treats information symbolically. Computers don't get physical, instead they work with weightless patterns of bits that represent real numbers, words, and graphics. It's like a game of Monopoly where, in the space of an hour, land is bought and sold, hotels rise and fall, fortunes are made and lost largely because players move tokens, not dirt, bricks, and dollars.
>
> Dr. Harold Goldes,
> "Performance Art," *The Prodigy Star* (December 1991)

What is a **computer**? According to Arno Penzias (2):

Stripped of its interfaces, a bare computer boils down to little more than a pocket computer calculator that can push its own buttons and remember what it has done. Obeying a stored sequence (or PROGRAM*) of instructions, it moves, adds, subtracts, multiplies, and divides numbers at blinding speeds, hauling them in and out of its memory as needed. Individually, each of these operations would require in human hands nothing more than paper and pencil. Computers merely add speed and diligence to the process. Most of a computer's operations come straight from mathematics (like addition and multiplication), while others come from logic (such as, If A = B, skip the next instruction).*

The hardware and software required for a computer-based information system (CBIS) will depend on the specific needs of the organization. The following pages discuss basic hardware and software components used in hospitality information systems.

	2008	2009	2010	2011	2012
Sales	$500,000	$600,000	$800,000	$975,000	$1,300,000
Check	$10.00	$10.50	$11.75	$11.50	$12.00
Covers	50,000	57,143	68,085	84,783	108,333

FIGURE 1-2. FIVE-YEAR SALES SUMMARY FOR RIBS UNLIMITED.

Hardware

Input Devices

Hardware refers to the physical apparatus of the computer systems, which consists of input devices, central processing units (CPU), storage devices, output devices, and communication devices.

1. **Input Devices.** A **KEYBOARD** is the most widely used device for entering text information into a computer. It is used in conjunction with a **MONITOR** or screen which displays the input and the user's response. When these two devices are linked, it forms a **TERMINAL**.

There are various keyboard layouts that improve typing efficiency and accuracy and prevent injury. The **QWERTY KEYBOARD** is the universally accepted arrangement of characters on 99 percent of typing devices. QWERTY was deliberately designed to slow down the human typist at a time when typewriter parts moved so slowly that they would jam if the operator typed too fast. The **DVORAK LAYOUT**, for example, minimizes finger movement by placing frequently used keys in the home row. **ERGONOMIC KEYBOARDS** are also available for those who spend long stretches at the keyboard and want to prevent hand or wrist problems, such as carpal-tunnel syndrome. An ergonomic keyboard divides the keyboard into two angled sections so that the hands are positioned at a natural angle when typing.

While typewriter keys are simply triggers, computer keys initiate electronic signals that are interpreted by the CPU. Computer keys must be converted into numbers (e.g., A = 01000001 where 8 bits = 1 byte or character). The computer uses two digits, 1 and 0, since its electronic circuits only have two states, on (1) and off (0). The meaning assigned to a key may be a symbol or task rather than a character. For example, a restaurant cash register keyboard could use a touch-sensitive membrane panel where a particular key represents the item for sale, such as French fries or a hamburger.

The greatest obstacle to computer use has been the method of inputting data. Before the keyboard, keypunch cards were used to input data. The user had to punch holes into computer cards using a special piece of equipment and then transport these cards to a compiler for processing. This process was very time-consuming and error-prone. Going from keypunch cards to a keyboard greatly expanded the number of users. Nonetheless, those with weak or nonexistent typing skills may find using a computer challenging. Unfortunately, there is nothing intuitive about a keyboard.

The keyboard represents a first-level interface. Subsequent input devices popular in the hospitality industry include the ubiquitous mouse and touchscreens. Most people who have used these input devices agree that they make it easier to use the computer.

Wireless keyboards are used in hotel rooms. For example, guest rooms at the Dream Downtown Hotel in Manhattan are equipped with Internet-ready 40" televisions with wireless keyboards.

TOUCHSCREEN monitors (screen keyboards) allow viewers to respond to the computer by simply touching the screens. Touchscreens have become more affordable and reliable.

When is Memory *not* Memory?
A: When it is storage.
There are two parts of your computer that are often misunderstood. They are the hard disk and the Random Access Memory, or RAM as it's most often called. The relationship between the RAM and the hard disk is much like that between a factory and a warehouse. The hard disk, like the warehouse, stores all the programs and data your computer uses. RAM, like the factory, runs programs and processes data.
RAM, like the factory, has a set work capacity. In search of greater computing power, some users believe that they will have increased processing capacity if they get a bigger hard disk. Then they discover that disk is like having a larger warehouse. Having more storage room doesn't mean increased production if nothing has changed at the factory. Your old RAM, like the factory, still has to operate in the same working space it had before the new hard disk was added.
If you find that you cannot load large programs, you may need more RAM. Or, if you have a lot of data to store such as duplicate data for multiple companies, you may need a larger hard disk.
RAM INC.
1 GB Factory
2 Terabyte WAREHOUSE

FIGURE 1-3. DIFFERENCE BETWEEN SECONDARY (HARD DISK) AND PRIMARY (RAM) STORAGE.

Source: Fisher Restaurant Systems, Marietta, GA

Various hospitality environments, including casinos, restaurants, hotels, theme parks, cruise ships, and airports, use touchscreen technologies. Diners at California-based Stacked Restaurants, for example, input orders using tableside iPads.

Voice or speech recognition technologies have advanced rapidly in recent years, making the Star Trek vision of human/computer interactions a reality. **Interactive voice response (IVR)** systems use computer-based voice recognition and software algorithms to conduct human/computer interactions (3). IVR can be used to control almost any task where the interface can be broken down into a series of simple interactions, such as a customer requesting the location of a restaurant.

A **voice portal**, the voice equivalent of Web Portals, provides a unique way to access the Web from mobile locations. A voice portal includes a voice browser allowing customers to access Web information from a telephone, cell phone, or smart phone. Automatic speech recognition connects a user directly to the Web site with voice prompts without a personal or handheld computer. This speech-enabled customer extends the reach of travel-related Web sites to a much wider and mobile population. In 2006, an airline inquiry voice portal was launched in Dubai to provide callers with up-to-the-minute airline schedules for flights in and out of Dubai International Airport. The first of its kind in the Arab world, this voice portal can recognize multiple accents and dialects in both English and Arabic. In 2011, Best Western International launched an advanced conversational voice portal for members of its Best Western Rewards loyalty program, enabling them to quickly obtain account information, redeem awards, and get details about program benefits.

Pen-based systems are portable or handheld computers with pen-like styluses for handwriting and pen gestures (e.g., tapping menu choices or keyboard letters). These systems can be used for taking notes, completing forms, or as a paperless signature system. For example, customers can sign for their credit card purchases on LCD tablets or screens, reducing paper waste.

Some handheld computers are also called **smart phones** (e.g., iPhone) and **personal digital assistants** (PDAs). Some of them operate by single touch or multi touch, allowing gestures and interaction with multiple fingers and hands. Others have small keyboards. Both can be equipped with wireless data transmitters for checking in hotel guests, tracking inventory, taking food orders as well as accessing online travel information and reservation systems. The transmitters are also used to connect to satellite-based navigation systems or global positioning systems (GPS). Tourists use a GPS to find specific locations. For example, BMW, an auto manufacturer, has teamed with Micros, a property management systems vendor, and VingCard Elsafe, a hotel lock and safe vendor, to enable BMW drivers to use their vehicles' GPS and Internet search features to book and pay for room reservations from the car and then to bypass the hotel front desk and open their guest rooms using their near-field communication (NFC – short–range wireless technology) equipped car keys.

Some input processes can be automated using **scanners** and **bar code readers**. A scanner is a photocopier-like device that takes a snapshot of a page (e.g., legal document, business card) and electronically saves it, enabling it to be easily accessed when needed. Bar code readers interpret bar codes, convert them into numbers, and then input the numbers. Bar code readers are used to identify such things as inventory items, luggage, and packages. Federal Express, which has more computers than it does employees, uses bar code technology to track every single package distinctly. Restaurants can use bar code technology to count inventory and upload it directly into an inventory software system.

A **SENSOR** is an input device that collects specific data (e.g., temperature, humidity, pressure, light, occupancy, movement, smoke, etc.) directly from the environment and then transmits it to a computer. In hotels, occupancy sensors are used to reduce energy usage by lighting and HVAC systems in unoccupied spaces (e.g., conference room, guestroom). In restaurants, wireless temperature sensors alert managers via cell phone text messages when cooling unit temperatures surpass food safety thresholds.

RADIO-FREQUENCY IDENTIFICATION (RFID) tags or electronic labels could eventually replace bar code labels. RFID technology uses wireless communication in radio frequency bands to transmit data from tags (microchips) to readers. It automatically identifies objects or people with RFID tags. Transmitted tag data often acts as input to further data processing. Wireless identification systems can be used for safeguarding and tracking inventory and assets, guestroom and building access control, cashless payment systems, baggage handling, customer safety, and public monitoring. The KeyLime Cove Water Resort in Gurnee, Illinois, for example, is deploying an RFID wristband system. It provides customers with automated cashless point-of-sale (POS), keyless entry to hotel rooms and lockers, and cashless vending and spending in the arcade. The Star City Casino in Sydney, Australia placed RFID tags on 80,000 uniforms. This reduced the number of lost and stolen garments as well laundry bill discrepancies.

Another method for identifying people is to use a **BIOMETRIC SYSTEM** to evaluate one or more biological traits (e.g., fingerprints, earlobe and hand geometry, iris and retina patterns, voice waves, etc.). Unique characteristics are captured through biometric scanners, converted into digital forms using software, and are then stored in databases. Later, to verify a person's identity, a new record is captured and compared with the previous record. If the new data matches what is in the database, the identity is confirmed. Biometric applications include recognition of VIP customers and access controls to physical locations and equipment, computer systems, and time and attendance systems. Many hospitality companies are using biometric time clocks to eliminate buddy punching and unauthorized early-in and late-out punches. The Venetian Macao-Resort-Hotel, Macau, Taipa Island, for example, uses face readers to authenticate 12,000 employees at the front entrance when a new shift starts and fingerprint readers to control access to restricted areas. The 1,200-room Hilton Americas-Houston, Houston's largest hotel, is using facial recognition technology to locate missing suitcases by following the luggage piece using a search based on color and object from the time it entered the hotel through to its present location. More than 7,000 items are reported missing each year at this hotel.

CPU

2. **CPU.** The heart of a computer is the CPU where data is processed. The CPU's internal circuitry consists of:

Arithmetic/Logic Unit

a. *An Arithmetic/Logic Unit (ALU).* The ALU unit performs computations on data.

Control Unit

b. *A Control Unit.* This unit supervises the execution of program instructions, directs input and output, and controls the flow of information within the machine.

Primary Storage

c. *Primary Storage.* This is where data and programs are held for processing on a temporary basis. Once data is processed it is permanently stored on a secondary storage medium for later use. Common secondary storage devices include a USB flash drive, hard disk, and magnetic tape. These items will be defined in later paragraphs (see Figure 1-3).

Primary storage or main memory consists of **RANDOM-ACCESS MEMORY** (RAM) and **READ-ONLY MEMORY** (ROM). Unlike ROM, the CPU can read and write data in RAM, enabling the user to modify data until it is ready for printing or storage. ROM contains a program that informs the computer where to find and load the computer's operating system, which is required for the computer to function and manage its operations. ROM program instructions are permanently stored and cannot be changed. However, when a computer is turned off, RAM is cleared of its contents. For example, a student working on a term paper 10 pages long must save his document to secondary storage before turning off the computer.

RAM storage capacity is measured in bytes. Most personal computers today are equipped with at least 1,000,000,000 bytes (1GB) of RAM. The number of bytes required depends on how much space the program and data occupy. The author can remember purchasing the Timex/Sinclair 1000 and using this machine to write a small program. After writing about half the program, a memory overflow error occurred. The program size had exceeded its memory capacity of only 8,000 bytes. The Timex/Sinclair 1000 was a short-lived product that failed because of its design and limited capabilities. It was a poor investment and now resides in the author's office as a reminder of the past.

Speed

d. *Speed.* The CPU affects the rate at which information is processed. The CPU of mainframe computers processes information more quickly than midrange computers and supports more users. CPU operating speed or power is measured in gigahertz (GHz) or million instructions per second (MIPS). It is important to make sure that there is enough processing power to handle all system requests. Otherwise, the system could "crash" or become too slow for users to carry out tasks efficiently and effectively.

The CPU is the electronic brain where all software commands turn into action. In a personal computer (PC), it is the biggest chip on the **MOTHERBOARD**, the main circuit board that connects to all the other components. There are various types of CPUs that operate at different clock speeds. The higher the CPU rating the quicker the computer's software will work. The first IBM personal computer ran at a 4.77 megahertz (MHz) with an 8088 processor. The newest processors operate at speeds greater than 3000 MHz or 3 GHz.

RAM (main memory), comprised of chips that are installed on the motherboard, also impacts a PC's speed. More RAM enables a program to run faster since more of it can be loaded into memory. Most lodging software, for example, will require at least at least 1 gigabyte (GB) of RAM to run comfortably. If more memory is required, additional RAM chips can be plugged into the motherboard in the form of memory modules.

Since CPUs are so fast, RAM is not the only thing that has trouble keeping up. When the CPU processes a chunk of data, it may encounter a bottleneck when sending it down an electrical path called a **DATA BUS**. The data bus connects the CPU, memory, and other hardware devices on the motherboard. The speed at which data travels between the hardware components is affected by the size of the data path – which is measured in bits. For example, a 32-bit bus can transfer four bytes at a time, whereas 64-bit bus can transfer eight bytes.

Storage Devices

3. **Storage Devices.** Since the contents of RAM are erased when the power is turned off, permanent or nonvolatile storage is required. Most of the data processed by a computer resides in secondary storage and is copied into RAM only when needed for processing and then *saved* or copied back to secondary storage. Thus, a secondary storage device is an input/output device with read/write capability. However, a key disadvantage of secondary storage is slow access time. Data can be read much more quickly from RAM than from a hard disk. For this reason, as much data as possible should be loaded into RAM to reduce the number of times data is accessed from secondary storage so that the program will run much faster. The following paragraphs discuss storage devices typically used with microcomputers:

Hard Disks

a. *Hard Disks.* This secondary storage device is capable of holding a large amount of data. Typical capacity ranges from 80 gigabytes to over one trillion bytes or one terabyte (1 TB) of storage. For example, a one-page word-processing document requires 2,000 bytes of storage. An 80-gigabyte hard disk, therefore, is capable of storing about 40 million pages. The size of the hard disk depends on program and data space requirements. Some hospitality systems have additional internal hard disks for storing duplicate or mirrored data. **DATA MIRRORING** involves copying data from the primary hard disk onto another. If one hard disk fails, the other one activates. There is no interruption in service. Data redundancy can also be achieved using a **REDUNDANT ARRAY OF INDEPENDENT DISKS (RAID)**, a storage technology that combines multiple disk drive components into a logical unit.

Data stored on hard drives needs to be backed up to a remote location (e.g., a data center in a different city) via the Internet or a private network or to removable media. Backups prevent loss of critical data due to fire, theft, flooding, virus attacks, hardware or software failures, and user errors. Backups ensure that data is safe and recoverable.

Some companies provide remote backup services. A key advantage is that copied data is in a separate physical location, protecting it from worst-case scenarios such as an

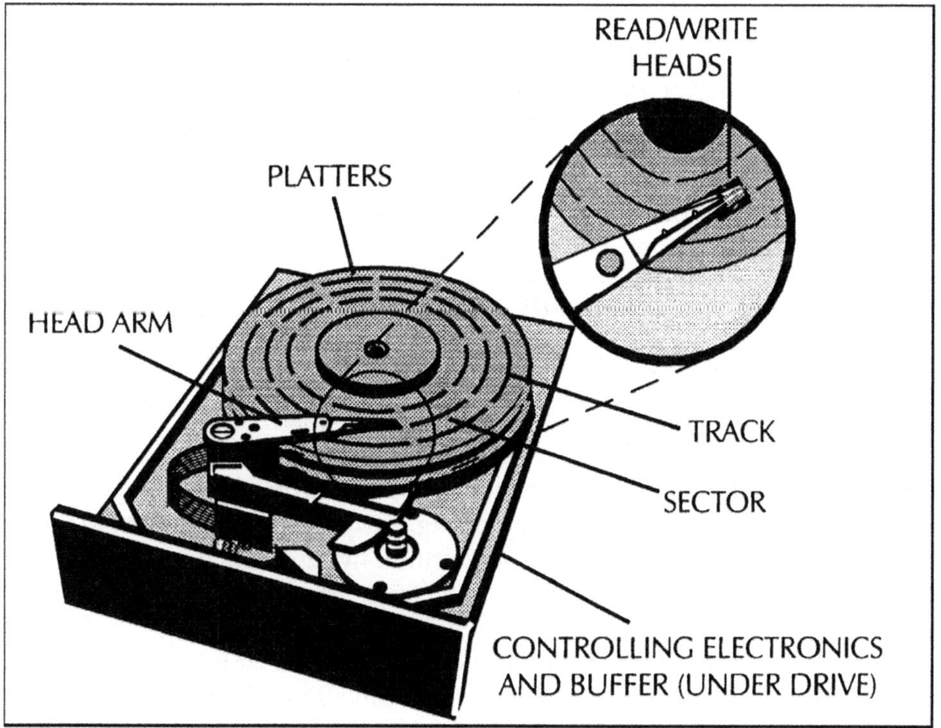

FIGURE 1-4. INTERNAL VIEW OF HARD DRIVE.

earthquake. Key disadvantages are that the Internet connection could be significantly slower than the speed of local backup devices, and a third party has control of sensitive data.

Removable media include external hard drives, flash drives, magnetic tapes, and optical discs (e.g., CD, DVD, and Blu-ray). In addition to backups, some removable media are also used for transferring files to other systems and for archiving historical data (e.g., guest folio history) to free up hard disk space.

Flash Drives

b. *Flash Drives.* These electronic devices are conceptually similar to RAM except that, once data is stored in it, it does not require electricity to be applied to retain the data–only to read and write it. When a universal serial bus (USB) flash drive is plugged into a computer's USB port, it is recognized as a removable drive and assigned a drive letter. The storage capacity (ranges from 4 GB to greater than 250 GB) and portability of this miniature mobile device makes it convenient to transfer data between a desktop computer and a notebook computer, or for personal backup needs. USB flash drives have replaced the 3 ½ inch floppy disks (1.44 MB storage capacity), once the only method to transfer data to another computer. USB flash drives also can include biometric fingerprint scanners for security or can be a platform for applications. iPads use internal flash storage, which is much more expensive than hard disk storage.

Magnetic Tapes

c. *Magnetic Tapes.* Because magnetic tapes are capable of storing and backing up large amounts of data (over 1 TB) quickly and cost effectively, they are commonly used with hospitality computer systems for making daily backups should the hard drive fail and data need to be restored.

However, since this information is stored sequentially, access time is slow, limiting its role to a backup medium. The hard drive is much faster because it directly accesses data. This can be compared to the difference between accessing a song on a cassette tape and a record. To play a song in the middle of a cassette tape, it must be wound forward. With a phonograph record (hard disk), you simply move the needle (read/write head) to the track containing the song (data).

A hard disk resembles a phonograph record where magnetized spots represent data. A hard disk is housed in a **DRIVE**, a device that spins the hard disk. It is also equipped with a read/write head that floats a few millionths of an inch from the disk's surface on a thin cushion of air produced by a rapidly spinning platter revolving at least 90 times per second. This can be compared to a Boeing 747 airliner flying six inches above the ground where the slightest obstruction can cause a crash (see Figure 1.4).

If the read/write head should encounter a small particle, for example, the entire unit will probably have to be replaced. To keep the hard disk clean inside, it is sealed air-tight and equipped with an air filtration system. The hard disk can also be damaged when it is moved if the read/write head is not parked, which is accomplished by turning the computer off.

Optical Storage

d. *Optical Storage.* This is the main alternative to magnetic storage (e.g., hard disk). Data is written to optical media, such as a **COMPACT DISC** (CD), **DIGITAL VERSATILE DISC** (DVD), or **BLU-RAY DISC**, with a laser for archival or backup purposes. While optical discs are more durable than tapes and less vulnerable to environmental conditions, they are slower than typical hard drive speeds and offer lower storage capacities. The storage capacity of a CD is around 700 MB, while a DVD and Blu-ray disc can store up to 18 GB and 128 GB respectively.

Output Devices

4. **Output Devices.** After data is processed, it can be either stored internally or transferred to external devices for viewing. The most common external devices are printers and monitors.

Printers

a. *Printers.* A printer prints out information on **HARD COPY** or paper. Various printers are designed to meet specific needs. Key features to consider when selecting a printer include:

Print Resolution and Speed

1. **Print resolution and Speed.** Print resolution or quality is typically measured in dots per inch (DPI). This represents the number of dots a printer can reproduce per

linear inch. For example, a 1200 DPI printer produces better print quality than a 600 DPI printer. Characters per second (CPS) and pages per minute (PPM) are common measures of printing speed. Depending on the printer type and model (e.g., laser), printing speeds generally range from 4 to 50 PPM. Many printers offer different print performance modes (e.g. draft, normal, maximum DPI) for the print quality and speed best suited to the task at hand. Draft quality uses fewer dots to form characters and would be appropriate for fast food receipts. A slow printer at a busy front desk is inappropriate. Labor productivity and customer satisfaction can suffer when it takes too long to print a guest folio. Print quality and speed can be improved by increasing the printer memory or RAM. Most print ers come with a small amount of memory (e.g., 1 MB).

Color

2. **Color.** Printers print in black and white or in color. Color printers, now affordable and smaller, enable hospitality operators to cost effectively create visually appealing menus, advertising flyers, brochures, coupons, table tent cards, and newsletters. Most hotel business centers have color printers. Some restaurants use two colors to highlight special food orders or cooking instructions (e.g., "no onions" printed in red).

Wireless and Remote Printing

3. **Wireless and Remote Printing.** Wireless printers use radio technology to communicate with networks over airwaves instead of cable, which reduces the clutter of cables in hospitality environments. They can be used anywhere and relocated in minutes to improve productivity and speed of service of employees and for customers at no additional cost. Some hotels provide remote printing services that enable guests to send Web pages, e-mail messages, e-mail attachments, and documents from any Internet-connected Web browser or wireless device (e.g., laptop) to centrally located printers for pickup.

Paper Handling

4. **Paper Handling.** The size of documents determines paper handling requirements. Small forms, like restaurant receipts or kitchen orders, may require a specialized printer feeding paper from a continuous roll. Use standard printers equipped with paper trays for business-size (8 ½" by 11") documents, like guest folios. The capacity of paper trays depends on the volume of business. A motel may only need a paper tray that holds 100 sheets, whereas a full-service hotel may require one with a 250-sheet capacity. It is important to have sufficient paper to accommodate peak periods and to replace ribbons and ink cartridges before print becomes light or illegible. This author witnessed chaos when a kitchen printer stopped printing food orders during the middle of a meal period due to a paper outage. Some printers have sensors warning that the paper needs replenishing.

Life Expectancy

5. **Life Expectancy.** The lifespan of a printer is one to five years, varying with how often used, location, care, throughput, model, and brand. For example, specially designed printers must stand the rigors of a kitchen environment. Printers have high failure rates because of so many moving parts. Consequently, some hospitality operators have spare printers on hand for areas where a printer failure will immediately disrupt the service system.

Cost

6. **Cost.** When selecting a printer, this is one of the most important considerations. The total cost of ownership includes the printer's initial purchase price and the cost of paper, ink or toner, as well as other supplies. Far more will be spent on supplies than is spent on the printer itself over the years.

A printer is classified as either impact or non-impact depending how it forms an image on paper. If the printer uses a mechanism to strike an image against an inked ribbon, it is called an **IMPACT PRINTER**. The impact printer used in hospitality operations is the **DOT MATRIX** printer. **A NON-IMPACT PRINTER** forms images by fusing or spraying ink onto paper without any striking movements. Non-impact printers used in hospitality operations are **LASER**, **INKJET**, and **THERMAL** printers.

A dot matrix uses dot combinations to represent various numbers, letters, and specific characters. Dots are achieved by pressing the ends of pins against the ribbon. Unlike non-impact printers, a dot matrix generates significant noise. Dot matrix printers produce draft and near-letter quality print. Dot matrix printers are used mainly for continuous feed preprinted forms (e.g., registration card with parking permit), for generating multiple copies of forms with carbons, and for printing customer receipts and food orders.

A thermal printer uses heated styluses to burn dots on specially treated paper. The print quality, comparable to a dot matrix printer, is commonly used by restaurants for credit card processing and for producing customer receipts and restaurant checks.

An inkjet printer sprays ink onto pages to form images of higher quality than produced by dot matrix and thermal printers. They are often used for generating business documents but are too costly to operate for high volume applications.

A laser printer fuses toner particles to paper much like a copier. Laser printers are fast, producing the highest quality output. They are used primarily for generating business documents. Hotels often use laser printers to print guest folios and registration cards as well as statements to groups, travel agents, owners, and others.

Technology Tidbits

"Your monitor is the window into your computer world, so choosing the right monitor is critical." ***www.pc.ibm.com***

Monitors

b. *Monitors.* These are TV-like devices displaying text, graphics, and video by lighting tiny dots called **PIXELS**. Pixels create the images on the screen. The two basic types of monitors are the **CRT** and the **FLAT PANEL MONITOR**. CRT monitors, like a television, use a cathode ray tube to generate a picture. The most popular type of flat panel monitor is the **LCD MONITOR**, which uses a liquid display crystal to display images on the screen. Many hospitality touch screen monitors featuring flat panel LCDs are countertop and wall mountable. LCD monitors have replaced CRT monitors in the vast majority of hospitality applications for several reasons. The thin design takes up much less desk space and provides a brighter picture with crisper text and sharper images, reducing eye strain. They are available in a wider range of screen sizes. Electromagnetic radiation and electricity usage are also less.

Digital Signage

LCD technology can also be found in **DIGITAL SIGNAGE**, an electronic display that shows menus, information, advertising, and other messages. For example, the Hyatt Regency Resort and Spa hotel in Waikiki features 11 LCD digital sign displays throughout the property to highlight meetings, restaurant menus, event and meeting room information, and food and beverage specials. Restaurants can use **LCD DIGITAL MENU BOARDS** to quickly update product offerings and pricing. Zippy's, a 27-store restaurant chain, updates digital menu boards remotely enabling real-time menu updates at all of their locations throughout Hawaii.

Communication Devices

Communication devices enable computers to be linked to together to form a computer network, which enables users to share hardware, software, and data and to communicate electronically with each other. Chapter 2 describes these devices in detail. Examples of communication devices are:

1. *Network Interface Card*: a device that connects a computer to a computer network.
2. *Router*: A device that connects an internal network to the Internet.
3. *Switch*: A device that connects network segments. Each segment can contain one or multiple computers.

There are basically two types of computer networks to manage:

Local Area Network

1. *Local Area Network (LAN).* This network usually links two or more computers together in the same building (e.g., point-of-sale system in a restaurant) using wires or radio signals. Multiple LANs can be tied together to form a **BUILDING AREA NETWORK**, used to connect environmental systems, such as heating, ventilation and air conditioning, and surveillance and security.

Wide Area Network

2. *Wide Area Network (WAN).* This network usually connects computers across a large geographic area (e.g., central reservation system or Web-based property management system) via the telephone network or radio waves. WANs are used to connect LANs to enable users and computers in one location to communicate with users and computers in other locations. Many hospitality LANs are connected to the Internet, the world's largest WAN. Hotels, for example, typically provide customers with access to the Internet via a wired and/or wireless connection. WANs also provide the backbone for **cloud computing**, which basically means that instead of storing and running applications on a hotel's computers, these tasks are performed by central remote servers (manages and stores data) on the Internet. This enables hospitality businesses to use applications without installation and to access their files at any computer with Internet access. Consequently, user hardware and software demands decrease. Although cloud computing is at an early stage of development, hospitality businesses may find it cheaper and more reliable than managing their own PCs, servers, and applications. Hotels, companies such as the Intercontinental Hotel Group, and Choice Hotels International, are moving key proprietary systems (e.g., room reservation and accounting software) into the cloud (4).

As computer networks evolve and converge in response to on-demand information and service applications, the need for even more powerful, affordable, and flexible solutions is critical. "Among the many areas of development are ad hoc networks, which can be created instantly as needed and can then be dismantled just as quickly, and networks of things, which can include virtually any item in a network through the use of technologies such as RFID tags" (www.linfo.org).

Software

Without a set of instructions, called **software** or **programs**, a computer is just a collection of metal and silicon. According to Roger Pressman and Russel Herron, authors of *Software Shock* (5):

> *Software is actually an information composite: It is information, it uses information, and it creates information. That's what makes it so difficult to understand, and that's also what makes it so powerful. Software is the computer programs that control the electronic hard ware and perform processing tasks for the user; it is the external manifestation of those programs seen by the computer user; it is the documents that describe how the programs work and how they are to be used; and finally, it is the data that are used by the programs as well as the data that are produced by them.*

There are two types of software: **system software** and **application software.** System software or the operating system is a master control program informing the computer how to function. While most of the work performed by system software is transparent to the user, a computer cannot operate without it. A specific job is performed by application software. **General-purpose business applications**, word processing, electronic spreadsheets, presentation tools, and database management, are programs providing end users with a framework to create and tailor generic business applications such as a report, budget, or sales analysis. There are also **industry-specific business applications** developed by hospitality software houses and corporate information system departments to address almost every phase of operations (see Figure 1-5). A number of these applications (front office, accounting, central reservations, food and beverage, etc.) are discussed in subsequent chapters.

Integrated Software

Integrated software (office suites) is an effort by the software industry to combine a number of software capabilities into a single package with a common set of commands and rules for its use. This allows a user to perform a variety of tasks without having to switch programs or learn different commands and procedures to run each one of them. Microsoft Office is an example of an integrated software package. It includes:

1. *Microsoft Word* – A word processing application
2. *Microsoft Excel* – A spreadsheet program.
3. *Microsoft PowerPoint* – An application for creating slideshows
4. *Microsoft Outlook* – An email program and personal information manager
5. *Microsoft Access* – A database application
6. *Microsoft Publisher* – A desktop publishing application
7. *Microsoft SharePoint Workspace* – An application for creating collaborative workspaces for sharing files and working on projects
8. *Microsoft InfoPath* – An application for designing and filling out forms to gather and reuse information throughout the organization

Google docs, which includes word processing, spreadsheet, and presentation tools, is a free Web-based office suite and data storage service offered by Google. It allows users to create and edit documents and spreadsheets online while collaborating in real-time with others. This keeps versions organized and available wherever and whenever users work. For example, employees involved in the budgeting process at Toronto-based Delta Hotels and Resorts now use Google Docs to share spreadsheets instead of emailing around Excel spreadsheets. Version control and a clear view of spreadsheet updates and changes have shaved eight weeks off the end-to-end budgeting process or a 30 % time savings.

Hospitality vendors also provide integrated software through **turnkey** or **interfaced** systems. A turnkey system, designed by a single vendor, consists of a modular suite of applications (e.g., front office, restaurant, spa, back office, event management, central reservations, etc.) where each module has access to the same underlying database. The more common interfaced system deploys stand-alone "best of breed" systems from different vendors with custom-built **interfaces**, which enable the exchange of specifically defined data sets between two disparate systems or applications (e.g., Micros POS interface to the WebRezPro PMS for posting a restaurant charge to a guest folio). A single, complete view of information (e.g., guest history) across a hotel chain is more easily achieved with a turnkey solution. However, this one-size-fits-all approach may not provide the desired application features and functionality found in interfaced systems. Although interfaced systems may have high interoperability, many times the business rules and data structures of each application and business unit have not been taken into account (e.g., customer contact information recorded in different formats), as they were developed independently of one another. This may cause employees to see only a portion of requested information (e.g., guest history) as well as preclude them from using the advanced application features and functionality provided by the vendor systems. Achieving **total systems integration**, the ability to deliver data, regardless of its origin, to whomever needs to work on it, for interfaced systems will not become a reality in the hospitality industry until rules and protocols which govern data exchange between disparate systems are standardized. Organizations, like Hotel Technology Next Generation (HTNG), a global trade association launched in 2002 by a small group of hoteliers who were frustrated on how difficult it was to share data consistently between various applications, are slowly tackling this task. For example, in 2012, HTNG introduced a standard for the sharing of customer profile data across hotel systems. Today's competitive environment requires information consolidation for decision support and streamlined workflow. This consequently increases the need for data integration.

> No one likes data integration. It's painstaking to automate and hard to measure in terms of ROI. Yet is required for making systems work together.
>
> Galen Gruman,
> "Whipping Data into Shape," *Infoworld* (February 2006)

Workflow Software

Workflow software involves the automated movement of documents or items through a specific sequence of actions or tasks related to a business process. At each stage in the workflow, an individual or group is responsible for a specific task. Once the task is complete, those responsible for the next task are notified by the software and receive data needed to execute it. For example, a hotel company could use workflow software (e.g., Guestware) to handle work orders and guest complaints and requests consistently from their onset to the final resolution. Lynk Software (www.lynksoftware.com), a developer of quality assurance software, has a workflow application providing customer service representatives with detailed account profiles and past complaint histories. Issues easily resolved are recorded and closed with automatic emails or letters to customers. For more complex complaints, customer service representatives are empowered to engage others in the resolution by assigning action requests or a new owner. Through a customized workflow, establishment of ownership, due date reporting, and automatic reminders, customers are more likely to receive timely and thorough responses. Workflow software tools can be utilized throughout the entire business process lifecycle, integrating technology, information, and human resources to improve control, save time, and reduce expenditures. For example, in 2012, the Panda Restaurant Group deployed an accounts payable workflow solution to reduce manual processing, while increasing accuracy and controls.

A workflow or business process is simply the way a particular task is accomplished. Before automating a process, it is critical to analyze it to insure that it will achieve the desired results. If there are problems in the process, fix them before automation. The improved process may expose new requirements for automation, or perhaps eliminate the need for it altogether. For instance, the U.S. Veterans Benefits Administration (VBA) made a sizable technology investment to speed the processing of benefit claims. The VBA failed to complete its analysis of claims-processing deficiencies before making a technology investment of $94 million. Consequently, only 6 to 12 days were trimmed from the average claims processing time of 151 days because the new technology addressed what turned out to be only a minor hitch in the claims process as a whole. A misjudgment like that can short-circuit technology's potential for a dramatic increase in productivity.

Operating System

An operating system (e.g., Windows) is a program that enables the computer to recognize the CPU, mouse, keyboard, drives, memory, and monitor. In addition, it provides the user with a means to communicate with the computer, and it serves as a platform from which to run application programs.

Hospitality Applications			
1.	Property Management System	13.	Customer Relationship Management
2.	Back Office/Accounting	14.	Call Accounting
3.	Central Reservations	15.	Condo/Timeshare
4.	Point of Sale	16.	Table Management
5.	Foodservice Management	17.	Energy Management
6.	Club Management	18.	Security/Electronic Locks
7.	Human Resources	19.	Kiosks/Remote Check in
8.	Engineering and Preventive Maintenance	20.	Payment Processing
9.	Sales and Marketing	21.	Surveys and Guest Response
10.	Catering and Events	22.	Mobile Customer Service
11.	Time and Labor Management	23.	Revenue Management
12.	Channel Management	24.	Spa and Recreation Management

FIGURE 1-5. HOSPITALITY APPLICATIONS.

Provides An Interface for Users to Communicate With The Computer

Operating System Tasks. When a computer is turned on, it performs a **BOOT**. This is an automatic routine that loads the operating system into memory to prepare the computer for use. As long as the computer is on, the operating system performs four primary tasks:

1. *Provides an interface for users to communicate with the computer.* In the beginning, personal computers had command-driven interfaces, which required users to type commands on the keyboards or to select commands from text-based menus. Today the computer's dashboard is a **GRAPHICAL USER INTERFACE (GUI)**. A GUI, such as Windows, uses a standard menu, mouse, or touch screen, and graphical icons, visual indicators, or special graphical elements to provide a more intuitive interface. For example, in one front office system the "Walk-in" task, represented by a pair of footprints, was selected by clicking the mouse pointer on an icon.

The most recent trend is **BROWSER-ENABLED** or Web-enabled hospitality applications. A browser-enabled application uses an Internet browser, such as Internet Explorer, to display application pages (e.g., reservation screen) in a GUI format. A **BROWSER** interprets the programming language of the Internet, HYPER TEXT MARKUP LANGUAGE (HTML), into the words and graphics that you see when viewing a Web page. "Most people today, particularly younger employees, know how to use a browser, with the familiar 'point and click' links, graphical displays, fonts, pictures, and graphs" (www.resortdata.com).

Manages the File System

2. *Manages the File System.* An operating system groups data into logical compartments for storage on the disk. These groups of data are called **FILES**. Computers store information in files, which may contain program instructions or data created or used by a program. Computers make storing millions of files easy. Retrieving files quickly makes business processes efficient. Files are kept organized by using a consistent naming scheme that is understandable and easily remembered by users (e.g., short, common names) and storing related files in the same directory.

A directory inside another directory is a subdirectory. Together, the directories form a hierarchy or tree structure. A hard drive, for example, can be compared to a warehouse filled with file cabinets (directories) with drawers (subdirectories) where the folders (files) are kept.

Performing file maintenance on a regular basis prevents the hard disk from becoming cluttered and full of obsolete files. The operating system enables files to be easily moved, copied, deleted, recovered, and renamed.

Manages the Hardware

1. *Manages the Hardware.* The operating system acts as an intermediary between programs and the hardware. It interprets commands to use memory and hardware devices

(e.g., printer) and keeps track of what programs have access to what devices. Windows provides a convenient way of changing the system configuration, such as installing and configuring a printer. For example, when a printer (e.g., Hewlett Packard Color Laserjet) is added in Windows, it is automatically accessible in all other programs.

Support Programs

2. *Support Programs*. Another major function of an operating system is to support other programs. For example, when a user requests a word processing program to list word processing document files available on USB flash drive, it calls on the operating system to perform this task. Other tasks include managing **virtual storage** (e.g., disk memory used to augment limited primary memory) and running **antivirus software**. As explained more fully in Chapter 2, antiviral software is used to prevent, detect, and remove **malware**, such as viruses, worms, Trojan horses, spyware, and keyloggers.

Examples of operating systems are Microsoft Windows, Mac OS, Unix, and Linux. Unlike Windows and Mac OS, Unix and Linux are based on open standards like the Internet, allowing them to run on virtually any type of computer. A browser-based operating system (just runs the browser) may also be used in conjunction with the aforementioned operating systems to enable cloud computing applications. Microsoft Azure, for example, is an edition of the Windows operating system that runs in the cloud.

A key consideration when selecting an operating system is the availability of the application. For example, a restaurant company selected Linux, a free operating system similar to Unix, because the software license fees and the computing costs were lower than other operating systems. It took the restaurant, however, five years to find a suitable Linux point of sale solution, a key application in any restaurant operation.

A rapidly growing number of hospitality applications have been designed for mobile devices (e.g., tablet, smartphone, and PDA), which require a **mobile operating system** for determining the available functions and features and which third-party applications can be used (mobile applications discussed in subsequent chapters). For example, the interactive restaurant menu application developed by Aptito for the Android tablet uses a Google (Ice Cream Sandwich/Gingerbread) operating system.

> It has collected more personal data than any other organization in human history. What will it do with that information ... Facebook is not above using its platform to tweak users' behavior, as it did by nudging them to register as organ donors ... Organ donor enrollment increased by a factor of 23 across 44 states. ... Advertisers, too, would be eager to know in greater detail what could make a campaign on Facebook affect people's actions.
>
> Tom Simonite,
> *"What Facebook Knows," Technology MIT Review, August 2012*

THE COMPUTER REVOLUTION

Advancements in information technology continue at a rapid and intimidating pace. The first large-scale computer, ENIAC, was introduced in 1946. The 30-ton machine, 18 feet high and 80 feet long, consisted of 17,468 tubes and more than 100,000 components. It was first used by the military to evaluate the feasibility of the hydrogen bomb. Since then, computers have shrunk while becoming extremely powerful. In the 70s, circuits were printed on very small silicon chips. When the entire CPU was placed on a chip weighing less than two grams, the microcomputer was born—a desktop computer far more powerful than the mammoth ENIAC. It enabled computers, which once required a specialized staff to operate and maintain them, to be placed in homes and in small businesses.

The author remembers glancing at a towering office building one night in Los Angeles. The well-lit offices revealed a computer on every desk. The author thought to himself: "The computer revolution has reached the fingertips of everyone." Between the years 1981 and 1982, the number of computers in the world doubled. In 1982, due to the pervasive impact of computers, Time magazine chose the computer as its "Man of the Year."

By the 1990s, anyone could create meaningful and useful digital content, whether working in a small or large business located anywhere in the world. The next breakthrough in the computer revolution allowed digital content to be easily shared and accessed via a global network called the **INTERNET**. Billions of users now view digital content (e.g., text, images, videos, and other multimedia) via the **WORLD WIDE WEB**, a system of interlinked, hypertext documents that was created in 1989. The Web has had a dramatic effect on business-to-business (salesforce.com), business-to-consumer (opentable.com) and consumer-to-business (e.g., priceline.com) transactions and communications. Sodexo, a business-to-business (B2B) company and provider of integrated food and facilities management services, uses a Facebook Fan Page for recruiting and is a channel for customer service and followup with applicants and interested parties. Advancements in wired, wireless, and mobile technologies make the Internet a very important medium for the hospitality industry. Almost 40% of the nearly 2,400 smartphone users surveyed by Atmosphere Research Group in 2012 said they intended to use their mobile device to book a hotel stay, while 27% indicated a willingness to use their iPhones to reserve hotel rooms, book car rentals and buy airplane tickets. Another recent study conducted by ComScore revealed that the majority of smartphone owners now access travel content via their devices.

The next generation of computers will be infinitely more intelligent than today's computers and much easier to use and operate. They will be wearable (e.g., eyeware), able to see, talk, understand speech, make decisions, learn and associate from past experiences, recognize user emotions, and perform physical tasks (e.g., flipping a hamburger patty).

In the future, mobile devices used in conjunction with indoor (e.g., RFID, Bluetooth, and WiFi) and outdoor (GPS) positioning systems could adapt service options based on the customer's location or proximity to physical objects in the real world. For example, the check-in icon could light up on the mobile screen when the customer enters the hotel lobby. Another scenario could be a Bluetooth (a wireless transmission standard) interaction between a mobile device and a public digital display that presents targeted and interactive

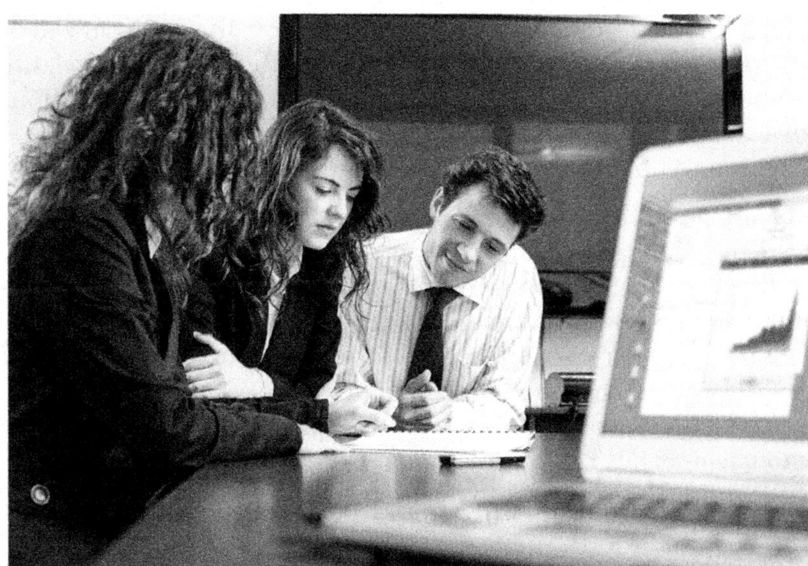

FIGURE 1-6. THREE BUSINESS PEOPLE.

Source: Image Copyright Zsolt Nyulaszi, 2008. Used Under License From Shutterstock, Inc.

content (e.g., mapping, event, menu, and shopping information) as well as value-added services. For example, a customer could request step-by-step directions to the casino through a navigationally-enabled phone. Directions could be given with arrows pointing in the right direction as a customer approaches one of the public displays. Providing turn by turn directions and other information via eyeware equipped with an ultra-miniature display connected to a mobile device via a wireless or wired link is another possibility. Microvision, an electronics company specializing in display and imaging products for mobile application, is developing mobile device eyeware that provides the wearer with a visual information overlay, while not losing awareness of their immediate surroundings (http://www.microvision.com/wearable_displays/index.html).

A change is occurring in who uses computers. In the past, computers were used by only a few people. They were mainly technical specialists, professionals, and managers. Today, however, technological advancements have moved intelligence to the front line of most organizations, where the action is. Consequently, the number of users has grown dramatically, and they want to shape and control the use of technology in their organizations. They understand that the effective use of technology will determine their personal and organizational success. They have become the leaders of the computer revolution that is altering the old ways of organizational computing.

Who Manages the CBIS?

There is no common title for the person in charge of managing the computer-based information system at the property level. In small operations, this responsibility may be assumed by the controller or manager. In larger properties, a person may be hired specifically to manage the information system. In this book, this position will be called the **INFORMATION TECHNOLOGY MANAGER** (see Figure 1-6). At the corporate level, the person responsible for the information system is typically called the Chief Information Officer (CIO) or Chief Technology Officer (CTO).

If an information technology manager is doing a good job:

1. The CBIS produces accurate, relevant data that is timely and easily accessible.
2. Users have the necessary resources to carry out tasks in the most efficient and effective manner. Making a front-desk clerk wait 10 minutes to print a guest folio, for example, is unproductive and a disservice to the guest. Providing employees with the necessary computer resources requires that each work area be closely analyzed to identify the users and the amount of computer time each user needs. For guest contact positions, it is important to provide the capability (measured in workstations) to accommodate peak business periods.
3. The CBIS is properly protected and maintained and downtime is kept to a minimum. Computer downtime can be very costly, especially in hospitality organizations that operate 24 hours a day. Keep the computer system running smoothly. Providing adequate protection entails the implementation of security measures for hardware, software, and the information database. Be prepared to deal with a variety of situations including fire, water damage, lighting strikes, theft, viruses, internal and external attacks, and employee tampering. Computer security is discussed in Chapter 2.

The information technology manager is also responsible for system maintenance (e.g., removing dust from hardware and deleting old, useless information from the database) and resolving routine system problems (e.g., printer jam). Properly maintaining the system and promptly responding and correcting system problems can significantly reduce downtime and enhance system performance. A major problem may require technical assistance from the vendor. There is typically a charge for this service. Hardware and maintenance contracts are discussed in Chapter 11.

4. The CBIS is scalable or can adapt to the increase demands for growth. A system that cannot scale can suffer from performance issues (e.g., slow transaction speed and throughput) when additional demands are placed upon it.
5. The CBIS is periodically evaluated to identify opportunities to enhance performance which better serves the organization. Be sure to consult with various employees before making any changes to the computer system; their feedback is invaluable. The evaluation could result in a variety of changes including modifying or installing new software and hardware. Assess how each change would impact users and its cost-effectiveness and compatibility with the existing system(s).
6. System utilization and acceptance are high. According to a study conducted by the Hospitality Information Technology Association and PKF Consulting, survey respondents identified a lack of training as a barrier to the use and implementation of technology. Due to the hospitality industry's high turnover rate, in-house training has been expensive and time-consuming. Consequently, most training

happens on-the-job where the information is handed down from one employee to another in an unstructured, ad hoc manner which tends to dilute knowledge of the system over a period of time. This diminishes system utilization and acceptance.

Providing employees with consistent, quality training accessible throughout all levels of the organization, including top and middle management, is one of the information system manager's most important responsibilities and greatest challenges. Proper training is the key to employees taking maximum advantage of the computer system and, ultimately, successfully competing in the "information age." Computer-based training as a tool for delivering cost-effective, personalized instruction discussed is in Chapter 11. Besides teaching employees how to use the hardware and software, standard operating procedures on the handling of computer-generated information should also be taught

Another important factor affecting system acceptance and utilization is **USABILITY**, the degree to which a system is easy to learn as well as satisfying to use. A hard to use program which ignores human factors can create a variety of problems including headaches, eyestrain, frustration, boredom, confusion, anxiety, and reduced worker productivity. In contrast, friendly software is adaptive, understandable, predictable, responsive, self-explanatory, forgiving, efficient, and flexible. Its design is not based on intuition but on a careful analysis of the human/computer interface (6).

Customer and employee hospitality applications for the Web are rapidly increasing. The models of navigation on the Web differ from those in desktop applications. If navigational schemes are not simple, logical, and understandable, users become confused. Users need to know where they are, where they can go, and how to get there. Other key factors affecting Web usability include screen or page layouts, design consistencies, content appropriateness, text readability, and download speeds. Customer Web sites are no longer online brochures but important direct-to-customer service channels. A small resort company, for example, increased online booking revenue from $300,000 to $2.3 million within one year after redesigning and optimizing the Web site.

Web-based and client/server applications designed for desktop PC screens usually do not render well on mobile device screens. Create Web-based and client/service applications just for mobile devices to ensure page layouts are mobile-friendly. **MIDDLEWARE** solutions can be utilized for automatically generating a display or new user interface based on the application and the associated device screen size and type. Middleware is a group of computer routines creating a communications interface between a high level application program and physical hardware. It insulates application programs from the idiosyncrasies of physical devices and provides modularity and portability. The interface design must support the limited attention of users often distracted by people, events, activities, or objects. Mobile user interfaces should not have complex menus. Simple and descriptive pages and an ability to connect on-screen information with the physical world are desirable (7).

7. There is a well-defined information plan that addresses the information needs and the technological architecture required to meet the mission, goals, and strategies of the enterprise. Many people believe that technology has not delivered sufficiently

higher productivity to justify spending scarce funds. Some blame this so-called productivity paradox on management's failure to relate business strategy to technology selection. Strategic investments in hospitality technology are complicated by difficulties in assessing their tangible and intangible benefits, a prevalent "front-of-the-house " mentality that puts a higher value on purchases that customers can see and touch, technological advances (e.g., cloud and mobile computing) and a blurring of customer and business technology. Chapter 8 discusses the use of technology as a strategic enabler. Chapter 11 identifies the steps involved in information system selection and implementation.

> "Technology represents intelligence systematically applied to the problem of the body. It functions to amplify and surpass the organic limits of the body; it compensates for the body's fragility and vulnerability ... Technological change defines the horizon of our material world as it shapes the limiting conditions of what is possible and what is barely imaginable. It erodes assumptions about the nature of our reality, the "pattern" in which we dwell, and lays open new choices."
>
> Shoshana Zuboff,
> *In the Age of the Smart Machine*

Advantages of Computerizing Information Processing

Why computerize? Today management is faced with an increasingly complex environment where pressures for quality information are paramount in remaining competitive. Manual methods of manipulating data are labor intensive, time consuming, ineffective, and untimely. Technological advances have encouraged many hospitality operators to rethink how data should be processed, stored, retrieved, and analyzed. Research has led to the implementation of various cost-effective applications addressing almost every phase of operations.

A computer system should be viewed as a tool for solving problems and effectively managing information, but, even more importantly, it will improve profitability through more effective utilization of resources. The additional profits generated by its implementation will usually cover its cost within two to five years, if the system has been fully utilized.

Technology Tidbits

A modern desktop computer is now much more powerful than a 20-year old supercomputer, which is capable of performing calculations that would take 3,840,000 labor hours. And smartphones are becoming more powerful than desktops of just a few years ago.

Improved Labor Productivity and Organizational Efficiency

The key advantages of a CBIS are as follows:

1. **Improved Labor Productivity and Organizational Efficiency.** Repetitive clerical tasks can be eliminated, resulting in labor savings in heavily staffed areas. For example, it may take 15 hours to post room and tax manually for a 600-room hotel; if this process was automated, it would take seconds.

A manual information system forces departments to frequently collect the same data because it is difficult to transmit it. On the other hand, a CBIS allows the sharing of data, which eliminates redundant data entry. Data is captured from the source only one time and stored in a centralized, on-line **DATABASE** (a collection of interrelated files containing data) for all who need it. For example, the sales and marketing department acquires reservation data to generate revenue forecasts.

Holyfields, a quick-service restaurant chain based in Germany, is lowering labor costs by having customers order from easel-like touch screen kiosks. The kiosks interact with devices handed to customers when they enter the restaurant that alert them when their orders are ready for pickup as well as link their transactions for settlement purposes at the cashier station.

Through technology, Taco Bell increased the span of control from one supervisor for five restaurants to one for 30. It operates 90 percent of its company-owned restaurants without a full-time manager. These locations are team-managed by young crews where the crew members are challenged to assume greater responsibility and learn more. John Martin, former Chairman and CEO of Taco Bell, explains:

> *Ask most young people who work at the crew level in the restaurant industry whether they'd rather chop lettuce or take the responsibility for transmitting a P&L (profit and loss) statement via computer to the main office. The fact is, many of them would rather chop lettuce. Why? Because most of them don't believe that they can do the other. They don't believe it because they haven't had the experience. But give them the experience. Change their beliefs. Prove to them that they can do the job. And much more often than not, they'll do it.*

Enhanced Decision Making Capability

2. Enhanced Decision-Making Capability. In the information age, access to timely, relevant information is necessary to make correct decisions. Getting information about an occurrence that happened two months ago may be too late for corrective action since some things, such as labor hours and sales activity, need to be monitored on a day-to-day basis. Unfortunately, many managers rely on a profit and loss statement which tends to lay blame rather than explaining where and when the mistake was made. Judging operational performance on a monthly profit and loss statement is like "reconstructing a novel based on the last page" (8).

A computer enables information to be retrieved in minutes or even seconds. Employees no longer have the arduous task of combing source documents (e.g., guest registration cards) to determine, for example, a breakdown of guests by geographical location or the purpose of their visit. One motel substantially increased its business by placing billboard advertisements along a highway when a computer report indicated that a significant number of its guests were truck drivers. Marketing data is invaluable.

A computer is a reliable storage vessel enabling important decision-making information to be passed on to new employees. At one historic hotel, for example, guest history remains only in the head of the reservations manager, a long-time employee. When she leaves, so does the information about guests' room preferences, desired bedding, and special needs.

The Donato's Pizza restaurant chain uses a **BUSINESS INTELLIGENCE SYSTEM (BIS)** or **DECISION SUPPORT SYSTEM**. This system consolidates data from different systems (e.g., point-of-sales data located in various transaction and customer relationship management systems), and provides a centralized reporting solution. After the data is consolidated into a master **DATA WAREHOUSE**, a place for storing enterprise data, it is immediately available for decision making. For example, a BIS could reveal real-time information on customer frequency, order trends, and coupon performance to capitalize on sales opportunities as they happen.

A BIS not only gathers data but also analyzes data and presents it to make business decisions easier. Typical information gathered and presented by a BIS includes (searchcio.techtarget.com):

a. Comparative statistics, revenues, and expenses.
b. Competitive sets or the selection of other competing hotels or restaurants by which a property or chain measures its own performance.
c. Budgets and forecasts.
d. What-if analyses or the consequences of different decision alternatives.

A BIS also enables a manager to be a detective. It identifies problems (e.g., downward trend in sales or guest satisfaction scores) and allows an executive to "drill-down" through layers of data to pinpoint exact causes. **DRILL-DOWN** refers to the ability to dig into information on the BIS screen and find out the background data that supports the totals or trends that are shown.

M3 Link, a hotel BIS, integrates property management system (PMS) data, Smith Travel Research (STR) reports, guest satisfaction surveys, and financial data in one place, across multiple brands. It allows hoteliers to read guest comments, compare competitive set index variances, analyze statistics, view trends, and drill-down into detailed data (e.g., Total Revenue > Restaurant Revenue > Lounge > Collins Bar).

Mobile BIS applications are expected to rise rapidly as format-friendly smartphones and tablet computers become more prevalent. According to the Aberdeen Group, a provider of fact-based research, mobile BIS applications can potentially improve business processes and employee productivity (e.g., time spent looking for information) and provide better and faster decision making and customer service and the delivery of real-time bi-directional data access to make decisions anytime and anywhere (http://www.informationweek.com/news/212300110). For example, a mobile BIS iPhone application developed by Alloso Technologies displays an information dashboard that enables hotel managers and executives to access real-time information, including profit and loss data, budget comparisons, revenue segments, expenses, and links to guest reviews.

Attributes and Similarities of Well Managed Data Warehouses and Fine Dining Restaurants

The following is based on an article authored by Margy Ross and Ralph Kimball of the Kimball Group, a consulting company specializing in data warehousing (www .kimballgroup.com).

Fine Dining Restaurant: The staff develops a delicious menu from raw ingredients and recipes.

Data Warehouse: The staff provides menus of available data available through output devices, such as a monitor.

Fine Dining Restaurant: The kitchen and dining room layouts are efficient, resulting in the timely production and delivery of food (throughput).

Data Warehouse: Is constructed from integrated data source systems to streamline and ensure the timely delivery of information to end-users (throughput). The databases are efficient and organized into logical structures: bit>character>data field>record>file>database. Patrons do not want to wait for information any more than restaurant patrons want to wait for their meals.

Fine Dining Restaurant: Menu item quality (outputs) depends on the raw material quality (inputs).

Data Warehouse: Information quality (outputs) depends on data quality (inputs). Incoming data, like lettuce, are checked for reasonable quality. Inconsistent data and wilted lettuce, for example, would be rejected.

Fine Dining Restaurant: The reputation of the restaurant depends on the delivery of consistent, safe, and quality food products

Data Warehouse: The reputation of the data warehouse depends on the delivery of consistent, high integrity, and quality information products. Consumers will not tolerate poor food or information.

Fine Dining Restaurant: The kitchen is off limits to patrons. Poor security could jeopardize food quality and production.

Data Warehouse: The same principle applies. Poor security could jeopardize information quality and processing. Customers stay outside of the preparation area, and are confined to the dining or authorized-user areas.

Fine Dining Restaurant: Restaurant managers monitor customer satisfaction and take quick action when problems arise.

Data Warehouse: Data warehouse managers monitor user satisfaction. If quick action is not taken when problems arise, patrons may locate to another "restaurant" that better suits their needs and preferences, wasting the dollars invested to design, build, and staff the data warehouse.

Reduced Operation Costs

3. **Reduced Operating Costs.** Other areas, in addition to labor, where costs may be reduced include: energy (e.g., energy management systems reduce utility bills), paper and postage (e.g., e-mailing reservation confirmations saves paper and lowers mailing expenses), and perishable and nonperishable products (e.g., inventory control systems reduce spoilage and theft).

Increased Information Accuracy

4. **Increased Information Accuracy.** A computer reduces the number of times data is handled by employees. This eliminates clerical and logic errors. For example, a survey revealed that handwritten restaurant checks were inaccurate 16% of the time, and 70% of these checks averaged a substantial undercharge (9).

Increased Revenues

5. **Increased Revenues.** Ensuring that all sales are captured and recorded properly can be a tedious task if done manually. Automation streamlines this process. For example, hotels frequently had difficulties in capturing and correctly accounting for sales transactions generated from various departments (e.g., restaurant, telephone, gift shop, etc.) until the process of posting remote charges to guest folios was automated. Furthermore, there are programs used to evaluate product pricing and cost in relationship to facility capacity. In fact, there are several sophisticated hotel programs which execute revenue enhancement strategies based on occupancy trends without management intervention. This capability is particularly useful in a volatile business environment. The following example is an illustration of one program strategy: "If occupancy in the groups discount class exceeds X percent with Y days before arrival, then move all group discounts to rack rate class."

Greater Customer Satisfaction and Loyalty

6. **Greater Customer Satisfaction and Loyalty.** Computers enable employees to be more efficient and well-organized, giving them more time to tend to customer needs. Wireless order taking, for example, enables servers to provide faster service and to spend more time on the floor interacting with customers.

Many hospitality operations are using computers to collect data about customer satisfaction to focus management and employee efforts on the customer who is, without a doubt, the most important aspect of the hospitality business. European-based Accor Hotels, for example, sends follow-up e-mails to guests immediately after a stay inviting them to take an online survey. The ratings for each hotel are shared with other Accor hotels to motivate them. However, the most detailed and compelling customer feedback is generated through open-ended survey questions. Scanning large volumes of free form responses is a time-consuming and tedious task. **Text analyzer software** expedites this task by sorting comments into complaint categories or clusters. It then distills the meaning of text into a concise form. It can also be used for complaint resolutions and tracking corrective actions.

Hospitality companies also gain feedback about their operations through **consumer generated media (CGM)** or blogs, discussion boards, hotel and restaurant review sites, social networks (e.g., Facebook and Twitter), etc. Approximately 300 million public comments are made online worldwide every day (10). The proliferation of online feedback and its vast exposure is leveling the playing field, despite disparities in marketing budgets. More and more customers are patronizing hospitality establishments because of previous guest experiences noted on the Web. Negative online comments, however, have a tendency to rank higher and spread faster than positive ones. **Reputation software** can be deployed to monitor online conversations and help reduce the impact and visibility of negative search results and promote positive reviews of the company.

Hoteliers can establish interactive relationships with customers via corporate-sponsored CGM initiatives. An example of such an initiative is the starwoodlobby.com, a site created by Starwood Hotels and Resorts. In 2007, Dunkin' Donuts created an online customer loyalty site (MyIcedCoffee.com) to appeal to younger women. Customers can sign up on the site for sweepstakes, giveaways, and refer-a-friend programs. Dunkin' Donuts can also gather specific consumer information, and promotions and communications about new products can be better targeted.

Hotels maintain guest history databases that track guest preferences, requests, complaints, and other important information, such as birthdays, anniversaries, and previous activities and arrangements. This information is used to personalize guest experiences and develop closer relationships. Ritz-Carlton, for example, collects immense amounts of information on their customers' needs and preferences, which is added daily to a chainwide database.

Improved Controls

7. **Improved Controls.** Automated systems are capable of generating detailed audit trails for tracking resources and ensuring that all financial transactions are properly handled. Since transactions can be identified by the employees who made them, greater individual accountability is also achieved. Employees can be evaluated on such things as sales productivity (e.g., number of bottles of wine sold and average guest check) and proper recording of payments and charges (e.g., number of voided items on checks).

Automated systems make it possible to collect money earlier and to spend it more intelligently. Notices on past-due accounts can be sent out more quickly, and management reports can result in earlier collection efforts. Money tied up in inventories can be reduced through better inventory and forecasting information. Targeted labor and food cost percentages have a better chance of being attained when the process is automated.

Technology and Information

IT associations' attempts to define **big data** often mention four characteristics: volume, variety, velocity, and value. The idea is that companies are rapidly amassing huge quantities of both structured data, things like transactions, folios and basic customer data, as well as unstructured data, such as social media messages, guest comment cards and video. Unfortunately, few are equipped with the right technology, or even a plan, to boil down the ocean of data into insights that help them run their businesses better.

Lisa Terry,
"Demystifying Big Data," Hospitality Tecnology, October 2012

According to Robert Wurman, author of *Information Anxiety,* "As information technology matures, the focus will turn from the machines themselves toward the information itself. The value of technology lies only in its ability to manage and exploit the product-information" (11).

Robert Waterman, author of *In Search of Excellence,* contends that successful businesses are those that can make the best use of information. Automated information systems are capable of generating hundreds of reports at a low processing cost. This capability, ironically, has overwhelmed managers who feel the need to read every report. Consequently, important information gets lost in the clutter. A manager must control the flow of information, selectively choosing relevant reports.

The format or organization of report information affects its usefulness. There are several ways to organize information:

Category

1. **Category.** Grouping information by category allows management to evaluate specific aspects of the operation. For example, over time hours broken down by job position pinpoints where corrective action is needed. Tracking sales by menu item allows management to discern fast and slow moving menu items. One South Florida country club operation had a high liquor cost percentage (cost/sales) because vending machine soft drinks, with a much lower markup, were included in liquor sales. This problem was corrected by creating a separate category for vending machine sales.

Time

2. **Time.** Certain events should be tracked by time period. Recording the number of meals served per hour assists in labor scheduling. Recording the number of meals served per day is helpful in determining food production requirements. Tracking financial information daily, such as sales, labor cost, food cost, and average guest check, enables management to quickly identify trends affecting profitability.

Location

3. **Location.** Organizing information by location makes sense when it comes from different locales or sources. For example, a property with multiple sales outlets or a hotel chain with 200 properties would require separate income statements. The executive vice-president of one hotel chain sent each general manager a report that contained the labor cost percentage for every property in the chain. Comparing performances incited healthy competition and, as a result, the corporation had a 10 percent lower labor cost.

Alphabet

4. **Alphabet.** When working with large bodies of information, it is common to arrange it alphabetically so that it may be more quickly accessed. This would include such things as a hotel telephone directory, accounts payable vendor list, and reservations file.

Continuum

5. **Continuum.** A scale may be used to arrange things in order of importance, rank, etc. Departments can be ranked from high to low on such things as absenteeism, labor turnover, or guest satisfaction.

The aforementioned organizing principles are necessary to structure information so that meaning can be extracted from it. It allows the analysis of information from different vantage points where insightful relationships between bodies of information can be established.

Data Miners

There is a new type of computer professional emerging whose specialty is "digging out nuggets of 24-carat knowledge from mountains of database dross or rubbish." This person is called a **data miner.** Data mining (see Chapter 9 entitled "Data Mining") has favorably impacted hospitality organizations' prediction and modeling capabilities. For example, it can identify potential new customers and ways of hanging on to existing ones. It can help predict what new menu items to offer customers based on past choices (12).

The data miner's first task is to find a suitable sample of the database and then to convert it into a uniform state for analysis. Cleaning up raw data can be a daunting task. **Data** are raw facts that describe the characteristic of an event or object There is one case where a retailer's database included 500 different ways of describing from which American state the information came.

The next task is not only to extract valuable information from the large amounts of data collected but to pull out trends, groupings, and connections that depend on many variables, linked together in complex ways. A **variable** is a data characteristic that stands for a value that changes or varies over time.

Successfully identifying patterns requires the use of sophisticated tools such as **neural networks**, computers that crudely mimic the brain's ability to find relationships in data by being shown examples. According to Robert Matthews, "Such networks are first trained on data samples showing, say, the relative proportion of customers who order particular appetizers, main courses, drinks, and desserts. The network then tries to classify each type of customer according to their preferences. At first, the classification is inaccurate, but the neural network's algorithms allow it to learn from its mistakes, revealing relationships between, say, orders for liqueurs after roast beef dinners"(13).

Various hospitality organizations are using neural network technology to forecast business volumes and workloads (e.g., meals, rooms, check-ins, phone calls, park attendance). By using all the conditions and variables affecting a particular business, such as weather, promotions, holidays, special events, etc., complex patterns are automatically created containing the same knowledge it would take a human forecaster months and years to gain. This tool gives managers the ability to forecast quickly and accurately.

Data mining techniques will reveal unexpected information. One company wanted to identify customers who were unlikely to pay their bills on time. Before carrying out the exercise, the company thought that those on low incomes were the worst offenders. It turned out to be urban achievers—white collar, good salary, and college educated.

One of the problems with data mining in the hospitality industry is developing rich, comprehensive databases. This should improve as diverse computer systems housing related databases are linked together forming a vast gold mine of electronic data.

Unleashing Your Brainpower

In your careers, you will use a variety of tools, such as Excel, to organize, process, and analyze data to answer questions and make informed decisions that will improve business performance. Figure 1-7 denotes point-of-sales data for the XYZ restaurant. The data highlight the following characteristics: menu item name, quantity sold, menu price, and menu food cost. This raw data does not offer much insight into menu item performance. For example, which menu item is the most profitable? Which item is the least profitable? To answer these questions requires the processing (calculating and sorting) of data into useful information, which is denoted in the second and third steps in Figure 1-7. The third step ranks the items based on their profitability from high to low (continuum organizing principle) to facilitate the analysis. The most profitable item is the Grilled-Fish Tacos and the least profitable is the Baja Burger. In the fourth step, the food cost percentage is calculated to provide further insight into menu item performance. For example, what can be done to improve the profitability of the Baja Burger? Because this menu item has the highest food cost percentage, management changes the food cost variable (reduces the cost to $2.65 by decreasing the portion size) to assess its impact on profitability or the total contribution margin, as denoted in the fifth step. Changing variables allows managers to create hypothetical or "what-if" scenarios to study future possibilities.

A computer is a creative tool that helps managers combine their linguistic, numerical, and analytical skills with imagination when working with information. It enables them to interact with information rather than simply receiving or reviewing it. It enables them to formulate, revise, and work with thoughts and ideas with speed and flexibility. But most importantly, "if information tools can help executives think, then they can help corporations flourish" (14).

Nobel Prize Laureate Arno Penzias writes: "As we review the needs and opportunities for advanced technology, we should also look for growth in human capabilities. Some of that growth can come from better use of the tools technology provides" (15).

XYZ Restaurant POS data for October

First Step

Menu Item	# Sold	Selling Price	Item Food Cost
Baja Burger	1200	$8.50	$3.11
Chicken Salad	3000	$7.95	$2.56
Shrimp Platter	1400	$16.95	$5.10
Grilled-Fish Tacos	6000	$9.95	$3.25
Baby Back Ribs	700	$19.95	$6.25
Classic Ribeye	500	$23.50	$8.00
Chicken Fajitas	4000	$11.50	$3.50

Second Step

Menu Item	# Sold	Selling price	Item Food Cost	CM	TCM
Baja Burger	1200	$8.50	$3.11	$5.39	$6,468.00
Chicken Salad	3000	$7.95	$2.56	$5.39	$16,170.00
Shrimp Platter	1400	$16.95	$5.10	$11.85	$16,590.00
Grilled-Fish Tacos	6000	$9.95	$3.25	$6.70	$40,200.00
Baby Back Ribs	700	$19.95	$6.25	$13.70	$9,590.00
Classic Ribeye	500	$23.50	$8.00	$15.50	$7,750.00
Chicken Fajitas	4000	$11.50	$3.50	$8.00	$32,000.00
Total					$128,768.00

Contribution Margin (CM) = Selling price - Item Food Cost
Total Contribution Margin (TCM) = # Sold X CM

Third Step

Menu Item	# Sold	Selling price	Item Food Cost	CM	TCM
Grilled-Fish Tacos	6000	$9.95	$3.25	$6.70	$40,200.00
Chicken Fajitas	4000	$11.50	$3.50	$8.00	$32,000.00
Shrimp Platter	1400	$16.95	$5.10	$11.85	$16,590.00

(continued)

Third Step (Continued)						
Chicken Salad	3000	$7.95	$2.56	$5.39	$16,170.00	
Baby Back Ribs	700	$19.95	$6.25	$13.70	$9,590.00	
Classic Ribeye	500	$23.50	$8.00	$15.50	$7,750.00	
Baja Burger	1200	$8.50	$3.11	$5.39	$6,468.00	
Total					$128,768.00	
Fourth Step						
Menu Item	**# Sold**	**Selling price**	**Item Food Cost**	**CM**	**TCM**	**FC %**
Grilled-Fish Tacos	6000	$9.95	$3.25	$6.70	$40,200.00	32.66%
Chicken Fajitas	4000	$11.50	$3.50	$8.00	$32,000.00	30.43%
Shrimp Platter	1400	$16.95	$5.10	$11.85	$16,590.00	30.09%
Chicken Salad	3000	$7.95	$2.56	$5.39	$16,170.00	32.20%
Baby Back Ribs	700	$19.95	$6.25	$13.70	$9,590.00	31.33%
Classic Ribeye	500	$23.50	$8.00	$15.50	$7,750.00	34.04%
Baja Burger	1200	$8.50	$3.11	$5.39	$6,468.00	36.59%
Total					$128,768.00	
Food Cost (FC) % = Item Food Cost/Selling Price						
Fifth Step						
Menu Item	**# Sold**	**Selling price**	**Item Food Cost**	**CM**	**TCM**	**FC %**
Grilled-Fish Tacos	6000	$9.95	$3.25	$6.70	$40,200.00	32.66%
Chicken Fajitas	4000	$11.50	$3.50	$8.00	$32,000.00	30.43%
Shrimp Platter	1400	$16.95	$5.10	$11.85	$16,590.00	30.09%
Chicken Salad	3000	$7.95	$2.56	$5.39	$16,170.00	32.20%
Baby Back Ribs	700	$19.95	$6.25	$13.70	$9,590.00	31.33%
Classic Ribeye	500	$23.50	$8.00	$15.50	$7,750.00	34.04%
Baja Burger	1200	$8.50	$2.65	$5.85	$7,020.00	31.18%
Total					$129,320.00	

FIGURE 1-7. XYZ RESTAURANT POS DATA.

Insights from an Expert

Technology and Leadership

Jon Inge
President, Jon Inge and Associates

Modern hotel management is very complex, requiring an unusually good balance between the warmth of personal interactions that form the very core of hospitality and the effective use of technology to support and enable them. Experience and gut feelings will always form the background to every decision – that's human nature – but successful hotel leadership is increasingly data-driven.

Guest relationship management has become very sensitive as each property strives to stand out through highly personal service. Travelers now expect that their regular preferences and past experiences are known to the hotel, and any errors in service therefore have a greater impact because expectations haven't been met. Outstanding service can't be achieved through staff training alone; it also requires making sure that the staff has instant access to the right amount of detailed and accurate profile information at each point of guest contact to anticipate and respond to their requests.

Revenue management is another challenging area. The rising use of mobile devices for booking reservations is encouraging ever-shorter lead times, and personalization of the travel experience has become a major decision factor. To be competitive a hotel needs to offer very specific packages to well-defined micro-segments of the market, and to do so at the times and on the channels where the target audience is most likely to see and book them. Further, the response to each offer must be monitored in real time so that unappealing packages can be pulled and successful ones expanded. This cannot be done manually; it requires the flexible and detailed analysis of booking trends and automated monitoring tools to guide the staff's expertise and help them distribute offers quickly and accurately.

As in most businesses hotel systems can generate massive amounts of data, but that's no help at all if it's overwhelming in volume and uncertain in accuracy. To get meaningful, actionable information out of it requires the best possible operations-wide integration between the systems, and powerful, flexible tools to identify trends and actionable priorities. Fortunately, we have both.

Ideally, each property would use a single, integrated system covering every aspect of the operation – reservations, front desk, housekeeping, guest activities, POS, S&C, accounting, supply chain management, workforce management, and so on. Such systems ensure that each piece of data is entered only once, at the source which has the best chance of ensuring its accuracy, and doesn't undergo any transformations to be available at any other point. They also make it relatively simple for useful guest profile data to be fed back to staff at restaurants, spas, and other guest-interaction points.

In many situations, however, a franchise brand will dictate which front desk and reservations systems will be used, and for full operational effectiveness these must be properly integrated with all the other non-brand-specific applications. This has become easier with the greater adoption of Web-services-based interfaces, but it is still leadership's responsibility to ensure that the right combination of systems is implemented, with the right interfaces. This may require the replacement of older applications which work well in their own environment but cannot share their data seamlessly with other areas.

Business intelligence systems can use the same comprehensive database that, in an integrated system, underpins revenue management and GRM. In more mixed environments, independent BI applications can consolidate data from many different systems for useful analysis and present it in easy-to-understand dashboards of KPIs. The sooner management can be made aware of trends and critical situations needing their attention, the more focused and effective their leadership can be.

Leadership also requires setting the right tone in making full use of the technology. Management has a key role in encouraging data accuracy, both at the first point of entry as well as in supporting the inevitably tedious work of keeping the database clean by identifying and merging duplicate records, keeping on top of changes of address, and so on. The same applies to the infrastructure; wired and wireless networks, computers, and printers must all be kept fully up to date if the systems are to operate at their best potential.

Staff training is of critical importance. Regular refresher training at least annually will ensure that both new and long-serving staff use the systems most effectively to leverage their skills and experience, and research has shown a direct correlation between training and bottom-line profitability.

Hospitality continues to be one of the most fascinating industries. It requires everyone involved to be very focused on personal interactions and on providing a warm, welcoming environment for the guests, but at the same time it embodies the most up-to-date convergence of mobile and personal technologies. Great leadership requires not just understanding and embodying this balance, but also ensuring that each department is working to its best potential and that each staff member has access to and confidence in the information s/he needs to do the job properly.

Tech News

Apollo Wills It!

Michael Schubach

The Greek God, Apollo, is most interesting to me for his credo: "know thyself". Apollo's watchwords were adapted by Socrates, who crystallized the essence of the thought into his now-famous observation that "the unexamined life is not worth living." All that classical stuff said, I think that we hotel folk should take a second look at our technology lives.

I support this call to reexamination based on a conversation I had with an equipment supplier who was very excited to see the interest that the hospitality community was showing in their latest generation of self-service equipment. To quote his sales team's reaction: "We are surprised to see this much interest in self-service platforms from the hospitality industry. We always thought of them as 'historically touchy-feely'."

Does the world still think that the hospitality industry is too much in touch with its touchy-feely side? I seriously doubt that – in this case I believe that we're dealing with an urban myth hangover. There was a time – once upon a time – when the dreaded computer terminal was viewed as the sworn enemy of high-touch personalized service. Hoteliers wanted the technology in the back room and the clerk with the caring smile out front at the desk. They hated that guest service agents would go "heads down" over a display rather than meet the guest at eye level. (I think we fixed that problem by installing bigger screens higher up, but let's not digress.)

As an industry, we finally realize and openly acknowledge that high-speed technology is the handmaiden of high-touch service. Today, with the rising tide of millennials and the ubiquity of personal computing devices, being one with the matrix is not just socially acceptable, it's ultimately cool. "Heads down" is now the posture-of-choice for both sides of the desk. For a growing number of travelers, self service is not only a viable option, but the way in which they actually prefer to be served.

The hospitality industry today has no problem with technology adoption – we're all over it like crazed fashionistas at a half-off shoe sale. Self-service equipment manufacturers and application writers can allay their fears, forget any lingering suspicion of hotelier touchy-feeliness and churn out next generation products as fast as they can. We want shiny somethings for everyone, and that enthusiasm is by no means confined to the I.T. staff. Point in fact, I.T. may be the *least* enthusiastic group in a technology stampede that encompasses virtually every other operating department, all of them feverishly seeking new technology solutions to make their business easier and their results more lucrative or satisfying … or lucrative.

This is the real reason that a reexamination of our technology-based life is due. Wanting, needing, or even buying each next new innovation isn't enough – maintaining and leveraging technology is every bit the challenge that evaluating, acquiring, and deploying represents. I am always amazed when I speak with hotel operators who can find the money for yet another snap-on attachment that offers the promise of everyone-wants-this market pull, but they haven't been able to find budget dollars for boring fundamentals like server replacement, software upgrades, and staff training. The network chain is only as strong as its weakest link, and the information it contains is only as valuable and usable as the input source is reliable. Yes, the vendor community has an obligation to keep producing new products and has its own vested interest in keeping the shiny quotient as high as possible. And the hotelier's willingness to investment in new guest service technologies is both smart and admirable. But the sheer volume of technology options being deployed in some operations is more than enough to overwhelm the advantages that the component pieces offer. We try to respond to potential sources of income and then realize that income opportunities can arise from everywhere. We try to be in touch with our guests' wants and desires and then realize that those could be anything and everything. We try to be open to every possibility and we realize that means never being able to exclude any possibility. We set up to reach out to the entire world and realize that we must be ready to respond to the entire world when they answer.

These are not only noble objectives – they are examples of how the game is played today. However, the bigger question they beg is how the game is *won* today. In the absence of a deliberate strategic plan with specified outcomes for each device and investment, technology can be reduced to nothing more than a lot of stuff of questionable value that may or may not be delivering the promised return on investment. The strategic plan needs to include a realistic assessment of how the hotel views its market and guests, whom it wishes to serve, and how it wishes to grow. Technology must serve those objectives or be retired, and each new project has to compete with other departments and other projects for the limited supply of budget dollars.

Surrounding one's operation with some of everything doesn't support the notion of knowing thyself ... really knowing thyself. Your technology array should demonstrate what your business is and tell a story of where it's going. "Unlimited possibilities" may sound Olympian but it isn't very practical. Besides, Apollo didn't ask you to "know thy universe." He, too, functioned on a more realistic plane. From a technology perspective, I think the philosophical statement that makes the most sense is "know thyself, make thy plan and remember that the unexamined stuff is not worth buying."*

(*To give proper credit and make certain that the quotation is accurately cited, that was Socrates, Apollo, and me all sort of shoved together at once.)

Royal Caribbean Rolls out Self-Service Drink Fountains with RFID Technology

Bob Midyette

With 22 innovative ships, and more than 270 destinations in 72 countries across six continents, Royal Caribbean International is always looking for ways to increase guest satisfaction and sales.

For several years, the firm has offered a popular beverage package featuring Coca-Cola products. This beverage package entitles guests to unlimited fountain soda for a set price at the beginning of their cruise vacation. While this package yielded a very high penetration rate among guests and became one of Royal Caribbean's single most popular offerings in food and beverage, it did not rate high on guest satisfaction.

The majority of the adverse comments we received from guests centered on their inability to refill their soda in the timely manner that they felt entitled to receive. After careful examination and extensive testing, the company implemented two unique solutions that completely changed guests' experiences while increasing sales.

Rfid Technology

In early 2008, Royal Caribbean commissioned both their souvenir cup manufacturing partner, Whirley DrinkWorks, and their sister company ValidFill to develop a self-service soda fountain machine prototype that would allow the company to better control and elevate their soda beverage packages.

The prototype used radio frequency identification (RFID) technology, which allowed guests who purchased the unlimited fountain soda packages to serve themselves while restricting service to guests who chose not to purchase the package.

After two years of testing, the company unveiled a specially designed souvenir cup from Whirley DrinkWorks with an embedded microchip and next-generation soda fountain dispensers retrofitted with the RFID technology from ValidFill. The dispenser instantly reads the microchip at the bottom of each cup, validates access to the beverage package, and pours the correct amount of soda, preventing guests from filling other cups or containers. Because liquids can adversely affect electrical signals, the RFID readers are contained in a waterproof stainless cabinet below the soda dispenser and special antennas are sealed in the drip tray.

Says Bob Midyette, director of fleet beverage operations for Royal Caribbean International and Azamara Club Cruises, "For the first time, guests are not dependant on an employee for timely service."

Ultraviolet Technology

Taking things a step further, the firm then asked themselves in-depth questions, "What if the self-service program is as successful as anticipated?" and "What demands would that success place on the firm's operation?" Traditionally, several thousand souvenir cups were unwrapped each week per ship, washed in a dishwasher, dried, lids placed back on and then sold.

It was a time-consuming process and the company became concerned that even a marginal increase in soda package sales could quickly overwhelm their workforce with the additional work and limit sales. With this in mind, the company began benchmarking best practices from various theme parks and discovered that sanitizing cups at the point of production rather than the point of sale reduced labor and allowed the firm to provide the highest level of assurance to guests and crew members alike.

In a process approved by the United States Public Health organization (USPH), a division of the Centers for Disease Control (CDC) that regulates the cruise ship industry, the souvenir cups now come to the ships pre-sanitized and cleaned. Each cup goes through an ultraviolet (UV) tunnel cleaning process before being packaged and shipped to Royal Caribbean. The UV lights use different wavelengths to ensure the cups are bacteria-free and safe for guests. Thanks to UV technology, there is a reduction in overtime and labor and staff are freed up to better engage guests.

Improved Sales and Guest Satisfaction

These technology solutions helped to change several business processes for Royal Caribbean, starting with the sales process. The self-service dispensers are a great sales generator because once guests learn that a souvenir cup is required for access, most choose to purchase an unlimited fountain soda package, and we've experienced a significant increase in soda sales since the dispensers were implemented.

The serving process also has improved. An excellent example of this can be seen at the pool deck, a very high volume bar, where in the past a significant percentage of guests would wait for a bartender to refill soda. Now, guests serve themselves, which allows the company to provide faster and more frequent service to guests requesting drinks other than soda.

Since the deployment, guest satisfaction has increased significantly. Crew members also benefit because they can focus on providing great service and selling premium cocktails. And, based on testing one ship, Royal Caribbean's sales expanded by 107 percent.

Royal Caribbean is committed to elevating the guest experience; with RFID and UV technologies, the company has dramatically improved guest satisfaction while increasing efficiencies, productivity and sales, and experiencing a return on their investment of over 1,000 percent since implementing these changes fleetwide.

References

1. Penzias, Arno, *Ideas and Information,* New York, NY: Touchstone, 1990, p. 30.
2. Tallon, Paul, and Pinesonneault, Alain, "Competing Perspectives on the link between strategic information technology assignment and organizational agility: insights from a mediation model," *MIS Quarterly*, June 2011, pp. 463–484.
3. Miller, Delyana, Halina, Bruce, Gagnon, Michele, Talbot, Vincent, and Messier, Claude, "Improving older adults' experience with interactive voice response system," *Telemedicine and E-Health,* July 2011, pp. 452–455.
4. Babcock, Charles, "Companies Getting Real Results from Cloud Computing," *InformationWeek,* January 2011, pp. 1–5.
5. Pressman, Roger, and Herron, Russel, *Software Shock*, New York, NY: Dorset House Publishing, 1991, p. 15.
6. Shneiderman, Ben, and Plaisant, Catherine, *Designing the User Interface: Strategies for Effective Human-Computer Interaction*, Upper Saddle, NJ, 2010.
7. Collins, Galen, "Usable Mobile Ambient Intelligent Solutions for Hospitality Customers," *Journal of Information Technology Impact,* 2010, pp. 45–54.
8. Sill, Brian, "Future Computer Applications," *Restaurant Business,* June 1989, p.136.
9. Kelly, Thomas, and Carvell, Steven, "Checking the Checks: A Survey of Guest-Check Accuracy," *Cornell Quarterly,* November 1987, pp. 63—65.
10. Talbot, David, "A Social-Media Decoder," *MIT technology Review,* November/December 2011, p. 44.
11. Wurman, Richard, *Information Anxiety,* New York, NY: Bantam Books, 1990, p. 297.
12. Matthews, Robert, "Planning for Data," *New Scientist,* May 25, 1996, pp. 30–33.
13. *Ibid.*
14. Boone, Mary, *Leadership and the Computer*, Rocklin, CA: Prima Publishing, 1991, p. 274.
15. Penzias, *op. cit.*, p. 165.

CHAPTER 2

Networks and System Security

"In a few hundred years, when the history of our time will be written from a long-term perspective, it is likely that the most important event historians will see is not technology, not the Internet, not e-commerce. It is an unprecedented change in the human condition. For the first time - literally - substantial and rapidly growing numbers of people have choices. For the first time, they will have to manage themselves. And society is totally unprepared for it."

Peter F. Drucker

CHAPTER OUTLINE

INTRODUCTION

The manner in which people communicate has come a long way since 1084 BC when news of the fall of Troy was transmitted by fires lighted on mountaintops. Today, people are linked by wires or air (wireless) carrying data, voice, video, and computer signals via the telecommunication systems. This method of information delivery is referred to as **DATA COMMUNICATIONS**, the combination of **TELECOMMUNICATIONS** (any system for communicating over a long distance) and **DATA PROCESSING**. The union of these two technologies has resulted in greater information access.

More specifically, data communications refers to the electronic transfer of information (e.g., data, text, still pictures, graphics, voice, and video) from one computer to another via direct cable or wireless connections (LAN) or via telecommunication links involving the telecommunication systems and modems (WAN). The linkage of computer systems by means of communication lines or channels (e.g., fiber optic, microwave, satellite, telephone line, 802.11) is called a **COMPUTER NETWORK.**

Data communications has had a pervasive impact on the world of business for several reasons:

1. It enables information to be accessed and transmitted quickly. According to Karen Nickel, a writer for *Fortune* magazine, "The lifeblood of business is information. And since information is perishable, it needs to be disseminated quickly." For example, Chuck E. Cheese Restaurants corporations use **Automatic Data Collection** or **Polling** systems for gathering data daily from each restaurant's point-of-sale system with the help of a WAN. In addition, the restaurant chain updates the menu changes with a touch of a button in more than 400 units. Before the installation of a WAN, Chuck E. Cheese used to update menu changes to POS system manually which took months. Reporting tools quickly make processed data available. Alerts can then be sent to select managers via e-mail, pager, cell phone, or other means when an important report is ready or a vital metric exceeds its preset variance (e.g., labor cost exceeds 35%).
2. It allows the storing of information in a centralized database that may be shared by a few users in a small computer network or by thousands of users in a large computer network. This eliminates duplicate processing, redundant information, delays, errors, and misunderstandings (1).
3. It facilitates centralized management and decentralized operations (e.g., restaurant chain). As a result, businesses are becoming increasingly global. With a centralized database and an advanced computer network, an international hotel corporation can maintain control of properties around the world (2) yet they can install and use specific software that the entire chain does not have to use. For example, not all hotels will need to use catering system, such as MeetingMatrix, but all hotels in a chain need to be part of the central reservation system.
4. It links business processes performed by independent computer systems to improve organizational efficiency and effectiveness. For example, central reservation systems can be linked into the gigantic distribution networks (i.e., Global Distribution Systems such as Travelport Worldspan) to expand the selling function to travel agencies, or a telephone system can be linked to the front office system via call accounting system for recording timely and accurate phone charges on guest folios.

5. It links a business to its customers. Communication devices, such as smart phones (i.e. iPhone, Samsung Galaxy) and tablet devices enable business people to always be in touch with their clients.
6. It links businesses to businesses. Businesses save a lot of money by connecting their systems together, therefore eliminating the need for manual connections. For example, McDonald's company's Point of Sale System (POS) is connected to its suppliers. Each time a BigMac is sold, the POS keeps track of the ingredients used. This way, at the end of the day, a purchase order is automatically generated (i.e., 50 dozen of burger patties, 50 gallons of frying oil), based on the items that were sold on that day. This eliminates the generation of purchase order manually, therefore saving a lot of money. Similarly, a hotel's Property Management System (PMS) can be tied to a corporate travel agent's reservation systems, allowing hotel reservations to be done automatically.
7. It links customers to customers. In this age of networks, customers generate their own content to be used by other customers. TripAdvisor.com is a great example of consumer generated material. The reviews about hotels and restaurants in TripAdvisor.com are very powerful in influencing hotel customers' choice. Similarly, social networking allows consumers to exchange information about businesses that influence decision making. The impact of consumer generated, unsolicited information is much more powerful than the advertising that the company does by itself.
8. It changes the organizational hierarchy. Economist Peter Drucker explains that middle management disappeared because information systems took over the communication of information upward and downward through the hierarchy. The consequent "flattening" of corporate structures is leading to a new model in which teams, not individuals, form the basic corporate unit. Drucker concludes that "the structure of the team-based organization of the future will resemble that of a symphony orchestra: bands of semi-autonomous professionals coordinated by central management, much as a conductor keeps the violins in step with the woodwinds" (3).

Computer Networks

In the computer world, the term computer network or simply network refers to a collection of computers and network hardware interconnected by communication channels that allow sharing of resources and information such as printers, applications, and databases (i.e., hotel central reservation system). Computer networks have become a "**mission critical**" component of hospitality businesses. Can you imagine a hotel company with its reservation website down? Or its central reservation system down? Probably not because the hotel reservation website and the central reservation system are significant sources of business. Both of them are part of a computer network that needs to be maintained and serviced.

> "What a computer is to me is the most remarkable tool that we have ever come up with. It's the equivalent of a bicycle for our minds." (Steve Jobs in film "Memory & Imagination," 1990)

Local Area Network (LAN) Hardware and Software

Local Area Network (LAN). By definition, LAN is linkage of computers in a specific geographical area (usually within an office or building) such as in hotels, restaurants, or country clubs using a transmission medium such as twisted pair wire or coaxial cable. The first LANs were limited to a range of 600 feet and no more than 30 computers. Today, it is possible to connect several hundred computers in a wider area to a LAN. However, to manage the LAN effectively, small logical areas called workgroups are created. Figure 2-1 shows a small LAN with a workgroup. To create a LAN, several types of hardware and software components are needed.

Wireless Networks

Wireless Networks. Today, more and more wireless LANs are replacing traditional wired LANs. Some of the advantages of a Wireless LAN that drives this change are:

1. Wireless LANs are simple to set up. It literally can take 10 minutes for a simple wireless network to be set up.
2. Wireless LANs are cheap to create.
3. When it is not possible to wire, Wireless LANs may be a viable choice. For example, in a golf course or the Grand Canyon, wired LANs are very difficult to install. However, with wireless LANs, it is possible.
4. Security is the biggest downside of wireless LANs. However, the recent standards, such as 802.11n, are increasing the security of wireless LANs.

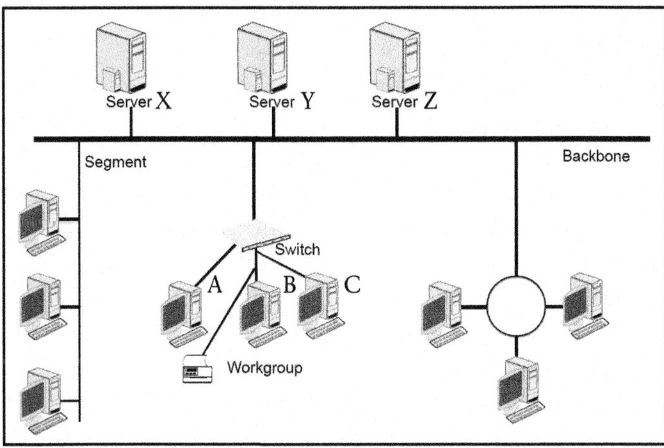

FIGURE 2-1. A SMALL LAN WITH THREE DIFFERENT TOPOLOGIES.

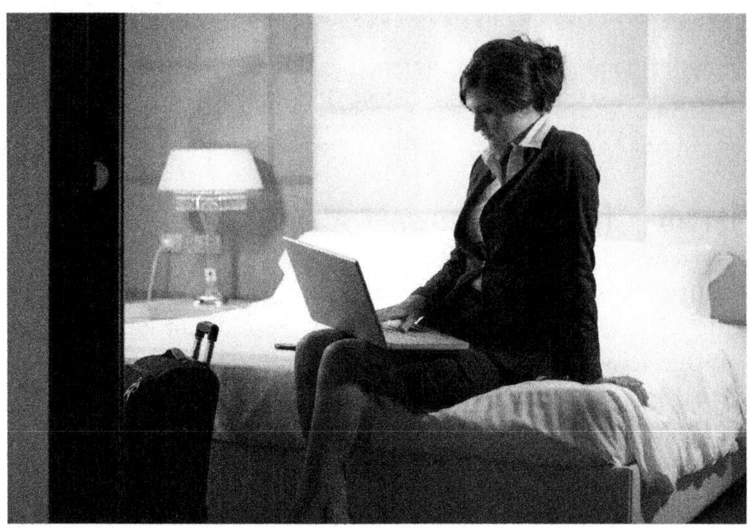

FBI'S INTERNET CRIME COMPLAINT CENTER WARNED OF A SPATE OF INCIDENTS OF TRAVELERS ENCOUNTERING BOGUS SOFTWARE UPDATE POP-UPS WHEN THEY USED HOTEL INTERNET CONNECTIONS OVERSEAS.

Source: © Stefanolunardi, 2013. Used under license from Shutterstock, Inc.

By connecting all the components and peripheral devices within a hotel restaurant or club, an organization could provide wide access to a valuable database such as a centralized reservation system or maximize the productivity of a laser printer or high capacity hard disk. A LAN's high speed communication capability (i.e., 10 Gigabits per second) enables a user to access remote devices as if they were directly attached to the user's workstation. A LAN consists of the following basic hardware and software components:

Network Operating System

1. **Network Operating System (NOS).** It runs the networked computers, providing the ability to share files, printers, and other devices across the network. Devices that share their resources are called **SERVERS**. Network operating programs that give the ability to use those shared resources are called **CLIENTS OR NODES**. Network software can be added to the system, such as Artisoft's LANtastic or Novell's Netware, or it can be part of an operating system, such as Microsoft's Windows 12 Server.

Workstation

2. **Workstation.** In LAN environment, a workstation, also called "node" or "client," refers to any computer that is connected to the network. However, it is important to note the difference between a workstation and client. A workstation is a computer that can request resources from the network while a client is any network entity

such as a printer or fax that can request resources from the network. In other words, workstations can be clients, but not all clients are workstations.

A HOTEL NETWORK SERVER ROOM WITH COMPUTERS.

Source: © Dotshock, 2013. Used under license from Shutterstock, Inc.

Server

3. **Server.** A server provides resources to the clients on the network. Servers are usually powerful computers that run network operating software (NOS) such as Linux, Novell or Windows Server 2012 that controls and maintains the network. For small properties, a server can handle multiple tasks such as a file server, print server, or web server. However, bigger properties may utilize separate servers for different purposes. Common servers are:

- File Server: holds and distributes files
- Print Server: handles printing jobs from clients
- Proxy Server: performs a function on behalf of other computers
- Application Server: hosts a network application (i.e., Marriott's central reservation system, Marsha)
- Web Server: handles web pages and other web content (i.e., Marriott.com, Hilton.com, Starwood.com)
- Mail Server: hosts and delivers electronic mail.
- Audio/Video Server: Audio/Video servers bring multimedia capabilities to Web sites by enabling them to broadcast streaming multimedia content. Streaming is a technique for transferring data such that it can be processed as a steady and continuous stream.
- Telnet Servers

A Telnet server enables users to log on to a host computer and perform tasks as if they're working on the remote computer.

- Voice over IP server: handles telephone calls over Internet Protocol (IP)

Hosts

4. **Hosts.** In LAN environments, all other networking devices are called "hosts."

Network Interface Card

5. **Network Interface Card (NIC).** A network card, network adapter, LAN Adapter, or NIC (network interface card) is a piece of computer hardware designed to allow computers to communicate over a computer network (See Figure 2-1). Each NIC has a unique address called Media Access Control (MAC) address. Even though the MAC of an NIC may be changed at the software level, it is used in switches to recognize the stations attached to a network.

Switch/Hub

6. **Switch/Hub.** A network switch is a computer networking device that connects network segments. Figure 2-2 shows a network cable connected to a switch. A switch

FIGURE 2-2. A NETWORK CABLE CONNECTED TO A SWITCH.

Source: © Kubais, 2013. Used under license from Shutterstock, Inc.

builds a table of all media access control (MAC) addresses of all stations and sends the requests for data transmission to appropriate stations, clients, or nodes. Before switches, a device called a "hub" was widely used. A hub does a similar job to a switch; however, a hub transmits all data to all nodes regardless of the source and destination. A switch, on the other hand, transmits the data only to the destination computer.

For example, in Figure 2-1, if workstation A wants to transmit data to workstation C, the data will first go to the switch. The switch will scan the MAC address table and locate workstation C and then send the data to workstation C only. However, if a hub is used instead of a switch, the data would to be sent to the hub first. The hub would then send the data to all nodes in the network (workstation B, workstation C, server X, server Y, server Z). Even though a hub is cheaper than a switch, it has two important constraints:

1. clogs the network: since a hub sends the data to all stations on the network, the network traffic increases.
2. poses security risk: since a hub sends the data to all stations on the network, unauthorized users may have access to sensitive data.

For these reasons, almost every hospitality organization replaced their hubs with smart switches.

Network Interface Board

7. **Network Interface Board.** Each workstation or microcomputer on the network contains an interface board. A cable is inserted into the adapter card and connected to network media (e.g., twisted pair, coaxial cable, or wireless). It is important to select reliable network interface cards that are compatible with the network and that can transfer data from the microcomputer to various servers quickly. Most computers today will include a LAN interface card and wireless interface card (i.e., 802.11a, n, g, or b).

Cable

8. **Cable:** A wired LAN requires cables to connect the computers together. There are several type of cables:

    1. Twisted-pair cable (TPC) consists of multiple, individually insulated wires that are twisted together in pairs. Sometimes a metallic shield is placed around the twisted pairs, which is then called "shielded twisted-pair cable". TPC are rated in the following categories: a) Category 1 (Cat 1), Category 2 (Cat 2), Category 3 (Cat 3), Category 4 (Cat 4), Category 5 (Cat 5), Cat-gory 5 enhanced (Cat 5e), Category 6 (Cat 6), Category 7 (Cat 7). Cat 5 and higher are also referred to as "Ethernet Cable." (See Figure 2-3) The most common cables used in LANs

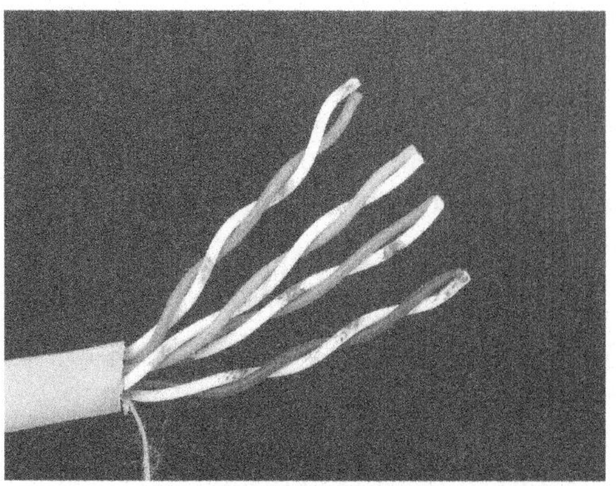

FIGURE 2-3. THE TWISTED PAIR WIRES OF COMPUTER NETWORK CABLE.

Source: © Georgios Alexandris, 2008. Used under license from Shutterstock, Inc.

FIGURE 2-3A. A TWISTED PAIR CABLE IN THE FORM OF CAT 5E.

Source: © Amlet, 2008. Used under license from Shutterstock, Inc.

FIGURE 2-4. A COAXIAL CABLE.

Source: © Johnny Lye, 2008. Used under license from Shutterstock, Inc.

are CAT 5 and CAT 5e. Cat 5 supports data transmission up to 100 Megabits per second (Mbps) while Cat 5e supports up to 1 Gbps and Cat 6 supports up to 10 Gbps. For new networks, it is better to use the most advanced cable (i.e., Cat 7) because as the category level increases, the quality and speed of the data that the cable transmits increases.

2. Coaxial cable: contains a center conductor, made of copper, surrounded by a plastic jacket, with a braided shield over the jacket. Many of you have seen this cable at your homes when connecting cable TV to your TV set (See Figure 2-4). This cable is usually found in older networks.

3. Fiber-Optic: An optical fiber is a glass or plastic fiber that carries light along its length. This cable is the fastest and most expensive transmission medium in the world today (See Figure 2-5). Since data is transmitted with light, it travels very fast. Fiber cabling was provided to only big businesses, however, recent advances in fiber-optic cabling have now made it viable for households and small businesses. Currently, Verizon offers fiber optic Internet access that can support data transmission up to 40 Gbps.

Some advantages of fiber-optic cable are:

- Superior System Performance
- Greatly increased bandwidth and capacity
- Lower signal loss
- Immunity to Electrical Noise
- Immunity to noise (electromagnetic interference [EMI] and radio-frequency interference [RFI]
- Lower bit error rates
- Signal Security
- Difficult to tap
- Lightweight

Some disadvantages of fiber-optic cables include: the cost (even though the cost of fiber-optic cable is very high right now, it is expected to be less expensive over time). Similarly, connectors for fiber-optic cable are expensive. Fiber-optic cables are also sensitive; they do not handle extensive bending.

Network Topology

9. **Network Topology.** The manner in which workstations are connected together physically and logically is referred to as a **NETWORK TOPOLOGY**. There are three basic network topologies (refer to Figure 2-6):

FIGURE 2-5. FIBER OPTIC CABLE AND CONNECTORS.

Source: © Yegor Korzh, 2008. Used under license from Shutterstock, Inc.

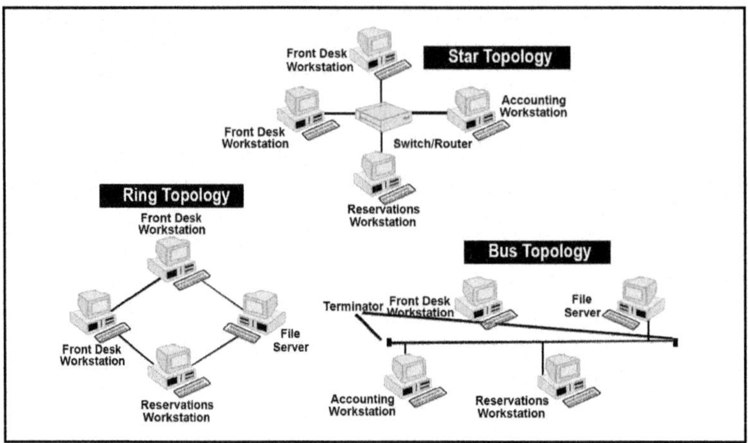

FIGURE 2-6. NETWORK TOPOLOGIES.

- *Bus topology.* This permits the connection of workstations and peripheral devices along a central cable. Bus topology is simple and cheap to set up, however, there are often problems when two clients want to transmit at the same time on the same bus.

  The advantages of bus topology:

- *Easy* to implement and extend.
- *Requires* less cable length than a star topology.
- Well suited for temporary or small networks not requiring high speeds (quick setup).
- Cheaper than other topologies.

  Disadvantages:

- Limited cable length and number of stations.
- If there is a problem with the cable, the entire network goes down.
- Maintenance costs may be higher in the long run.
- Performance degrades as additional computers are added or on heavy traffic.
- Proper termination is required (loop must be in closed path).
- Significant Capacitive Load (each bus transaction must be able to stretch to most distant link).
- It works best with limited number of nodes.

  Bus topology is almost never used in the hospitality industry today due to its limitations.

- *Ring topology.* This permits workstations to be connected to each other forming a closed loop. A ring network requires less cable than a star network and is less sensitive to distance than a bus topology since each workstation in the ring regenerates the signal. The primary disadvantage of a ring network is that a failed workstation might break the ring. In a star network, a disabled workstation does not affect other workstations. Ring topology may be used in departments that handle sensitive data, such as accounting and human resources.

- *Star topology.* Star topology is the most common network. With the advances in switches and routers, it is relatively simple to create a fast local area network using star topology.

  In its simplest form, a star network consists of one central switch, hub, or computer, which acts as a conduit to transmit messages. This permits workstations to be connected to a central point or hub. The switch, as explained above, is similar to a telephone switch because it directs all network requests. It is easy to pinpoint hardware problems in a star network topology. A star network, however, requires more cable than a bus or ring network.

Wide Area Network (WAN)

Wide Area Network. A WAN links computers in a LAN set up over a great distance using telephone lines, fiber-optic, satellites, microwave stations, cellular broadband technology or a combination of these transmission media. At least two LANs should be connected to each other to be able to create a WAN. Figure 2-7 shows a simple WAN network between two hotels.

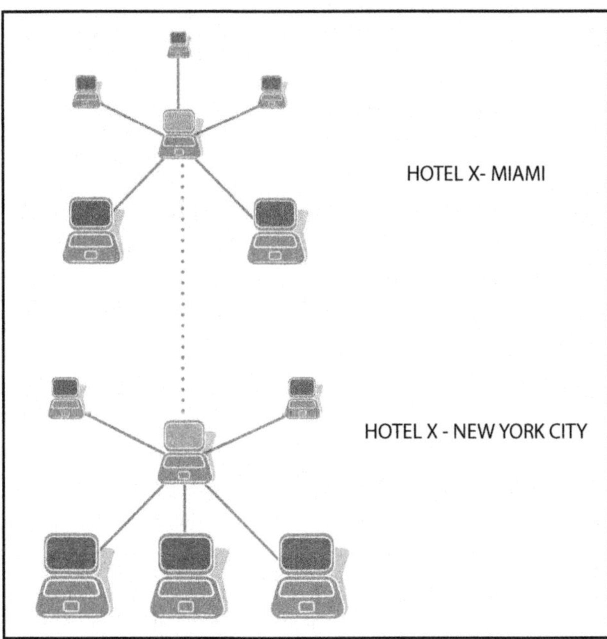

FIGURE 2-7. IMAGE COPYRIGHT SMITH&SMITH, 2008. USED UNDER LICENSE FROM SHUTTERSTOCK, INC.

Source: © Smith&Smith, 2008. Used under license from Shutterstock, Inc.

Organizations use common carriers to be able to create a WAN. Common carriers provide two basic types of services: a private line and a dial-up line (14).

A **Private Line** is leased from the carrier, usually on a monthly basis. The charge for this channel is based on both the channel capacity (bits per second) and the distance (air miles). A T-1 line, a 1.544 Mbps point-to-point dedicated and digital circuit, is an example of a private line. A T-1 line is frequently used to connect remote LANs or a PBX to the telephone company's central office. Another level, the T-3 line, transmits data at 44.736 Mbps.

A variation of a private line is **frame relay**, a telecommunication service designed for cost-efficient data transmission for intermittent traffic between local area networks (LANs) and between endpoints in a wide area network (WAN) utilizing existing T-1 and T-3 lines. Frame relay puts data in a variable-size unit called a frame and leaves necessary error corrections (retransmission of data) up to the endpoints, which speed up overall data transmission. For most services, the network provides a permanent virtual circuit (PVC) which means, for example, that each property in a hotel chain has a continuous and dedicated connection without having to pay for a full-time leased line. Carriers figure out the route each frame travels to its destination and charge based on the usage (*www .whatis.com*). Frame relay is offered by a number of carriers, including AT&T and Sprint, and may be used by hospitality organizations for their **virtual privatenetworks (VPNS)**. A VPN is a way to use a public telecommunication infrastructure, usually the Internet (IP), to provide properties and restaurants with secure access to their organization's network. An IP VPN is less expensive than a frame-relay VPN.

Microwave technology allows a company to transmit data over a wireless, low end radio channel. Because radio signals travel in a straight line, any tall object (e.g., trees, tall buildings, mountains) can interfere with microwave signals. Consequently, microwave dishes are often found atop sending and receiving towers or tall buildings. Furthermore, microwave transmissions have a range of about 60 miles. To extend the range, land based repeater stations can be used to regenerate signals. A regional hospitality corporation, for example, might find installing microwave equipment less expensive than leasing private lines. Microwave technology has been used extensively by the broadcast and cable television industries, as well as in other telecommunications applications, since the early 1950s. Today, microwaves are employed by telecommunications industries in the form of both terrestrial relays and satellite communications.

For geographically dispersed corporations, such as Sheraton, land based repeater stations are replaced with satellite relay stations to overcome the 60-mile distance limitation. A satellite relay enables a microwave transmission to reach locations anywhere in the world, enabling computers in Paris, France to communicate with computers in New York City. Although a satellite channel must be leased from a common carrier, it is generally less expensive than a terrestrial channel of equivalent capacity and is not vulnerable to natural disasters such as hurricanes and earthquakes. Satellite channels are used to transmit such things as reservation data, credit card authorizations, and customer orders (see Figure 2-8).

VSAT is a satellite communications system. It requires an integrated receiver decoder (IRD) at the receiving location to interface between the computer and an outside dish antenna with transceiver.

Figure 2-8 shows satellite dish hardware. The transceiver receives or sends a signal to a satellite transponder in the sky. A satellite transponder is a device on an orbiting satellite that receives incoming signals over a range, or band, of frequencies and then retransmits the signals on a different band at the same time. Geostationary Earth Orbit (GEO) satellites, located at 22,282 miles above the equator, serve as the central relay between a terrestrial hub and a wide-area network of small and inexpensive terrestrial transceivers with dish antennas as small as 16 inches in diameter. A VSAT handles data, voice, and video signals (*www.whatis.com*). VSAT is used by hospitality organizations. Especially, the units that are remote from DSL or Cable prefer VSAT technology because it can be set up in anywhere in the world. Border Foods, which owns approximately 80 Pizza Hut franchises in Minnesota, Iowa, and Wisconsin, has developed a broadband satellite network to enable its stores to receive online orders. The results are faster service, increased spending by customers, and greater in-store efficiency.

FIGURE 2-8. SATELLITE DISH.

Source: © Ramon Grosso Dolarea, 2008. Used under license from Shutterstock, Inc.

Various pieces of equipment are required to transmit data between computers in a wide area computer network.

Modem Technologies

Modem (Modulator/Demodulator) is a device that converts digital data into analog data and vice versa (4). Regular telephone networks work with analog technology. However, computers work with digital technology. To carry electronic data on an analog telephone line, a modem must be used. In the beginning days of the Internet in the 1990s, the majority of the users used a modem to connect to an Internet Service Provider (ISP) for Internet service. However, today, only a minority of users use modems to carry data over telephone lines. **Bandwidth**, the amount of data that can be transmitted in a fixed amount of time, is usually expressed in bits per second (bps). Dial-up modems, used by only a minority of users, have standard speeds between 28.8 Kbps (kilobits per second) and 56 Kbps (5). Dial-up modems are being replaced with affordable digital lines, such as **Digital Subscriber Lines** (DSL) and **Cable Modem Networks**. Each of these broadband technologies can provide the necessary bandwidth to satisfy the demand for high-speed Internet connections (6).

DSL

DSL is the one of the modem technologies for businesses using telephone copper lines. Assuming that a business location is close enough to a telephone company central office that offers DSL service, an individual connection can provide from 756 Kbps to 6 Mbps, (higher prices apply for higher rates of data transfer speed) and about 128 Kbps upstream (www.dsl.com). According to Elahi, xDSL refers to the general category of DSL services and also represents the different variations of DSL, such as **Asymmetrical DSL** (ADSL) and **Symmetrical DSL** (SDSL) (7). The "x" is a place keeper for the term describing the type of DSL connection.

ADSL is "asymmetric" because most of its two-way or duplex bandwidth is devoted to the downstream direction, sending data to the user. ADSL is an appropriate choice for business users using the Internet primarily for downloading information (www.dsl.com). SDSL is "symmetric" because its bandwidth is equally shared in the upstream and downstream directions. SDSL is an appropriate choice for business users uploading as much information to the Internet as they download (*www.dsl.com*).

Cable Modem Networks

Delivering data services over a cable network requires the allocation of one television channel for downstream traffic to businesses and another channel for upstream traffic. A Cable Modem Termination System (CMTS) communicates through these channels with cable modems located in subscriber businesses to create a virtual local area network connection (8). The CMTS is located at the head end, a facility at a local cable TV office that originates and communicates cable TV services and cable modem services to subscribers. Most cable modems are external devices that connect to a PC through

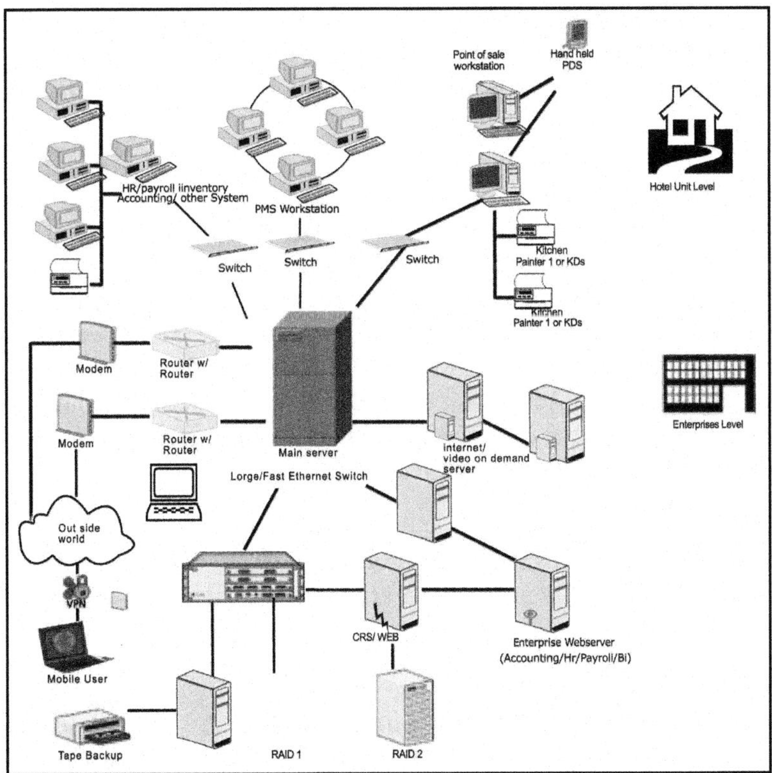

FIGURE 2-9. ENTERPRISE HOTEL NETWORK.

a standard Ethernet card or Universal Serial Bus (USB) connection. An individual cable modem subscriber may experience access speeds from 1.5 Mbps to 30Mbps or more, depending on the network architecture and traffic load.

Providing high-speed Internet services requires cable operators to build an end-to-end Internet Protocol (IP) networking infrastructure in each community that is robust enough to support tens of thousands of data subscribers. Consequently, the implementation of a cable modem network poses serious engineering and operations challenges (*www.cabledatacomnews.com*).

Wireless Cable Networks

Wireless cable is emerging as a viable local-access platform for the delivery of high-quality data. A **Wireless Cable Network** is similar to a wired cable network (*www.smarthomeforum.com*). A cable modem router and related networking equipment are installed at the wireless cable operator's head end. Then, digital signals, such as Internet content requests, are modulated onto the radio frequency (RF) channels for broadcast transmission to rooftop antennas at subscriber locations. Coaxial cable is run from the antenna to a down converter, which first shifts the microwave signal frequency into the cable television band before it enters the cable modem inside the customer premises. Wireless cable requires a direct line of sight between the transmitter and the receiving antenna. Dense tree cover, hills, tall buildings, mountains, and heavy precipitation can hinder reception.

Network Management

Since networks have become the assembly line, warehouse, and delivery system for many hospitality organizations, they need to be properly managed. In some cases, networks can be very large, making it necessary to be managed on a daily basis. In hospitality organizations where the average staff turnover rate is higher than other industries, managing networks becomes even more important to ensure the security of guest, company, and staff data. According to Fred Simonds, "Network management is a systematic approach to planning, organizing, and controlling networks" (16). The five basic functions of network management are:

Fault Management

1. **Fault management.** This is the detection and correction of errors. Common problems include defective network interface cards, damaged cabling, and server configuration errors.

Configuration Management

2. **Configuration management.** This involves cabling, configuration issues, design and planning, and upgrades. The network configuration is typically in a constant state of flux. Cable may need to be added or deleted to accommodate device changes. New devices must be assigned network addresses and configured correctly. Configuration of a printer, for example, might entail the prioritization of print jobs. Users must be added and deleted from the database. User login identifications and passwords need to be set and changed periodically.

Performance Management

3. **Performance management.** Does the network deliver satisfactory response times and meet the business purpose for which it was intended? In a hospitality environment, it is critical that a network delivers prompt responses to inquiries and requests. For example, waiting 20 seconds for a central reservation system to generate a reservation confirmation is unacceptable.

Security Management

4. **Security Management.** This entails user authentication and authorization, encryption techniques, antivirus measures, and physical security. This function grows in importance as the enterprise-wide user community expands.

Accounting Management

5. **Accounting Management.** This entails usage statistics, costallocation, and making sure that software licenses are not violated.

In many hospitality organizations, costs associated with networks and Internet access are distributed to revenue centers. Network management software helps accountants to determine the level of usage of network resources by each department, unit, or staff member.

Computer Networks are viewed as an essential ingredient in meeting tomorrow's challenges because they provide the critical information linkages required for global competition, improved guest services and property yields, and reduced training and support costs.

Most hotel organizations have three networks to manage: a property or local area network for front and back office applications, a wide area network for telephone, central reservations, credit card processing, corporate data, and Internet connectivity, and a guestroom network which now exists as cable TV, in-room entertainment such as video on demand or video games, and telephone service (i.e., Voice-over IP telephony). In today's age, hospitality organizations converge all of these systems. This is called network convergence. In new hotels, instead of several cables that serve each of these services, only one fiber-optic cable is run to the room to handle telephony, in-room entertainment, and all other networks such as electronic locking and energy management systems.

Network Importance and Vulnerabilities

How important are computers to hospitality organizations? Turn the computer system off during a rush period and observe the consequences. Food orders cannot be printed in the kitchen.

Reservations cannot be made. Guests cannot be registered or checked out. Charges cannot be posted to guest folios or restaurant checks.

Computers can deliver a paralyzing blow when they stop functioning. The flow of information is disrupted, making it difficult to complete transactions (e.g., reservation), to access critical information (e.g., room status and reservation availability), and to maintain guest service levels. Keeping computer downtime to a minimum in guest-related areas (e.g., reservations and front desk) is critical. When a central reservations network is down, for example, potential sales are being redirected to competitors every minute. When it takes more than 10 seconds for your hotel's website to upload, the visitors will go to other websites. People have less patience when it comes to technology. Lengthy computer downtime can result in substantial revenue losses. In fact, many types of businesses, such as banks and insurance companies, would go bankrupt in just a few days if their computer systems stopped working. Hospitality businesses became heavily dependent on technology because **"mission-critical"** systems are all technology based. Mission-critical systems are systems whose reliable performance is crucial to the successful performance of the organization in which it is used. For a hotel, mission-critical systems are central reservation systems (CRS) and property management systems (PMS). For a restaurant, a mission-critical system is Point-of-Sale system (POS). To make sure that these systems are up and running, there needs to be a systematic approach to maintain them. The remainder of this chapter will address the steps necessary to ensure that all systems are properly protected and maintained, working efficiently, and safely and securely accessed.

Networks are becoming synonymous with information technology and are grown extensively impacting all aspects of business, with the hospitality industry being no exception. In every level of hospitality management, networks are involved. We live in a connected world. In every stage of our lives, we are connected. At the property level, there are local area networks where property management system, reservation system, sales and catering system, point-of-sale, menu engineering, inventory, payroll, accounting, human resources, and other systems reside (20). At the corporate level, the LAN within the hotel or restaurant is usually connected to the head office or corporate headquarters via some kind of connectivity such as Dial-up, cable, DSL, or frame relay. Individual units are required to send information either continuously (real-time) or several times during the day (polling) to the corporate office. In addition, hotels or restaurants may offer wireless or wired high speed Internet access to their guests in the hotel/restaurant or in private dining, public and meeting areas (21). This has resulted in the creation of "backdoors," a mechanism secretly introduced into a computer system to facilitate unauthorized access to the system comprising computer security (22).

At the user level, the user accesses the hotel/restaurant website to make reservations and to get information about the hotel/restaurant. This level of interaction in a network environment increases the accessibility of the whole computer system, thus creating enormous potential for information and network security problems as any information sent on Transmission Control Protocol/Internet Protocol (TCP/IP) can be potentially captured by unauthorized individuals if the information is not well protected and encrypted. The magnitude of the problem is enhanced by the fact that the person who is responsible for information technology in the restaurant is usually someone who does not have expertise in technology but who happens to be familiar and comfortable with computers (23).

The continued growth of the global Internet have also made networking between computers much easier, yet, more challenging to manage. Any computer that is connected to an Internet Service Provider (ISP) is part of the biggest network of networks: the Internet. Even the smallest hotel or restaurant can be part of a WAN using connection mediums such as cable, digital subscriber line (DSL), or satellite technologies.

Even though the advancement of the Internet and networks have brought substantial innovations to the way hospitality organizations do business (i.e., accounting, training, operations), they have also brought significant challenges. One of these challenges is the security of hospitality networks.

Businesses are subject to various disruptions, such as fires, floods, earthquakes, vandalism, stealing, human errors, power outages, and malicious threats from outsiders or misuses. Unless firms prepare in advance, disasters inevitably shut down business operations. And the longer a firm's operations are shut down, the more likely it will never reopen for business.

Many companies have developed a disaster contingency recovery plan (DCRP) (24). Although a DCRP is vital, it is primarily a reactive approach (i.e., a corrective control) and not a comprehensive plan for risk management. In contrast, a business continuity plan (BCP) seeks to eliminate or reduce the impact of a disaster condition before the condition occurs.

Common Causes of System Failure

Business Continuity Planning (BCP) is an interdisciplinary concept used to create and validate a practiced logistical plan for how an organization will recover and restore partially or completely interrupted critical function(s) within a predetermined time after a disaster or extended disruption (25).

Let's look at the common causes of system failure:

> "The only truly secure system is one that is powered off, cast in a block of concrete and sealed in a lead-lined room with armed guards."
>
> Gene Spafford (26)

Operator Error

1. **Operator Error.** Various operator errors can cause system failure. Common errors include improper handling of lengthy processing routines (e.g., end-of-day audit), database maintenance (e.g., changing and deleting data), and hardware (e.g., moving a hard disk without parking the read/write head). Providing thorough training and establishing careful procedures reduce operator mistakes.

A small restaurant chain, four units in the same city, had frequent point-of-sale (POS) system crashes. These crashes went on for more than a year before it was discovered that the culprit was incorrect database information. The general manager of the chain, after updating one unit's database, had been copying it on magnetic tape and then loading it into the other three POS systems to save time and money. However, the general manager did not realize that the database copy included a printer configuration (identifies printer type and location) inappropriate for the other three restaurants. As a result, it took longer to print requests, which slowed down response times and caused the POS systems to "freeze" during peak business periods. The author, acting as a consultant, made the following recommendation: *"Each restaurant database should be reconfigured from scratch by a qualified technician. Future modifications should be handled specifically for each restaurant on a scheduled basis where databases are not mixed."* Another example of user error also happened in a restaurant in New York City. The night manager shut down POS while taking "Z-Report" (end of the day report). The database structure was corrupted and the next day the POS system did not work. The restaurant manager had to call the support of the POS vendor and paid a hefty amount for it to be fixed.

Hardware Failure

2. **Hardware Failure.** All hardware components are susceptible to failure, particularly those with moving parts (e.g., printer).

The PMS system of Pan Pacific Hotel in Bangkok, Thailand was 11 years old. Even though it was DOS based, it was functioning normally. However, one day, the 10 MB hard drive of the server crashed. The hotel had backups so they bought a new hard drive and restored everything.

The only problem was that they could not find 10MB hard drive any more. The smallest hard drive that they found was 1GB. The 484 server did not handle 1GB hard drive well. So, the hard drive crashed again in 6 months. The hotel finally decided to buy a new system along with new hardware.

Three basic measures reduce hardware malfunctions:

Keep the Temperature and Relative Humidity at the Appropriate Levels

a. *Keep the temperature and relative humidity at the appropriate levels.* Controlling atmospheric conditions may require air-conditioning, a higher ventilation rate, or humidifying equipment.

While electronic components function, they get warm although newer models of computers generate low heat (27). Internal fans are used for cooling. However, blocked ventilation slots, an overly hot office, or excessive exposure to direct sunlight can result in overheating. This may lead to chip failures, loss of data, drying out of disk drive lubricants, or damaging of secondary storage media (e.g., hard disk – See Figure 2-11).

A dry atmosphere causes static electricity, which can ruin a circuit board. For example, electronic door locks at one hotel were zapped by guests during a cold, dry spell. Static buildup can be minimized by spraying the carpet with a static eliminator, touching a metal object before touching the computer, grounding equipment, or using an anti-static strip on the keyboard (28).

Keep Equipment Clean

b. *Keep equipment clean.* Dust, smoke particles, and hair have a "sandpaper effect" on disk surfaces and read/write heads. A large accumulation of interior dust balls can literally suffocate a computer system.

In a kitchen area, airborne grease can interfere with a computer's circuit board and cable connections. If a hotel is located in a destination beach area, guests may insert sand-laden key cards into electronic door locks, rendering them dysfunctional over time (See Figure 2-12).

For this reason, some resorts prefer Radio Frequency Identification (RFID) based electronic key systems where the guests do not have to insert the key physically to the card slot but just wave it. Even though RFID based key locks are more expensive than slot-based electronic key locks, over time, using RFID based electronic key locks may save money.

FIGURE 2-10. MAJORITY OF THE HARD DRIVES HAVE MOVING PARTS, MAKING THEIR LIFE LIMITED. USUALLY A HARD DRIVE LASTS 3-4 YEARS. NEW TECHNOLOGY ALLOWS FLASH HARD DRIVES WITH NO MOVING PARTS ALTHOUGH THEIR CAPACITY IS MUCH LOWER THAN TRADITIONAL HARD DRIVES.

Source: © Alfred Bondarenko, 2008. Used under license from Shutterstock, Inc.

FIGURE 2-11. A GUEST INSERTING A MAGNETIC STRIPE KEYCARD INTO AN ELECTRONIC LOCK.

Source: © Paul Velgod, 2008. Used under license from Shutterstock, Inc.

A computer's external surfaces (monitor, keyboard, printer, disk drives, and system unit) should be cleaned at least once a week, especially in high heat, grease environments such as the kitchen display system in the kitchen. The interior should be cleaned biannually. Cleaning supplies and equipment commonly used include (29): "anti-static video screen wipers, cotton swabs, disk drive cleaning kit, degreaser/cleaner, rubbing alcohol, magnetic head-cleaning spray, miniature vacuum cleaner, protective keyboard cover, canned compressed air, tape head demagnetizer, and WD-40 lubricant."

Computers can be damaged by moisture. Placing a computer next to a dishwasher or spilling a beverage on a keyboard may result in irreparable damage.

c. *Keep magnets away from computers:* Magnets can cause permanent loss of data on hard disks. Electric motors or electromagnets produce magnetism. There are magnets in phones that ring instead of beep, speakers, monitors, magnetic screwdrivers, magnetic clip and paper holders, and magnets themselves. It is best to keep anything magnetic away from computers and disks.

d. *Keep water and corrosive agents away from computers:* Liquids can be very hazardous to the computer's health. These are caused by operator spills, leaks, and flooding. Certainly operator spills can be controlled by not having liquids near the computer. However, some leaks and flooding are not always preventable (30).

Establish a Preventative Maintenance Program

e. *Establish a preventative maintenance program.* In addition to clean ing equipment, it is important to check the following components on a regular basis.

   a. System fan.
   b. Circuit board connections.
   c. Cable connections. Examine monitor, keyboard, and printer cables.
   d. Disk drives. Check for misaligned read/write heads and test drive speeds. Flash drives (USB drives/Thumb drives) also need to be checked frequently.

Equipment maintenance is often neglected because maintenance activities are rarely incorporated into a systematic schedule. An effective maintenance schedule will:

   a. List maintenance activities and the necessary information to properly perform maintenance tasks.
   b. Provide a timetable for performing maintenance activities.
   c. Indicate who is responsible for performing maintenance tasks and the date each one was completed.
   d. Indicate whether any problems were identified and what was done to correct them.

This proactive approach uncovers potential problems that may lead to hardware failure. Sofware, such as Schedule+ from Microsoft or even Microsoft Outlook can be used for hardware preventive maintenance schedules. As an additional measure, some companies use fault-tolerant computer systems for critical functions. A fault-tolerant computer is equipped with a backup system enabling it to function despite the failure of certain internal hardware components such as a hard drive or disk controller card. Data redundancy in computer data storage is achieved through disk arrays Redundant Arrays of Inexpensive Disks (RAID), which in the case of disk failure, all or part of the data stored on the array can be recovered.

One hospitality corporation uses a **fault-tolerant** mainframe for its central reservations network. The moment a failure is detected, a backup system is immediately brought online. This backup system may be off premises. This ensures that in the case of a disaster on premise, the backup data would be safe. In the 9/11 World Trade Center tragedy, it was found that most companies did have backups, however, they were on premises. Some financial institutions lost all of their records due to this. An off-premise fault-tolerant system would have saved the organizations' data. Off-premise fault-tolerant systems are also supported by a Storage Area Network (SAN) (See Figure 2-12).

A SAN is an architecture to attach remote computer storage devices such as disk arrays to servers in such a way that, to the operating system, the devices appear as locally attached (31). A benefit of SAN includes the ability to allow servers to boot from the SAN itself. This allows for a quick and easy replacement of faulty servers since the SAN can be reconfigured so that a replacement server can use the logical unit number (LUN) of the faulty server. So, to the system, everything is the same even though the server is now served by a SAN.

If this failure lasts for more than one minute, a computer generated message is sent to the manufacturer who ships out the replacement part to the IT team. The design of this mainframe makes it easy to replace internal components. Replacing a circuit card, for example, is like pulling out a file cabinet drawer (system unit), lifting out a file (defective circuit card), and replacing it with a new one. These steps can be done in seconds.

Power Problems

3. **Power Problems.** Power line trouble causes 70 percent of hardware and software failures. Symptoms include burned components, garbled transactions, memory loss, corrupted data, lost data, and unexplained intermittent problems. To avoid power disturbances, the following measures should be implemented.

Surge Protection

a. *Surge protection.* A computer system can be plugged into an inexpensive electrical device called a surge protector that prevents overvoltages damaging its circuitry

FIGURE 2-12. A TECHNICIAN REPLACES HOT-SWAPPABLE HARD DISK IN A OFF-PREMISE BACK UP UNIT WHICH IS PART OF STORAGE AREA NETWORK (SAN).

(See Figure 2-13). Power failures and lightning can cause potent surges capable of frying circuits instantly. However, most surges are small and come from business equipment and appliances. Smaller surges eventually cause circuit damage, too.

The author, while installing a computer system at a Caribbean hotel, witnessed a power surge that killed fish in the accounting office's aquarium.

Proper Wiring and Grounding

b. *Proper wiring and grounding.* Electric noise from equipment, such as a food mixer or photocopy machine, can interfere with a computer system plugged into the same power circuit. The source of interference can be physically moved by plugging the food mixer into a different receptacle or eliminated by using a power line filter or a **DEDICATED LINE**, an electric line supplied directly from the building transformer to the computer system.

It is also important to make sure that computer equipment is properly grounded and not exposed to unwanted energy flow. Inadequate grounding is a frequent cause of system failure.

Uninterruptible Power Supply

c. *Uninterruptible Power Supply.* A power failure clears RAM of its contents and requires the reinputting of data not saved to secondary storage. Also, a power failure during a lengthy processing routine (e.g., posting room and tax) can damage the database.

FIGURE 2-13. AN END USER-LEVEL SURGE PROTECTOR.

Source: © Anthony Berenyl, 2008. Used under license from Shutterstock, Inc.

To avoid such problems, an uninterruptible power supply system (UPS) can be added to the computer system (See Figure 2-14). This device has a battery providing continuous power to the computer system during a commercial power outage for up to 30 minutes or more, during which time work in progress can be saved before shutting down the computer. This preserves the integrity of critical data. Power surges, spikes, brownouts, and even complete power blackouts can cause a computer to reboot or crash unexpectedly (32). When this occurs, hours of unsaved work are irretrievably lost. In extreme cases, a sudden system interruption can potentially corrupt open system files, resulting in more serious subsequent startup problems. A UPS prevents data loss and system corruption. It detects the loss of alternating current (AC) and switches over to battery power. The switchover takes only a few milliseconds (thousandths of a second), and the PC never detects the difference.

Software Bug

4. **Software Bug.** A bug is a logic error in the program preventing it from working properly. For example, one hospitality accounting program aborts if the user forgets to turn on the printer before printing a financial statement.

Most hospitality operations rely on software developers for program debugging, the process of locating and correcting logic errors. And no one knows when they will get around to fixing the problems or releasing a "bug-free" version. Therefore, it is important to test a program thoroughly before making a purchase. Also, remember older products typically have fewer logic flaws because of having been subjected to greater industrial use. In every industry, software bugs exist. In 2005, automaker Toyota announced a recall of 160,000 of its Prius hybrid vehicles following reports of vehicle warning lights illuminating for no reason, and cars' gasoline engines stalling unexpectedly. But unlike the large-scale auto recalls of years past, the root of the Prius issue wasn't a hardware

FIGURE 2-14. UNINTERRUPTED POWER SUPPLY FOR A COMPUTER.

Source: © Pakhnyushcha, 2008. Used under license from Shutterstock, Inc.

problem—it was a programming error in the smart car's embedded code. The Prius had a software bug (33).

System Overload

5. **System Overload.** Placing too many demands on a computer can greatly diminish its performance and may cause system failure. Causes of system overloads include:

Insufficient CPU Clock Speed

a. *Insufficient Central Processing Unit (CPU) Clock Speed.* The CPU clock speed determines how quickly it can process tasks. The original IBM personal computer, for example, which had a CPU clock speed (8088 chip) of only 4.77 MHz (4.77 million cycles per second), was easily overwhelmed by processor-intensive tasks. However, today's microcomputer CPUs (e.g., Quad-Core Intel® Xeon® Processor or Intel® CoreTM 2 Duo Processor), with clock speeds over 3000 MHz or 3 GHz, are performing tasks dramatically faster than the original personal computer. They have enough under-the-hood horsepower, in fact, to perform **MULTITASKING**, which is the ability to open and work with several programs at once, to operate sophisticated software applications, to support multiple users accessing programs and data at the same time, and to work with powerful operating systems such as UNIX, Linux, Windows Vista Server, Windows 7 and Windows 8 easily.

The type of CPU depends primarily on the number of users and the software applications being used. As a CPU is pushed to full capacity, there will be a degradation in response time to user requests. If the CPU capacity is exceeded, computer operations will be halted. Either situation may be resolved by reducing unnecessary usage of the computer, scheduling processor-intensive routines during slow periods, replacing the existing CPU with a more powerful one, or adding a second processor (dual processing), which is particularly helpful for multitasking.

Inadequate RAM

b. *Inadequate Random Access Memory (RAM).* A computer may have a powerful CPU but processing speed might be impaired by insufficient RAM. Inadequate RAM is one of the most common reasons for computer failure. One of the best ways to improve the performance of a slow PC is to add memory (RAM).

When instructions and data are too large to fit into RAM, the computer system will "freeze" unless they are stored on the hard drive as a RAM extension (**VIRTUAL MEMORY OR SWAP FILE**) or RAM is expanded (see Figure 2-14). Virtual memory techniques cause delays up to 30 seconds or more because the CPU must stop while information is retrieved from secondary storage (hard disk). Therefore, expanding RAM (adding more RAM chips) is the best solution because it allows the CPU to operate more efficiently by reducing the number of disk accesses.

Slow Mechanical Components

c. *Slow Mechanical Components.* The rate at which data is exchanged between the hard drive and CPU (input/output operations) is also affected by the type of hard disk and disk controller and the manner in which disk files are stored.

Hard drives vary in how quickly they identify the location of data and transfer it to the CPU. A hard drive that either has a slow access time or transfer rate delays processing activities. A good measure of data throughput is how fast the disk spins. This is expressed in **rotations per minute (rpm)**. The higher the disk's RPM, the faster the hard drive can locate and send requested data. Today's hard disks spin between 5400 to 15,000 RPM. A hard drive with 7200 RPM is considered good for an end-user laptop or desktop.

Monitors also operate at different speeds. It is important to use monitors with prompt screen-update speed, particularly when visual output is necessary to complete customer transactions such as a room reservation.

File Fragmentation

d. *File Fragmentation.* Even though the hard drive may have a good performance rating, response time will deteriorate as more files are added to the hard disk and others are deleted. Since DOS stores data in a random order, it will break up files (fragmentation) to fill in holes left by deleted files (see Figure 2-15). Consequently, pieces of files are scattered all over the disk. Although this does not affect the integrity of program and data files, it takes much longer (up to 10 times longer) to read or write files from the disk. This also results in greater wear and tear on hard drive components (e.g., more time is required moving read/write head) and significantly increases the likelihood of a head crash or disk damage. File fragmentation, however, can be corrected. There are programs which assemble broken files into complete, contiguous files.

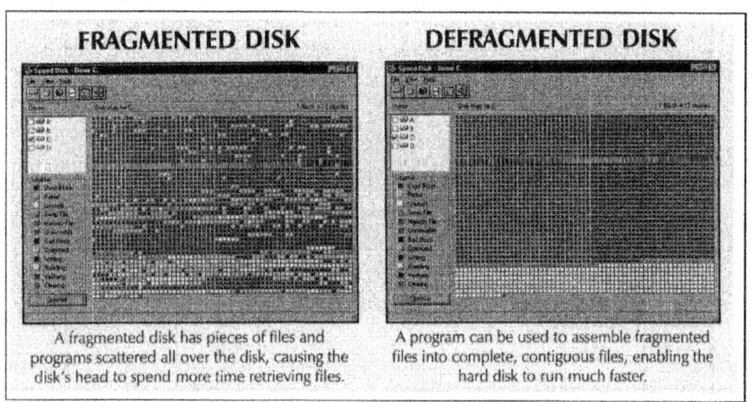

FRAGMENTED DISK
DEFRAGMENTED DISK
A fragmented disk has pieces of files and programs scattered all over the disk, causing the disk's head to spend more time retrieving files.
A program can be used to assemble fragmented files into complete, contiguous files, enabling the hard disk to run much faster.

FIGURE 2-15. FRAGMENTED DISK.

Inadequate Disk Storage

e. *Inadequate Disk Storage.* A computer must provide adequate storage capacity. Early microcomputer systems would only allow the storage of 20 or 30 million bytes (MB) of information. Most of the storage space would be monopolized by one or two software applications. Foreseeable space shortages would trigger frequent, visual warnings commanding the deletion of outdated file information to prevent the 'freezing up of the system.' Unfortunately, this old, useless data was often guest history information which, if kept, could have been profitably used in marketing and sales applications.

The size of the hard disk depends on the space (expressed in bytes) required by each software application (e.g., word processing, spreadsheet, front office, accounting, food cost) and any foreseeable applications that may be added (see Figure 2-16). The needs of the operation may unexpectedly change (e.g., property adds 100 rooms), however, requiring greater data storage.

Increasing disk capacity may also be avoided if housekeeping tasks are regularly performed on the hard drive. This would include removal of useless, obsolete, or duplicated files and/or transfer of files to floppy disks or magnetic tapes such as guest folio histories and accounting information. Performing file management tasks may require knowledge of operating system commands. However, with falling prices of hard drives, it is very easy to add additional hard drive space to computers. Newer computers come with racks where the users can buy swappable hard drives and insert them easily to increase hard drive space.

Another way of freeing up hard disk space is to store dated files offline using **REMOVABLE-MEDIA DEVICES**, such as **OPTICAL DRIVES** (i.e., DVD) and external hard drives. External hard drives are capable of holding more than 1 Terabyte (TB or 1000 Gigabytes) (See Figure 2-17).

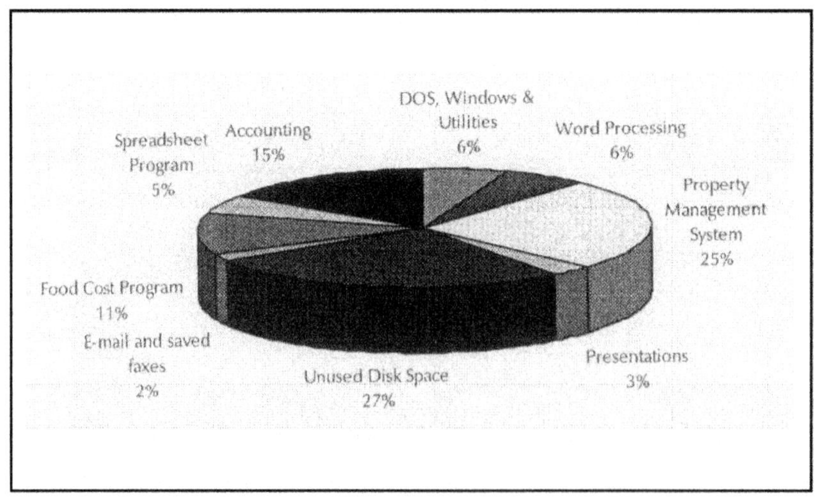

FIGURE 2-16. USED AND UNUSED DISK SPACE (100 GIGABYTES OF STORAGE CAPACITY).

FIGURE 2-17. EXTERNAL HARD DRIVE THAT CAN BE CONNECTED TO THE PC/MAC BY USB OR FIREWIRE.

Source: © Jaroslaw Solty Siak, 2008. Used under license from Shutterstock, Inc.

Virus

6. **Virus.** If programs take longer than normal to load or intermittent or unusual error messages are being displayed, the computer may have a virus. A computer virus is a program mimicking influenza. It spreads by copying itself from one program to the next, changing or destroying each program that it infects without the user knowing it.

Virus-infested programs are transmitted via e-mail, floppies (which are hardly used now), USB drives, and networks (e.g., a website).

There are a wide variety of viruses, some of which proceed slowly and insidiously while others quickly invoke chaos and mass destruction. Although most viruses are designed to damage databases and programs, some do attack hardware and hurl mechanical components such as a disk read/write head into costly convulsions or slow down a computer system with unnecessary commands. Also, there are harmless viruses flashing prank messages and special effects on computer screens. One virus named "Falling Tears," for example, causes all the characters on the screen to fall to the bottom in a pile, unsettling the user.

The carrier of a virus is a program that appears legitimate called a Trojan Horse, named after the hollow horse that was given as a gift to the Trojans by the Greeks. Unaware that the horse was filled with Greek soldiers, the Trojans allowed it into the city. The Greek soldiers crept out to open the gates of Troy to their army.

Trojan horses also carry Time Bombs or Logic Bombs which are not activated until certain conditions are met such as a date or event (e.g., Friday the 13th or April Fool's Day). Such bombs can cause swift destruction when detonated.

Motives for creating viruses range from vandalism to revenge. Robert Morris, a 23-year-old Cornell graduate student and the son of a computer security expert for the National Security Agency, created a virus in 1988 that incapacitated 6000 computers on six continents. It involved computers at M.I.T., Rand Corporation, University of California at Berkeley, three NASA facilities, and Los Alamos and Lawrence Livermore national laboratories, and was the first virus that affected a worldwide network.

Unfortunately, the proliferation of computer networks has enabled viruses to reach an epidemic level. According to a recent survey of companies conducted by the National Computer Security Association, 98 percent reported virus infections resulting in an average loss of $8,000 per incident. There are now more than fifty thousand known software viruses. However, only a small number of viruses account for most of the infections.

Since the arrival of computer viruses in the early 1980s, federal and state laws have been enacted to penalize computer hackers who introduce malicious viruses into computer systems. Robert Morris was convicted in 1990 under the Federal Computer Fraud and Abuse Act of 1986 and was placed on three years of probation, fined $10,000, and ordered to perform 400 hours of community service.

Despite the growth in legal remedies, it has been difficult to prosecute perpetrators. Consequently, most operations have taken a defensive posture by purchasing antivirus programs such as Norton or McCaffee to detect viruses, Spyware, and Trojan horses to assist in the deletion or repair of infected files. An antivirus program, however, is not a cure-all. It can fight only those viruses it was designed to recognize. One of the things that needs to be done is keeping the antivirus software up to date. Since every single day, there could be potentially a new virus; the database of the antivirus software needs to be current with new viruses. Most antivirus software offers subscription plans which allow users to download the new virus definitions on a daily or weekly basis so that the user will be protected from new viruses. Antivirus software can automate this process so that it can check the antivirus software database online to see if there are new definitions. If yes, it will download them automatically.

A computer security study was conducted among restaurant managers. Twenty-four percent of the restaurant networks had a computer network attack within the last 12 months. On average, the restaurants received 1-5 network attacks within the last 12 months. A Security Index (SI), the total number of security tools utilized, was created for each respondent. The size of the restaurant (number of units) was positively correlated with the SI, and the total number of network security tools utilized by restaurants. Regarding attack types, "Virus Attack" (71.4%) was reported most frequently, followed by "Insider Abuse of Net Access" (57.1%), "Laptop Theft" (42.9%), and "Spoofing" (39.3%) (using someone else's resources for spam or illegal activity). In terms of protection from these attacks, restaurant IT managers reported that the most used protection tools are antivirus software (86.2%), hardware firewalls (79.3%), and physical security (75.9%). The least used network security tools are honeypots (7.7%) and biometrics (14.8%).

It is interesting to see from the results that only 87 percent of the restaurants use antivirus software. Antivirus software is one of the easiest ways of implementing computer security, yet about 13 percent of the restaurants do not use it. Not using an antivirus application is an open invitation to all sorts of problems.

This study also found that the restaurants surveyed do not have dedicated IT personnel. IT functions are typically inherited by operations managers that know more about computers than the others in the company. This fact shows that these people who have other major responsibilities cannot spend enough time on network security issues. For that reason, some restaurants may not even know that they are vulnerable or that they are being attacked by internal or external hackers. This particular fact is scarier than the attacks known by restaurateurs because when an attack is detected, prevention tools can be applied, but if not known, then nothing can or will be done.

New viruses emerge on a daily basis, such as Melissa. This self-replicating, e-mail virus can quickly overwhelm e-mail servers and cause them to crash. In 1999, about 60,000 users were infected at the company that made the first complaint. Two strains, called "Melissa.A" and "Mad Cow" have recently appeared, emphasizing the importance of downloading antiviral program updates on a regular basis.

Furthermore, it is also necessary to make regular backup copies of data files and to closely scrutinize new programs of questionable origin before using them. "In the majority of computer virus infections, the carrier was traced to a commercial program, usually a pirated copy." Martin (38) suggests the following steps in the case that a computer is believed to be infected with a virus:

1. Isolate and disconnect

The first thing to do is to physically disconnect your computer from the network. An infected machine endangers all computers on the network. It is essential that your computer stay isolated until you are sure it has been restored thoroughly.

If you're not sure whether another computer has been infected as well, act as though it has. Remove it from the network and go through the same steps. It's counterproductive to clean off one machine while an infected computer is still connected to the network, waiting for you to plug back in so it can continue its path of infection.

2. Remove the virus

Once the computer has been isolated and removed from the network, you must remove the code that caused the damage in the first place. The most reliable method of getting rid of a virus, worm, or Trojan horse from your computer is to use removal tools written for that specific code. Your antivirus software should have updates or patches available for the specific security threat, released as soon as the malicious code is discovered. Leading vendors make both removal tools and updated definitions available as soon as a threat is discovered.

Simply deleting the virus program or infected file is not enough. Most viruses, worms, and Trojan horses copy and spread themselves in different forms, hiding in and infecting other programs and documents. Trojan horses can install back doors in your system, leaving an entry point for hackers or additional malicious code. Even if you destroy the

Trojan file, the security hole remains. Downloading a removal tool or patch for that specific Trojan will help eliminate additional vulnerabilities.

You should also check for security alerts that are released whenever new viruses are found. Alerts warn you about the spread of a new virus, the forms it comes in, and the methods you should use to remove it if you've already been infected.

3. Restore your data

You may experience varying degrees of data loss from an attack, ranging from altered file names to total obliteration. A nasty virus may render your applications useless, or an annoying worm may rename your Word documents. Regardless of the extent of damage, you'll need to restore your computer to its original state.

Reinstall programs:

Some viruses can completely destroy an operating system. In this case, use a "quick restore" CD, if your computer came with one. The CD will return your computer back to its state at the time of purchase. You will lose any applications you have installed or data files you have stored if you reinstall your OS. To restore applications, gather your documentation together, including original software, licensing, and drivers where applicable. You will need the documentation to register the software when you reinstall these programs.

Scan for viruses:

Once you are up and running, perform a thorough antivirus scan. Scan all files and documents, and keep track of those that have been altered. If your data files are stored in a central location, such as a server, they should be scanned there as well. Scan all computers on the network, including your server.

Restore files:

If your data files are stored on your individual machine, your data loss will depend on the virus' payload and how recently you backed up your files. If the virus attacked applications, you may find your data files have been left untouched. Unfortunately, some viruses specifically target data files. If you keep a regular schedule of backing up to tape, CD, or other media, your loss will be contained to the time period between your last backup and the virus attack. If you don't observe a schedule of backups, your files will be lost permanently.

Before restoring the backup files to your computer, you may wish to make an image copy of your system. This will allow you to quickly restore the machine to a known clean state in the event of future compromise.

Scan each file with antivirus software as you restore it to your system. Watch for unexpected macros or documents with extensions like ".vbs," which maybe viruses.

Document the process:

Document the steps you took to repair your system after the attack, including which files and applications you restored and the method you used to restore them. If something else goes wrong, you can retrace your steps, or use the information for future reference.

4. Prevent future infection

After all this trouble, you'll want to keep your system free of viruses in the future. It is imperative that you run antivirus software and keep the definitions current, preferably with a program that automatically updates them for you. If you aren't running antivirus software, start now. If you are, immediately update the virus definitions from your vendor site. Then download the latest security patches for your operating system and all of your applications to fix any known security holes.

Next, change all of your passwords, including Internet Service Provider (ISP) access passwords, File Transfer Protocol (FTP), email, and Web site passwords. This is a free, easy, and effective way to boost security. Some malicious code can capture passwords or crack them, so a security breach may be evidence that they have been tampered with. It's a good idea to change your passwords regardless. Any secure data on your computer should have a password, and it should be created or changed at this time. Passwords should be at least eight characters long, combining capital and lower case letters, numbers, symbols, and punctuation. Avoid using recognizable words, phrases, or names.

5. Learn from your mistakes

Although the wreckage of a virus attack can be difficult to remedy, consider it an opportunity to assess your security practices. If a virus got in this time, it could infiltrate your network again. It's important to evaluate the security measures, if any, you were using and why they weren't effective. Do you need a firewall? Are employees downloading files without scanning them? Are you opening attachments from unknown users? Are your virus definitions up to date?

Did you lose data in this breach that could have been restored using backups? Create a regular backup schedule that involves copying files from the computer onto removable media like CD or tape, and storing a set of them offsite. Make frequent backups part of your routine and in the future you won't be at a loss.

6. **Virus.** A virus attack can cost you time, money, and frustration. Prevention is the best security policy. But if your network has been compromised, follow these steps to get up and running again as quickly as possible so you don't lose your data — or more.
7. **Spyware.** Spyware is computer software that is installed secretly on a computer to intercept or take partial control over the user's interaction with the computer, without the user's informed consent. Some spyware could collect and track the user's web activity such as surfing history so that marketing could be targeted accordingly. However, some spyware could be much more dangerous. It can also interfere with user control of the computer in other ways, such as installing additional software, redirecting Web browser activity, accessing websites blindly that will cause more harmful viruses, or diverting advertising revenue to a third party. Spyware can even change computer settings, resulting in slow connection speeds, different home pages, and loss of Internet or other programs. Unlike viruses and worms, spyware does not usually self-replicate. The main drive for spyware is commercial gain and hacking. Most of the time, users will not realize that spyware is installed in their computer

unless they protect and scan their computers. The distributor of spyware usually presents the program as a useful utility such as free MP3 download software. Users down load and install the software without immediately suspecting that it could cause harm. Luckily, there is software such as Ad-aware (free), Windows Defender (free), Spy Sweeper, and CounterSpy that will scan and find spyware. (See Figure 2-18)

Spywareguide.com is a website which keeps tracks of known spyware. Some examples of spyware include "CoolWebSearch" that directs traffic to advertisements on Web sites and "180 Search Assistant" that transmits logs of every web page a user visits.

How to Protect a Computer from Spyware:

According to Microsoft Corporation, a user should do the following to protect a computer from a spyware:

1. *Install a firewall:* Firewall is a hardware/software that controls incoming and outgoing Internet traffic for a computer.
2. *Apply patches for your software:* Every major software company will release free of charge security patches. For example, Microsoft releases their patches every second Tuesday of the month. When a patch becomes available, one should apply it immediately.
3. *Adjust web browser settings:* Every major web browser will have security settings that will prevent spyware from being installed on computers. Users need to make sure to view these settings and set them accordingly.

FIGURE 2-18. SPYWARE CAN BE DANGEROUS AS IT CAN BE USED TO STEAL YOUR PRIVATE INFORMATION SUCH AS SOCIAL SECURITY NUMBERS AND CREDIT CARD NUMBERS STORED ON YOUR COMPUTER.

Source: © Tyler Olson, 2008. Used under license from Shutterstock, Inc.

4. *Use an antivirus and spyware software.* There are several different anti spyware programs. Some of them are free such as Windows Defender or Ad-Aware Free. Some companies charge for anti-spyware such as Spy Sweeper and Country Spy.
5. *Read fine prints:* Make sure to read security warnings, license agreements, and privacy statements associated with any software you download.
6. Download software from sites you trust.

Technology Tidbits

Operating a hard disk without backing up data is like driving without insurance.

Backup Strategies

The best insurance for any computer system is a backup. An operation cannot be careless about making backups. Eventually hard disk data files will be damaged or disappear and, without a backup, it may take hours, days, or even months to reconstruct them. Therefore, it is important to establish standard operating procedures that cover the following areas.

Backup Frequency

- **Backup Frequency.** Since most hospitality operations are open seven days a week, it is probable that files will be added or modified daily. Consequently, data files must be backed up **at least** once a day. This responsibility is typically carried out during the night reset (Night audit is now called night-reset because it takes only few minutes to do the night audit tasks in new property management systems as opposed to several hours in the old PMSs) because it puts a substantial drain on most computer systems and avoids the problem of backing up data files being updated by employees. In fact, many hospitality programs require the user to perform a backup to successfully complete the night reset or end-of-day routine.

Backup Method

- **Backup Method.** Magnetic tapes and removable-media devices (e.g., 1TB external hard drive) are the most common methods for backing up a hard disk. How much data needs to be backed up determines the most appropriate storage media.

Another backup method is a remote hard disk via a local or wide area network connection or an internal hard disk. Some hospitality computer systems are equipped with two internal hard disks where data is backed up to a second hard disk. The backup hard disk may also be programmed to mirror the first hard disk where every transaction is copied as it occurs without employee intervention. The mirror hard disk immediately comes online if the first one fails. Since this may be transparent to the user, the system should be periodically checked. Otherwise, a hard disk failure may go undetected until the backup hard disk fails. However, since both of these drives reside on the same physical place, the data may not be saved if a natural disaster such as flooding happens. Therefore, it makes great sense to keep the backup tapes or drives off premises.

An internal hard disk backup may be more convenient but it is more vulnerable to environmental hazards such as fires, floods, and power disturbances. On the other hand, removable storage media (tapes or external hard drives) can be safely stored in a fireproof vault.

Some alternative ways of backing up includes a SAN (previously defined in this chapter), which is a computer architecture to attach remote computer storage devices to servers in such a way that, to the operating system, the devices appear as locally attached. Several hospitality companies use SANs as a backup method.

In addition, a user can back up programs and data by using an online backup service company. These companies allow users to access an online storage space and store data. Since the online storage is off-premise, it will be safe in the case of a disaster.

The best method of backup is not relying on one single method. A hospitality professional would do best by employing more than one backup method just to be on the safe side. For example, a hotel may use external hard drives (different one for each day of the week) to back up data on a daily basis. It can also use an online backup company to back up incrementally on a weekly basis.

Rotation of Secondary Storage Media

8. **Rotation of Secondary Storage Media**. A magnetic tape or even external hard drive or disk array has a limited life expectancy. A hotel lost its computer system during a small front-office fire. The database had been backed up to a magnetic tape and stored in a safe, but could not be restored because the magnetic tape was defective. Therefore, backup storage media should be replaced at least once a year using a different tape or set of tapes or hard drives for each day of the week. If for some reason the latest backup becomes unusable, there would be six other backups.

Hardcopy

9. **Hardcopy.** What happens if the computer system goes down at 8:00 AM due to a hard drive failure? How will charges be posted and guests checked out? The hotel must have a well-defined manual backup system that employees know how to use or pure chaos will erupt. As part of the computerized night reset, consolidated guest and city ledger folios should be printed (hardcopy), which can be used for settlement and for creating a handwritten guest and city ledger if the computer system is not quickly repaired. Other information commonly produced during the night audit can be used for tracking room status. Most PMSs have "emergency reporting" capability, which is printed every 4 hours. The emergency report will

include the house list, check-ins and -outs with balances, and a room status list. At least, in the event of emergency or system failure, the staff members will be able to operate the business.

Should a restaurant POS system go down where guest checks and food order slips are computer generated, servers must be prepared to write out orders, provide food production areas with handwritten order slips, and prepare guest checks for settlement.

When the computer system is revived, it must be brought up-to-date as soon as possible, especially for time-dependent transactions such as reservations. However, this may require additional labor hours.

Computer Security

People pose the greatest threat to maintaining the integrity of an information system. The majority of computer crimes are perpetrated by employees seeking access to such things as hardware, client lists, trade secrets, employee files, and accounting information for financial gain or revenge. Security violation examples include:

- Salespeople copying the hotel client list onto a USB drive and selling it to a competitor.
- Front-desk clerks receiving cash to settle guest folios, but instead pocketing the cash and transferring the outstanding balance to a bogus city ledger account or "black hole" account.
- Employees gaining access to payroll records and changing wage rates.
- Small operations without insurance and alarm systems having all of their computer equipment stolen.
- Servers voiding entree items off guest checks after collecting cash.
- Tapping a corporate central reservations network to access group bookings for hotels in a particular geographical area in order to lure business away with better accommodations at a lower rate.
- Assistant restaurant managers copying the recipe database onto USB drive for friends opening restaurants with a similar theme.

There are various ways of accessing information systems without authorization.

The Keyboard

1. **The keyboard.** All computer systems are exposed through keyboards. The most common method for restricting employee access is passwords. Passwords, however, can be bypassed by:

Using Obvious Passwords

- *Using obvious passwords.* Passwords should not be obvious but easy enough to remember without being written. A pet name, for example, may be easy to remember but also easy to guess (see Figure 2-19). According to one study, about 30 percent of the restaurants use vendor provided passwords (i.e., admin/admin). This is a very

Mnemonic Passwords			
How Chosen	Example	Number Possibilities	Average Time to Discover
Name (short/long)	Ed/Victoria	2000 (name directory)	5 hours
Word (short/long)	a/mangelwurzel	60,000 (spell checker)	7 days
Two words together	fish/bird	3,600,000,000	1,140 years
Mix of initials & dates	HRM86NYRO9	3,700,000,000,000	1.2 billion years

FIGURE 2-19. MNEMONIC PASSWORDS.

Source: Computer Security (Alexandria, VA: Time-Life Books, 1990) P.24.

clear security risk because hackers try to break into systems by using these common passwords.

Not Regularly Changing Passwords

- *Not regularly changing passwords.* Change passwords periodically. Passwords lose effectiveness with time. One operation which had not changed its password scheme in several years experienced frequent cash shortages because everyone knew the password required to void transactions. Also, delete all passwords used by former employees. Do not let them leave with the "soft" keys. Only half of the restaurants have a method of authorizing new accounts and getting rid of old accounts. This is also a very clear security risk as disgruntled employees are one of the major reasons of security breaches.

Hackers and Encryption

- *Hackers.* An effective security measure is to **encrypt** or scramble data to make it unreadable once it is accessed. However, data encryption requires up to a threefold increase in disk space and can significantly slow down the system as files are encrypted and decrypted. In the case of transmitting data over the Internet protocol, using a secure, encrypted way of communication is also a key to secure data transmission. Computer encryption is based on the science of cryptography, which has been used throughout history. In a very basic way, encryption entails a "code" or "formula" which is only known by the intended party. To give a simple example, let's say that Party A wants to send "Hello" message to Party B in an encrypted way. If the encryption "code" or "formula" is "character + 2", then the message will be converted to "Jgnnq". The code or formula is called "public key." What it did to the message of "Hello" is that it took every letter of the word and replaced it with two down from it in the alphabet. So, the letter "h" became "j." The same formula is applied to all letters of the word. This encryption will be done at the source computer. Once it is transmitted, even if it is hacked, the hacker will not be able to understand the word "Jgnnq". He/She has to have the formula to decode the encryption. In reality, the encryption formulas are far more complicated than the one we gave here as an example (Character +2). The destination computer will be able to decrypt the message with the help of a private key.

So, public-key encryption uses a combination of a private key and a public key. The private key is known only to your computer, while the public key is given by your computer to any computer that wants to communicate securely with it. To decode an encrypted message, a computer must use the public key, provided by the originating computer, and its own private key.

To implement public-key encryption on a large scale, such as a secure Web server might need, requires a different approach. This is where digital certificates come in. A digital certificate is basically a bit of information that says that the Web server is trusted by an independent source known as a certificate authority. The certificate authority acts as a middleman that both computers trust. It confirms that each computer is in fact who it says it is, and then provides the public keys of each computer to the other.

A popular implementation of public-key encryption is the Secure Sockets Layer (SSL). Originally developed by Netscape, SSL is an Internet security protocol used by Internet browsers and Web servers to transmit sensitive information. SSL has become part of an overall security protocol known as Transport Layer Security (TLS) (See Figure 2-20).

An additional security measure used in conjunction with password security is magnetically encoded cards or biometric features such as fingerprint or face recognition. Biometrics is the study of methods for uniquely recognizing humans based upon one or more intrinsic physical or behavioral traits. In recent years, several hardware and software

FIGURE 2-20. YOU CAN UNDERSTAND IF A WEBSITE IS SECURE AND THE INFORMATION IT WILL TRANSFER IS ENCRYPTED FROM THE "S" AT THE END OF THE HTTP.

companies produce biometric devices. For example, Saflok produced finger print electronic key locks. Similarly, Radiant created a POS system which has a fingerprint scanner. The Aloha POS software that works with Radiant hardware requires the supervisors to scan their fingerprint in void and cancellation approvals. Normally, POS systems require management to approve voids and cancellations with a password (often a 4-digit number), however, in busy a restaurant environment, this password is known by all staff members, therefore, making this "check" obsolete. Figure 2-21 shows a fingerprint being scanned by a fingerprint scanner and matched to a database of fingerprints. If there is a correct match, then the person is given access to whatever the procedure is.

Having said that biometric technology is not free of disadvantages. One of the major disadvantages is the security of the data. Everyone knows that if one person loses a credit card or a password, it is easy to cancel the old one and issue a new one. However, if one's fingerprint is stolen, it will not be able to issue a new fingerprint, at least not easily. Therefore, there may be a resistance to the use of biometric technology by users, especially by guests.

How do people break into a computer? According to one computer security study, most people guess or steal passwords or create a ploy to discover them. The study also determined that the most protection is needed for employee records, followed by financial data and budgets, executive correspondence, production data, product and marketing plans, research and development data, customer lists, electronic and voice mail, and employee correspondence.

A U.S. government report noted that Defense Department computers were illegally accessed 30 times between April 1990 and January 1991, including a computer that directly

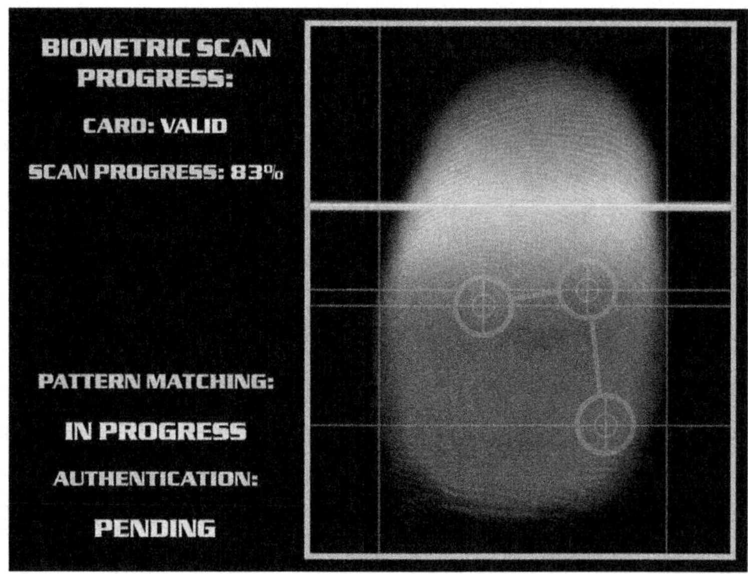

FIGURE 2-21. THUMB SCAN.

Source: © Andy Piatt, 2008. Used under license from Shutterstock, Inc.

supported operations in the Persian Gulf War. Those security violations resulted from poor password management and inadequate computer security expertise.

Communication Line

2. **Communication Line.** Computers that can be accessed through Internet Protocol (IP) networks allowing computers to communicate with each other, are the most difficult to protect because anyone who has a computer and an Internet connection has the potential to breach security from anywhere in the world by guessing passwords correctly. Certain measures, such as a software and/or hardware firewall, however, offer protection against this by restricting which computers can access the source computer.

Another problem is the interception of data that is sent over communication lines. Encrypting this data before transmission is an effective safeguard as previously explained.

Internet

3. **Internet.** More and more hospitality organizations are connecting their private networks to the Internet to take advantage of technological opportunities, such as cheaper email, new distribution channels, and access to vast databases. Figure 2-22 shows that hotels nowadays are interconnected to each other and with a central office (i.e., chain or franchisor) with the help of a wide area network which is supported by Internet communication technologies. Yet there are risks associated with the corporate use of the Internet because of the lack of security. Consequently, companies are protecting sensitive data (e.g., credit card numbers) through encryption methods and the installation of **firewalls.** A firewall provides reliable and secure access to Internet services and prevents any unauthorized connection to and from the Internet.

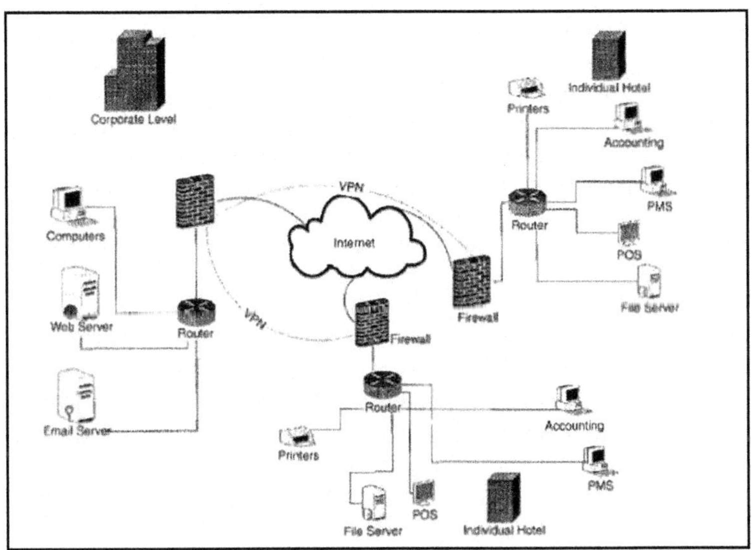

FIGURE 2-22. HOTEL WAN.

Physical Access

4. **Physical Access.** Stealing computer equipment from NORAD's (North American Aerospace Defense Command) heavily guarded computer facility is impossible because it is buried deep in a Colorado mountain with two steel entry doors three feet thick weighing 25 tons apiece. But large hospitality operations are vulnerable to theft and vandalism because computer equipment is usually scattered throughout the property with numerous points of entry. Actually, one IT audit/professional hacking company tests the physical access reliability by dressing up one of their audit members as a Dell employee with the Dell uniform and car with Dell logo. The audit member reports to the hotel, claiming that he/she is there to service the server. A majority of the time, they are given access to the hotel server. The IT audit person unplugs the server, takes it outside, takes a picture with it, and brings it back to the hotel. Measures physically protecting computer equipment and software are:
    a. *Install Locks.* Lock offices with computers after hours. A system for issuing keys and changing locks when employees leave should be established. Locks should also be installed on equipment storage cabinets as well as on equipment enclosures housing expensive removable components. Computer equipment may also be bolted down, a particularly effective deterrent to daytime theft when doors are unlocked and alarm systems are deactivated. A network security audit firm, as part of their audit, sends one of their staff members disguised as a Dell employee with Dell name tag, Dell employee dress and a fake Dell work order. He/She reports to the hotel and claims that he/she will take the server for service. Eight out of 10 times, the auditor has not had a problem accessing the server. This is something that should never happen in any business.

Most corporate computer facilities have closed-circuit television monitors and badge readers at access points.

    b. *Install Alarm Systems.* Alarm systems are especially effective in protecting areas with windows and expensive computer equipment. Computer areas should also have fire alarms. It is important to remember that water-based suppression systems cause irreparable damage to computer equipment. Therefore, gas suppression systems (Halon) must be used to protect important electronic equipment. Some operations also keep rolls of plastic sheeting nearby for use when the first drop of water appears.
    c. *Conduct Equipment Inventories.* Equipment logs or system maps, which identify the locations of equipment and the employees using it, are used for performing equipment inventories. With regular inventory audits, equipment losses are lower because employees are held accountable. Furthermore, employees must be instructed to report equipment losses immediately to expedite the investigation of losses and the correction of problems.

A company label should be attached to each piece of equipment for easy identification in the case of theft. Some computers are equipped with an electronic homing beacon (a radio transmitter) or a radio frequency identification (RFID) tag to track down stolen or missing equipment. RFID tags are intelligent bar codes that talk to a networked system.

d. *Hire Honest Employees.* Many computer crimes can be eliminated by being careful about hiring the personnel who have access to the information system. It is important to remember, however, that loose controls can even tempt employees with impeccable records.

Software piracy or the illegal copying of programs (e.g., Microsoft Excel) costs the software industry hundreds of millions of dollars each year. Various schemes have been devised to prevent the unauthorized duplication of programs. Software pirates, however, have been able to circumvent each copy-protection method. Most vendors now rely on legal remedies to thwart software thieves.

Many operations are confronted with various ethical dilemmas on the proper use of copyrighted software such as the sharing of programs among colleagues. An operation should strictly adhere to the conditions stipulated in the purchase agreement.

In summary, a risk analysis should be performed to identify threats to an information system and appropriate, cost-effective security measures should be taken. Figure 2-23 shows the different computer and network security tools and techniques used by restaurants.

	Use	Do Not Use
	Percentage	Percentage
Anti-virus Software	86.2	13.8
Hardware Firewall	79.3	20.7
Physical Security	75.9	24.1
Software Firewall	72.4	27.6
Access Control	71.4	28.6
Encrypted Login	64.3	35.7
Intrusion Detection System	50.0	50.0
Reusable Passwords	39.3	60.7
Encrypted Files	32.1	67.9
Internet Security Systems Scanner	33.3	66.7
Vulnerability Assessment Scan	25.0	75.0
PCMCIA	23.1	76.9
Image Servers	21.4	78.6
Digital IDs	13.8	86.2
Biometrics	14.8	85.2
Honeypots	7.7	92.3

FIGURE 2-23. THE LIST OF COMPUTER SECURITY TOOLS AND TECHNIQUES AS USED BY RESTAURANTS.

Furthermore, a disaster-recovery plan is needed if an information system is vulnerable to "acts of God" or natural forces such as floods, earthquakes, and hurricanes.

IT Compliance

As explained earlier in this chapter, information technology has become an integral part of hospitality businesses. IT is no longer viewed as a cost center, rather the hospitality companies see IT as a strategic enabler. This fact makes the hospitality companies depend on IT more than ever. Above, we discussed the importance of keeping computer network systems safe and secure. However, there is one more component that is also very important in keeping IT systems in line with local, state, national, and international level laws, regulations, standards, and policies. This is called "compliance." Compliance is a process, effected by management and other personnel, designed to provide reasonable assurance that transactions are executed in accordance with 1) laws governing the use of budget authority and other laws and regulations that could have a direct and material effect on the financial statements or required supplementary stewardship information and 2) any other laws, regulations, and government wide policies identified in audit guidance. The second point here is called "standards" because they are not government created. These standards, which will include regulations and policies, are created by organizations that are not part of the government and do not have the force of law behind their requirements; failure to comply with those requirements may well disqualify an entity from participating in certain businesses. One good example of this could be the Payment Card Industry Data Security Standards (PCI DSS), which are created by major credit card companies (i.e., Visa, Master, Discover). Not complying with PCI will not make a business illegal (at least for now); however, in the case of a credit card holder breach, the businesses will be subject to a series of fines by financial institutions (acquirers) and actions to follow up. If a company is not interested in accepting credit cards as a form of payment, it is not required to comply with the PCI standards. However, anyone wanting to accept credit cards is required to contractually agree to comply with the PCI standard.

Being noncompliant may have serious consequences for hospitality operations. For example, Dave & Buster's restaurant systems were hacked by hackers. As a result of this breach, more than 5000 credit cards were stolen and hackers spent about $600,000 with the credit cards that they stole. According to Nebel, an independent PCI DSS auditor, the reason for this breach is that Dave & Buster's IT security system is not fully compliant with PCI DSS. So, Dave & Buster's now face very serious fines from financial institutions and they are now considered a "Level 1" (more than 6 million credit card transactions a year) merchant, which will require them to undergo very intensive, expensive security testing and programs.

Cougias, Halpern, Herold, and Koop list laws, regulations, policies and standards that a business may be subject to below. This list is enough to show the complexity of "compliance."

Sarbanes Oxley

- Sarbanes-Oxley Act (SOX)
- PCAOB Auditing Standard No. 2
- AICPA SAS 94
- AICPA/CICA Privacy Framework
- AICPA Suitable Trust Services Criteria
- Retention of Audit and Review Records, SEC 17 CFR 210.2-06
- Controls and Procedures, SEC 17 CFR 240.15d-15
- Reporting Transactions and Holdings, SEC 17 CFR 240.16a-3
- COSO Enterprise Risk Management (ERM) Framework

Payment Card

- PCI DSS (Payment Card Industry Data Security Standard)
- PCI DSS Security Scanning Procedures
- VISA CISP: What to Do If Compromised
- American Express Data Security Standard (DSS)
- MasterCard Wireless LANs - Security Risks and Guidelines

U.S. Federal Security

- FTC Electronic Signatures in Global and National Commerce Act (ESIGN)Uniform Electronic Transactions Act (UETA)
- FISMA (Federal Information Security Management Act)
- FISCAM (Federal Information System Controls Audit Manual)
- FIPS 191, Guideline for the Analysis of LAN Security
- Clinger-Cohen Act (Information Technology Management Reform Act)
- The National Strategy to Secure Cyberspace

International Standards Organization

- ISO 73:2002, Risk Management - Vocabulary
- ISO 13335, Information Technology - Guidelines for Management of IT Security
- ISO 17799:2000, Code of Practice for Information Security Management
- ISO 17799:2005, Code of Practice for Information Security Management
- ISO 27001:2005, Information Security Management Systems - Requirements
- ISO/IEC 20000-12:2005 Information technology — Service Management Part 1
- ISO/IEC 20000-2:2005 Information technology — Service Management Part 2

This list is only partial of the whole list that Dorian, et al listed in their book. One of the most important standards is the PCI DSS.

Payment Card Industry Data Security Standards

Payment Card Industry Data Security Standards

The Payment Card Industry is a consortium of credit card issuing brands: Visa, Incorporated; American Express, MasterCard World wide, Discover Financial Services, and JCB International. They have formed this consortium to improve the security of the global payment system by protecting consumers, merchants, and banks from frauds and hacks. The consortium has created a set of Data Security Standards governing the protection of all sensitive cardholder data stored electronically or on paper. The Payment Card Industry Data Security Standards (PCI DSS) applies to every organization including hospitality businesses that process credit or debit card information and merchants and third-party service providers that store, process, or transmit credit card/debit card data.

The PCI DSS entails twelve major standards comprised of over 200 specific requirements established by the PCI, which address minimum standards of security for both paper and electronic transactions and reports of transactions. The Data Security Standards are owned and maintained by the PCI Security Standards Council (SSC). Enforcement of the standards is done individually by each card issuing brand (i.e., Visa), typically via the acquiring banks (i.e., Chase) that service the merchants. PCI DSS requirements are applicable if a Primary Account Number (PAN) is stored, processed, or transmitted (see Figure 2-24). If a PAN is not stored, processed, or transmitted, PCI DSS requirements do not apply.

	Data Element	Storage Permitted	Protection Required	PCIDSS Req. 3.4
Cardholder Data	Primary Account Number (PAN)	YES	YES	YES
	Cardholder Name*	YES	YES*	NO
	Service Code*	YES	YES*	NO
	Expiration Date*	YES	YES*	NO
Sensitive Authentication Data**	Full Magnetic Stripe	NO	N/A	N/A
	CVC2/CVV2/CID	NO	N/A	N/A
	PIN/PIN Block	NO	N/A	N/A
* These data elements must be protected if stored in conjunction with the PAN. This protection must be consistent with PCI DSS requirements for general protection of the cardholder environment. Additionally, other legislation (for example, related to consumer personal data protection, privacy, identity theft, or data security) may require specific protection of this data, or proper disclosure of a company's practices if consumer-related personal data is being collected during the course of business. PCI DSS; however, does not apply if PANs are not stored, processed, or transmitted.				
** Sensitive authentication data must not be stored subsequent to authorization (even if encrypted).				

FIGURE 2-24. PCI SSC'S TABLE OF STOREABLE AND NON-STORABLE DATA TYPES.

Source: Payment Card Industry Standards Security Council Website (https://www.pcisecuritystandards.org/tech/pci_dss.htm).

Merchant Levels: The issuing brands (i.e., Visa) classify merchants (i.e., Marriott) into various levels by volume or risk assessment. Acquirers (i.e., Chase) and brands have the latitude to classify any merchant to a higher level for essentially any reason they choose. All merchants at any Level need to comply with the DSS in full, but the reporting and verification requirements vary according to Merchant Level. For example, according to Visa (http://usa.visa.com/mer-chants/risk_management/cisp_merchants.html),

- Level 1
  - Any merchant—regardless of acceptance channel—processing over 6,000,000 Visa transactions per year.
  - Any merchant that has suffered a hack or an attack that resulted in an account data compromise.
  - Any merchant that Visa, at its sole discretion, determines should meet the Level 1 merchant requirements to minimize risk to the Visa system.
  - Any merchant identified by any other payment card brand as Level 1.
- Level 2
  - Any merchant—regardless of acceptance channel—processing 1,000,000 to 6,000,000 Visa transactions per year.
  - Level 3 Any merchant processing 20,000 to 1,000,000 Visa e-commerce transactions per year.
  - Level 4 Any merchant processing fewer than 20,000 Visa e-commerce transactions per year, and all other merchants—regardless of acceptance channel—processing up to 1,000,000 Visa transactions per year.

Payment Card Industry Data Security Standards

The core of the PCI DSS is a group of principles and accompanying requirements, around which the specific elements of the DSS are organized:

Principle 1 – Build and Maintain a Secure Network

Requirement 1: Install and maintain a **firewall** configuration to protect cardholder data.

Requirement 2: Do not use vendor-supplied defaults for system passwords and other security parameters.

Principle 2 – Protect Cardholder Data

Requirement 3: Protect stored cardholder data.

Requirement 4: Encrypt transmission of cardholder data across open, public networks.

Principle 3 – Maintain a Vulnerability Management Program

Requirement 5: Use and regularly update antivirus software.

Requirement 6: Develop and maintain secure systems and applications.

Principle 4 – Implement Strong Access Control Measures

Requirement 7: Restrict access to cardholder data by business need-to-know.

Requirement 8: Assign a unique ID to each person with computer access.

Requirement 9: Restrict physical access to cardholder data.

Principle 5 – Regularly Monitor and Test Networks

Requirement 10: Track and monitor all access to network resources and cardholder data.

Requirement 11: Regularly test security systems and processes.

Principle 6 – Maintain an Information Security Policy

Requirement 12: Maintain a policy that addresses information security.

All of these requirements have sub requirements. For more information, you can visit PCI SSC website at https://www.pcisecuritystandards.org. It is easy to list these requirements; however, it is not so easy to implement these requirements, especially in the hospitality industry.

REFERENCES

1. O'Dell, P. (1989). *The Computer Networking Book* (pp. 3–4), Chapel Hill, NC: Ventana Press, Inc.
2. Nickel, K. (1992). *The New Shape of Business*. Prodigy Services Company.
3. Saffo, P. (1992). *Commentary: Things to Come*. Prodigy Services Company.
4. Elahi, A. (2001). *Network Communications Technology* (pp 101–107). Stamford, CT: Delmar.
5. 5Thomas, B. (August 31, 2001). *IT Trends: Global Wireless 2001–2004, IdeaByte* (p. 1). Cambridge, MA: Giga Information Group.
6. Dimitrova, N., Koenen, R., Yu, H., Zakhor, A., Galliano, F., & Bouman, C. (1999). Video Portals for the Next Century, *Proceedings of the Seventh ACM International Conference on Multimedia*, 271–275.
7. Elahi, *op cit.*, pp. 101–107.
8. *Ibid.*
9. Gerwig, K. (2001). Wireless Fixations: Service Providers focus on Point-to-multipoint Rollouts, *National ITFS Association*, p. 1., Retrieved December 31, 2001, from http://www.itfs.org/articles/WirelssFixations.html.
10. Martin, J. (1988). *Data Communication Technology* (p. 9). Englewood Cliffs, NJ: Prentice-Hall.
11. *Ibid.*, p. 383.
12. Strehlo, C. (July 1988). A 10 Point Prescription of LAN Management, *Personal Computing*, pp. 110–118.
13. O'Dell, P. *op. cit.*, p. 118.
14. Long, L. (1991). *Introduction to Computers and Information Processing* (p. 146). Englewood Cliffs, New Jersey: Prentice-Hall.
15. Elbert, B. (2001). *The Satellite Communication Ground Segment and Earth Station Handbook*. Boston, MA: Artech House.
16. Simonds, F. (1994). *LAN Communications Handbook* (pp. 383–414). McGraw-Hill.
17. Redi Consultancy. (1991), Electronic Data Interchange [Brochure].
18. Schaefer, C. Jo. (April/May 1992). Ideas and Information: An Interview with Nobel Prize Laureate Arno Penzias, *IAHA: The Bottomline*, p. 19.
19. *Ibid.*
20. Cobanoglu, C., & Cougias, D. (2003). Security: What to watch for and how to prevent attacks. The Annual International Foodservice Technology Conference and Exhibition, Long Beach, CA.
21. Zhang, F., & Zhou, S. (2003). Honeypot: a Supplemented Active Defense System for Network Security. *Proceedings of the Fourth International Conference on Parallel and Distributed Computing, Applications and Technologies*, 231–235.

22. Inge, J., Cobanoglu, C., Patrick, R., Barbieri, D., Bloss, R., Furrer, A. & Perkins, D. (2006). Property Management Systems: How Do You Refresh Something so Mature? 6th Hospitality Operations and Technology Conference, Dallas, TX.
23. Panko, R. R. (2004). *Corporate Computer and Network Security*. Upper Saddle River, NJ: Prentice Hall.
24. Cerullo, V., & Cerullo, M. J. (2004). Business Continuity Planning: A Comprehensive Approach. *Information Systems Management, 21*(3), 70–78.
25. http://en.wikipedia.org/wiki/Business_continuity_planning
26. http://ravichar.blogharbor.com/blog/Quotablesecurityquotes
27. http://www.cio.com/article/31764/Cool_running_Low_Heat_Laptops
28. Beechhold, H. (1987). *Microcomputer Troubleshooting and Maintenance* (p.77). New York: Prentice-Hall Press.
29. *Ibid.*, pp. 74–93.
30. http://www.millbury.k12.ma.us/hs/techrepair/cleaning.html
31. http://en.wikipedia.org/wiki/Storage_area_network
32. Tech Support *Smart Computing, 18* (8), August 2007, 89.
33. Garfinkel, S. (2005). History's Worst Software Bugs, Wired. Retrieved from http://www.wired.com/software/coolapps/news/2005/11/69355
34. Hsu, J., & Kusnan, J. *The Fifth Generation: The Future of Computer Technology,* Blue Ridge Summit, PA: Tab Books, 1989, pp. 40–43.
35. *Ibid.*
36. Tech Support *Smart Computing, 18* (8), August 2007, 89.
37. Cobanoglu, C. (2007). A critical look at restaurant network security: Attacks, prevention tools and practices. *Journal of Foodservice Business Research, 10*(1), 31–50.
38. Martin, K. (2006). 5 Steps to Recovery. *Small Business Technology Magazine,* 10. Retrieved from http://www.sbtechnologymagazine.org/magazine/read/archives/articles/article.php?ProposalOnlineID=295
39. http://en.wikipedia.org/wiki/Spyware
40. http://www.microsoft.com/protect/computer/spyware/prevent.mspx
41. Cougias, D., Halpern, M., Herold, R., & Koop, K. (2007). *Say What You Do: Building a framework of IT controls, policies, standards, and procedures.*
42. Savage, M. (May 14, 2008). Trio indicted in restaurant data security breach, SearchSecurity.com. Retrieved from http://searchsecurity.techtarget.com/news/article/0,289142,sid14_gci1313708,00.html

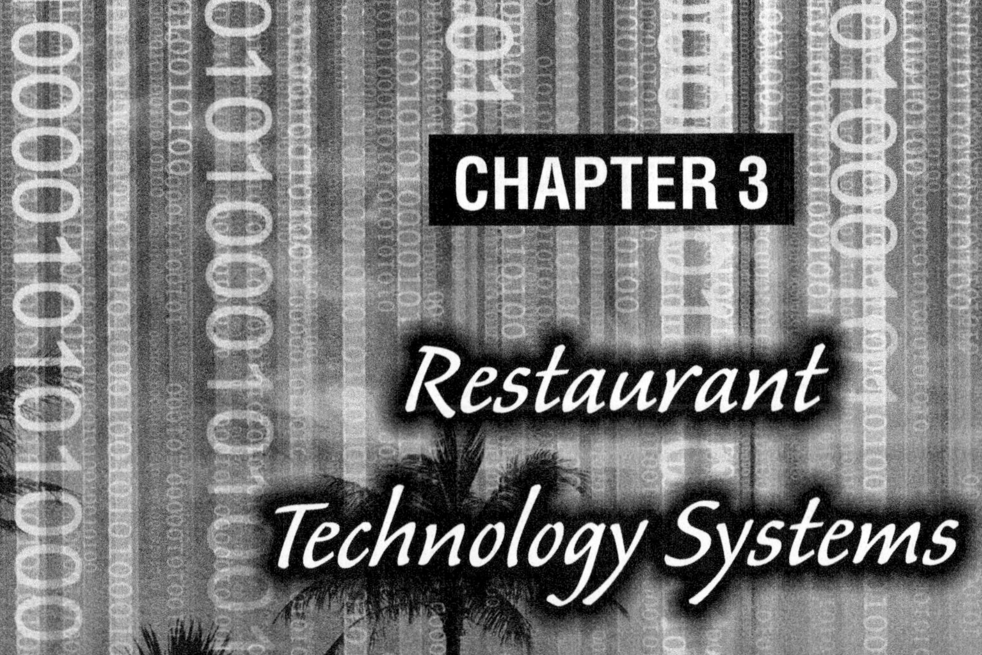

CHAPTER 3

Restaurant Technology Systems

"During the past decade a technology revolution has taken place in the restaurant industry. What once was viewed as equipment and systems that made economic sense for only large, multi-unit restaurants, are now common place even among smaller, one-restaurant independents" (www.restaurantowner.com).

Julie Woodman, "The Byte Stuff 1991," Restaurants and Institutions

CHAPTER OUTLINE

Introduction

According to Brian Sill, principal of Deterministics, a food service management and consulting firm: "To compete effectively in the markets of today, and tomorrow, all stages of the restaurant production and service chain must act in concert, so as to ultimately deliver quality products at the right prices to the right guests at the right times. Failure to do so can result in excess inventory, poor food quality, poor guest service, underutilized capacity, and unnecessary cost. Restaurant technology helps management monitor and coordinate these activities in a more timely and focused manner."

Restaurant technology also provides management with the right information at the right time resulting in fewer costly mistakes, better forecasting, higher productivity, and improved marketing know-how (1). Large volumes of paperwork are replaced with computer generated reports that reveal previously hidden dynamics (2).

The Information Age has produced a wave of technological applications, changing the way restaurants process and monitor transactions. Applications covered in this chapter include point-of-sale (POS) systems for table service restaurants, table management systems, home delivery, frequent dining and gift card programs, inventory control systems, and menu management systems.

Point-of-Sale Systems

A **POS System**, a core foundational application, can enhance decision-making, operational control, guest service, and revenues. However, not all POS systems offer the same features and potential for profit improvement. The purpose of this section is to discuss those factors which are critical to POS system selection for table service restaurants (3).

A POS system is a network of cashier and server terminals that typically handles food and beverage orders, transmission of orders to the kitchen and bar, guest-check settlement, timekeeping, and interactive charge posting to guest folios. POS information can also be imported to accounting and food cost/inventory software packages. A variety of reports can be generated including open check (list of outstanding checks), cashier, voids/comps, sales analysis, menu mix, server sales summary, tip, labor cost, etc. Sophisticated POS systems can generate hundreds of management reports.

Although POS systems are becoming more affordable, they still represent a substantial financial investment. The average cost of a POS system, including installation, is about $15,000 and must be replaced or upgraded every three to five years. Some restaurant operators spend $50,000 or more for their POS systems (4). Although many claim that a POS system can improve profitability by 20 to 60 percent with a payback of less than two years, a few restaurant operators remain skeptical. Attitudes are changing, however, as POS systems become more robust, flexible, powerful, user-friendly, and cost effective. The disadvantages of standard cash registers compared to POS systems are hard to ignore.

Elimination of Arithmetic Errors

1. **Elimination of arithmetic errors.** A guest-check survey conducted in 1987 revealed that handwritten checks were inaccurate 16% of the time where 70% of these checks averaged a substantial undercharge. Undercharges were brought to the restaurateur's attention 36% of the time as opposed to 91% for overcharges. This study concluded that restaurants using handwritten checks have lower tipping and a substantial loss of potential revenue (5). A POS system would eliminate those errors due to miscalculations, which could increase revenues up to 1.5%.

Improved Guest Check Control

2. **Improved guest check control.** Guest check control under manual conditions is one of the first items to be neglected. Failure to audit missing checks and to reconcile guest check sales with cash register readings often results in a lower sales volume and higher cost ratios. With a POS system, a server must place the order through a server terminal for it to be printed in the kitchen or bar. This ensures the recording of all sales and provides line cooks with legible orders. It also electronically tracks open checks, settled checks, voids, comps, discounts, and sales for each server, as well as employee meals. Consequently, sales abuses associated with manual systems are eliminated without much effort. It also ensures that employee meals, waste, and guest comps are rung up and discounted accordingly.

Increased Average Guest Check

3. **Increased average guest check.** Since orders are transmitted to the kitchen printer, travel time to the kitchen is reduced. This allows more time for suggestive selling and servicing guests. Also, a POS system provides a detailed summary for each server, listing average guest check, items sold, and total sales (see Figure 3-1). This information can be used for job evaluations, motivational programs (e.g., wine contest), and assessing merchandising skills (e.g., average guest check and item sales) and server efficiency (e.g., sales per hour).

Faster Reaction to Trends

4. **Faster reaction to trends.** A POS system can provide a wealth of information on a real-time basis. Most POS systems can easily track sales and cost information by time period (e.g., hour, daily, weekly), employee, meal period, register, outlet, table, and menu item. This allows a restaurant operator to quickly spot and react to problematic areas affecting profitability such as a declining average guest check during lunch, excessive labor hours in the kitchen, a changing menu mix, or sluggish liquor sales. It also enables operators to quickly identify and capitalize on sales trends (e.g., items largely sold at 6:00 PM versus 9:00 PM help chefs create specials tailored to each crowd). Some POS systems provide information on table turnover and utilization. This can be used to evaluate station sizes, dining room table mix, service style, server and kitchen efficiency, and seating and reservation policies.

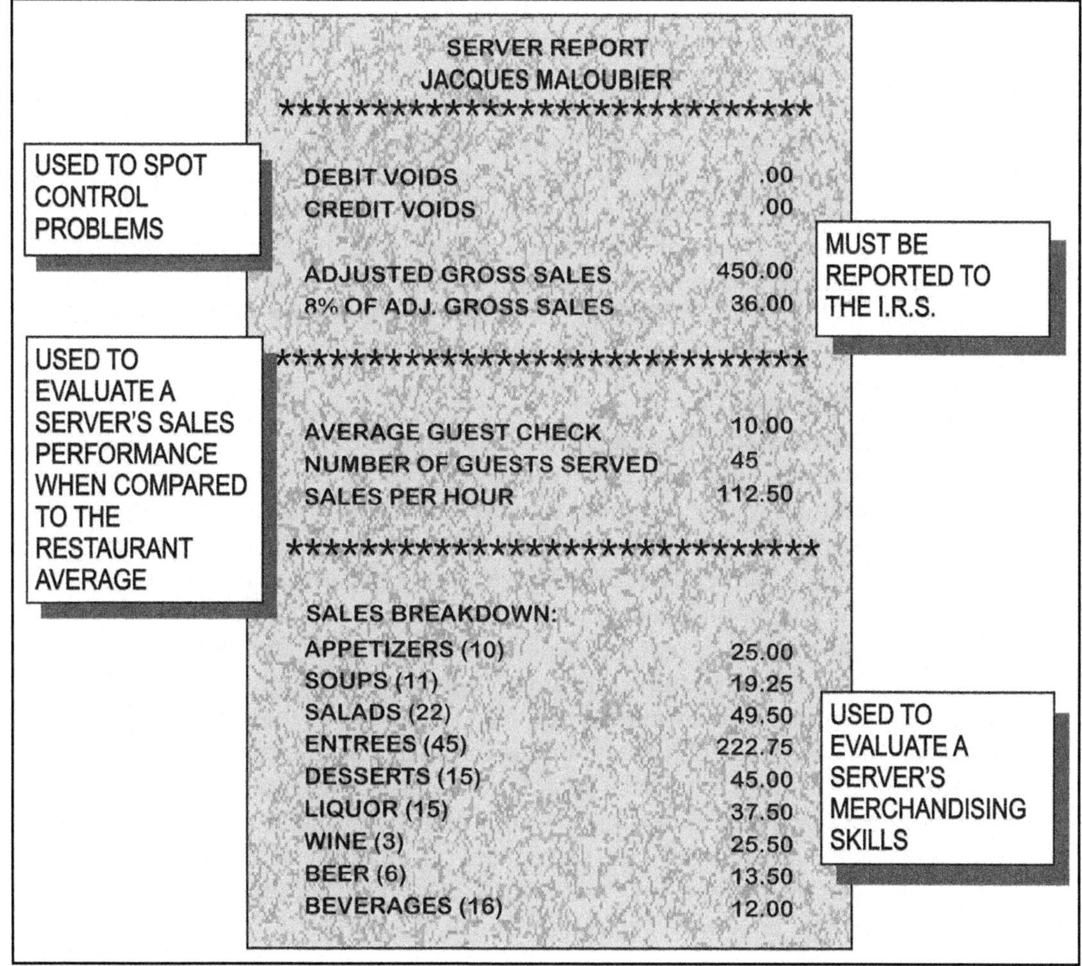

SERVER REPORT
JACQUES MALOUBIER
****
USED TO SPOT CONTROL PROBLEMS
DEBIT VOIDS .00
CREDIT VOIDS .00
ADJUSTED GROSS SALES 450.00
8% OF ADJ. GROSS SALES 36.00
MUST BE REPORTED TO THE I.R.S.
****
USED TO EVALUATE A SERVER'S SALES PERFORMANCE WHEN COMPARED TO THE RESTAURANT AVERAGE
AVERAGE GUEST CHECK 10.00
NUMBER OF GUESTS SERVED 45
SALES PER HOUR 112.50
****
SALES BREAKDOWN:
APPETIZERS (10) 25.00
SOUPS (11) 19.25
SALADS (22) 49.50
ENTREES (45) 222.75
DESSERTS (15) 45.00
LIQUOR (15) 37.50
WINE (3) 25.50
BEER (6) 13.50
BEVERAGES (16) 12.00
USED TO EVALUATE A SERVER'S MERCHANDISING SKILLS

FIGURE 3-1. A PARTIAL SERVER REPORT.

Unfortunately, many managers rely on profit and loss statements to judge operational performance, which tends to lay blame rather than explaining where and when the mistake was made (6).

Reduced Labor Costs and Greater Operational Efficiency

5. **Reduced labor costs and greater operational efficiency.** In the 1980s, a 140-seat South Florida restaurant with sales in excess of $4,000,000 was using a mechanical cash register. Managers spent a considerable amount of time auditing guest checks, collecting dups from the kitchen to derive a sales mix and hourly cover count, and closing out the register. The implementation of a POS system eliminated much of the paperwork and resulted in a leaner management staff who refocused their efforts on guest related issues.

Since cover count information is retained on an hourly basis for each day, managers can use this to sense changes in daily workloads (forecasting) and take the required action (managing). This will help reduce unused labor capacity.

A POS system can streamline employee tasks to save time and improve productivity. For example, a POS system provides the opportunity to eliminate cashier positions by assigning this responsibility to servers who carry their own personal banks. Combining certain technologies such as wireless handheld order entry systems with kitchen display systems significantly reduces service delays and labor requirements and increases table turnover. The aforementioned technology combination was used to slash at least 20 minutes off the total guest experience and eliminate the need for a window-person dealing with orders entering the kitchen at a busy T.G.I. Friday's restaurant (*www.micros.com*).

Reduced Credit Card Expenses

6. **Reduced card-related expenses.** Most POS vendors offer credit (and debit) card interfaces. The server slides the credit cards through magnetic stripe readers attached to the POS terminals which automatically call for authorization, display approval on the screen, and produce checks to be signed. This eliminates the need for stand-alone credit card terminals, which pays for the credit card interface in less than a year in most cases. One telephone line or Internet connection (used for faster credit card processing) is needed to support a POS network. The expense of multiple phone line installations and monthly phone line usage costs is saved. Input errors are virtually eliminated because information does not need to be rekeyed manually. The amount of the sale will always match the amount of the charge on the credit card, which also eliminates the need to go back and match individual sales when the credit card batch does not match credit card sales. Also, when the cashier is overwhelmed with too many credit card approvals, the servers can carry out this task. Furthermore, POS vendors can offer clients very competitive credit card commission rates through arrangements negotiated with banks or financial organizations. Transaction fees are further reduced when restaurants allow customers to pay with debit cards. A recent development is the **Mobile Payment System** (e.g., Square Wallet). It enables customers to pay with their mobile devices, such as smart phones. This provides the opportunity for operators to streamline payment processes as well as save on credit and debit card transaction costs. On the horizon are **Invisible Payment Systems** that use smart phone global positioning system technology for detecting a customer's presence. "You can actually walk into a merchant, keep your phone in pocket, keep your wallet in your pocket, and a picture of you pops up on the register. You can just say 'I'm Laurie, and I'd like a cappuccino,' and your card is charged in the background" (http://money.cnn.com/2012/08/14/technology/startups/square-dorsey).

Reduced Late Charges

7. **Reduced late charges.** Ensuring that food and beverage charges are posted to a folio before guests check out can be a problem if done manually. The most effective

measure at reducing late charges is to interface POS terminals in the food and beverage outlets with an automated property management system. Along with providing timely and accurate charge posting, it checks the status of a guest's room or credit.

AUTOMATED BEVERAGE DISPENSING SYSTEM

American Business Computers manufactures a computerized beverage dispensing system that can dispense over 1200 different drinks and account for liquor, cocktails, cordials, wine, beer, and soft drinks. It pours a complete drink within two seconds after pressing a preset key or ente-ing a PLU #.

TERMINAL DESIGN VARIES

Terminal Design Varies. POS terminals come in different shapes and sizes. However, there are two terminal types. A **SERVER** or **PRECHECK TERMINAL** is used for entering orders only, while a **CASHIER TERMINAL** has a cash drawer. A cashier terminal, which can be used for both entering and settling checks, may support up to four cash drawers.

A terminal may consist of a display screen and keyboard, touch screen and keyboard, or just a touch screen. It may also have a guest check printer, pole or customer display, and **MAGNETIC STRIPE READER**, an input device that can retrieve information from the magnetic film strip found on the back of credit cards or employee identification cards (see Figure 3-2). Some POS terminals are equipped with **FINGER PRINT READERS**. Employees place fingers on a small sensor which authenticates identity and logs them on. These biometric security devices can be used in place of cumbersome passwords or magnetic swipe cards to simplify the logon process and to enhance security measures against fraudulent behavior. The latest development is a POS **RFID READER**, which can trigger an automatic logon at a POS station when a server wearing a RFID wristband is within range. The KeyLime Cove Water Resort in Gurnee, Illinois, has deployed an RFID wristband system (another example of a mobile payment system) developed by Precision Dynamics Corporation. It provides customers with automated cashless POS with a simple wave of their wrist. Cash is electronically loaded and deducted on the RFID wristband for instant purchases throughout the resort.

For inputting orders, there are typically four options: the standard 101-key models found with computers, touch screens, handhelds, and programmable keyboards. **PROGRAMMABLE KEYBOARDS** use touch-sensitive, wet-proof membrane panels where the keys are flat. POS input keys can be classified as:

PRESET

1. *Preset*—These keys are identified by item name or icon (e.g., press key titled **HAMBURGER** to enter order) and also maintain the price.

FIGURE 3-2. EXAMPLES OF POS DEVICES.

Courtesy of Menusoft Systems Corp.

Price Look-up

2. *Price look-up (PLU)*—The number of preset keys appearing at once is limited by the size of the keyboard or screen. To enter menu items not appearing on the keyboard or screen, enter its PLU # (e.g., enter 113 for lamb special on the numeric keypad).

Numeric Keypad

3. *Numeric keypad*—This is used for entering PLU numbers and transactions requiring numeric input, such as entering a server number or ordering five steaks.

Payment

4. *Payment*—When settling a check, the cashier can choose from a number of payment keys (e.g., cash, Visa).

Cooking Instructions

5. *Cooking instructions*—These keys are used for preparation instructions to the chef that appear on the kitchen printout.

Hard

6. *Hard*—These keys assist in processing transactions such as void and clear. Unlike the other keys, these keys cannot be reprogrammed.

Item Recipe Look-up

7. *Item recipe look-up*—A bartender can look up drink recipes. A server can look up photographs and ingredients of menu items. Customers increasingly want to know the nutritional value of menu choices. Moreover, servers with convenient access to detailed ingredient information are more likely to advise customers with food allergies correctly.

Customer Look-up

8. *Customer look-up*—A server can look up information about customers to repeat or modify their past orders (e.g., automatically reorders a round of drinks without having to reorder each drink manually), to learn about their preferences and special needs (e.g., allergic to garlic), and to provide them with rewards updates for those enrolled in a frequent dining program.

When using a touch screen to input orders, the user selects keys by pressing the screen at the appropriate place. This input option is popular due to its flexibility and ease of use. Another input option gaining in popularity are **Mobile Pos Devices**, which typically involve a handheld terminal, tablet PC, or smart phone. Mobile restaurant operations, such as food trucks, particularly benefit from Mobile POS systems.

Wireless handheld terminals were first introduced in 1977. Numeric keypads were used to enter PLU numbers and infrared technology to relay this information between the handhelds and POS systems. Later handheld terminals used radio frequencies for transmitting information. Handheld terminals were not popular during the 70s and 80s. The public did not accept them. At some restaurants, servers were instructed to step away because of customer complaints. Some restaurateurs wanted technology to remain behind the scenes. In addition to negative perceptions, there were other drawbacks. Some servers found the handheld screens difficult to read and to navigate. Unit prices were expensive, and many restaurant operators feared handhelds would be damaged, stolen, or lost. Units sometimes malfunctioned in hot weather or were disrupted by other FM transmitting devices. There were also problems with the recording and timing of orders. However, the current generation of handheld devices, ruggedized and restaurant hardened, have overcome most perception and technical problems and are becoming easier to use. Furthermore, improvements in wireless technology (e.g., RF and Ethernet) have significantly extended the transmission or distance range. Handheld terminals are most commonly used in outdoor recreational areas without electricity, such as resort pools or golf courses. "Nevertheless, while you will probably find that some bars and restaurants use them for patio dining, they have yet to make major inroads to the main dining room–but that may be changing," according to restaurant veteran Joe Erickson (7).

Specific benefits include:

1. Delivery of food is quicker resulting in higher average checks and greater table turnover.
2. Servers have more time for servicing guests and suggestive selling resulting in higher tips and satisfied guests. For example, handhelds at the Oak Forest Bowl in Chicago, Illinois eliminated the need for servers to walk back and forth across a 20,000 square foot beer garden to take and input orders into the POS system. Servers at Washington, D.C.'s Royal Mile Pub use handhelds to quickly list all of the 83 single-malt scotches the restaurant serves.
3. Training time is significantly reduced. With easy access to the menu, including daily specials, server menu knowledge is enhanced and menu memorization reduced.
4. Handhelds can be equipped with portable belt printers and credit card swipes for printing customer receipts and performing tableside settlement. This provides quicker service, for curbside and takeout service especially, and also safeguards guests from credit card fraud.
5. Handhelds inform the servers when items are out of stock or orders are ready, although this task can also be accomplished through waiter paging systems. Silent (no beeper noise) paging systems are available. Servers receive an unmistakable vibration when an order is ready.
6. More tables can be assigned to servers without compromising the service.
7. Customer, ingredient, and nutritional information can be accessed easily.
8. Errors and omissions due to transferring orders to the POS system are significantly reduced.
9. Lines at POS terminals are eliminated.
10. The system can prompt a server to read each order back to verify accuracy before hitting send.
11. Hardware-related costs can be reduced. Five fixed POS stations, for example, can be replaced with two fixed stations and eight to ten handhelds, reducing energy consumption. Handhelds may have the capability of texting or e-mailing receipts, reducing the cost of reordering thermal receipt paper and printers.

Recent developments in handheld ordering systems are write-on handhelds, tablet PCs, (e.g., iPad), and smart phones (e.g., Android). Write-on handhelds, instead of trying to compress touch screen interfaces onto tiny PDA screens, allow servers to simply write the orders down using styluses. Handwritten information is then transformed into menu items using handwriting recognition software. "As the server writes, all items containing the letters or codes he or she has written are displayed in the Selection Window. As soon as the server sees the correct item, he or she may tap it once to add it to the order" (http://www.rmpos.com).

A growing number of operators are using Apple's iPad as part of their POS systems, from arming servers with them to installing them on dining tables. iPad's larger display enables more POS keys to be shown, making it a more attractive sales and information tool (8). In a recent survey conducted by Technomic, a food industry consulting and research firm, customers are receptive to trying new restaurant technologies, especially tableside touch screen devices that enable them to self self-order and pay, view menus, and tie in digital rewards with loyalty programs. According to recent studies, tablet menus increase sales in most restaurants. Menu information can be presented in multiple languages. They contain more information than paper menus, offering high-resolution pictures of dishes and easily accessible allergy and nutritional information. In 2012, New York-based OTG equipped tables with self-ordering and payment iPad tablet PCs at five table-service restaurants and common seating areas at JFK, LaGuardia and Minneapolis-St. Paul airports. According to Rick Blatstein, chief executive of OTG, which operates 150 restaurants, gourmet markets, food courts, and other food service points of distribution at 10 airports, the self-service tablet technology has resulted in a double-digit increase in sales due to faster seat turns, higher average guest checks, and higher levels of service. Servers no longer have the burden of recording and entering order details.

SoftTouch, a restaurant point-of-sale (POS) provider, created a Mobile POS system called DineBlast Mobile used for table service, quick service (QRS), takeout, or curbside ordering. Restaurant diners self-order and self-pay using Wi-Fi (a wireless transmission standard) enabled personal devices (e.g., Palm Treo, Blackberry, iPhone, and iPod Touch). Customers can also page and text servers (e.g., need extra Italian dressing), request drink refills, complete customer satisfaction surveys, and access their order and payment history. A designated printer provides hard copies of receipts customers can sign on their way out (http://www.softtouchpos.com).

In 2007, Microsoft introduced **Pixelsense Computing** (formerly called Surface Computing), an interactive tabletop technology with unique capabilities and possibilities for evolving future dining table experiences. PixelSense computing has four key attributes (www.microsoft.com/surface):

1. *Direct interaction with a touch-sensitive screen*—Users can use their hands to "grab" digital information and to interact with content by touch and gesture without a mouse or keyboard.
2. *Multi-touch*—Many points of contact are recognized simultaneously, not just with one finger like on a typical touch screen but up to dozens of items at once.
3. *Multi-user*—The horizontal form factor makes it easy for several people to gather around surface computers providing a collaborative, face-to-face computing experience.
4. *Object recognition*—Users can place physical objects, such as credit cards or room keys, on the surface to trigger different types of digital responses, including the transfer of digital content.

Sheraton Hotels and Resorts used this expensive technology at five properties to enable guests to order and pay for food and drinks as well as to browse and listen to music, send photos home, download books, etc. PixelSense computing and technologies like it provide a rich platform for future hospitality applications. For example, a "customer simply sets a wine glass on the surface of a smart dining table, a restaurant could provide them with information about the wine they're ordering, pictures of the vineyard it came from and suggested food pairings tailored to that evening's menu. The experience could become completely immersive, letting users access information on the wine-growing region and even look at recommended hotels and plan a trip without leaving the table" (www.microsoft.com).

The following are various criteria for evaluating what POS systems are best for your operation:

1. *How quickly must orders be processed?* To evaluate speed, obtain the time values associated with opening a check, adding items, voiding items, modifying orders, settling the check, and capturing a credit card authorization. For most POS systems it will take 10 to 20 keystrokes to process a typical guest check. The speed at which these keystrokes are executed primarily depends on the responsiveness of the terminal and how quickly a server can identify the required keys. Look for terminals where descriptions of PLU numbers can be quickly accessed, screen and keyboard layouts are well-organized and not too crowded, and order modifications and substitutions are easily executed. The POS program should enable a server to input the order just as the guest has ordered it without delay (e.g., server looks for a manager to determine whether fries can be substituted with a side salad).

Handheld Devices Carve Restaurant Niche

Handheld technology is slowly transforming the restaurant industry and soon the waiter's order pad may become a relic of the past.

Richard Webster (www.qsrweb.com)

2. *What system provides the most effective interaction?* When choosing a POS system, it is important to assess the user's skill level and training needs. Most people feel touch screen systems provide a more natural interaction, making it easier to learn and use. However, experienced, older employees at a busy restaurant might prefer a programmable keyboard. An operation with a high turnover and low literacy may find that keyboard buttons dedicated to the icons of the various products (e.g., hamburger, fries, milk shake) provides the best interaction. (9) Terminal selection should be based on the needs and quirks of the user. Provide employees with the opportunity to experiment with the POS systems under consideration. Observe their reactions to them, perhaps administering a survey for additional feedback.

3. *How are menu changes handled?* Restaurants with frequent menu changes would find touch screens easier to manage than flat programmable keyboards, which require typed **Menu Boards** to overlay the keyboard surface for identifying the function of the key. This board must be retyped when menu items (preset key descriptions) are added, deleted, or changed. A different board may also be required for each new meal period (e.g., breakfast, lunch, and dinner). This might pose a significant problem in a 24-hour operation where meal periods overlap. Another consideration is the reconfiguration of desktop or full-screen menus for mobile POS devices. Client/server applications designed for desktop PC screens usually do not render well on mobile device screens. **Middleware** solutions can be utilized for automatically generating a display or new user interface based on the application and the associated device screen size and type. Middleware is a group of computer routines creating a communications interface between a high level application program and physical hardware. It insulates application programs from the idiosyncrasies of physical devices and provides modularity and portability (10).
4. *How many preset keys and PLU numbers are needed?* It is extremely important that the system can identify every item sold. This allows the restaurateur to easily discern fast and slow moving menu items and to differentiate between desirable and undesirable food cost items for various parts of the day. As a result, menu items with a high percent of sales and low food cost may be promoted. This information is also needed by the back office for calculating standard usages of raw goods for inventory and cost control. POS keys also need to appropriately categorized or grouped (e.g., Food Sales, Soft Beverage Sales, Liquor Sales, Beer Sales, Wine Sales, etc.) according to industry standards specified in the **Uniform System of Accounts for Restaurants**, a book published by the National Restaurant Association. This enables potential cost issues to be isolated (e.g., liquor cost is measured against liquor sales; wine cost is measured against wine sales, etc.) and allows restaurant operators to gauge their performance compared to others (e.g., XYZ Restaurant: Wine Cost/Wine Sales = 39% ; Industry Average = 35%)
5. *What should the POS terminal configuration be?* Terminal placement and the number of terminals needed primarily depends on the layout of the dining area, volume of business, average length of a transaction, restaurant theme or concept, and terminal size.

The restaurant operator should locate terminals which are easily accessible to servers, minimizing travel and waiting time. A terminal can normally handle three to eight servers. A 40-seat restaurant may require only one terminal. Placing terminals in a large restaurant with several rooms requires careful planning. Vendor recommendations should be carefully considered. They have the sales-driven tendency to recommend more terminals than are actually needed. If placing a terminal in a particular area is questionable, install the necessary communication cables that would allow a terminal, if needed, to be quickly brought online. A spare terminal, for example, could be used in a banquet room that is sometimes used for Sunday brunches.

Terminal visibility or obtrusiveness is another consideration. Exposing terminals to guests may take away from the restaurant's ambiance. POS terminal dimensions vary significantly. Small terminals can be tablesunk, making them virtually transparent to the guest. Bulky terminals are difficult to conceal and are usually found around side stations and back-of-the-house areas. On the other hand, a flat, touch screen terminal can be placed almost anywhere, including being hung from the ceiling or mounted on the wall like a picture.

Technology Tidbits

In 1992, the first touch screen handheld was introduced.

Servers or tables equipped with mobile POS devices eliminate terminal placement and capacity considerations. However, wireless technology is not limited to handhelds and portable computers. Full-size terminals are also available.

Wireless POS systems provide the maximum design and redesign flexibility. They enable POS terminals to be placed virtually anywhere and relocated where the employees and customers are in minutes to improve productivity and speed of service at no additional cost. Cost requirements posed by wired installations are also reduced.

Are Server Terminals Always Needed?

Are server terminals always needed? In some operations, servers never touch a terminal. The cashier is responsible for entering and settling all guest checks. A cashier-only system offers the following advantages:

1. No more than three terminals are needed for most operations, greatly reducing the hardware cost.
2. Training servers to operate a POS terminal can be eliminated. Many feel that training is a waste of time in a high turnover industry. This time can be spent on merchandising and service skills.
3. Since there are fewer inexperienced users, there are fewer POS problems.
4. Tighter product and cash control results.

Choosing a cashier-only POS system may be an appealing option, particularly for smaller operations (annual sales less than $1,000,000) with limited resources and a compact dining room layout.

Technology is finding its place at the restaurant table, according to the National Restaurant Association's 2012 Restaurant Industry Forecast. Nearly 4 in 10 consumers say they would likely to use an electronic ordering system and menus on tablet computers at table service restaurants. About half said they would use at-table electronic payment options and a restaurant's smart phone app to view menus and make reservations. At quick service restaurants, about 4 out of 10 consumers say they would place online orders for takeout, use in-store self-service ordering kiosks, and use smart phone apps to look at menus and order delivery (www.restaurant.org).

Pos Printers

POS printers. When selecting printers, noise, speed, reliability,special features, and costs must be considered. POS printers produce credit card slips and receipts for customers and order slips for the kitchen and bar staff.

Dot matrix and thermal are two commonly used slip and receipt printers. A dot matrix printer is an impact printer that forms text by pressing the ends of pins against a ribbon. A thermal printer is a non impact printer that forms an image by moving heated styluses over specially treated paper. Both of these printers use continuous roll paper.

Dot matrix printers typically cost $200 to $400 and are more appropriate for use in the kitchens where the ambient temperatures are enough sometimes to prevent thermal printers from working effectively. Thermal printers typically cost $100 to $500. They are better suited for printing credit slips and receipts, and the only option for tableside printing. Fewer moving parts make them quieter, faster, and more reliable than dot matrix printers. The cost of thermal paper is roughly equivalent to the cost of paper and ribbons for dot matrix printers.

Order items can be routed to different printers. For example, hot food items can be directed to the hot food prep station and drinks to the bar or drink prep station. One kitchen printer will probably be sufficient for most restaurants. If a restaurant, however, has different stations which handle different dishes, a printer for each station may be preferable if it enables employees to more easily keep up with and time the items for which they are responsible.

Kitchen printers should be compact, allowing them to be placed in areas that are easily accessible without occupying valuable space. Order slips should remain partially attached to each other before being separated to keep them from getting lost and out of sequence.

Order slips should be easy-to-read. There should be ample spacing between lines and clear and adequate menu descriptions (at least 16 characters) that can be read from a distance. Character size is a primary concern. Orders can also be printed in two colors, which is useful in highlighting preparation instructions.

The system should also inform the user when a printer problem exists. Common problems include running out of paper and printer jams. If a printer should jam, order slips and paper guest checks should be redirected to another printer. It is important that printers have sufficient paper to accommodate peak periods and to replace ribbons before the print becomes too light or illegible. The author witnessed pure chaos when a kitchen printer stopped printing food orders during the middle of a meal period due to a paper outage. Some printers have sensors that sound warnings when paper is out or nearly out.

Among POS components, printers have the highest failure rate because they have the most moving parts. Consequently, some restaurant operators own spare backup printers.

Course Firing

Course Firing (Hold and Fire). This allows servers to place entire orders, after which the system sends the different courses of the orders to the kitchen printer at time intervals selected by the servers or requested by the customers (e.g., bring out appetizer with entrée). Course firing is particularly helpful in placing hotel room service breakfasts, typically ordered via doorknob cards. After the cards are collected in the early morning, the orders are first entered into the POS system and then printed in the kitchen automatically at the appropriate time. Not only does this save time, it also enables the kitchen staff to review all the pre-entered orders when they arrive to quickly gain a sense of the morning's workload.

Video Monitor or Kitchen Display Systems

Video monitor or kitchen display systems. Video monitors are typically used in quick-service and high-volume restaurants to expedite preparation and tracking of orders. Orders placed through POS terminals appear on a kitchen video monitor and can be routed to one or more displays, with the ability to route items based on sale type. The display sequence may be based on a certain priority, such as preparation time. In addition, the display screen can be customized to help kitchen employees time the preparation of food orders (e.g., cold food orders appear blue) and to identify special cooking instructions (e.g., "No Salt" blinks). When the order is ready, it is cleared from the screen by pressing a "bump" bar. Video monitors are also gaining acceptance in the mainstream table service environment, especially as an aid to expediting orders quickly and efficiently (11).

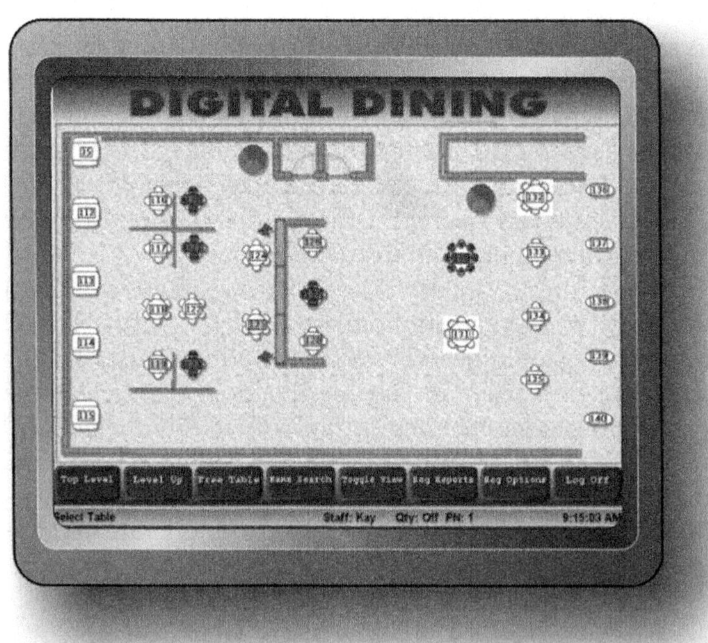

FIGURE 3-3. AN EXAMPLE OF A WINDOWS-BASED POS SCREEN.

Source: Menusoft Systems Corporation, Springfield, VA.

Today, restaurant operators can purchase surveillance systems displaying POS data atop normal video pictures. This is done with video technology called text insertion. Any data entered via the POS keyboard will appear on the video monitor. The combination of visual and textual data is helpful in spotting theft and fraudulent transactions involving no-sales, voids, discounts, excessive sales amounts, etc. For example, if the surveillance system shows a bartender handing out three beers, the sale of those three beers must appear on the screen for it to be a legitimate transaction. Video surveillance systems can also be used to help train employees by monitoring their actions and watching what new menu items are purchased and if employees are making menu items properly and safely. For example, Vision Enabled Training from Elmwood Park, N.J.-based Sealed Air pairs advanced algorithms with high-quality cameras to record employees in food preparation areas and to detect any noncompliance with health regulations and safety codes.

Hardware Platforms

Hardware platforms. The widespread adoption of standard personal computer architecture signifies the beginning of the end for proprietary POS systems (see Figure 3-4). POS systems built on personal computer (PC) platforms provide management with greater software portability, enhanced internal controls and transaction processing technology as well as improved report generation. PC-based POS systems are also more robust with the capability of connecting any type of peripheral from smart card readers to biometric scanning devices.

POS systems are manufactured and serviced by a range of firms and run on a range of operating systems, including DOS, Windows, Linux and Unix. Most restaurant operators have POS software running on Windows-based networked systems. Small installations run peer-to-peer local networks and larger installations incorporate a dedicated server. In a cloud- or web-based POS network, the server is located offsite. The Internet is used to collect data from POS terminals and to transfer it to a remote server. Restaurant POS terminals will continue to function if the Internet connection is lost. Data will be available once the Internet connection is restored. A cloud-based POS network offers a restaurateur, especially with multiple locations, a number of benefits. Onsite server support tasks are eliminated. The analysis of data across outlets is simplified because the data is stored in a single database. Price and menu changes, employee schedules, and product orders are easily made and can be applied to a single restaurant or an entire chain. With a Web connection, employees can check work schedules anywhere. Owners and managers can access up-to-the-minute information (e.g., sales, labor, and promotions) about their operations anytime. Business intelligence capabilities are improved. Trends can be spotted immediately and acted upon enterprise-wide. Another significant advantage of cloud-based POS systems is interconnectivity with customer mobile devices. They make it convenient for customers to order, pay, and participate in loyalty programs using their own smart phones or tablets.

Advancements in POS software design and user interfaces have resulted in shorter learning curves and offer a number of possibilities for improving employee effectiveness and efficiency. Order entry screens have become more informative and easier to use.

Colorful graphical icons can replace character-based computer functions (e.g., selection of a hamburger by touching an icon). A Windows-based POS system, for example, allows servers to view the dining room layout graphically, displaying the location of station and table assignments (see Figure 3-3). In addition, it enables the attachment of photos and video as well as animation clips for such things as online promotions (e.g., picture of chef special) and training (e.g., video clip of how to make a Vodka Martini).

System Evaluation Begins With a Detailed Checklist

System evaluation begins with a detailed checklist. The basic functionality of POS software does not vary much from one package to the next. However, as more features are added, the software becomes more complex and expensive. It is important to devise a detailed list of all the things you want a POS to do. Without clearly defining selection criteria, it is difficult to differentiate POS products.

The next step is to test the POS System to validate performance capabilities and evaluate ease of use. How certain tasks are handled may make a difference in system selection. Providing more than one check per table, for example, is much easier if the system tracks orders by seat number rather than by check or table number. Such a system can generate a soft check for each seat, any combination of seats, or the entire table

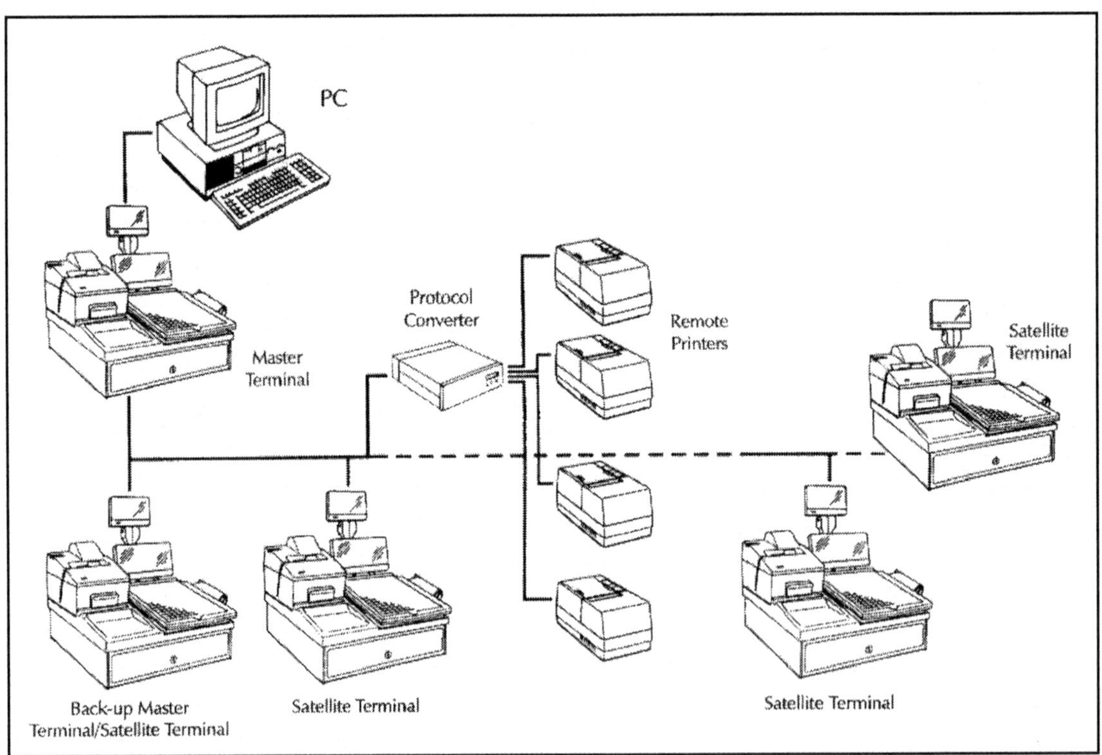

FIGURE 3-4. AN EXAMPLE OF A POS HARDWARE PLATFORM USING SPECIALIZED EQUIPMENT.

Source: System Concepts, Inc., Scottsdale, AZ.

without any additional steps and check responsibility. It might also have the capability of splitting the cost of any item on the menu between two or more customers.

It is important to investigate what systems a POS system can be interfaced with and whether it is compatible with existing systems. The best POS systems can communicate data to a variety of third-party software programs (e.g., payroll, food and beverage, front office). Avoid POS systems with limited interface options; otherwise, an operator may not be able to take advantage of applications which can reduce data entry, improve efficiency, and provide meaningful information.

There should be controlled access to the system. This can be achieved through passwords, electronic key locks, magnetic cards, or fingerprint and RFID readers. This prevents unauthorized employees from performing supervisory tasks such as making changes to the database, opening and closing servers, adjusting checks and punch-in and punch-out times, etc.

The POS payment application and debit card personal identification number (PIN) device must be compliant with the Payment Card Industry Data Security Standard (PCI-DSS – see Chapter 2 for more information), which contains a set of regulations or rules developed jointly by the leading card companies (e.g., American Express, Visa, MasterCard, etc.) to prevent cardholder data theft and to combat debit and credit card fraud. Restaurants regained the title as the most breached industry -- representing 57% of the investigations according to the 2011 Global Security Report authored by Trustwave, a provider of on-demand data security and payment card industry compliance management solutions. Many restaurateurs do not understand the magnitude of this problem. It takes one card breach to potentially put a restaurant out of business. Restaurants are frequently targeted by organized thieves because of the high volume of card transactions and the low level of security in place. The threats of theft are increasing as sophisticated techniques to hack into systems evolve. Expert assistance is often needed to identify appropriate tools and services to achieve compliance. An owner of a restaurant, for example, assumed that a new POS system safeguarded the operation from a security breach until it was hacked and the affected parties started demanding make-good payments. Unfortunately, the restaurant had to close because of hundreds of thousands of fines and fees.

Also be sure to safeguard the system against power fluctuations. The system should be equipped with an uninterruptible power supply (UPS) where electric lines are supplied directly to the POS network from the building transformer. This minimizes electric noise in the power supply circuit, which can cause garbled transactions, scrambled memory, device failures, and downtime.

Selecting the right POS system can significantly improve accounting controls, efficiency, and profitability. However, the wrong system can be disruptive and a constant source of frustration.

Table Management Systems and Home Delivery Software

Table management systems. Some POS systems provide table-management functions or can be integrated to dedicated table management systems for selected tasks. Table management systems reduce guests' waits, improve service, drive revenue through online bookings, and increase turns by lowering the number of decisions a host or hostess must make, balancing server workloads, shortening the time a table sits empty between the departure of the last party and the arrival of the next, and improving communication between employees and between employees and guests. Tasks performed by table management systems include:

Reservations Processing and Wait List Management

Reservations processing and wait list management. A table management system can keep track of all call-in and walk-in reservations and project the waiting time based on the desired seating time (e.g., 90 minutes) and current table status information. A computer monitor located at the host station can graphically display which tables are occupied, reserved, or vacant and whether a table has been bussed or its check has been open, printed, or paid. This information enables tables to be seated more quickly since a host or hostess does not have to walk the floor to determine table status and helps predict when a particular table might become available. It can also identify which tables have been seated longer than the desired seating time, triggering an appropriate tactical response to turn the table. For example, a couple who have finished their dinner and are enjoying a lingering conversation could be gently persuaded to leave their table by having the restaurant manager invite them for complimentary after-dinner drinks in the restaurant's lounge. Sophisticated table management systems can handle group and private room reservations. They may also be able to accommodate multiple locations and to check availability across multiple outlets within the same operation as well as transfer reservations from one outlet to another.

Table Assignments and Balancing

Table assignments and balancing. Evenly distributing server workloads is extremely important in achieving the desired throughput and service quality. Triple seating a server, for example, cannot happen with a table management system because it automatically assigns each server station with the same number of guests and tables and auto matically matches a guest's seating preference to an appropriate table (e.g., 4-top in nonsmoking section).

Restaurant-Wide Communication

Restaurant-wide communication network. Table management systems use Internet links, pagers, video monitors, NETWORK hardwired or wireless transmitters, personal keypads, and mobile devices to electronically link key communication processes found in the service cycle:

1. *Reservation taking.* A table management system can be linked to an online RESTAURANT RESERVATION SYSTEM enabling customers to book tables, place waitlist requests, and access wait times via mobile or desktop devices. It may also enable customers to select tables of their choice, preorder, share table-booking information with others, and send booking reminders through e-mail and text messages. A table management system can also be interfaced with a **CALLER IDENTIFICATION SYSTEM** for immediately recognizing existing customers when they call and automatically populating reservations with their contact information.

2. *Guest greeting and waitlist management.* Handhelds permit greeters to compile and manage waitlists away from the host terminal. The GuestBridge table management system (acquired by OpenTable in 2009) can instantly recognize guests carrying RFID-enabled Guestbridge VIP/ID cards. The VIP card is recognized by antennae placed at the entryway. When a VIP arrives, the software immediately displays the guest record to the host stand and/or wireless handheld devices. "This enables staff to greet guests by name before they even have to speak, and their favorite drink can be waiting for them at their favorite table" (*www.guestbridge.com*).
3. *Table and wait alert.* When a hostess selects a waiting party, the software automatically notifies guests through mobile phones, pagers (e.g., coaster blinks and vibrates) , or a video messaging center, a guest-facing display that can also show the waitlist. NoWait, an iPad waitlist app,for example, sends a text message with the wait to the customer's cell phone until their table is ready. Those with smart phones can also click on a link for information about their place in line. A wait alert pager, if equipped with an LCD display, can also provide automatic updated wait times to waiting guests (e.g., your table will be ready in 10 minutes). When a waiting guest is approaching or has exceeded the quoted waiting time,the system can also automatically make the party name flash on the waitlist. Some restaurant operators feel that guests are willing to wait longer if the wait process is fair and they can see progress being made.
4. *Table seating.* When the host touches the picture of the table on the floor plan, the server is paged to alert him that a new table has been seated in his assigned station.
5. *Table service.* Guests can page servers.
6. *Table delivery and order pickup.* The kitchen can page servers when their food orders are ready to deliver. RFID location tracking technology can be used to identify where to deliver the food in self-service restaurants. For example, at Panera Bread, a fast food bakery chain, a customer receives a coaster after ordering, finds a place to sit, and then places the coaster on the table. The coaster recognizes an RFID tag underneath the table and then transmits this information back to the kitchen so staff can instantly correlate the food order to a table. Another approach is to provide customers with handheld pagers so they can be summoned to pick up their orders, which Cosi, a fast casual restaurant chain, uses in its higher-volume stores to save the time employees formerly spent walking around the dining room calling out ticket numbers.
7. *Table status.* Using a keypad or a handheld or wearable (e.g.,watch) device, a busser can change the status of a vacated but dirty table to vacant and clean.

Customer Relationship and Marketing Management

Customer relationship and marketing management. Table management systems capture valuable information about customers, such as contact information (e.g., e-mail and mailing addresses and cell phone number), important dates, (e.g., birthday), historical data (e.g., past wait times, number of prior and future dining reservations booked and number of no shows and cancelled dining reservations) and preferences (e.g., favorite table and server). This information is used for marketing to conduct an e-mail or direct mail promotional campaigns and to personalize future customer visits. One system, for example, generates slips containing key information about customers. These slips are used by servers to greet guests by name and to know their preferences, past histories, and dietary restrictions. Table management systems can also track referrals and establish incentive programs for concierges. The online restaurant reservation feature also helps create an online presence by providing useful restaurant information, such as location and driving instructions (e.g., Google map), customer reviews, pictures, and menus.

Detailed Service Analysis

Detailed service analysis. Table management systems are most appropriate for high volume restaurants with multiple dining rooms or dining rooms with obstructions that prevent a clear view from one vantage point. In addition to handling reservations and table-related activities, they can provide information on table turnover and utilization, average wait time, average seating time, number of guests served, etc. This can be used to evaluate station sizes, dining room table mix, server and kitchen efficiency, and seating and reservation policies.

Home Delivery Software

Home delivery software. Delivery options are no longer limited to pizza and Chinese food. Although home delivery has been around for a while in the fast food arena, it is becoming more prevalent in table service restaurants. Home delivery software addresses the growing outside delivery market by providing restaurants with easy access to the repeat customer's order history: address, directions to home, phone numbers, past orders, etc. When orders are phoned in, the user simply enters the caller's phone number and the caller's name and address appear on the screen. The order is entered and then printed in the kitchen. Features such as one-touch ordering, which automatically enters a past customer order, and suggestive selling prompts (e.g., try our new chicken wings) enhance the ordering process. Home delivery software can improve delivery times and driver productivity by tracking delivery driver production, efficiently routing drivers to minimize drive time, and printing street maps that highlight routes and optional turn-by-turn directions. The delivery receipt or label also has delivery in structions and any useful information about the customer's location, such as "the door is on the left side of the building." Home delivery software also can be integrated with a caller identification system. This feature saves time by immediately identifying repeat customers and bringing up their previous ordering information.

Many customers prefer to order online or with a mobile application. For example, online ordering is available at all Domino's and Papa John's pizza restaurants across the nation. "Customer's like the system because they can see the restaurant's entire menu and review it at their own pace, allowing them to feel in control of the ordering process" (www .crmdaily.com). Domino's now uses pizza tracking technology to keep the customers better informed. When customers place an order at Domino's, they can go to www.dominos.com and click on the Pizza Tracker icon. They will see a horizontal bar that lights up red as each step in the process is completed. Customers will see confirmation of their order being received by the store and when it is being prepared, baked, boxed, or en route. The Andromeda POS system uses a more sophisticated GPS-based tracking program, which allows customers to track on an online map exactly where the pizzas are. Customers are also automatically notified via text when their deliveries are en route and the estimated time of arrival.

Frequent Dining and Gift Card Programs

Frequent dining. The purpose of frequent dining programs is to create and maintain customer loyalty while increasing revenue. Such programs play a major role in customer relationship management (CRM). Frequent dining programs, similar to frequent buyer and flyer-miles programs, reward return customers with points, which can later be exchanged for free desserts, half price specials, or dollars off their meals. Restaurants typically issue frequent diners membership cards that are swiped at POS terminals to track transactions. POS systems make frequent diner programs available to small restaurants, which in the past have been the domain of large chains.

Restaurants can award points based on the number of visits, the menu items purchased, or the item dollar amounts. For example, higher point values could be assigned to low-performing or high-profit items to give them a boost. Frequent dining programs enable customer purchasing behaviors to be monitored and analyzed. This information can be used to influence the purchasing habits of customers. Customers, for example, who rarely order takeout food can be targeted with a takeout promotion. This information also enables the tracking of frequent diner complaints and the issuing of customized coupons prompted by specific complaint reasons. Charlie Brown's Steakhouses, the largest steakhouse chain in New Jersey, has a successful frequent dining program providing members with the following benefits (*www.charliebrowns.com*):

- Two $10 vouchers for 300 accumulated points. Members, who earn one point for every dollar spent, can access their accounts online.
- Free gifts for active members on birthdays and anniversaries.
- Triple points all day on Mondays at all locations.
- Exclusive members-only offers and events.

Frequent dining or loyalty programs have flourished, increasingly migrated to online media, and become more creative. Chipotle's program (called Farm Team) rewards participants based on their knowledge of its food. Farm Team members access a special Chipotle Website to learn where Chipotle's food comes from, take quizzes and polls, play games, and watch videos about the company. As customers make their way through the Farm Team site to different levels they earn points, which they can exchange for food and other prizes. Customers of Menchie's Frozen Yogurt can sign up for its new mySmileage reward program at menchies.com, through Facebook or Twitter, or in-store with a mobile phone number, then pick up a mySmileage wallet and keychain cards in-store. Members earn one "Smile" for every dollar spent at Menchie's. Menchie's automatically loads $5 in "Menchie's money" onto the mySmileage card each time a customer earns 50 "Smiles" (12).

Gift Cards

Gift cards. Many POS systems have gift card modules to track gift cards and certificate sales to ensure that they are being sold and redeemed securely and correctly. Cards are swiped at POS terminals for card issuances, transactions, and balance inquiries. Some POS systems provide customers with online access to gift card balances. Key benefits of gift card programs are advanced cash flow, increased sales, new customers, the frequency and nature of customer transactions are tracked, a higher profit margin because not all gift cards are redeemed, and the refilling and reusing of them by customers. Starbucks, the specialty coffee retailer, has benefited greatly from its gift card program, which accounts for 10% of all transactions. Furthermore, over a third are being refilled and reused because it saves customers time in line, since swiping gift cards speeds the transaction process. Starbucks gift cards can also be loaded onto the Starbucks mobile app for even a faster checkout. To pay for a beverage, for example, the customer holds the bar code appearing on the smart phone for the selected card up to the 2D scanner, and the purchase will be deducted from the balance.

Getting Back to Basics

As successful operators have always known, the basic disciplines make more money for a food service operation than any system, manual or automated, ever could. And two of these two basic disciplines are inventory and receiving. In many cases, a reduction of 2–3% of sales can be accomplished by tightening up on the basic disciplines of inventory and receiving.

Three basic rules seem to work every time for operators who want to reduce food costs substantially.

1. *Increase the frequency of taking inventory.*
2. *Reduce the level of inventory.*
3. *Receive goods like a fanatic.*

The Food Tracker,
A Food Cost Management Newsletter by System Concept's, Inc., First Quarter, 1990

Inventory Control System

An **inventory control system** tracks product quantities and prices and provides accurate information on inventory activities in a timely manner, enabling management to better control food costs. Also, the system makes taking and extending inventories and ordering and receiving easier. The following paragraphs discuss the mechanics involved in constructing and operating an inventory control system.

Create Vendor and Product File

Step 1. Create vendor and product file. Each vendor and product is assigned a number for tracking purposes including work in process (e.g., tuna salad). A vendor file usually contains the name, address, telephone number, and contact person for each vendor. A product file usually contains the vendor identification, product code, product description, product brand, inventory unit (e.g., bag, case) inventory location, and general ledger account number for each product. To save time, inventory items and prices can be imported from a food distributor order guide (e.g., Shamrock Foods).

Design Inventory Worksheet

Step 2. Design inventory worksheet. The order of the items on the worksheet should reflect the sequence of items on shelves to expedite inventory taking.

Take Inventory

Step 3. Take inventory. If the International Foodservice Distributors Association (IFDA) makes bar code labels a mandatory field, use of handheld bar code readers for inventory taking could become wide spread, eliminating inventory worksheets and greatly reducing inventory time.

Using handheld devices, such as Palms, equipped with scanners make taking inventory easier, quicker, and more accurate. Information is downloaded to the handheld from the inventory control system and can be organized by storage location (e.g., freezer, dry storage, prepwalk-in). Inventory items are called up by entering a product name or index number, scanning the product bar codes or UPCs, or by pressing the "next" key if following the inventory sequences established in the inventory control system. The inventory control software may also be capable of generating bar code labels for products without manufacturer bar codes. In addition to inventory counting, handhelds can also be used for orders, transfers, requisitions, receiving, and more.

Handhelds are also used for taking liquor inventory. There are three common methods for estimating what is left in a partial bottle. The "tenth" method basically has the employee eyeball the bottle and estimate, to the tenth, how much is left. The second method has the employee scan the product's bar code or UPC and then the handheld displays a silhouette of the brand's bottle. The employee draws a line with a stylus indicating the level of alcohol left inside. The third method has the employee scan the product's bar code and then place the bottle on a digital scale. The net weight is sent automatically to the handheld through a wired or wireless link. Partial liquor inventory information, however, can be automatically accessed through a **WIRE LESS FREE-POUR SYSTEM**, in which each bottle spout contains a unique microchip that transmits pour data to a computer via radio frequency. This type of system is also capable of tracking who's pouring what and when as well as the cost of the liquor served. It can also be linked to handhelds located in the bar areas to provide immediate feedback about each drink poured. This information can help bartenders tolearn and maintain pouring accuracy and a proper pouring style. Management can also use handhelds to access real-time reports to identify and resolve problems, including graphics that show the current liquor level of any bottle.

Radio-Frequency Identification (RFID) tags or electronic labels could eventually replace bar code labels. RFID technology uses wireless communication in radio frequency bands to transmit data from tags (microchips) to readers to automatically identify objects with RFID tags attached. Tagging inventory items could automate most inventory counting tasks, as well as streamline workflows involved in the ordering, receiving, production, and selling of food and beverage products.

The Blue C Sushi restaurant in Seattle, Washington, deployed an RFID system to improve both inventory management and customer service. Blue C Sushi serves sushi on plates that are placed on a conveyor belt that travels around the restaurant. Customers remove the plates of sushi that they want to eat. The restaurant previously used a bar code system where the bottom of each sushi plate was labeled with a bar code, enabling the restaurant to track when plates were added to the conveyor belt and when they were removed by customers. The RFID system, which uses specially designed RFID tags to withstand high-temperature dishwashing and harsh cleaning chemicals, provides far more information, including what type of sushi is on a plate and which chef prepared it, how long each plate has been on the conveyor, and which types of sushi inventory are running low. Chefs access this information in real-time from touch screen workstations to determine which sushi to prepare next to avoid making items that will not be eaten and to ensure the availability of items desired by customers. "It can also determine the sale patterns of its menu items according to the time of day or day of the week, which allows it to better plan inventory purchasing quantities and schedules. The improved purchasing has enabled the restaurant to pare down its sushi suppliers to one and reduced wasted sushi by avoiding over-orders" (*www.rfidupdate.com*).

At the Cheeky, a Latino restaurant in Georgia, customers use RFID-enabled cards to pour their own glasses of beer (restricted to 40 ounces) from a wall of eight beer taps and then pay the exact amount consumed. This self-serve beer system monitors and accurately records every ounce of beer that is dispensed, eliminating issues of spillage, theft, giveaways, and over pouring and significantly increasing the number of beers served per keg.

Print Reports

Step 4. Print Reports. Various meaningful reports are produced by inventory control systems.

Inventory Extension Report

- **An Inventory Extension Report** contains the value of the inventory on hand. Inventory adjustments can be automatically posted to the general ledger if the two systems are interfaced.

Food Usage Report

- **A Food Usage Report** shows the food cost, food cost percentage, purchases, inventory, sales, and customer count and may highlight those food items which varied the most from their historical average usage (see Figure 3-5). Significant changes in product usage may indicate poor portion control, pilferage, spoilage, or the need to adjust inventory levels because of a decrease or increase in product demand.

REORDER QUANTITY REPORT

- **A REORDER QUANTITY REPORT** suggests reorder levels based upon forecasted sales, par levels, minimum and maximum order quantities,lead time, and historical usage statistics. An accurate purchase order prevents waste and having too much cash tied up in slow selling items, and guarantees that popular menu items will be available.

PURCHASE ORDER

- **A PURCHASE ORDER** itemizes all products on order from a vendor, indicates the order and tentative receiving date, and projects invoice costs for the order. This minimizes misunderstandings and reduces ordering mistakes.

6 day period ending 12/ 6/87 | Your Place | Page 1 12:36 PM

THE FOOD-TRAK (R) SYSTEM
MANAGEMENT SUMMARY

GENERAL INFORMATION:

Actual Food Cost :	$7,619.70	37.87 %	Sales Reported :	$20,115.46	Customer Count :	5,757
Average Food Cost:	$7,697.65	38.25 %	Year-to-Date Sales:	$864,834.93	Inventory Value:	$11,318.94
Net Variance :	-$77.95	-.38 %				

FOOD USAGE RANKINGS:

Name of Food	Inv Unit	Actual Usage (Units)	Avg Usage (Units)	CHANGE in Units	CHANGE in Dollars	CHANGE % Sales	Days Left	Beginning Inv (Units)	Purchases in Inv Units	Ending Inv (Units)	Cost per Inv Unit	Inventory Ending Value	Index
Top 15 Overused:													
COD	BOX	11.00	3.17	7.83	$151	.8	10.4	24.00	6.00	19.00	$19.250	$365.75	F00006
CHK FIL	LB	47.00	9.97	37.03	$134	.7	3.8	41.00	48.00	42.00	$2.356	$98.95	F00144
CATFISH	LB	301.38	235.00	66.38	$132	.7	9.8	225.38	570.00	494.00	$1.989	$982.57	F00007
REG MIX	TANK	11.00	8.49	2.51	$69	.3	20.2	31.00	17.00	37.00	$27.500	$1017.50	F00090
TAR SAUCE	GAL	14.50	5.30	9.20	$47	.2	3.7	5.50	18.00	9.00	$5.143	$46.29	F00108
TOMATOES	CASE	5.75	2.96	2.79	$43	.2	2.1	1.75	6.00	2.00	$15.500	$31.00	F00020
GARLIC	LB	4.00	-.05	4.05	$39	.2	12.0	12.00	.00	8.00	$9.600	$76.80	F00046
BULK SAUS	LB	26.00	4.71	21.29	$38	.2	.0	26.00	.00	.00	$1.787	$.00	F00004
S VEG MX	CASE	12.00	9.13	2.87	$37	.2	4.0	4.00	16.00	8.00	$12.980	$103.84	F00034
SLAW MIX	BAG	21.00	12.90	8.10	$33	.2	1.1	2.00	23.00	4.00	$4.130	$16.52	F00116
EGG BOILED	LB	13.00	4.09	8.91	$32	.2	6.9	35.00	-7.00	15.00	$3.594	$53.91	F00124
STEAK	BOX	28.00	26.38	1.62	$32	.2	6.4	33.00	25.00	30.00	$19.690	$590.70	F00002
SEASONING	BAG	.00	-.61	.61	$31	.2	****	1.00	.00	1.00	$50.070	$50.07	F00047
PORK CHOPS	CASE	6.00	5.02	.98	$30	.2	12.0	10.00	8.00	12.00	$30.420	$365.04	F00005
CHKN, FULL	LB	70.00	57.43	12.57	$27	.1	1.1	23.00	60.00	13.00	$2.145	$27.89	F00096
					$879	4.4							
Top 5 Underused:													
BAY SHRIMP	LB	87.63	136.27	-48.64	-$191	-1.0	15.7	166.38	150.00	228.75	$3.933	$899.67	F00012
RIBEYE 5OZ	CASE	1.25	5.54	-4.29	-$183	-.9	19.2	2.25	3.00	4.00	$42.750	$171.00	F00156
CH POT PIE	SG	.00	14.85	-14.85	-$115	-.6	****	.00	.00	.00	$7.728	$.00	F00142
TBONE 10OZ	CASE	.00	1.86	-1.86	-$88	-.4	****	.00	.00	.00	$47.410	$.00	F00137
FLOUNDER	BOX	17.00	24.53	-7.53	-$87	-.4	10.9	18.00	30.00	31.00	$11.544	$357.86	F00152
					-$665	-3.3							

Prepared 5/12/88 FOOD-TRAK is a Registered Trademark

FIGURE 3-5. FOOD USAGE REPORT.

Source: System Concepts, Inc., Scottsdale, AZ.

> *It is a good control procedure to obtain price quotations from three purveyors for each food item, although a shortage of local purveyors might make this impossible.*
>
> James Keiser and Elmer Kallo,
> *Controlling and Analyzing Costs in Food Service Operation*

Bidding Module

Adding a **Bidding Module** to an inventory control system helps management identify the most economical products adhering to purchase specifications. It stores price bids that management will review when selecting vendors for purchases. The Food-Trak System by Phoenix-based System Concepts, Inc., for example, enables vendors to submit bids via a Web portal and can place an item on a purchase order automatically for the vendor offering the best price.

Purchase orders can be sent electronically to food distributors across private or public networks. Online purchasing or **e-procurement** can save time, reduce paperwork, improve supplier integrity, drive both buyer and supplier compliance, and lower transaction costs. It also enables a restaurant to route purchase orders for approval and to inquire about product prices as well as availability and order status.

Receiving Report

- **A Receiving Report**, which identifies all products received and discrepancies between quantities ordered and received, is used to ensure that accurate invoices are inputted into the accounts payable module.

Discrepancies requiring the invoice amount to be adjusted include price and quantity errors (e.g., three cases of ribs are denoted on invoice but only two cases are received in shipment), damaged goods (e.g., jelly jar is broken during shipping), incorrect items (e.g., 24 loaves of French bread are ordered but 24 loaves of rye bread are received in shipment), and extension errors (e.g., 10 bags of cabbage with a unit price of $7.95 is incorrectly invoiced at $87.45).

In a fully integrated restaurant management system, data reflected in the receiving report updates accounts payable invoice information, inventory quantities and costs, and recipe ingredient costs found in the menu management system.

Menu Management System

A Menu Management System enables a restaurant operator to price, control, and monitor the entire menu. It provides the operator with a detailed item analysis and insight into what inventory usage and cost of sales should be. The following paragraphs discuss the mechanics involved in constructing and operating a menu management system.

> *Recipes are the backbone of the operation. For most operations, every operating expense, every salary and wage, and every penny of profit must come from the difference between the selling price and the cost of recipes.*
>
> WILLIAM SCHWARTZ,
> PRESIDENT OF SYSTEM CONCEPTS

In order to track menu item costs, it is necessary to create ingredient, recipe, and menu item files. Nutritional values and allergens provided by the restaurant operator and/or U.S. Department of Agriculture can be entered for raw ingredients to automatically generate nutritional and allergen information for recipes and menus, which can be printed (e.g., fact sheet, label) or viewed (e.g., POS terminal, Web site). In March 2010, Congress passed a national law requiring chain restaurants with 20 or more outlets to list calories and other nutrition information on menus and menu boards.

Create Ingredient File

Step 1. Create ingredient file. Every ingredient used in menu items must be inputted into the system. To reduce data entry, menu management systems may have a preloaded database so that it will not take extra time to input every ingredient into the system.

Information inputted into the **INGREDIENT FILE** typically includes:

- Ingredient description (e.g., bacon)
- Unit description and cost (e.g., case, cost per case = $144.00)
- Portions per unit (e.g., 480 bacon slices per case)
- Portion cost (e.g., $.30 per bacon slice)

The ingredient file must be complete before entering data for recipes.

Create Recipe File

Step 2. Create recipe file. All recipes are stored in the **RECIPE FILE**. A recipe lists the ingredients along with preparation procedures (text, audio, photo, and/or video) to help maintain consistent food quality. Recipes can be quickly resized (e.g., increase portions from 50 to 100) automatically adjusting the ingredient quantities and costs.

Menu management systems allow for the creation of **SUBRECIPES**, recipes placed inside other recipes, to make the construction of complex recipes easier.

Information typically inputted into the recipe file includes (See Figure 3-6):

- Recipe description.
- Cost and quantity of ingredients used.
- Serving weight after processing. This reflects the shrinkage and evaporation factor in a recipe.
- Recipe or batch cost.

- Servings per batch.
- Portioning tool.
- Serving portion.
- Serving portion cost and selling price.
- Cost as a percentage of price.

Create Menu Item File

Step 3. Create menu item file. After the recipe file is complete, the final step is to set up the MENU ITEM FILE. Information inputted into the menu item file typically includes:

- Category description (e.g., Breakfast)
- Menu item description (e.g., Two eggs, bacon, and potatoes)
- Serving price (e.g., $6.95)

THOUSAND ISLAND DRESSING			
Ingredients	**Quantity Used**	**Portion Cost**	**Total Cost**
Mayonnaise	160 OZ	.026	4.16
Tomato Puree	50 OZ	.029	1.45
Pickle Relish	32 OZ	.029	.93
Freeze Dried Chives	16 TSP	.049	.79
Onion	12 OZ	.020	.24
		TOTAL BATCH COST	**$7.57**
		COST PER OUNCE	**$ .033**
Servings per Batch	= 116		
Serving Size	= 2 oz.		
Portioning Tool	= 2 oz Ladle		
Cost per Serving	= .066		
Price per Serving	= .85		
Food Cost Percentage	= 7.76%		

FIGURE 3-6. RECIPE EXAMPLE.

- Accepted food cost percentage (e.g., 33 %)
- Actual food cost percentage (e.g., 35.25%)
- Ingredients. Figure 3-7 shows the ingredients found in a breakfast menu item.

Post Quantities Sold and Generate Menu Analysis Reports

Step 4. Post quantities sold and generate menu analysis reports. At the end of each day's activities, the quantity of each menu item sold is manually or automatically (if interfaced to the POS system) entered into the menu management system to calculate theoretical usages of all inventoried products and to generate various reports evaluating menu and cost control performance.

Product Cost or Menu Mix Report

A **Product Cost Or Menu Mix Report**, as shown in Figure 3-8, contains the selling price, the ideal cost (recipe X quantity sold), the food cost percentage, the percentage of

TWO EGGS, BACON AND POTATOES			
Ingredients	**Quantity Used**	**Portion Cost**	**Total Cost**
Eggs	2.00 EGGS	.16	.32
Oranges	1.00 SLICE	.05	.05
Jelly	1.00 PACKET	.20	.20
Whipped Margarine	.50 OZ	.10	.05
Coffee	20.00 OZ	.04	.80
Toast	.20 OZ	.037	.01
Half and Half	1.00 CREAMER	.10	.10
Sugar Packets	2.00 PACKETS	.05	.10
Bacon	2.00 SLICES	.30	.60
Parsley	1.00 SPRIG	.03	.03
Grill Shortening	.20 OZ	.052	.01
Potatoes	4.00 OZ	.045	.18
TOTAL COST FOR MENU ITEM			**2.45**

FIGURE 3-7. MENU ITEM INGREDIENTS.

Theoretical Usage Report Example

Item	Unit	Unit Cost	Actual Usage	Actual Usage Cost	Ideal Usage	Ideal Usage Cost	Variance Quantity	Variance Cost	Variance %
Apple	Each	$.54	20.00	$10.80	13.00	$7.02	-7.00	-$3.78	-0.03%
Bran	Each	$.47	15.00	$7.08	19.00	$8.96	4.00	$1.89	.0.02%

6 day period ending 12/ 6/87 | Your Place | Page 1 11:40 AM

THE FOOD-TRAK (R) SYSTEM
PRODUCT CONTRIBUTION REPORT

P R O D U C T   C O N T R I B U T I O N   S U M M A R Y

Name of Product	Selling Price	Ideal Cost	Gross Margin	Ideal Food Cost %	Sold this Period	Sold Year to Date	Avg per Day	Total Dollars Sold	Ideal Contri-bution	% of Total Sales	% of Gross Contrb	Index	Rank
Top 15 Contributors:													
STEAK DINNER	$3.99	$1.04	$2.95	26.07	565.0	2568.0	92	$2254.35	$1669.01	11.21	12.41	P00027	1
ICE TEA UNSWEET	$.69	$.06	$.63	8.70	1745.0	7762.0	277	$1204.05	$1104.58	5.99	8.21	P00005	2
STEAK & CHICKEN	$4.99	$1.22	$3.77	24.45	243.0	1072.0	38	$1212.57	$917.08	6.03	6.82	P00144	3
CHICKEN DINNER LARGE	$4.89	$1.52	$3.37	31.08	246.0	1146.0	41	$1202.94	$830.25	5.98	6.17	P00031	4
SODAS	$.79	$.24	$.55	30.38	1279.0	5590.0	200	$1010.41	$700.89	5.02	5.21	P00111	5
CHICKEN DUMPLING DINNER	$3.79	$1.14	$2.65	30.08	255.0	1052.0	38	$966.45	$675.24	4.80	5.02	P00024	6
CHICKEN REGULAR	$3.89	$1.03	$2.86	26.48	220.0	953.0	34	$855.80	$628.54	4.25	4.67	P00030	7
CATFISH DINNER	$6.69	$3.45	$3.24	51.57	192.0	837.0	30	$1284.48	$622.08	6.39	4.62	P00049	8
COFFEE	$.69	$.08	$.61	11.59	883.0	3867.0	138	$609.27	$537.75	3.03	4.00	P00003	9
FLOUNDER	$4.99	$1.85	$3.14	37.07	149.0	582.0	21	$743.51	$468.16	3.70	3.48	P00165	10
PORK CHOP LARGE DINNER	$5.19	$2.13	$3.06	41.04	112.0	424.0	15	$581.28	$342.50	2.89	2.55	P00026	11
CHICKEN LIVERS DINNER	$3.49	$.73	$2.76	20.92	124.0	481.0	17	$432.76	$342.36	2.15	2.54	P00028	12
SEAFOOD COMBINATION	$6.79	$2.54	$4.25	37.41	68.0	283.0	10	$461.72	$289.34	2.30	2.15	P00073	13
PIE WITH ICE CREAM	$1.79	$.61	$1.18	34.08	244.0	1170.0	42	$436.76	$289.14	2.17	2.15	P00122	14
SEAFOOD PLATTER	$7.29	$3.44	$3.85	47.19	67.0	258.0	9	$488.43	$257.75	2.43	1.92	P00050	15
Totals:	$2.15	$.64	$1.51	29.61	6392.0	28045.0	1002	$13,744.78	$9,674.67	68.34	71.92		
Bottom 5 Contributors:													
FISH FREE	$.00	$.75	-$.75	.00	112.0	532.0	19	$.00	-$83.89	.00	-.62	P00032	144
CHICKEN FREE	$.00	$.45	-$.45	.00	164.0	817.0	29	$.00	-$74.29	.00	-.55	P00033	143
PEANUT BUTTER & JELLY	$.00	$.32	-$.32	.00	28.0	138.0	5	$.00	-$8.85	.00	-.07	P00036	142
GREEN SALAD SUBSTITUTE	$.40	$.44	-$.04	110.00	129.0	505.0	18	$51.60	-$5.55	.26	-.04	P00143	141
FRUIT PIE	$.00	$.61	-$.61	.00	8.0	19.0	1	$.00	-$4.84	.00	-.04	P00135	140
Totals:	$.12	$.52	-$.40	443.84	441.0	2011.0	72	$51.60	-$177.42	.26	-1.32		

FIGURE 3-8. PRODUCT COST REPORT.

Source: System Concepts, Inc., Scottsdale, AZ. Used With Permission.

total sales and the gross contribution margin (sales less food cost) for each menu item. This information is helpful in analyzing profitability, food costs, customer preference, menu structure, trends, promotion effectiveness, product performance, and contribution. Menu items on this report may be ranked according to their contribution to profits, enabling management to discern desirable and undesirable menu items quickly.

> *Probably the most important concept with a menu is the menu mix. The more items on the menu, the more difficult it is to monitor the overall menu pricing. The goal is to determine the correct mix of meals which will yield the highest profits. While you must sell what the customers want, you need to provide these items at the most advantageous price.*
>
> WILLIAM A. OLEKSINSKI, JR. AND MICHAEL G. OLEKSINSKI, P.C. *FOODSERVICE SPREADSHEET APPLICATIONS*

Menu Price Analysis Report

A **Menu Price Analysis Report** shows the impact of price changes on the food cost percentage. It may indicate the food cost percentage for the current menu item prices, the previous menu item prices, and the proposed menu item prices. It may also allow a manager to test speculative menu item prices and to make cost comparisons between various menus.

Theoretical Usage Report

A Theoretical Usage Report compares ideal usage, the amount which should have been used based on customer sales and recipe requirements, to actual usage. The exact loss of any food item can then be readily identified.

Perpetual Inventory Report

A Perpetual Inventory Report identifies theoretical inventory levels based on the beginning inventory, purchases, and customer sales. This information is compared to actual inventory counts to compute inventory variances, which are caused by product waste (e.g., burnt steak), poor controls (employee steals two bottles of vodka), and failure to enter invoices into the menu management system (e.g., report indicates 5 cases of ribs but the actual count is 10 cases). Daily reconciliation of the perpetual inventory report for high cost items, such as meats, liquor, and seafood, greatly reduces inventory losses.

In the sample section of the theoretical usage report on the previous page, two types of muffins are evaluated: apple muffins and bran muffins. The actual usage of apple muffins exceeds the ideal usage, or what was entered into the POS, by seven muffins. That means that more muffins were consumed than the POS accounted for, resulting in a revenue loss and an unfavorable variance of $3.78. Contributing factors could have been spoilage, spillage, pilferage, etc. For bran muffins, the opposite is true. This is likely due to a counting error or keystroke error in the POS.

Perpetual Inventory Report Example						
	Beg. Inventory	Inventory Received	Sold	Theoretical Inventory	Actual Inventory	Variance
Napa Ridge Merlot Bottles	10	9	6	13	15	2

Insights from an Expert

TECHNOLOGY IN RESTAURANTS

MICHAEL FODOR
VICE PRESIDENT OF MARKETING AND SALES, F&B MANAGEMENT

For a restaurateur, time and data are the most essential commodities. However, in the restaurant world mismanaged time and data frustrates ownership personally and professionally, as well as staff, and guests. Technology used properly offers a solution. Smart phones, tablets, electronic inventory and point of sales systems streamline staff administration and provide pertinent real-time information by efficiently using time and resources.

With the current available technology, a restaurateur's day is laid out before even entering the building. By simply checking a smart phone, a manager or owner can access previous day's numbers, notes, inventory, projected sales, and staff schedules. In this manner, one device saves hours of meticulous data analysis and allows the manager to spend time resolving more immediate issues.

In addition to mobile devices, intuitive inventory programs have the ability to automate several time consuming tasks in one place. An inventory program allows the manager to calculate theoretical costs and costs of sales in order to analyze the profit margin; the system is then able to create accurate grocery and liquor orders that can be electronically sent to vendors. This guarantees that proper amounts are ordered and waste is eliminated. Additionally, managers can use a handheld computer or tablet with a scanner to take an electronic inventory to compare theoretical with actual costs provided by the system. With the information, one can determine exactly which items help with the margin and simultaneously conduct menu analysis. By using this tool the manager will see a reduction in food and beverage costs and an increase in time to work with guests and staff.

Historically, gut feelings or hours of data examination have determined decisions to help prepare for a shift. With new real-time, up to the minute point of sale (POS) systems, managers have access to information from one or more restaurants available to them on a smart device in their pocket; information such as when employees' shifts begin and end, current sales and labor costs, and how the restaurant compares week to week or even year to year. They can see which employees up sell well and have good table turns as well as taking reservations online, the current wait at the front desk and if the front of house quotes the wait time accurately. Once assessed, these times can be compared to cook times in the kitchen. The times are then adjusted by the system to accommodate for average cook times by item and even down to how long a rare steak cooks, compared to a well done steak; in this manner, all items for each table leave the kitchen at the same time, prepared properly. Such efficiency ensures that everyone works together to give the guest the best experience possible.

Because all inventory and staff are properly accounted for, the devices are able to provide fraud prevention alerts. A software program scans all transactions instantaneously and alerts that manager to potential theft by determining the variance between purchased and sold items. The program also has the ability to look for scams that employees use to defraud the restaurant such as the "Wagon Wheel," where an employee sells an item multiple times while purchasing the item from the house only once. As a result, the system constantly evaluates and ranks the staff based on the reports. In addition to theft prevention and discrepancy detection, the program in the POS system monitors all social media sites and reports on negative or positive reviews. Allowing the manager to identify and address customer dissatisfaction before the guest leaves the building generates a proactive approach to better dining reviews. Because of the efficient and expedient process, managers can quickly discern and resolve any problems either in lost capital or customer satisfaction.

New technology not only benefits management. Above and beyond posting reviews, guests also have the ability to interact firsthand with the restaurant by ordering food online, checking loyalty points and gift card balances, and even accessing their checks while in the restaurant. Once inside, customers have the ability to add items to the check, pay the bill on their smart phone, send themselves a receipt, and call their server to the table.

In an industry where time is money, technology is critical. Tighter controls, more accurate margins, and instantaneous data add breathing room to a restaurant manager's hectic day. Instead of spending time resolving tedious accounting issues, managers and owners have the opportunity to interact with their customers on a personal level. In a voraciously competitive industry that demands long hours and hard work, extra time on hand is a priceless asset.

Tech News

iPad App Gives Shula's a Competitive Edge by Dave Shula

Once in a great while a game-changing innovation comes along in the restaurant business that enables those who embrace it to gain a competitive edge. My father and I both began our careers in football then established ourselves in the restaurant business. The latest innovation we have introduced in our restaurants reflects our focus on excellence and execution.

At Shula's, we pride ourselves on offering the best possible dining experience and, of course, the best steak money can buy. Our guests value the wide selection of wines we offer and choosing the right wine to complement their meal is an integral part of their dining experience. Shula's has recently rolled out the Hospitality Pad across its locations in order to further enhance each visit. Developed by Hospitality Social, this iPad solution enables our guests to select wines easily in a variety of ways.

Food pairings: Guests can pick a menu item and see a list of suggested wines for the entrée they have chosen.

Flavor preferences: Guests can decide on a wine by its flavor profile such as a full bodied white wine or a sweet wine with a rich fruit flavor.

The 90 point club: Customers can restrict the wines they wish to browse to those with a point rating greater than 90.

Free-form search: This gives guests the maximum flexibility in searching for a particular wine they may know by some characteristic but not by name. For example, they can simply enter the word "cherry" to find all wines having a cherry flavor.

Once a diner has found a particular wine, he or she can view its tasting notes and see a picture of its label. The most important aspect of this application is that it gives customers the confidence to spend money on a special bottle of wine by enabling them to make a much more informed decision. The Shula's in Naples, Fla. has already enjoyed increased wine sales since the Hospitality Pad was introduced.

Bottom Line Benefits

Since moving wine lists to the iPad, changes are much easier and efficient. Lists can be easily updated so out of stock vintages are removed from the wine list immediately. New varieties can be added quickly and guests can be made aware of the latest offerings and rare finds. This can be done without any reprinting costs or delays. More importantly, customers are no longer disappointed by listed wines that are not available.

Shula's has received positive feedback from diners that have used the application. The elegant form factor of the iPad combined with Hospitality Social's intuitive interface has made it a big hit with customers. Handing customers an iPad with an interactive wine list creates excitement and distinguishes the dining experience we create from our competitors.

Shula's has found that the iPad application improves server interaction with patrons. It's a conversation starter and enhances each server's ability to educate clients.

The Hospitality Pad also allows customers to see a cooked steak as they are discussing their menu choices with servers. Shula's has enjoyed positive customer feedback on this application and it complements Shula's premium branding.

Making the Connection

Another important aspect of this wine application is that customers can enter their email address to receive the detail of the wine they enjoyed while dining at Shula's. Hospitality Social also enables guests to connect through Facebook. With most new business being generated from word of mouth, this feature will introduce Shula's to a fresh clientele and increase customer loyalty.

The Keys to Success

The dining experience is the key to success in this business and this application enhances it in ways that were never before possible. Three elements to success in the restaurant business are: keep customers coming back, increase average check size, and find ways to bring in new business. The new iPad application from Hospitality Social delivers on each of those. It has enabled Shula's to engage with loyal customers, increased wine sales, and through the social media connection, introduced Shula's to new customers. It's an investment that will pay for itself several times over, and will continue to be a benefit well into the future.

References

1. Woodman, Julie, "The Byte Stuff 1991," *Restaurants and Institutions*, December 18, 1991, pp. 85-86.
2. Sill, Brian, "In the Age of Computer Technology, Information is the Competitive Edge," Nation's Restaurant News, May 22, 1989, p. 30.
3. Collins, Galen, "Evaluating and Selecting a Property Management System," FIU Hospitality Review, Fall 1991, pp. 36-49. (Most of the discussion on POS systems is based on the contents of this article.)
4. Erickson, Joe, "Programmed for Success: How to Work With Your POS Programmer for Maximum Profitability," Restaurant Startup and Growth, October 2012, pp. 25-30.
5. Kelly, Thomas J., and Carvell, Steven, "Checking the Checks: A Survey of Guest-Check Accuracy," Cornell Quarterly, November 1987, pp. 63-65.
6. Sill, Brian, op. cit., p. 30.
7. Erickson, Joe, "POS In the Palm of Your Hand: A Wireless Hand-Held Review, Restaurant Startup & Growth, 2011.
8. Liddle, Alan, "iPad POS Use Rising Among Restaurants," Nations Restaurant News, December 20, 2010.
9. Dale, Archibald, "Between Mind and Medium," Training, May 1990, pp. 20-21.
10. Collins, Galen, "Usable Mobile Ambient Intelligent Solutions for Hospitality Customers," Journal of Information Technology Impact, 2010, 10 (1), pp. 45-54.
11. Switzer, Paul, "The ABCs of POS System Selection," Foodservice Tech Advisor, May 6, 2002, p.1.
12. American Express, "Frequent Diner Programs: How Well Are They Working," American Express Market Briefing, October 2011. Retrieved 2012-11-27, from http://www.technomic.com/_files/Newsletters/Marketbrief/marketbrief_10-11.pdf

CHAPTER 4

Lodging Technology Systems

"Selling a hotel room used to be simple; business would literally walk in off the street. No more. As the number of channels a customer can use to book a hotel room grows, hoteliers will be forced to take a more holistic view of their technological infrastructure."

Bruno des Fontaines, Vice President Amadeus Hospitality Business Group

CHAPTER OUTLINE

Introduction

Research has led to the implementation of various cost-effective applications addressing almost every phase of lodging operations. One such lodging technology application that has had a significant impact on the hospitality industry is a property management system (PMS), a foundational lodging technology system. A PMS normally performs both back and front office functions as well as supports a variety of other applications and functions such as housekeeping, sales, catering, energy management, and customer relationship management. Property management systems have been designed for motels, hotels, resorts, and condominiums and rely on computer hardware and software to process information.

One of the first property management systems was installed at the Sheraton Waikiki in 1970. It had only 12 megabytes of storage and it cost between $400,000 and $500,000. Today, the same system, boasting a dramatic increase in performance, would cost considerably less. The first property management systems were designed for very large hotels interested in streamlining reservations and accounting and reducing costs in these areas (1).

In June, 1982, NCR announced that the 4200 front desk mechanical posting machine, which had dominated the lodging industry with thousands of installations since the early 1970s, would no longer be sold. This announcement stunned the industry. Six months later NCR announced that supply parts for the 4200 were no longer available. This left the hotel industry dependent on a product (4200) that had reached the end of its useful life cycle. The only product that NCR had to offer was its Model 250, an electromechanical version of the 4200. The industry responded by looking for alternatives.

In the early 1970s, a few large companies dominated the PMS business (e.g., EECO, MICOR, Sigma Data, Philips, and American Express). At that time, computer growth was hampered by price, complexity, difficulty of training, and the dominance of NCR's 4200.

In the late 1970s, less expensive minicomputer-based property management systems were introduced by such vendors as IHS, HIS, EECO, and CLS. They were installed in many hotels with more than 250 rooms. An increase of large hotels in the late 1970s created a significant demand for property management systems and firmly established the need for hotel automation.

The cost, however, was still too high for smaller hotels and motels, the number of which was increasing rapidly during the 1980s. With the advent of the microcomputer

Evolution of Property Management Systems

Dave Berkus, inducted into the International Hospitality Technology Hall of Fame in 1998, has identified the following generations of Property Management Systems (2). The author has added cloud computing services as the seventh generation.

First Generation: Proprietary Systems. *Minicomputers were inexpensive and small enough to permit automation at the local hotel level for a large number of properties. The systems were initially used to reduce costs. Later they were used to increase revenues and enhance customer service.*

Second Generation: Open systems: *The arrival of personal computers and UNIX and then NOVELL-based systems (LAN network operating software) gave comfort to the industry that solutions selected were "portable," avoiding reliance upon one brand of hardware. Prices for hardware dropped significantly as competition between vendors increased.*

Third Generation: Database-driven Systems: *Although not common at the property level, several hotel chains deployed reservation systems based upon fourth generation tools and relational databases. Relational databases permitted more rapid database alterations when requested.*

Fourth Generation: Client-Server Systems: *The next evolution led to deployment of databases at the central or local level using intelligent workstations or clients, which made requests of the server, processed the data request, and sent the result to the client. A few such systems, created using fourth generation tools, found their way into the hotel industry.*

Fifth Generation: MS Windows Graphic User Interfaces: *The current generation of systems, such as the Best Western central reservation system, has deployed a graphic user interface, which is generally consistent with most users' experience with horizontal products (e.g., word processors). Windows systems are usually client-server systems by design.*

Sixth Generation: Virtual Private Networks: *It is based upon the creation and deployment of virtual private network (VPN)s, where a hotel's database may be located at the hotel or a regional or corporate headquarters or scattered in a number of logical locations—all accessible by any authorized workstation on the private network. Communications between workstations and the database may be a local or dedicated line or may make use of secure links across the Internet to create a virtual private network at a significant cost savings over other wide area network technologies. Hotels, for example, may be able to deploy their resources in the following ways:*

- *Night audit and back office staffs can be centralized by region with instant access to live data as if located at any property.*
- *Data warehousing will permit instant access to records for guests with a history of stays at any group property, even if the guest is a walk-in.*
- *Ad hoc questions by senior management will be responded to with graphic answers provided by the executive information system located centrally, efficiently able to combine information and statistics by region or hotel group.*

Seventh Generation: Cloud Computing Services or Software as a Service: *The seventh generation is emerging. Cloud computing services entail the migration of computing resources (e.g., hardware, software, and data) to a remote data center, managed by a vendor. It allows lodging employees to access different computing resources (e.g., PMS application and data) via the Internet using mobile and desktop devices. Unlike a VPN, a cloud computing services vendor provides data processing capabilities. While cloud computing offers a flexible, scalable, and cost-effective platform, worries about privacy, control, security, and connectivity are barriers to its adoption.*

in March, 1981, the prices of reservation and front and back office systems were reduced allowing most properties, some as small as 25 rooms, to automate.

NCR's decision to stop supporting the 4200 resulted in a flood of new PMS vendors. Today, more than 80 PMS suppliers specialize in various types of lodging accommodations.

Different types of lodging establishments (e.g., resort, commercial, residential, transient, timeshare, and fractional ownership), have varying computer needs. The types of technology found in hotels are influenced by the following factors:

Departmental Needs

1. **Departmental needs.** Software applications have been written for almost every operational phase including food and beverage, housekeeping, telephone, front office, reservations, sales, catering, engineering, accounting, guest services, and security.

Guest Amenities

2. **Guest amenities.** Many of the guest amenities found in hotel rooms today are technology-based such as Internet access (WiFi), entertainment, climate control, cell phone charging, business and guest services, in-room checkout, minibars (e.g., eTrays that monitor snack consumption), and minisafes. For example, all guestrooms at the Atlanta Marriott Century Center have high-speed Internet access and plug-in technology panels for all electronic devices. This generation of guests, which relies heavily on the Internet for conducting business and staying connected to the world, will not tolerate sluggish, fluctuating Internet connections. The cost of providing ever-increasing bandwidth to meet guests' demands is significant. Tablet computers (e.g., iPad) may also become a common fixture in tomorrow's guestroom. A survey of iPad usage in 53 hotels conducted by software company Intelity revealed that eight in ten guests used the iPad during their stay, mostly for in-room dining. At a Scotland boutique hotel, CitizenM Glasgow, hotel guests use a Philips Moodpad to program everything from mood lighting and music, to live-TV, movies-on-demand, window shades, heating, and air conditioning.

Service Level and Customer Relationships

3. **Service level and customer relationships.** Delivering quality service is a challenging task in an industry with high employee turnover, rising labor costs, and shortages of skilled workers. Consequently, technology applications, such as self check-in/out via a lobby kiosk or Web check-in/out, have been developed to enhance the delivery of service while reducing the labor burden. Recent applications enable guests to interact digitally with the hotel through their smart phones, tablets, or laptops to access a variety of services, ranging from setting the time for a wake-up call to requesting turndown service. Hotel Brussels in Belgium, for example, provides guests with the option of using their mobile phones as room keys to bypass check-in and wait lines.

Lodging Interactive's **GUEST REVIEW SYSTEM** enables in-house guests to post comments about their experiences on the hotel's Web site. This enables hotel staff to quickly identify problems and resolve them before guests leave the property or have the opportunity to post negative reviews on third-party sites.

An **INTEGRATED GUESTROOM SERVICES NETWORK**, a seamless interfacing of various guest service applications (e.g., room controls and entertainment), enables the personalization of service delivery by capturing guest preferences from previous stays, such as room settings and TV channel lineups, and reflecting that in future visits.

Applications have also been developed to improve the quality of guest and employee interactions. Customers remember hotels that gave them personalized care. For example, a computerized reservation system with a guest history module (discussed later in this chapter) enables clerks to know their guests' rooming preferences. Improved guest experience and satisfaction was rated as the biggest advantage of technology according to a survey of lodging executives conducted by the American Hotel and Motel Association in 1990. In a 1995 Survey by HITA/PKF, 81 percent of the respondents felt that technology enhanced customer satisfaction. According to a 2002 lodging-technology study conducted by HITA and *Hospitality Technology* magazine, guest service enhancements and **CUSTOMER RELATIONSHIP MANAGEMENT (CRM)** received the highest allocation of information technology dollars. Today, hotels continue to invest heavily in guest service and CRM tools. A 2008 survey of American Hotel and Lodging Association members overwhelmingly agreed that technology is important for increasing customer satisfaction (3).

CRM is an information industry term for methodologies, software, and usually Internet capabilities that help an enterprise manage customer relationships in an organized way (See Figure 4-1 for an example of a CRM system). (*www.whatis.com*). Hilton Hotels, for example, uses a CRM system to assist in the consolidation of guest history information or the linking

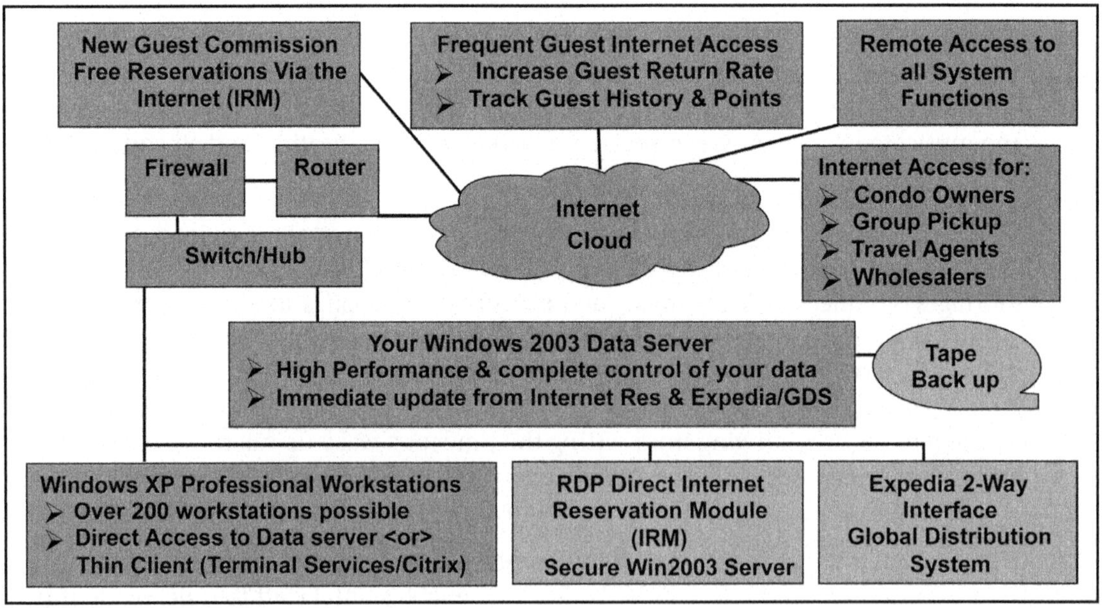

FIGURE 4-1. A DIAGRAM OF A CRM SYSTEM OFFERED BY A PMS VENDOR.

Source: Resort Data Processing, Vail, Colorado.

of chain-wide guest history information to one guest record. Consolidated guest history information can be used to develop expanded and customized service offerings and mined for target-marketing campaigns. Loyalty programs, such as Hilton Honors and Marriott Rewards, and e-marketing are becoming standard ways for hotel companies to practice CRM. "And because of that, CRM systems are adapting to meet the needs of hotels big and small. They are going deeper, detailing information about guests' preferences and keeping an itemized history" (4). For example, Accor Hotels is discovering more about its loyalty members and their interests by reviewing their (public) social media profiles and then selecting related check-in gifts.

CRM tools are available through application service providers (ASP), which are third-party entities (e.g., Guestware.com) that manage and distribute software-based services and solutions to customers across a wide area network from a central data center. "This model allows the smallest hotel to rent space on the service provider's hardware and spreads costs across the entire client base instead of requiring each client to make their own investments in hardware and software. For this class of applications the ASP platform is far more efficient than a client/server approach. This efficiency has increased the number of hotels willing and able to commit to sophisticated CRM strategies and tactics" (www .hospitalityupgrade.com).

Providing comprehensive, chain-wide CRM solutions can be a challenging task. It requires owners, management companies, and the franchiser to share data. This may not happen if their interests are misaligned. It also requires the interfacing and consolidation of data from different sources, which is a cumbersome task if the technologies used at the property level are not standardized. For example, one hotel chain had to manually enter customer data into its CRM system for several properties that did not have the chain's standard property management system.

Facility Size and Layout

4. **Facility size and layout.** Software and hardware requirements vary according to the property size and layout. A 900-room luxury resort would need to purchase a much larger computer system than a 100-room limited service motel to adequately handle its transaction volume (e.g., number of folio postings, reservations, check-ins/outs, accounting entries) and reporting requirements. The number of communication links to tie a system together (e.g., food and beverage point-of-sale system interfaced with front office system) is also more complex in larger properties, particularly ones with multiple retail outlets that are spread out over a wide geographical area.

Organizational Structure

5. **Organizational structure.** The manner in which reporting relationships are defined determines information distribution: who needs what, at what time, to make a decision. If the organization is part of a corporation or chain affiliated, information may also need to be distributed to and from a regional or central office. Various communication applications (e.g. central reservations) have been designed to facilitate the flow of information in a geographically dispersed organization. Enterprise-wide Web- and cloud-based computing applications are the latest development. They enable centralized or remote servers to support workstations, mobile devices, and printers

throughout a hotel group or chain. In 2007, Choice Hotels International deployed its proprietary Web-based hotel PMS, ChoiceAdvantage, the first massively-distributed, cloud-based PMS. A cloud-based solution enables Hyatt Hotels and Resorts to provide email, instant messaging, and social collaboration applications for all of its employees, including deskless workers such as bellhops and housekeepers. By providing access to information and tools across the enterprise, Hyatt has boosted organizational productivity and communication. According to Mike Blake, CIO at Hyatt Hotels and Resorts, guests are happier, too, because their needs are met more quickly.

Globalization

6. **Globalization.** Hotels that cater to international travelers may need to store data in multiple languages and currencies. A more sophisticated PMS enables rates to be quoted and displayed in alternate currencies and guest documents (reservation confirmations, folios, and invoices) to be displayed and printed in a preferred language. An international hospitality chain may also require flexibility to change the language of the user interface for Web and PMS applications. For example, multi-language fields may be required to support worldwide operations in an official language while enabling local staff to use home languages.

The remainder of this chapter discusses basic features found in a PMS reservation, front office, sales and catering system, and other related systems and modules.

Reservation System

A reservation system typically performs the following basic functions: 1) selling individual reservations, 2) selling group reservations, 3) displaying room availability and guest lists, 4) tracking advance deposits, 5) tracking travel agent bookings and commissions, and 6) generating confirmations and various reports.

Selling Individual Reservations

Selling Individual Reservations. A PMS reservation module al lows a reservationist to enter, review, modify, or cancel a future hotel booking. The process begins with a phone call where the reservationist must access the following information to determine room availability (see Figure 4-2).

Arrival Date

1. *Arrival date, requested room types, party size, and number of rooms and room nights.*

Rate Code

2. *Rate code.* Identifies special discount rates such as government, corporate, and senior citizen. Entering a rate code overrides the standard rack rate. There is usually no other way to override a rack rate unless a management password is used.

After the above data is inputted, availability and daily rates are displayed for requested room types (e.g., king, double) within seconds. Some systems can also quickly display

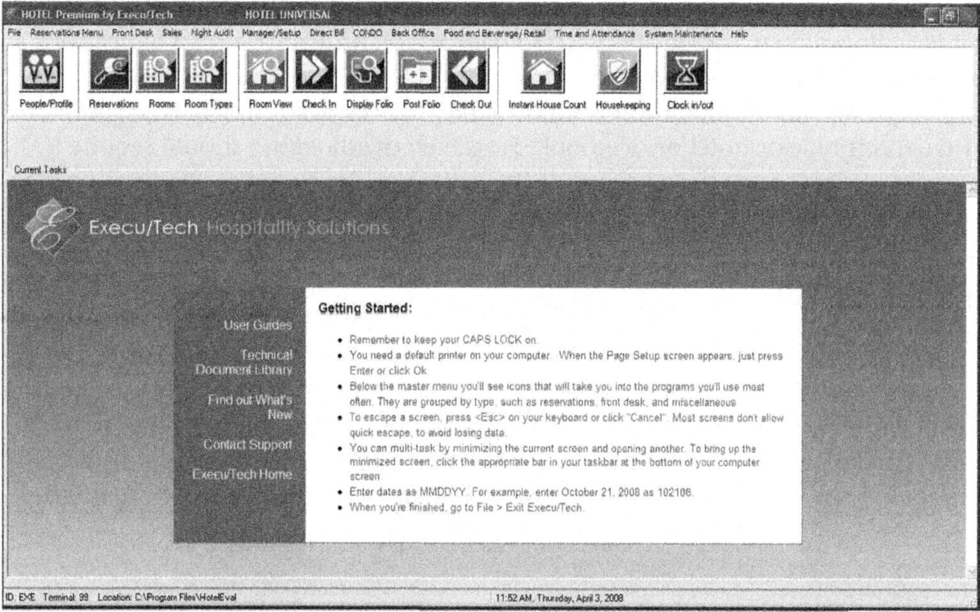

RESERVATIONS HOTEL UNIVERSAL

Exit Log on

Group code:
Arrival date: 90108 Mon Days: 7 Mon
No. of rooms: 1 Share-with
Room type: DD
Room number: 101 Find Lock Room
Adults/child: 2 0
Rate code: 2
Room rate: 150.00 view/edit re-calc
Company:

0020000040 01
Date made: 4/03/08 by EXE

Total room and tax: 1134.00 Net due: 1134.00

Guest Name: FRANKLIN, FRED
Address: 12345 ALASKA STREET
City: AKRON
State/country: OH
Postal code: 44321
Email address: fred@franklin.com
Home phone: 850-747-0581
Bus. phone: 850-747-0491
Comment 1: VIP!!!
Comment 2:
Comment 3:

Travel agency:
Guarantee code: VS
Account no: 4444333322221111
Expiration dt: 1212
Deposit req'd/ date due: .00 82508
Market/Source: AIR INT
Master folio: 0
Tax exempt?: N
Confirm letter?: Y
Split folio?: N
Maid service: D

Save Cancel resv Reverse cnx Display deposits Notes More names Guest profile

FIGURE 4-2. RESERVATION SCREEN.

Source: Execu/Tech Systems, Inc., Panama, FL.

the availability of particular rooms by specifying the desired features (e.g., ocean view and wet bar). Rooms can also be allocated to package plans. Package plan allocations are reduced when reservations are booked.

If the requested accommodation is unavailable, the reservationist may suggest an alternative room type or hotel or overbook. However, overbooking should require a management override code or password. If the caller decides to book a reservation, the following information is commonly collected:

GUEST NAME AND ADDRESS

3. *Guest name and address.* If the reservation system has a **GUEST HISTORY MODULE**, the reservationist must first ask callers for their names (see Figure 4-3). For repeat guests, the reservation screen prefills with information from prior stays. This minimizes data entry and personalizes the selling process by identifying rooming preferences and special needs such as a portable refrigerator or bed board. A guest history module is an in valuable marketing tool that also has the following capabilities:

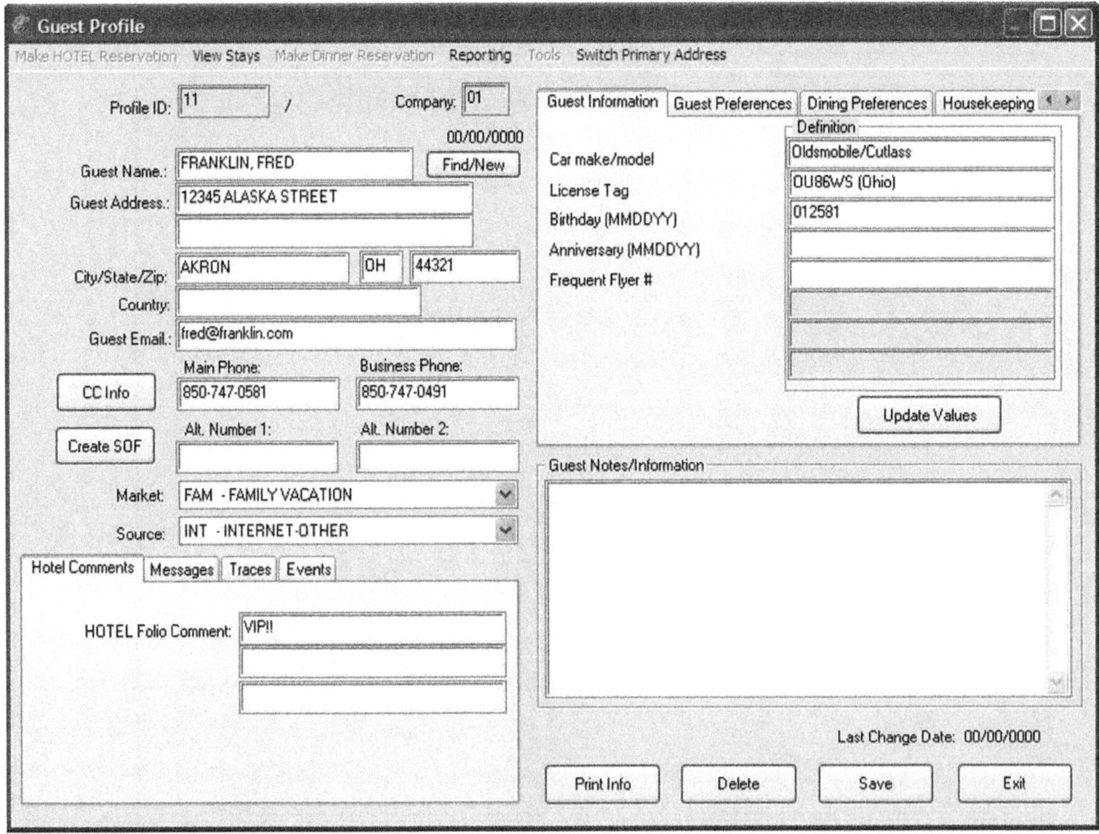

FIGURE 4-3. GUEST HISTORY SCREEN.

Source: Execu/Tech Systems, Inc., Panama, FL.

- Generates mailing labels, lists, and user definable letters (if integrated with a word processor) according to user criteria (e.g., "Print mailing labels for all guests from the state of Vermont").
- Captures all folio information and revenue totals such as room,telephone, and food and beverage.
- Maintains statistics such as number of stays and cancellations by guest, company, or travel agent.
- Allows guest history information to be entered manually or captured at guest check-out.
- Displays reservations currently linked to a guest history name.
- Contains remarks made by hotel staff. For example, if a guest raved about a particular room during his last stay, the guest history record could be marked: "Mr. Collins has a strong preference for room 107." Knowing guests and their reactions help to keep them satisfied.
- Maintains a list of undesirable guests.
- Captures guest e-mail addresses, enabling e-mails to be sent to all, or part of, a guest history or database without postage cost. It also provides a way to alert past guests of special promotions and packages. Marketing e-mails can also be linked to an **ANALYTICS MODULE** to measure the results of specific promotions or campaigns. However, guest marketing e-mails must be used wisely. According to a 2010 study released by the Chief Marketing Officer Council, loyal guests that are inundated by irrelevant and impersonal e-mails may switch brands (5). Consequently, guests should have an **OPT-OUT** option, which will prevent the e-mail system from sending them mass e-mails in the future.
- Enables a property to determine which markets to pursue, how to meaningfully segment business, and when to take actions. It identifies who the property's guests are, what they are buying, and which promotions are attracting them.

A guest history module, for example, would enable a resort to extract a list of guests who have used the XYZ cafe to encourage repeat usage and help determine the profile of potential customers who have yet not tried this particular restaurant.

In addition to a guest history module, the PMS may have a **FREQUENT GUEST** or **LOYALTY MODULE** to track guest visits. The points awarded for each stay can be based on things like total dollars spent and room types. Guests can use points when they make reservations as a method of payment. A history can be kept of all point reservations. Members of frequent guest programs are about twice as likely to return to a hotel compared to nonmembers. They typically spend more per room, are less sensitive to price increases, and are more satisfied with their hotel experiences (www.hotelmotel.com).

MARKET CODE

4. *Market code.* Identifies the type of reservation (e.g., business, leisure, airline crew, truck drivers). This enables statistics, such as total revenue, occupancy, and average daily rate, to be tracked by the market segment. Based on this

information, the property can target advertising and mass mailings to the most profitable markets.

Package Plan

5. *Package plan.* Identifies how revenue is allocated among revenue centers for each package plan. For example, a $300 weekend package at a golf resort may require a daily posting of $60.00 to room revenue, $40.00 to food and beverage revenue, and $50.00 to golf revenue.

Phone Number

6. *Phone number.* Identifies telephone number and extension and whether it is a home, business, or travel agent number.

Guarantee Method

7. *Guarantee method.* Identifies method of guaranteeing a reservation such as an advance deposit, direct bill, or credit card.

Requests and Additional Guest Information

8. *Requests and additional guest information.* Identifies special guest needs such as a crib, nonsmoking room, or extra bed and any other information related to their stay, such as time of arrival and type of transportation.

VIP Identification

9. *VIP identification.* This identifies reservations made by valued guests and companies and is linked to a **VIP MODULE** showing year-to-date revenue and hotel bookings.

Room Blocking

10. *Room blocking.* A room may be **PRE-BLOCKED** or pre-assigned to ensure its availability when the guest arrives. A reservation that contains multiple rooms and names is split into separate reservations so that guests may be blocked specific rooms or checked in.

Travel Agent Identification

11. *Travel agent identification.* This identifies reservations made by travel agents and is linked to the travel agent module discussed later in this chapter.

Business Source

12. *Business source.* Identifies who made the reservation, such as a reservation service, airline, individual, or hotel. It may also identify how a guest found out about the hotel, a friend or an ad in *Travel Magazine* for example. This information allows a property to determine the effectiveness of its marketing efforts. For example, if the ad in the *Travel Magazine* costs $50,000 a year and it only generates $20,000 in total revenue from this source of business, perhaps it's time to find an another magazine.

After completing the reservation, a confirmation number is generated. A confirmation letter may also be printed or automatically faxed, texted, or e-mailed in Adobe or other formats. Confirmations contain information concerning reservation arrangements, deposit requirements and receipts, cancellations, and changes. Some reservation systems enable confirmation letters to include customized messages, hotel logos and pictures, directional maps, and other hotel-related information (see Figure 4-4). Affinia Hotels provide a Web

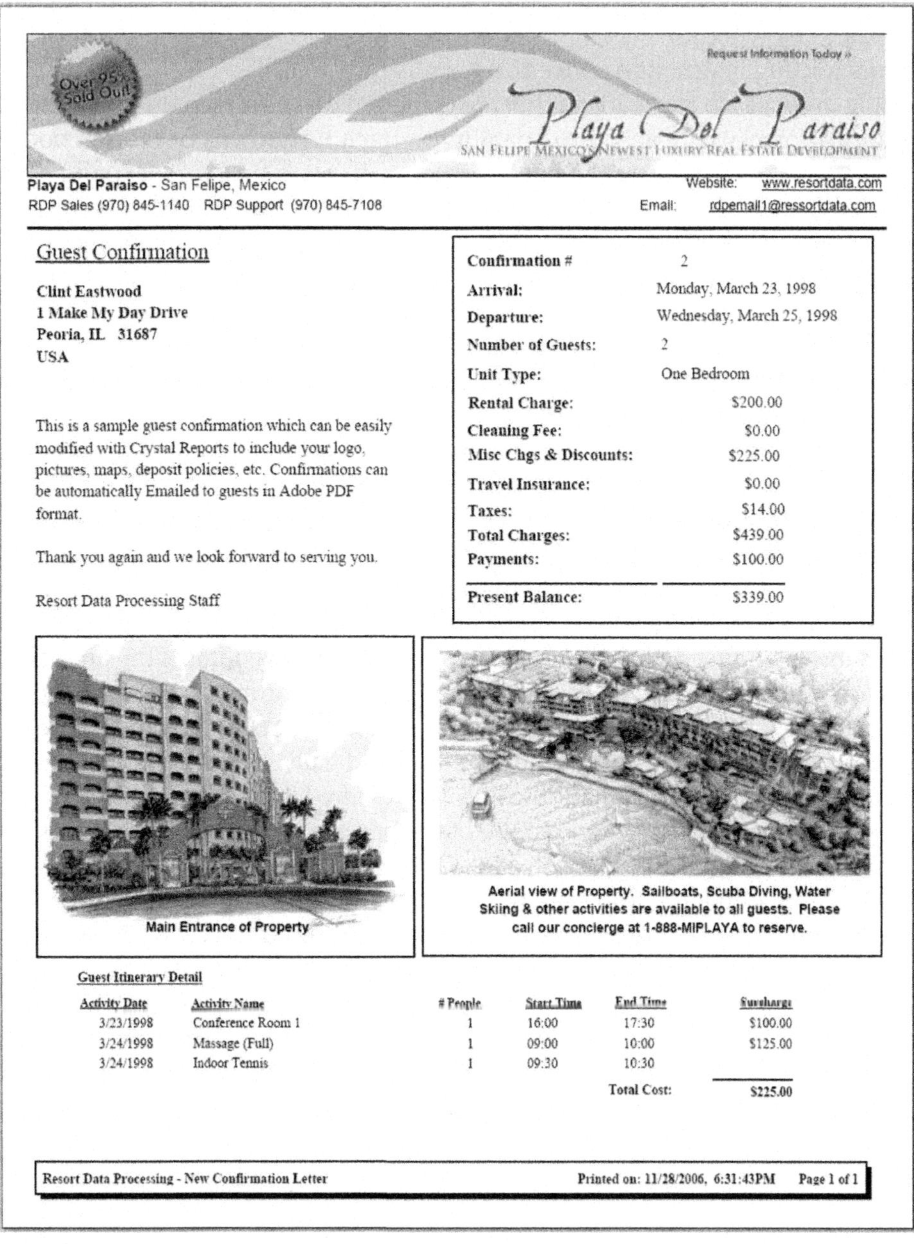

Request Information Today »

Over 95% Sold Out!

Playa Del Paraiso

San Felipe Mexico's Newest Luxury Real Estate Development

Playa Del Paraiso - San Felipe, Mexico Website: www.resortdata.com

RDP Sales (970) 845-1140 RDP Support (970) 845-7108 Email: rdpemail1@ressortdata.com

Guest Confirmation

Clint Eastwood
1 Make My Day Drive
Peoria, IL 31687
USA

This is a sample guest confirmation which can be easily modified with Crystal Reports to include your logo, pictures, maps, deposit policies, etc. Confirmations can be automatically Emailed to guests in Adobe PDF format.

Thank you again and we look forward to serving you.

Resort Data Processing Staff

Confirmation #	2
Arrival:	Monday, March 23, 1998
Departure:	Wednesday, March 25, 1998
Number of Guests:	2
Unit Type:	One Bedroom
Rental Charge:	$200.00
Cleaning Fee:	$0.00
Misc Chgs & Discounts:	$225.00
Travel Insurance:	$0.00
Taxes:	$14.00
Total Charges:	$439.00
Payments:	$100.00
Present Balance:	$339.00

Main Entrance of Property

Aerial view of Property. Sailboats, Scuba Diving, Water Skiing & other activities are available to all guests. Please call our concierge at 1-888-MIPLAYA to reserve.

Guest Itinerary Detail

Activity Date	Activity Name	# People	Start Time	End Time	Surcharge
3/23/1998	Conference Room 1	1	16:00	17:30	$100.00
3/24/1998	Massage (Full)	1	09:00	10:00	$125.00
3/24/1998	Indoor Tennis	1	09:30	10:30	
				Total Cost:	$225.00

Resort Data Processing - New Confirmation Letter Printed on: 11/28/2006, 6:31:43PM Page 1 of 1

FIGURE 4-4. CUSTOMIZED CONFIRMATION.

Source: Resort Data Processing, Vail, Colorado.

link in e-mail reservation confirmations enabling customers to select additional amenities such as fitness kits, gel eye masks, contact lens solutions, golf putters, and specialty pillows (e.g., buckwheat, hypoallergenic, memory foam, etc.).

Other useful features found in well-designed reservation systems include:

- An audit trail that denotes each change to a reservation, when it was made (date and time), and by whom.
- Charge routing instructions once the guest is in-house.
- Tagging messages to reservations that are displayed on the screen during guest check-in.
- A wait list for any date and the capability to track turndowns or refused bookings. This is useful in evaluating the need to change the rate structure, expand room capacity, or shift demand to non-peak days. A wait list function can be integrated with a Web-based reservation module, enabling guests to add themselves to wait lists during online inquiries. An e-mail is automatically sent to a wait-listed guest when a room becomes available. A wait-listed reservation is then converted into a "real" reservation when the guest confirms it.
- The capability to inquire about a reservation using various search criteria such as guest and company name, arrival date, or group code.
- A **SPECIAL EVENTS POP-UP SCREEN** that denotes events occurring during the guest's stay. This feature promotes guest service and helps build overall revenues. Message pop-ups can also be used on hotel Web sites. For example, a customer is looking at a resort booking website, paying particular attention to golf and restaurants. While the customer is browsing, a message pops up offering a package plan that includes 3 hotel nights, two rounds of golf, and dinner at the resort's highly acclaimed seafood restaurant.
- An extensive on-line help facility (**ON-LINE CONCIERGE**) that contains the answers to the most frequently asked questions. It may provide information about the location, amenities, facilities, nearby attractions, the best restaurants in town, a detailed map of the area surrounding the hotel, group resumes and daily events maintained by sales and catering, etc. This information could be presented in a multimedia format allowing the reservations agent to view a picture of the hotel or requested guest room from different angles. Any employee can access this function to help a guest. This feature is an effective training tool for new employees and ensures that questions are answered in a consistent manner. On-line concierge services may also be accessed by guests through mobile applications without them having to interact with any employees. However, the mobile concierge application should provide guests with the option of calling or text messaging if additional assistance is required (e.g., on the concierge request page: "feel free to contact us for dining priority and event tickets") (6).
- The ability to **SCRIPT** interactions between reservation agents and guests to reduce miscommunications. Best Western International has its central reservations agents read the following script at the end of a reservations booking:

  End Call

  Are there any additional reservations I can help you with BOB JONES. Let me review your travel plans.

I have BOB JONES confirmed at the

B/W EXEC PARK-DOWNTOWN in Phoenix, Arizona

Arriving on Nov 17, 2009

for 1 2 DOUBLE BEDS, COFFEE MAKER rooms(1) 2 person(s) RACK RATE at the rate of 99.00 USD

Cancel by: 4PM on 11/13/09

Your confirmation # is 794224948

Thank you for calling Best Western. We appreciate your business.

- The ability to track the type of calls received (e.g., information calls, brochure requests, reservations).
- The ability to track reservationist productivity and system performance: average length of a call, conversion rate, and reservations booked per hour. These statistics indicate employee and system efficiency (average cost per call) and effectiveness (average revenue generated per call) and the need for training, software/process redesign, or software replacement.
- The ability to interface with a **RECREATIONAL SCHEDULING PROGRAM**. This enables reservationists to schedule workouts, golf tee times, tennis and dining reservations, and spa treatments (e.g., treatment type, service provider, time, and facility). Hotels with spas may have a **SPA MANAGEMENT SYSTEM** that links guest health information to room reservations for evaluation of guest preferences and booking patterns. Reservation confirmations may be configured to reflect complete guest room and recreational reservations.
- The capability for two or more guests to share the same room (share-with). Each share-with can have a folio with split room charges and different arrival/departure dates and rates.

Selling Group Reservations

Selling Group Reservations. This requires the creation of a group master where a block of rooms is allocated by room type or "run of the house" with the room type assigned as individual reservations are made or when a rooming list is received. Several important features include:

- The tracking of rooms that have not been picked up or sold. Management uses this information to evaluate the need to release or to add rooms to the group master.
- The capability to quickly input a rooming list where information in the group master can be used to prefill guest information in individual reservations.
- The capability to block a large number of rooms at one time to save time.
- The establishment of group rates by room type with an optional reserve rate for members staying longer than the group.
- The setup of charge routing instructions to the group master or a city ledger account.

- The capability to forecast sales and revenue for future dates using tentative bookings.
- The capability of preassigning rooms to facilitate group check-ins and checking out the entire group or those due to leave with one entry.
- The capability to create a customized Web site for each event that provides detailed information about the hotel and its amenities and to select how reservations are accepted: Web, fax, and/or phone.
- The capturing of historical information for every group, conference, company, and organization. "Historical information is useful when negotiating with a returning group. For example, the group may have negotiated a deep discount last year based on a projection of 400 room nights. They may have only booked 150 room nights. This information may lead to a lower discount, increasing average daily rate and profits" (*www.resortdata.com*).

Displaying Room Availability

Displaying Room Availability and Guest Lists. Before selling a reservation, most reservation systems provide several types of screens for reviewing availability where information may be depicted graphically.

Today's Inventory

1. *Today's inventory.* This screen is used to maintain tight inventory control. It identifies the number of rooms available for sale and may also include occupancy statistics, house count, and room rates and revenue (see Figure 4-5).

Future Date

2. *Future date.* The reservationist selects the date for displaying the same information denoted in today's inventory.

7 to 14 Day Availability

3. *7 to 14 day availability.* Displays one or two weeks of availability where only available rooms by room type are shown.

Blocked Rooms

4. *Blocked rooms.* Displays information about the blocks for a specific room number or room type. Scheduling conflicts that arise when a blocked room has been assigned to another guest through an override are denoted by the system.

Guest name lists are displayed on the screen or printed according to various criteria such as arrivals for date with special requests or guests with package plans or guaranteed reservations. Other criteria for generating a guest name list include guests checked in on a specific date, guests departing on a specific date, cancellations for guests who have a deposit on file, reservations with deposits not yet received, guests now in-house, market segment, VIP identification, travel agent identification, business source code, and address information.

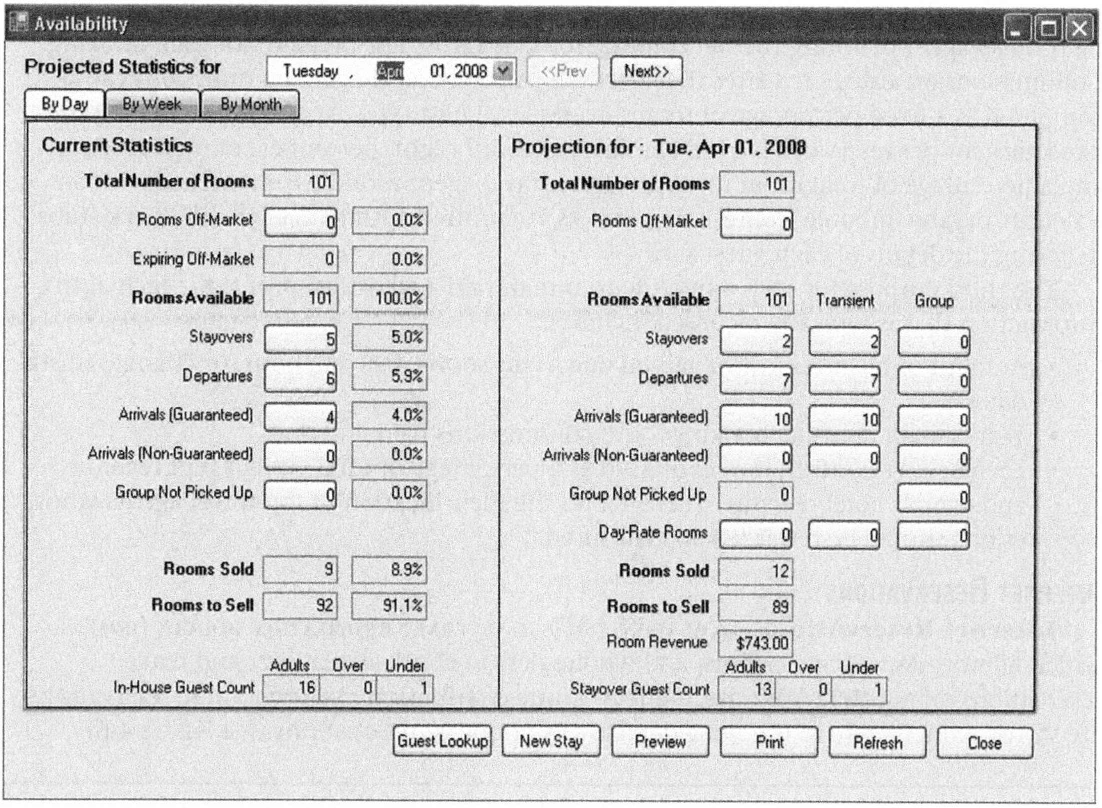

Availability

Projected Statistics for Tuesday , April 01, 2008 <<Prev Next>>

By Day | By Week | By Month

Current Statistics

Total Number of Rooms	101	
Rooms Off-Market	0	0.0%
Expiring Off-Market	0	0.0%
Rooms Available	101	100.0%
Stayovers	5	5.0%
Departures	6	5.9%
Arrivals (Guaranteed)	4	4.0%
Arrivals (Non-Guaranteed)	0	0.0%
Group Not Picked Up	0	0.0%
Rooms Sold	9	8.9%
Rooms to Sell	92	91.1%

	Adults	Over	Under
In-House Guest Count	16	0	1

Projection for: Tue, Apr 01, 2008

		Transient	Group
Total Number of Rooms	101		
Rooms Off-Market	0		
Rooms Available	101		
Stayovers	2	2	0
Departures	7	7	0
Arrivals (Guaranteed)	10	10	0
Arrivals (Non-Guaranteed)	0	0	0
Group Not Picked Up	0		0
Day-Rate Rooms	0	0	0
Rooms Sold	12		
Rooms to Sell	89		
Room Revenue	$743.00		

	Adults	Over	Under
Stayover Guest Count	13	0	1

Guest Lookup | New Stay | Preview | Print | Refresh | Close

FIGURE 4-5. AVAILABILITY SCREEN.

Source: Multi-Systems, Inc., Phoenix, AZ.

Tracking Advance Deposits

Tracking advance deposits. Money sent to guarantee an arrival is an **ADVANCE DEPOSIT**. The amount of money sent is usually based on one night of room revenue, length of stay, or a fixed amount. Advance deposit information is kept in an **ADVANCE DEPOSIT LEDGER** that records all deposits received, refunded due to cancellations, or transferred to folios upon guest check-in. An advance deposit module may also provide a means of automatically generating refund checks when it is interfaced with the accounts payable module.

Tracking Travel Agent Bookings and Commissions

Tracking travel agent bookings and commissions. A **TRAVEL AGENT MODULE** contains information for each travel agent such as address and commission rate. This information is available to reservationists for linking to guest bookings where confirmation slips may be sent either to the travel agent, guest, or both.

The second purpose for a travel agent module is to generate commission statements for each travel agent denoting the net commission due (gross less prepaid) for each booking. Commissions are calculated after the guest's departure. Travel agent commissions can be computed as a fixed percentage of room revenue by guest type, fixed amount per guest, fixed amount per reservation, fixed amount per room night, percentage of total revenue, and a percentage of total room revenue. If the travel agent module is interfaced with an accounts payable module, commission checks are printed automatically with check stubs denoting the details of each guest stay.

The third purpose for such a module is to maintain a statistical profile for each agent. Information that is typically recorded includes:

- Amount of business lost or gained due to no-shows, cancellations, or changes in stay dates.
- Year-to-date revenue, bookings, and commissions paid and due.
- Each agent's contribution expressed as a percentage of total travel agent revenue and overall hotel revenue. This enables the identification of top travel agents whose efforts should be rewarded and nurtured.

Internet Reservations

Internet Reservations. Most PMSs have an **INTERNET RESERVATION MODULE (IRM)**, which allows guests, travel agents, and wholesalers to check availability and make reservations on a Hotel's Web site, a direct online distribution channel. These reservations are stored immediately in the same database as phone-in reservations (see Figure 4-6).

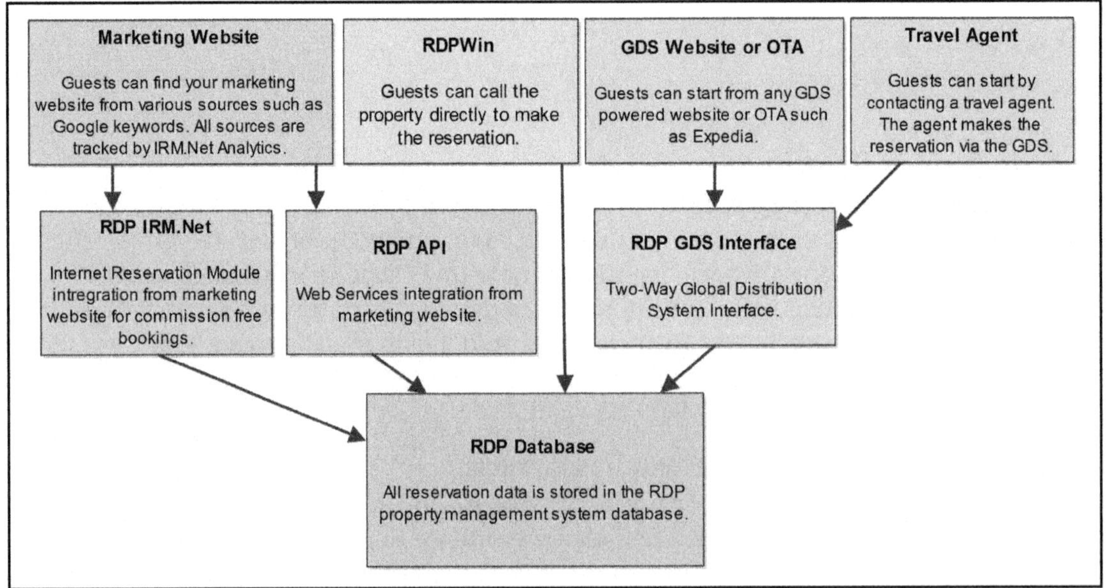

FIGURE 4-6. RESERVATION SYSTEM.

Source: Resort Data Processing (RDP), Vail, Colorado.

When guests book reservations through a hotel's Web site, room revenue increases because fees are not being paid to a third party reservation service (e.g., Expedia). When third parties are involved, hotels may pay out 12 percent or more of the room price.

Greater amounts of inventory are being sold to guests via hotel Web sites. Roughly 57 percent of all travel reservations are made on the Internet. Sixty-five percent of same day hotel reservations are made via smart phones. Consequently, more budget dollars are being earmarked for the marketing of hotel Web sites (desktop and mobile versions). However, maximizing online bookings requires a well-designed and up-to-date Web site with relevant and compelling content. For example, a small resort company's online booking revenue increased from $300,000 to $2.3 million within one year after redesigning and optimizing the Web site. The company launched a robust, full-scale Internet marketing campaign to advertise the site (www.hospitalitynet.org).

Hotel web sites (e.g., room77.com and Tripkick.com) may enable guests to find detailed room information (by actual room number), including virtual room views (e.g., what would it look like standing in the balcony of a room), interactive floor plans (e.g., high or low floor), and interior photos. At the Hyatt Regency Waikiki, for example, rooms 1010 and 1410 are Deluxe Ocean View Doubles. On Room 77, however, the former looks into the Waikiki Police Station; the latter, over the top of it. Bonnie Buckhiester, a noted revenue management consultant, predicts consumer demand for detailed room information will grow and force hoteliers to provide room categories that are more discriminating. "No longer will the hotelier be able to lump rooms into a single category that have been judged by the guest to be inferior" (7).

Central Reservations

Central Reservations. Central reservations processing is a crucial and expensive decision for a lodging chain. It is a lucrative direct distribution channel. A PMS reservation system may be interfaced to a **central reservation system (crs)** provided by a lodging chain or an **independent representation or reservation service (irs)**, an outsourced CRS managed by a third party (ihotelier). The voice center, a facility in which reservation agents take calls for reservations, may also be operated by a third party. Central reservation systems offered by the major chains began in the 1960s. In the 1980s, there was a surge in PMS installations. Many properties had two on-site reservation systems (property and central) that did not talk to each other. Additional labor was required to keep both systems up-to-date. Since the property reservation system was tied into guest registration and accounting, it was necessary to quickly update it with CRS-generated reservations. The same sense of urgency did not exist for entering property-generated reservations into the CRS. Consequently, the CRS frequently had inaccurate room availability resulting in lost sales or inadvertent overbooking. Today, property management systems can be interfaced to a CRS so that both are updated whenever either party makes a reservation.

In 1995, the Holiday Inn chain launched the first Web site with a full online reservation system. Others followed because of the popularity of this channel and to compete with third party travel Web sites or **travel portals**, such as Expedia, Hotels.com, and Travelocity, which were selling many discounted hotel rooms. Since 2003, hotel chains have regained more control of their rooms and prices by offering best-rate guarantees. If customers who book a room on a hotel chain's Web site find a room at a better rate on another site, the best-rate guarantee will be honored (e.g., Marriott: 25% discount from lower room rate).

Chain and property Web sites will continue to be the focus of hoteliers. These direct online channels are the cheapest form of distribution and preferred by customers.

Hotel chains, such as La Quinta Inn and Suites, Omni Hotels, Choice Hotels International, and Starwood Hotels and Resorts, have developed mobile applications allowing customers to book rooms and access customer loyalty programs as well as other property-specific information. In March 2009, Choice Hotels International was the first major hotel chain to introduce an iPhone booking application. iPhone's built-in GPS technology also generates a list of Choice properties in the vicinity and provides directions to the hotel locations. The cost to develop the application was recouped within the first 40 days according to Chris Brya, Director of User Experience and E-commerce Projects at Choice Hotels International (8).

Global Distribution Systems (GDS)

Global Distribution Systems (GDS). A CRS or IRS can be linked to one or more GDSs to enable traditional travel agents from around the world to book hotel rooms in real time. About 19% of hotel inventory in the United States is sold via a GDS. This percentage is expected to decline as more hotel rooms are sold via brand Web sites (e.g., Hilton International). Global distribution systems such as Travelport Worldspan, which were originally designed and operated by airlines, were later extended to travel agents as sales channels. GDSs, which are no longer owned by airlines, are also accessible to consumers through travel portals (e.g., Orbitz, Priceline.com, Travelocity) for hotels, rental cars, airline tickets, and other services.

Connecting a CRS and IRS to a GDS requires a **distribution switch** (provided by Pegasus Solutions) or a bidirectional interface providing travel agents and consumers with direct access to hotel central reservations systems. When a reservation is transmitted to a hotel from a GDS or Web site (desktop or mobile version), the system "switches" the computer message instantly into a unique format and queries the hotel central reservation system database. Once the reservation is confirmed, the information is available immediately to the requestor (www.pegs.com). GDS and switch fees are incurred for each reservation transaction.

A hotel chain will interface its CRS to those GDSs with the greatest concentration of travel agents in the target market. For example, if a lodging organization wanted to secure a market share in Europe, it might link its CRS to the Amadeus GDS.

Alternative Distribution Systems (ADS)

Alternative Distribution Systems (ADS) or Online Travel Agencies (OTA). These are indirect online channels with distribution through global travel portals as well as small, regional ones. They number in the thousands, providing exposure to millions of consumers booking online. They include companies such as Expedia.com, hotels.com, TravelNow.com as well as StarCite, a group function/meeting planning site. Like GDS channels, ADS channels are losing market share to direct online channels.

Electronic Distribution Management (EDM)

Electronic Distribution Management (EDM). According to John Burns and Jon Inge, two noted hospitality technology consultants, few people have the mental bandwidth or time to manage more than five to seven channels manually. Distributing the right proportions of room inventory across the most productive selling channels at the right times and at the right rates is difficult as conditions change not only daily but even hourly. Thus, this requires automation or the implementation of an EDM system. An EDM solution enables a hotel to seamlessly control and distribute hotel inventory in all sales channels (PMS↔CRS↔GDS↔ADS↔hotel/chain Web site) from one single point of entry. This allows a PMS to automatically open and close the rates available to various channels according to occupancy and other factors and to have these changes ripple through all the appropriate distribution channels (e.g., consumers via 400 travel portals and brand Web site, 600,000 travel agents via GDSs, etc.) in real time. An EDM system might also have a **rate-tracking module** to identify where the hotel's rates are being distributed and the mark-ups that travel portals are adding to the net rates. Rates and the strategies and tactics used by competitors to establish rates are also tracked. This rate-intelligence information helps the hotel maximize room revenue.

> *Revenue management needs to focus more on optimal channel mix to maximize profit.*
>
> Beverly Ramsook
> VP of Revenue Management and Distrubution, Denihan Hospitality

Revenue Management

Revenue Management. This computer-aided program determines whether the pricing and room allocation for a particular rate or market segment (e.g., group, transient, corporate, travel agent) should be increased, decreased, or closed based upon an analysis of demand and competitive pricing conditions. Revenue management decisions are then implemented through the reservation system. In 2009, InterContinental Hotel Group (IHG) deployed an advanced large-scale enterprise revenue management system (referred to as a price optimization module). By 2012, it had achieved $145 million in incremental revenue for IHG (9).

A Revenue management program (also called **yield management**) identifies booking patterns by room type and market segment (*pattern recognition*) by analyzing variables (e.g., weather, historical bookings, booking lead-time behavior, length of stay distributions, walk-ins, local events, no-shows, denials, competition, client and group profiles, current reservations, seasonal variations) and then compares it to a set of rules (*heuristics*) formulated by management to spot trends and to recommend or automatically initiate management defined actions or strategies such as, "If my occupancy in the group discount class exceeds X percent within Y days before arrival, then move all remaining group discounts to rack rate class." For example, the revenue management system at one particular hotel revealed that the sales office was selling more low cost-cost group rooms than their booking goals would have permitted. In response, hotel management wrote a strategy that sent them an electronic message when unauthorized discounting was detected (10). Revenue management rules can be established for (11):

1. **Overbooking** – determining the optimum number of rooms to overbook based on such factors as forecasted no-shows and late cancellations.
2. **Discount control** – limiting the availability of discounted rates to prevent turning away high-value guests.
3. **Length of stay control** – determining the length of stay restrictions to ensure that short stay guests do not displace longer stays or that longer stay discounted sales do not displace shorter, high rate guests.
4. **Product class control** – managing room types to ensure that business is not turned away due to the unavailability of specific room types when other substitutable room types may be available.
5. **Group evaluation** – assessment of whether or not to accept a group, taking into account group size, room rate, banqueting and other revenue generating services, and complimentary rooms relative to the revenue which would otherwise be generated by guests.
6. **Optimization** – using all costs (e.g. distribution channel costs, package costs) and revenues (e.g. margins on package elements, strategic value of frequent guests) associated with a rate code configured in the reservation system.
7. **Lead times** – pricing rooms to encourage advanced bookings, such as offering travelers who book seven days in advance discounted, nonrefundable rates.
8. **Packages** – pricing package plans based on the forecasted demand for all components as well as suggesting alternate dates and times that would push demand to slower periods and offer guests lower-cost options.

The primary advantages of a revenue management system are that it:

1. Forces management to clearly define selling strategies that increase the average room rate (close lower rates when hotel reaches X percent occupancy), occupancy percentage (open discounted rates if hotel occupancy falls below X percent occupancy), and contribution margin (close travel agent or group bookings at X percent occupancy). Revenue management systems typically increase room revenue from 3 to 8 percent.
2. Provides the capability to quickly extrapolate and react to short- and long-term patterns affecting profitability and improving management productivity and effectiveness.

Revenue Management Strategies

In a "Down Market":

- aggressively monitor competitive moves and react appropriately.
- make immediate pricing recommendations in reaction to demand trends.
- monitor/interpret changes to the economy and the impact–manage mix.
- explore new distribution channels to gain market share and verify rooms are available.
- pair with Sales Force to determine new business sources for the hotel.

In an "Up Market":

- proactively monitor demand.
- filter demand in order to accept only the best business for the hotel.
- monitor and evaluate pricing strategies to maximize revenue.
- ensure inventory is available to sell through all distribution channels.

Revenue management technology enables operators to optimize rate strategies across properties and distribution channels. For example, Vintage Hotels, a three-property group in Ontario, Canada, sells rooms from any channel without being concerned about overselling and rate inconsistencies because the revenue management system utilizes a single database system platform.

Front Office System

Reservation information is transferred to the front office system during registration when a guest is assigned a room and a folio is created for documenting charges and payments. Other functions performed by a front office system include rooms and housekeeping management, cashiering, night audit, and guest check-out.

Guest Registration

Guest Registration. The front desk staff is provided with information on each reservation on the arrival day. Registration cards for new arrivals are printed in alphabetical order during the night audit or morning shift. An expected arrivals list is also printed detailing such things as name, arrival and departure dates, blocked room, room type and rate, balance, special requests, guarantee status, and share-with information.

Guest registration entails four steps:

Retrieve Reservation

Step 1. Retrieve reservation. A guest's reservation is retrieved by entering either the guest name or the confirmation number. If the name is misspelled or incomplete, the screen displays a listing of similar names from which to choose.

Assign a Room

Step 2. Assign a room. A front desk clerk can either select a room by viewing available rooms via a *computerized room rack* or have the computer (desktop or mobile device) pick a room based on the requested room type and features (e.g., handicap room). A computerized room rack displays available room numbers that match reservation criteria. It may indicate connecting room numbers, whether vacant rooms are clean or dirty, and the number of consecutive nights each room number is available for sale. Guests can personally select rooms if the hotel has a self-service kiosk, which may visually display the rooms on a graphical map (e.g., rooms facing the waterfront). Self-service kiosks can also be used for issuing room keys, checking out, enrolling in a loyalty program, passport scanning, and airline check-in. Guests using the France-Based Ariane Systems kiosks, for example, typically complete check-in and check-out in a couple of minutes, in the language of their choice. Many hotels, like the airlines, also provide online or Web check-in. Today, customers can select airline seats over the Internet. Perhaps in the future hotel guests will select rooms the same way.

Wireless front office applications have also been developed for iPads and other mobile devices with remote PMS access. Staff can perform many of the functions of a wired PMS terminal anywhere a wireless signal is available, such as check-in and check-out (e.g., curbside, lobby, etc.), upselling, room changes, guest registration signature and credit card payment capture, group check-in and room blocking, and encoding of room keys.

The PMS may have a **baggage handling module** for tracking luggage, golf clubs, cars, and other items. "With each item collected, a voucher is printed and recorded to the guest folio, and can then be checked at any time to determine its status" (springermiller.com). In the future, hotel baggage handling systems may use radio frequency identification (RFID) tags to improve tracking capabilities. For example, McCarran International Airport began using radio frequency identification in 2006 to track bags checked in at downtown hotels along the Las Vegas Strip.

Collect Payment

Step 3. Collect Payment. If the payment by the guest is in cash, the system displays the full amount due for the entire stay. Cash is collected and a credit is posted to the guest folio. The front desk may have a credit card interface. The front desk clerk slides a credit card through a credit card swipe attached to the terminal, prefilling the check-in screen with the guest's name (if a walk-in or a guest without a reservation) and both the credit card number and expiration date. The credit card swipe is connected via a phone line or an Internet connection (used for faster credit card processing) to the card processor to allow immediate pre-authorization or payment and wire transfer of funds to the bank. Pre-authorizing the credit card at check-in reserves a "credit line" on the card based on the length of stay. This helps guarantee that the card will be good at check-out. The credit card authorization is automatically matched to the sale at check-out with any unused portion released back to the guest, which is required by credit card compliancy regulations. Otherwise, the hotel will be charged a higher fee and potentially subject to other penalties for noncompliance. Customer service will also be negatively affected by needlessly reserving a guest's available credit. Hotels must also comply with other Payment Card Industry (PCI) standards to ensure credit card security, which include:

- Restricting data to those who need to know the information.
- Assigning a unique code to each person with PMS access for tracking purposes.
- Restricting physical access to cardholder data.
- Protecting stored cardholder data. For example, one hotel company had to modify PMS software so that credit card data could not be recorded in nonsecured areas, such as special request fields.

Method of payment appears on a credit limit report that is printed during the night audit and circulated to food and retail outlets. This report indicates whether a guest has charging privileges or must settle by cash or check. It also lists the guest's credit limit, current balance, and amount over credit limit. A guest's outstanding balance may also be monitored by the cashiering module so that room charges are disallowed when a folio balance exceeds its credit limit and/or the operator is notified if any charge places the guest over his assigned limit.

Verify Room Status

4. *Verify room status.* The final registration step is to confirm the status of the assigned room as occupied or in-house. Later on, the guest may request a room change where the guest folio is assigned a new room number.

Room Status and Housekeeping Management

Room Status and Housekeeping Management. The front desk must have up-to-date and accurate room status information when selling rooms. Otherwise, a hotel may lose room sales or experience unnecessary delays in rooming guests. While the front office system denotes a change in status when a guest is checked out or registered, information is needed from the housekeeping department to verify room status, since a guest may leave or decide to stay longer without informing the front desk, and to change the status of rooms to clean.

The housekeeping department may provide the front desk with a list denoting the status of each room or enter the changes via a terminal located in the housekeeping office. If the phone, electronic locking, or entertainment systems are interfaced to the front office system, room status is promptly updated by room attendants via room telephones, door locks, or TVs. Wireless handhelds can also be used for automatically updating room status.

A **guest detection system**, typically a component of an in-room energy management system, instantly determines the physical occupancy of rooms using sensor technology. This real time information can be accessed by housekeeping, maintenance and minibar personnel via wireless handhelds or small corridor displays adjacent to guest room doors. This information can also be obtained at the front desk and executive housekeeper's office and by security personnel via remote central display panels. Guest detection systems prevent guest interruptions and are helpful tools for identifying intrusions or sleep-ins in unsold rooms and for determining which rooms need to be evacuated during emergencies as well as for checking housekeeping discrepancies.

Discrepancies in room statuses between the front desk and housekeeping do occur. A **DISCREPANCY** is a room which was reported occupied by housekeeping but vacant by the front desk and vice versa. Room discrepancies are denoted in a daily reconciliation report (**ROOMS DISCREPANCY REPORT**) and/or through a visual warning when updating the housekeeping status of rooms.

A **ROOM STATUS REPORT** is printed during the night identifying expected stayovers and check-outs. It also shows the next date the room is blocked and what work must be done the next day as well as the current room statuses, including an explanation of out-of-order rooms. It is used as a manual backup for the computer system.

Other useful features found in a well-designed housekeeping management module include:

- Displaying check-outs (room number and departure time) on the housekeeping terminal as they occur.
- Providing up-to-the-minute room status and forecasting reports to assist in employee scheduling.
- Scheduling room maintenance and repairs, which also may be linked to a **WORK ORDER SYSTEM** for automating the process of entering and completing work order requests. Wireless handhelds can be used to notify maintenance personnel and room attendants of tasks quickly. For example, when the front desk enters and assigns a work order to "fix the toilet in Room 101" using the Resort Data Processing (RDP) PMS, the request will appear on the wireless PDA of the person assigned to the task. The PDA can "beep" to indicate the arrival of a new, high-priority work order. When the task is completed, the information is transferred to the RDP system via the PDA. All workstations at the property are then aware the work order has been closed. The system can also send a warning notification for a high priority work order to one or more other employees if the task is not completed on time. The general manager and manager on duty, for example, could both be notified that the "toilet in Room 101" has not been fixed after 3 hours. Notifications can be sent to a manager's workstation, cell phone, or wireless PDA (resortdata.com).
- Generating inspection and inventory forms. Inspection and inventory information can be entered through wireless devices to save time. A wireless handheld can be used by a housekeeping inspector to update room status (e.g., ready for guest) and to alert maintenance and housekeeping staff of tasks (e.g., towels needed in room 101). A housekeeping module may also track the most common room-cleaning errors noted by inspectors, such as dust on the furniture or smudges on the windows. This knowledge can be incorporated into employee training. Comparison of room-cleaning attendant scores can be incorporated into an incentive program based on improving attendant scores. A **LINEN MANGAGEMENT SYSTEM** using RFID technology (linen with embedded RFID tags) can provide instant, accurate inventory information on all linen items as well as track them as they traverse through laundry chutes and machines and linen closets. This enables the housekeeping department to manage linens more efficiently and extend linen life.

- Generating a room assignment schedule (room number, status, and type and service required) for each room attendant, which may be printed or accessed via a wireless handheld. The system equally distributes workloads by assigning a value to each room type (e.g., suite 2 credits, king room 1 credit).
- Tracking of rooms not cleaned and vacated to assist in determining afternoon and night shift staffing requirements.
- Placing rooms off-market for a designated period of time and removing them from the hotel's total room inventory.
- Tracking labor productivity by identifying the average amount of time it takes each room attendant to clean a room. One PMS vendor provides a housekeeper-phone interface for capturing the exact cleaning time per room. The room attendant presses a key on the in-room phone to record the "start time" and presses another key to record the "end time." Reports are then available showing the actual cleaning time per room, as well as the expected cleaning time and variance.
- Tracking room revenue by room number or type to assist in rate determination and selling strategy.

Cashiering and Guest Check-Out

Cashiering and Guest Check-Out. In the cashier module, folios are created, transactions are posted, cashier shifts are opened and closed, and guests are checked out.

There are four basic types of folios: individual folios, master folios, city ledger folios, and control folios. **Individual folios** are created for each in-house guest. However, multiple folios can be created for each guest to separate the types of charges. For example, one folio may only record room and tax while the other records only incidental charges. Also, two people sharing one room may require separate folios for accounting purposes.

Master folios are typically created for groups. Individual folio postings are transferred automatically to the group master according to billing instructions (e.g., post only room and tax to group master) that defines the billing transfer start and stop dates.

When a guest checks out, the folio balance can be transferred to a **city ledger folio** for direct billing. The city ledger is a subsidiary ledger (discussed later in this chapter). It contains a list of customers who owe the hotel money (accounts receivable) and non-guest accounts with in-house charging privileges such as employees and business clients.

A **control folio** or a wash account (a control folio balance should always be zero) is set up in the city ledger so that all revenue and payments not directly recorded by the front office system will be reflected in the daily report. For example, a point-of-sale system interfaced to the front office system may only record room charges. Therefore, to enter food and beverage cash and credit sales into the system the following transactions must be posted to a control folio:

DEBITS: $1000 Food $500 Bar

CREDITS: $988.12 Cash $511.88 Credit Card

Different types of folio postings include (see Figure 4-7):

Charge Postings

- *Charge postings.* Charges are entered as a debit (+) and include such things as room and tax.

Payment Postings

- *Payment postings.* Payments are entered as a credit (–) and include such things as cash and checks.

Correction Postings

- *Correction postings.* A correction posting reverses an incorrect transaction only on the day that it occurred.

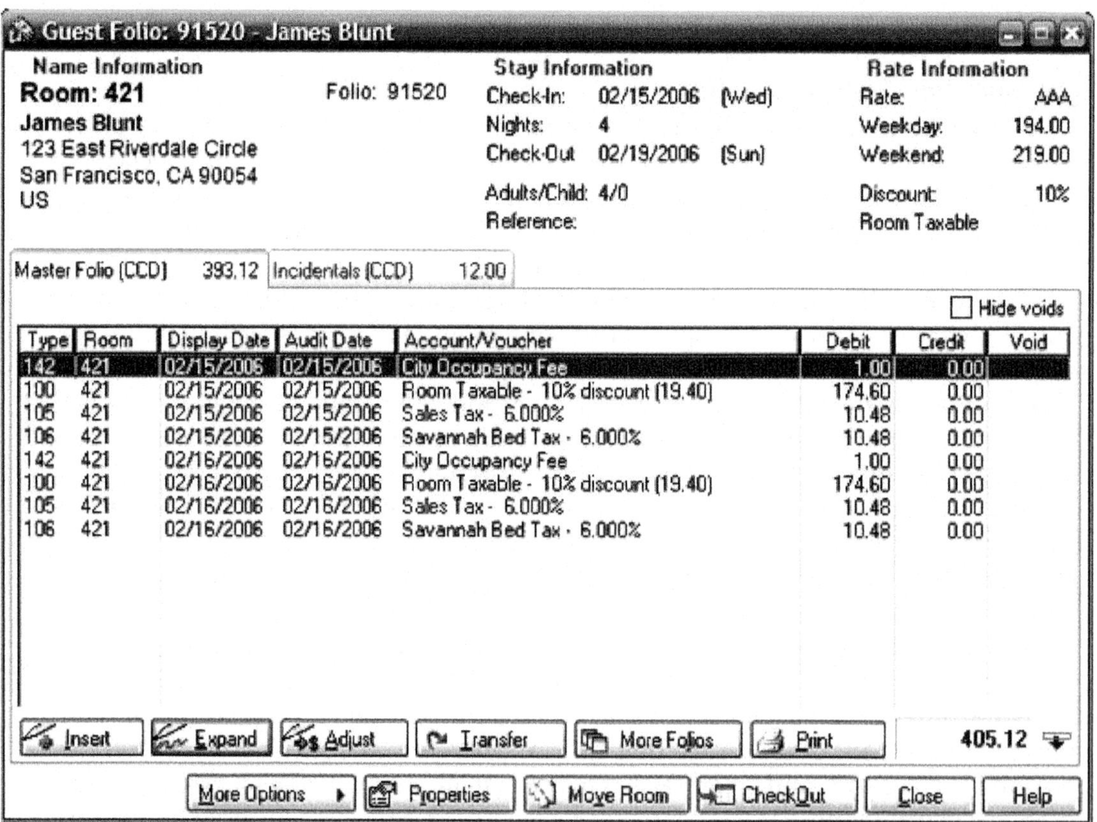

FIGURE 4-7. GUEST FOLIO SCREEN.

Source: Innquest Software, Tampa FL.

Adjustment Postings

- *Adjustment postings.* An adjustment posting is used when a posting mistake is made on a folio but not discovered until the next business day after the revenue and cash have been recorded by the system.

Transfer Postings

- *Transfer postings.* Postings are transferred to another guest, master, or city ledger folio.

Automatic Postings

- *Automatic postings.* These are postings that require no human intervention. If the system is interfaced to call accounting, point- of-sale, in-room video, or minibar systems, these charges are auto-posted to the correct guest account.

Posting a transaction typically requires the following information:

- Operator identification (GC).
- Department or payment code (RT – restaurant, CA – Cash).
- Amount.
- Room number.
- Source document or voucher number (restaurant check number 01200).
- Reference (Snacks).
- Folio identification.

Charges for a specific departmental code, such as gift shop, can be posted in the batch mode without retrieving each guest folio individually. This enables rapid charge posting.

The check-out process entails the following steps:

Print Folio for Guest Review

Step 1. Print folio for guest review. A folio can be printed on command detailing every charge. This reduces charge disputes since every transaction is well-documented. For example, if a guest disputes a restaurant charge, the voucher number can be used to quickly reference the source document (check with signature).

Folios can also be preprinted for departing guests to reduce the check-out time. However, if additional charges have been incurred, an updated copy must be printed. Late charges can be a problem when the front office system is not interfaced to retail outlets (e.g., breakfast charge) and the telephone system (e.g., long distance telephone call). The cashier module should have the capability to reinstate folios for late charges or corrections and to summarize folio details for long-term stays. Guests can also view their folio transactions on their in-room televisions if the PMS is interfaced to the movie or entertainment systems. Guests with a valid credit card on file can process their check-outs through the entertainment system without going to the front desk. Some hotels also enable check-out via the Web. The Hyatt Web Checkout, for example, enables guests to review their charges, check-out online, and have their receipts sent to their e-mail addresses.

Post Final Payment and Print Folio

Step 2. Post final payment and print folio. After the folio is settled, the guest receives a folio and the hotel retains a copy for accounting purposes. Most front office systems maintain folio history; therefore, folios can be reprinted for guests who misplace their settled folios and need a second copy to document business expenses.

Guest Check-Out

Step 3. Guest check-out. Once a folio has a zero balance, the system will prompt the clerk to check-out the guest. A guest check-out automatically updates the room status, house count, and reports. Some systems allow guests to check-out the night before and also track those who have requested late check-outs. The system may also automatically send a thank you e-mail after check-out with a copy of the folio and/or a guest satisfaction survey link. The Resort Data Processing PMS, for example, links guest survey results to the guest history and CRM modules. RDP also provides a variety of tools and reports for analyzing guest survey results and findings (e.g., display all guests who thought food quality was poor). See Figure 4-8.

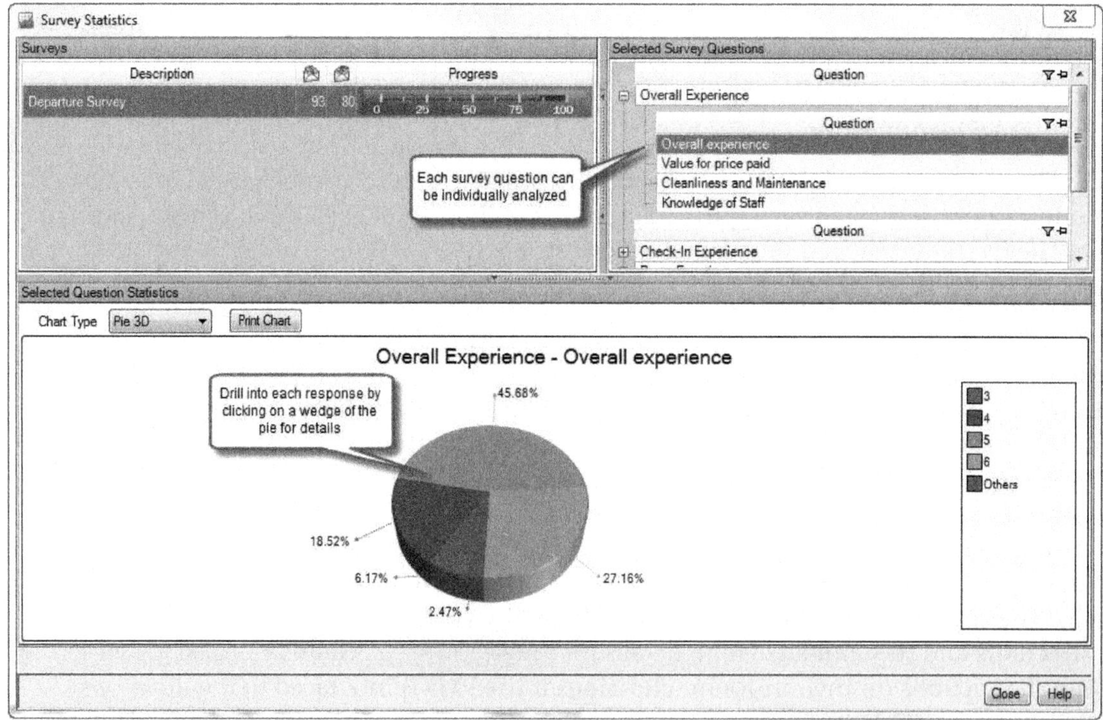

FIGURE 4-8. GUEST SURVEY RESULTS.

Source: Resort Data Processing, Vail, Colorado.

At the end of each cashier shift, a cashier report is printed which typically includes the following information:

1. All transactions posted by departmental code.
2. A summary of debit and credit totals, which should come out equal.
3. A comparison of actual cash deposited to cash posted to derive an overage or shortage (see Figure 4-9).

NIGHT AUDIT

A computerized **NIGHT AUDIT** simplifies and expedites the auditing process by:

RECORDING ALL TRANSACTIONS

1. **Recording all transactions.** It records all daily activities in the advance deposit ledger, city ledger, and guest ledger, generating an audit trail. Each transaction is described in detail (e.g., amount, departmental code, cross reference information, and operator ID). This facilitates the balancing of payments received and source documents (departmental control sheets, restaurant checks, vouchers, paid out slips, etc.) to system readings.

TENDER	TOTAL	NUMBER OF POSTINGS
Cash	1000.56	20
Check	221.87	4
Cash Received	1222.43	24
Less		
Cash Paid Out	(60.33)	3
SYSTEM DEPOSIT	1162.10	
Drawer Total	1704.56	
less bank	(500.00)	
ACTUAL DEPOSIT	1204.56	
ACTUAL DEPOSIT	1204.56	
less SYSTEM DEPOSIT	(1162.10)	
OVER	42.46	

FIGURE 4-9. CASH OVERAGE/SHORTAGE REPORT.

Posting Room & Tax

2. **Posting of room and tax.** It performs automatic posting of room and tax to all in-house guests as well as other automatic charges.

Producing a Trial Balance

3. **Producing a trial balance.** It automatically totals debits and credits determining whether the system is in balance.

> *The daily report is the written financial history of a 24-hour time period in the life of a hotel.*
>
> Charles Steadmon, *Managing Front Office Operations*

Generating Reports and Updating Statistics

4. **Generating reports and updating statistics.** A variety of reports can be automatically printed during the night or viewed later including:
   - *Downtime reports*. These reports, used when the computer system is not working, include condensed city and guest ledger folios for folio balances, a room status report to identify vacant and ready rooms, an occupancy forecast for reservations, and an in-house guest list for the front desk and telephone operator.
   - *Morning reports*. This includes pre-printed folios, an expected arrivals and departures list, a credit limit report, and preprinted registration cards.
   - *Night auditor reports*. Two important night auditor reports are the **RATE VARIANCE REPORT** and the **DAILY REPORT**. The rate variance report denotes rates that vary from the rack rate. The daily report is the primary accounting document of the day. It records the financial total for each charge or settlement category and is used for reconciling cash and revenues and as a posting reference for inputting financial data into an accounting program (Room Revenue Code—RM = General Ledger Code—1435.78). It also contains a reconciliation of the advance deposit, guest, and city ledgers.
   - *Management reports*. These daily flash reports provide management with information concerning both revenue performance and operating and marketing statistics.

Night Audit Steps

Night Audit Steps.

Step 1. Verify that all charges have been posted.

Step 2. Verify that all of today's guest departures have been checked out of the system.

Step 3. Cancel all reservations that were no-shows to release rooms to inventory and to undo preblocked rooms. Print a guaranteed no-show report and send to accounting for billing purposes.

Step 4. Turn off PMS interfaces. Only carry out this task once the POS system has been closed out for the day. The POS system allows food and beverage charges to be posted to the room. Checks settled to cash and credit cards must be posted to the food and beverage control account found in the city ledger. For example, a food check for $20.00 would be posted to the following keys: CA $20.00 RT $20.00. This account should always have a zero balance.

Step 5. Perform room rates audit for all occupied and complimentary rooms and rate overrides. The basic purpose of this step is to ensure that every guest is checked in at the correct rate. The night auditor should also compare the rate on the signed registration cards or forms, found in the "bucket" or "Pit," to the computer rates in the room rate audit report in order to identify any discrepancies.

Step 6. Close out the cashier, ending all daily activity.

Step 7. Post room and tax.

Step 8. Reconcile computer register readings with source documents, vouchers, cash collected, and credit card transactions report. To obtain computer register readings, print preliminary daily report. If discrepancies are identified during the reconciliation process, request a printed listing of detailed transactions for discrepant departmental codes or register keys to pinpoint the problem.

A. Reconciliation of department codes to source documents.				
		Register Reading	**Source Documents**	
PO	Paid Outs	____________	____________	(Voucher)
D1	Deposit Kept	____________	____________	(Voucher)
D2	Deposit Return	____________	____________	(Voucher)
D5	Deposit Paid	____________	____________	(Voucher)
RT	Restaurant	____________	____________	(Checks)
BR	Beverage	____________	____________	(Checks)
AX	American Express	____________	____________	(Credit Card Transactions Report)

B. Cash and credit card reconciliation.		
Register Reading: CA CASH RECEIVED	*Less*	______
PO PAID OUT	*Less*	(______)
D2 DEPOSIT RETURNED	*Less*	(______)
D5 DEPOSIT PAID OUT		(______)
CASH TO BE DEPOSITED		______
ACTUAL CASH DEPOSITED		______
If Cash > Computer Reading = OVERAGE OF		______
If Cash < Computer Reading = SHORTAGE OF		______
Credit Card Terminal Reading: AMERICAN EXPRESS, etc.		______
CREDIT CARD TOTAL TO BE DEPOSITED		______
ACTUAL CREDIT CARD TOTAL TO BE DEPOSITED		______
If Credit Card Terminal Total > Computer Reading = OVERAGE OF		______
If Credit Card Terminal Total < Computer Reading = SHORTAGE OF		______

Common Posting Mistakes

Common posting mistakes:

1. Posted a charge twice (overcharge).
2. Posted incorrect charge amount (overcharge or undercharge).
3. Charge to wrong folio (overcharged one guest and undercharged another).
4. Forgot to post a charge (undercharge).
5. Posted to wrong settlement key (received cash but posted payment as American Express, resulting in credit card shortage and cash overage).
6. Collected payment but did not apply payment to guest folio (cash overage).
7. Posted incorrect payment amount (cash overage or shortage).

Step 9. Print downtime reports before closing out the day when most software problems surface.

Step 10. Backup database.

Step 11. End-of-day routine. This closes out the business date, restarts daily activity totals, and updates monthly and yearly totals.

Step 12. Prints morning, management, and night auditor reports.

It is important to note that the night audit sequence varies from operation to operation, from simple to elaborate. Some computerized night audits are programmed to execute steps according to a predetermined order set up by the night auditor or management. Some PMS vendors provide a "one-button" or "one-step" night audit option that performs an instant audit without the need to shutdown interfaces while it automatically backups the database and generates daily reports.

Sales and Catering Systems

Almost everyone who works in a sales and catering office can remember when they had to rely on manila files for holding client account information, hand written phone logs, type written contracts and banquet event orders (a final contract for the client and a work order for the catering department), master card files for quickly obtaining addresses and phone colnumbers of clients and prospects, and the trace card file for reminding salespersons of contacts they must handle on a specific date. No longer do hotel sales offices have to rely on manual systems and books, such as the group control log for identifying the maximum colnumber of guest rooms it can sell to a group on a given day or the function book for scheduling and planning events and tracking function space availability.

An automated sales and catering system streamlines the sales and booking processes, eliminating the need to stand in line at the function book and reducing the amount of time spent on preparing reports, contracts, and proposals, tracking down information, calculating rates, typing up proposals, and drawing room layouts. It can also be integrated with a revenue management system to maximize revenue and results. Basic functions performed by a sales and catering system include:

Booking Management

1. **Booking Management.** This enables salespersons within a hotel or hotel chain to book business faster and more accurately since they can access up-to-the-minute availability, book rooms and functions from their own computers (desktop or mobile device) simultaneously, and provide customers with instant feedback about availability and rates. Customized event Web sites can be set up to enable attendees to book hotel reservations online. Each attendee type can also be provided a unique reservation URL.

Before Hyatt Corporation automated its booking of function space, a customer eager to book space would have to wait hours, sometimes days, if he or she called Hyatt headquarters in Chicago to book a function room in San Francisco. As a result, many would-be customers found space elsewhere. Through the new system (a wide area network with a centralized database server), Hyatt users can check availability and book function rooms at any connected hotel from any hotel on the network.

Contact Management

2. **Contact Management.** This provides an organized system of maintaining detailed information to help salespersons keep track of whom to contact and when to solicit business as well as a means for organizing daily tasks, including personal sales calls and follow-up visits.

Account Management

3. **Account Management.** This organizes and tracks all of a hotel's accounts, providing the sales staff with quick access to important information. The entire account history is listed, including sales activities, bookings, call reports, traces, names and phone colnumbers of decision makers, addresses, etc. This information is also used for marketing (e.g., targeted mailings) and generating various reports (e.g., statistical report).

Event Management

4. **Event management.** This provides the ability to plan and track events (for example, a lunch banquet scheduled in the Cyprus room on October 2, 2013 at 12:00 pm) which are displayed on daily, weekly, and monthly calendars. Event information can also be automatically displayed on guest reader boards or digital signage systems when interfaced with the sales and catering system. An event management module enables the assignment of AV media, of catering, of furnishing and staging, and of personnel events. It can generate banquet event orders, name tags, guest lists and table tents and track inventory items (e.g., potted plants, piano, tables) to determine what is available for any given function. It may also have the ability to produce dimensionally accurate, graphic drawings for creating meeting room layouts showing the placement of furnishings and equipment and architectural details—doors, windows, pillars, electrical, angled walls, folding walls, etc. (see Figure 4-10).

Reports and Queries

5. **Reports and Queries.** A sales and catering system allows managers to easily prepare reports on overall bookings by group market segment, lost business because of cancellations or turndowns, total bookings by time of year, budgeted revenue versus actual, and this year's revenue compared to last year. The sales staff can be evaluated by producing reports on the colnumber of phone calls they made on a given day, who they talked to, their next business steps, and whether they closed any business.

Utilizing and manipulating the data gathered by the sales and catering system is critical to remaining competitive. Predefined and custom queries are used to extract the desired information from the database. A query, for example, could identify how much business IBM brought to the hotel for Fridays in October or which meeting planners book the third week of October with a two-month lead time and more than 200 sleeping rooms.

Field Force Automation

Field Force Automation. Unlike property salespersons, field sales persons typically serve as brokers connecting room buyers with properties throughout the chain. In the past, managing a global field force was a difficult task for hotel chains since regional offices kept little hard information on the activities of the field force—making it extremely

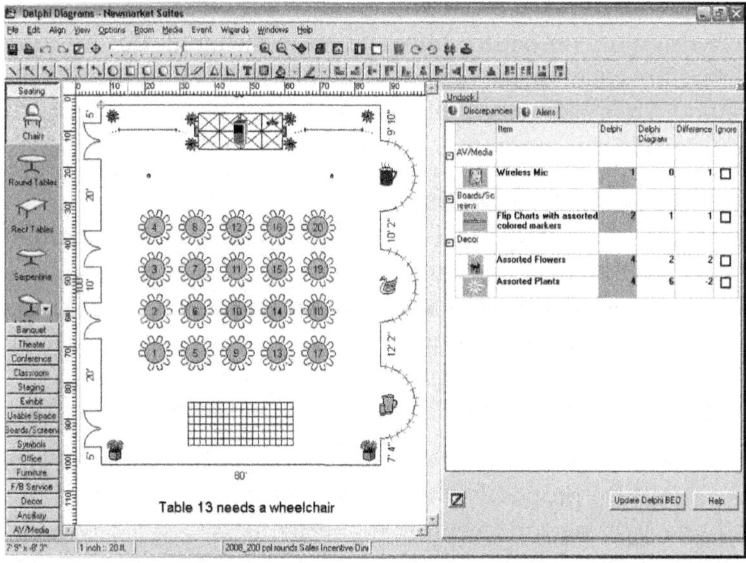

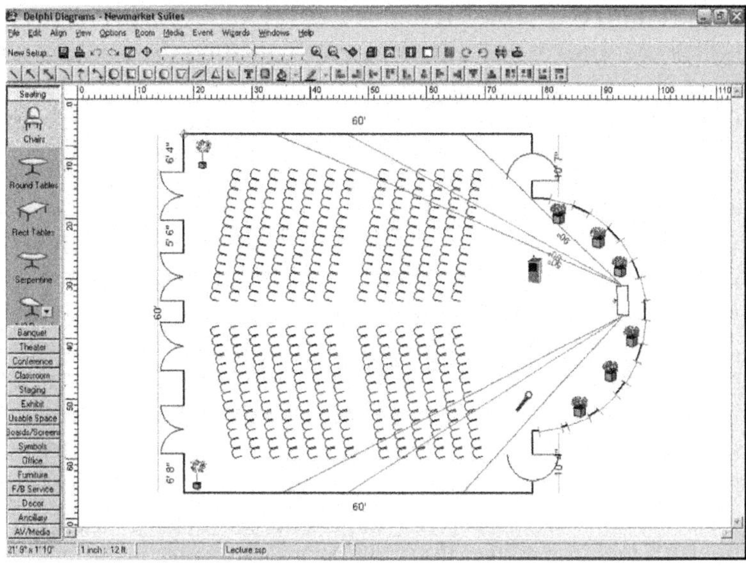

FIGURE 4-10. EXAMPLE OF A DRAWING PROGRAM FOR MEETING PLANNERS.

Source: Newmarket International, Portsmouth, NH.

difficult for the headquarters sales staff to consolidate data to track trends and analyze competition. Consequently, hotel organizations are providing field representatives with wireless notebook computers and other mobile devices that can plug into a corporate wide network. This enables them to have relevant information at their fingertips and to share information. One hotel corporation has developed a fairly comprehensive field force automation system. When a lead is passed by person A to person B, a tickler shows up on B's machine to prevent information from being lost and the client left hanging. When a contract is written or competitor information is gathered, this information is disseminated so that the entire sales force can operate as much more of a unit. The field force automation system has grown business and resulted in an increased sense of professionalism among field salespersons.

Lead and Proposal Management Systems

Lead and proposal management systems. The proliferation of sales channels has added to the complexity of tracking and responding to leads. A **lead management system** provides a suite of online tools for quickly assigning, responding to, and analyzing leads. All incoming leads can be distributed through a central routing point and as signed by channel, market segment, account, geography or any other user-defined rules. A lead management system enables a hotel organization to (www.newmarketinc.com):

- Respond to leads before the competition. Studies have shown that 85% of those first to respond to request for proposals (RFPs) win the business.
- Assign leads to the right person to eliminate bottlenecks.
- Establish business rules that prioritize responses to preferred accounts and automatically escalate leads until responses are sent.
- Analyze and track the sources of leads to determine which distribution channels are producing the most revenues and profits.
- Integrate lead management processes with enterprise systems to ensure the tracking of customer information and that excellent service is provided.

Hotel sales managers typically respond to RFPs via e-mail that includes attached files (Word, PDF, and image files). A sales and catering system can also be integrated with an online **proposal management system** to deliver compelling proposals, electronically eliminating the need for customers to download large and sometimes incompatible RFP files, For example, the Newmarket International proposal management system (eProposal), a browser-based application, allows hotel sales staff to deliver proposals in less than 60 seconds to meeting planner clients via a secure (unique user name and password assigned to client) and personalized hotel Web site with information tailored for their upcoming events at the hotel. The system also includes a prospecting Web site (e-Brochure - www.grandbohemianhotel.com/meetings/meetings.asp) designed exclusively for each hotel to showcase their property's meeting space, floor plans, accommodations, menus, and food and beverage operations.

Video marketing. Compelling and informative online videos can result in more leads and sales. Lead-generation videos can be posted via Flickr or YouTube or embedded on a hotel Web site. According to a study by Comscore, online video is significantly more effective than text in engaging customers and bringing them closer to purchase. For example, a video marketing campaign (desktop and mobile) for the Hotel Casa del Mar in Santa Monica, CA generated a 75% engagement rate and a 27% coupon and suggestive promo redemption rate (12).

Insights from an Expert

YOUR RELATIONSHIP WITH DATA

TODD DAVIS
CIO CHOICE HOTELS INTERNATIONAL

Early winter 2013, I was walking through the airport on my way from Arizona to Stockholm, Sweden for business. We all are people watchers, right? What else is there to do at the airport? Do you notice how technology has the ability to take an absolute firm grasp of everyone's attention? Families are sitting together waiting for planes, each totally engaged in the information on their personal mobile device. No talking, no family time, no interactions whatsoever. You see this behavior everywhere.

I use the word mobile loosely. With the proliferation of wireless devices such as smart phones, laptops, tablets, and slates coupled with the "Cloud", we now have ubiquitous computing. Information processing is integrated into everyday objects and activities. Jaron Lanier, a visionary on virtual reality, wrote in his book, You Are Not a Gadget, "What happens when we stop shaping technology and technology starts shaping us?" It's too late, at least for that family at the airport.

We have great consumer technology devices and Moore's Law* tells us technology advancements will grow at an exponential rate. However, devices themselves are not information providers; they are enablers, content delivery mechanisms. Is technology shaping you? Does it drive or influence your decisions on where you eat, how you travel, and what you buy? The engagement in personal mobile devices is in part due to the convenience of the technology device. However, the main influence is the personalized content delivered to the device.

How do you create influential content that creates absolute focused engagement and a relationship with you? The answer is through using massive amounts of raw data, referred to as "big data" that has been transformed into relevant, personalized, localized, and interactive content and delivered to your ubiquitous device on demand. Using your search criteria, gathering relative big data applying localization filters and leveraging predictive analytics, the content you receive is tailored to your needs and engages you in a customer/vendor relationship. Sample sources of big data in the hospitality industry come by aggregating data from internal and external systems. Table A provides examples of internal and external systems that are sources of data within the hospitality industry.

TABLE A. INTERNAL AND EXTERNAL HOSPITALITY SYSTEM EXAMPLES.

Internal Systems	External Systems
• Reservations	• Trip Advisor Reviews
• Property Management	• Google Marketing
• Customer Loyalty	• Smith Travel
• Point of Sale	• Competitive Pricing & Amenity Data
	• Customer Surveys

Wikipedia provides the following definition for predictive analytics: "In business, predictive models exploit patterns found in historical and transactional data to identify risks and opportunities. Models capture relationships among many factors to allow assessment of risk or potential associated with a particular set of conditions, guiding decision making for candidate transactions." Predictive analytics encompasses a variety of techniques from statistics, modeling, machine learning, and data mining that analyze current and historical facts to make predictions about future events.

I took data statistics at Northern Arizona University when I was a Hotel & Restaurant Management student in the 80s and loved it. I focused on probabilities and this is core to predictive analytics. I knew that as this discipline matured it would be vital to driving increased business and consumer value. At that time we did not have the technology we have today to make the data personalized and deliverable in real-time to the consumer at or before the purchase decision point. Big data companies like Amazon, Google, and Facebook now use predictive models including machine learning models in real-time to drive consumer behaviors and improve the likelihood of a sale. Content is king and using big data with predictive analytics provides the keys to the kingdom.

Big data and predictive analytics are expected to become a several hundred billion dollar industry generating all forms of new employment opportunities. Currently, there are very few courses focused on developing these capabilities. Therefore, in order to leverage these emerging capabilities in today's business world you need internal associates that know your industry and understand how to create the analytics used to drive business enablement. Today, I must leverage internal staff that has both the acumen for analytics and deep business knowledge to mature the capabilities of big data and predictive analytics.

Looking forward, the hospitality industry will thrive on real-time predictive analytics, electronic distribution of relative information based on those analytics, and the ability to properly manage the distribution channels where content is provided. Successful companies will have leaders and associates who understand how to create relative information in real-time that provide a meaningful, engaging, and personal relationship with your brand. These leaders and associates will be required to understand the power of technologies such as big data, business intelligence, data visualization, and predictive analytics.

Recently I attended an advisory meeting for a startup company. The leader posed a question, "If we were a public brand today, what brands out there would you desire to emulate?" Someone responded, "We should be the type of company where the customers are so loyal that they tattoo your logo on their body."

This level of loyalty can be obtained over time by leveraging big data and predictive analytics. Utilizing historical consumer purchases, product reviews, trending, and market information in real-time helps us to clearly understand customer needs. Delivering meaningful, engaging content, tailored and personalized to the individual on ubiquitous devices will drive customer satisfaction resulting in customer loyalty. You can have a relationship the likes of Harley Davidson, most likely though without the tattoo.

Tech News

Luxury Hotel Makes Website a Five-Star Direct Revenue Channel

Nick Aristou, Executive Director, Four Seasons in Limassol, Cypress

The Four Seasons in Limassol, Cyprus has been open since 1993 and is independently owned and operated by Muskita Hotels Ltd. The Five Star deluxe property boasts 304 rooms, six restaurants, four bars, and extensive conference facilities. The Hotel is situated on its own sandy beach, which has been awarded with the Blue Flag (a symbol of cleanliness and safety awarded by the European Community) and is eight kilometers East of Limassol city center.

The hotel's website is an important marketing tool that helps the property to attract and retain elite guests from all over the World. The objective was to increase its impact, make the hotel web page more user friendly, and convert as many site visitors into customers as possible by making it easy for them to complete bookings. It became obvious that the hotel's online persona needed a business chat solution to provide prompt interaction 24/7 and supply prospects with accurate information.

The first step to discovering a solution was doing a thorough review of available products, including several market leaders. However, none matched the Four Seasons' specific needs. The main limitations were the lack of multilingual support, patchy compatibility with tablet users and the absence of robust archival features. LiveWebAssist, a chat solution deployed on the site of IceWarp – a provider of business messaging solutions, was the first to meet all the Four Seasons' requirements.

As a SaaS, the deployment of LiveWebAssist is painless. It takes just several minutes to open accounts on the LiveWebAssist website and define operators. Then the solution generates a short code that is imbedded into the site and it was ready to launch.

The IceWarp team helped do additional customization to make the window color scheme more in line with the Four Seasons' website design and embedded pictures of its operators. To ensure that employees were comfortable using the new system, a mirror page of the hotel's website was created before going live. Operators were taken through a colnumber of mock scenarios, fine-tuning the workflow and the use of knowledgebase (prefabricated content insertable with just a few mouse clicks). This helped to avoid any major work disruptions once the system launched.

The Four Seasons also activated the LiveWebAssist Direct Chat Technology, a VIP connection that gives dedicated access to key IceWarp support personnel. This option makes it possible to reach the important contacts no matter where they are – at their desktop, off-site, or on the road.

From the very beginning, the Four Seasons' customer service team was making the most of LiveWebAssist's multilingual interface and knowledgebase support features to interact with customers in English, Greek, and Russian. The property's sales and marketing team started to see the positive effects of LiveWebAssist almost immediately with a definite increase in bookings. Analysis showed that customers were making buying decisions, because they were given real-time explanations through the chat service.

The Four Seasons technology team also likes LiveWebAssist's capability to recognize returning website visitors. This feature helps an operator to resume a conversation from the same spot where it was ended or interrupted. That makes users spend, on average, seven to eight minutes on the site, a very high indicator.

In an approach radically different from other chat products, LiveWebAsisst supports the InLine no-flash chat architecture, eliminating pop-up windows. This design allows more visitors to initiate chat sessions, because they don't have to deal with pop-up blockers. It also assures usability for visitors using tablets like iPad or Android to access the site. Additionally, this option gives actionable information about the visitors' behavior. The operators can tell exactly where the user is on the site, so they can offer them immediate assistance, tell them where to go and answer questions with a high degree of relevancy.

Predicting Sales Patterns

LiveWebAssist's analytical capabilities helped the hotel to optimize its Internet marketing strategy. The property's marketing analysts are now able to locate sources the customers are coming from and what browser they are using. It's a very effective tool, especially when used in conjunction with Google analytics.

The Four Seasons' team found is the LiveWebAssist Knowledgebase a very practical tool to employ. At any point of the conversation, it allows operators to insert preapproved messages (such as terms and conditions, cancellation policy, etc.). Operators don't have to think about how to phrase these messages and URLs and graphics are added with a single click. In the near future, the Four Seasons is planning to extend the knowledge base with images and, possibly, videos.

Four Seasons is now expanding the LiveWebAssist functionality and considering using it on mobile devices. Another possibility is adding automated translation and integration with a new CRM system.

Immediate Returns

LiveWebAssist was showing compelling ROI from the day it was implemented. The colnumber of bookings that have been converted directly through LiveWebAssist, paid for the solution almost immediately.

Usually, hotel bookings for five+ star hotels are a very high-value item—usually $5,000–6,000 per transaction. There are many issues that potential customers should understand before they actually commit to book. Anything that can give a customer greater confidence and prompt him to make a decision to buy is very valuable. LiveWebAssist provides that for the Four Seasons.

Ten Steps to Simplify a Complex Distribution World

Cindy Estis Green

Adapted from *Distribution Channel Analysis: A Guide for Hotels, published by the HSMAI Foundation.* Written by Cindy Estis Green, CEO and co-founder at Kalibri Labs, an analytics firm that specializes in building tools that provide insights for hotels, hotel brands, and management companies on business acquisition and overall performance. She can be reached at cindy@kalibrilabs.com.

Content and user experience are key variables that can drive online consumers to one site over another. However, it is important to keep in mind that because travel shoppers visit so many sites and are touched by so many promotional contacts in the run-up to a booking, a presence on multiple sites and at multiple consumer touch points is likely to be appropriate. Following are ten points to keep in mind:

1. Compelling Content
   Make your content compelling and relevant, whether it is on your own website or syndicated to many other sites where you have a presence. Investing in great content is a highly effective differentiator given the colnumber of hotel websites from which a traveler can choose. Content is a form of merchandising and should be developed with that in mind. Look at sites like Roomkey.com, Trip Advisor or the Kayak search engine as examples of how a hotel's content can be distributed and "plugged in" to external sites where users want a range of options. The consumer books using the hotel booking engine, but may find a point of entry to this content on another site. Recognizing that any effort spent on content should take in account both the content on the hotel's website as well as what consumers may see elsewhere on the shopping path.
2. Great User Experience
   Make sure the user experience on your website and your booking engine is easy, enjoyable and/or efficient. The most important rule—make sure your website and booking engine allow your site visitors to accomplish what they came to do and continually evaluate this to make sure you get it right all the time. There are tools that are low cost or no cost that can be tapped to survey consumers and ask them about their experience. This feedback is essential to be sure your primary portal is functioning well for the users that depend on it for information and that it facilitates the booking process.
3. Know Your Customers
   Research the path your customers take on their way to a booking with you. Examine each step along that path for opportunities to have a meaningful presence that engages and builds the relationship, whether that is online or off-line. Some of this information can come from the analytics tool used to indicate the website visited before reaching

your site. Knowing where shoppers stop along the way and testing the use of your hotel content on some of these stops can yield better results for a hotel.

4. Build an Online Strategy
   Consumers can typically have 10–15 interactions with various sources of hotel information before they make a booking. The process is complex. Review your online strategy against the travel process to ensure you have considered actions at each step to create a bias among your customers and prospects to consider you. Look at each touchpoint and review a list of websites that serve that need for your consumers, then determine how you would like to present your hotel in these sites.
5. Create Bias for Your Preferred Channels
   You can't make travel shoppers choose one channel over another, but you can put out bread crumbs along their path that are so compelling that they will choose your route because it is appealing and helps them accomplish their goals better than the alternatives. This doesn't mean only using your own website. By collaborating with others, you can get travelers to choose sites in which you can deepen your relationship with them as you lead them to your booking engine. Some new sites may emerge that provide valuable content and help travel shoppers sort the many options they may have in any given destination; these sites will likely send the

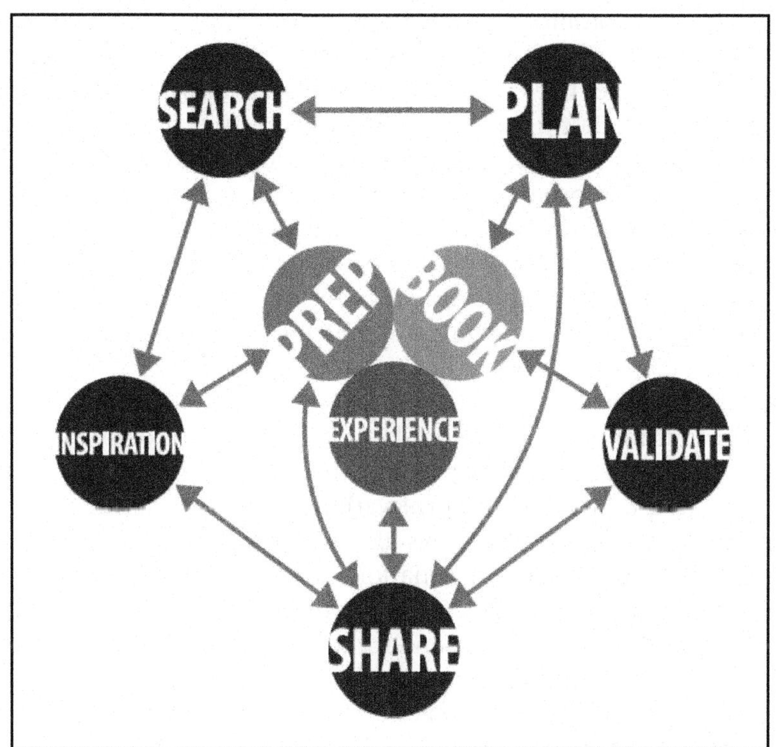

consumer to your booking engine, after providing some valuable guidance on their choices.

6. Get Social
   Consumers are all about social. Figure out a way to be there in appropriate ways. Master the social sites used by your consumers. Think of social sites as places to build relationships and if you sell or incorporate your booking engine into a social site, put it in a place that makes sense for the way the social site is naturally used. Keep an eye out for an evolution of hybrid sites that may include consumer reviews, other elements to allow social interaction, and offers. Social, seach and mobile are all merging into integrated platforms and consumers want an more interactive experience where they can ask questions and acquire dynamic and live content that is relevant to their own interests.
7. Test and Monitor
   Whatever you do online, you should track results in all places possible. If you partner with a website (social, transactional, or informational) to promote your hotel, be sure you can track the results from it, whether it is a booking or other form of interaction. If you decide to test a new option, try to remove other factors that would muddy the results.
8. Attribution Models
   Be sure to calculate promotional lift from all your marketing channels, not just the ones that are vocal about claiming credit for it. Likely every one, including promotional messages like email, banner or display ads, and some off-line campaigns are contributing to making the cash register ring. Many attribute credit for bookings to either the last place the hotel shopper visited before coming to your site (last click attribution) or to the first place a consumer entered in their shopping expedition. However, this is unlikely the case given the colnumber of places a consumer may look on their shopping path. Look hard at the data to be sure you can quantify what each channel brings in terms of benefit from an added presence and test many sites until you figure out which ones get you the bookings at the lowest overall cost.
9. Distinguish Yourself
   It is helpful to think about how your brand (independent or chain) differs from the others. Hotel brands have a tendency to look very similar in their content and messaging. It is hard to cut a unique swath from that cloth; this has been most successfully done in regional settings like boutique brands in major metro areas or in resorts. On a national or international basis, there is a tendency to dilute a brand's uniqueness with messages that resonate with so many consumer profiles that they fail to distinguish the brand for any particular customer cohort. Ensure that your content and interaction sets you apart with the audience that matters most to you in your market; your market is all that matters to the consumer when they are booking into your destination.

10. Seek Sustainable Profit

As much as every hotel would love the simplicity of one-step promotions that deliver immediate revenue, few consumers buy without having some kind of relationship first, an outcome that usually requires multiple interactions. Focus on engagement. A customer that does not refer others or return is worth far less than those who do. Spend your time and money on those who will refer or repeat. If you allocate resources in terms of acquisition, persuasion, and retention, remind your team that if you are spending too much time on the first two steps, you may find yourself cycling through too many customers and chasing your tail. Focus your resources on the channels that contribute the most profit and have long-term potential.

References

1. Merrick, B. (1989). *Property management systems: A guide to implementation and staff planning* (p. 12). Madison, WI: Magna Publications, Inc.
2. Berkus, D. (1999). Next Generation Lodging Products. *The Horner Technology Report.* pp. 19–20.
3. Brewer, P., Junsun, K., Schrier, T., & Farrish, J. (2008, May). *Current and Future Technology Use in the Hospitality Industry Report.* Washington, DC: American Hotel and Lodging Association.
4. Oliva, R. (2002, September). Today's customer relationship management strategies demand high-tech systems. *Hotels Magazine,* p.1.
5. Chief Marketing Officer Council. (2010). *The leaders in loyalty: Feeling the love from the loyal clubs.* Palto, CA: Author.
6. Day, R. Hotel concierges: Capitalizing on the mobile web. *Hotel Business Review.* Retrieved October 19, 2012, from http://hotelexecutive.com/business_review/3041/hotel-concierges- capitalizing-on-the-mobile-web.
7. Buckhiester, B. (2011, May). Revenue management: Social media's impact. *Hotel NewsNow.com.* Retrieved October 14, 2012, from http://www.hotelnewsnow.com/articles.aspx/5550/Revenue-management-Social-medias-impact.
8. Kirby, A. (2009). Hotels get app happy: Mobile downloads are the new frontier for Online Booking. *Hotels.* Retrieved October 24, 2012, from http://www.hotelsmag.com/article/CA6686816.html?industryid=47565.
9. Koushik, D., Higbie, J., & Esiter, C. (2012). Retail price optimization at intercontinental hotel group. *Interfaces, 42*(1): 45–57.
10. Berkus, D. (1988, June/July). The Yield Management Revolution. IAHA: Bottomline. pp. 13–15.
11. Adams, W. (1995, April). Hotel Yield Management - New Tool Brings New Opportunities. *Horner Technology Report.* p. 11.
12. Lodging Interactive. (2012). Destination visibility: How hotels & resorts market online. *White Paper.* Parsippany, NJ: Author.

CHAPTER 5

Accounting Information Systems

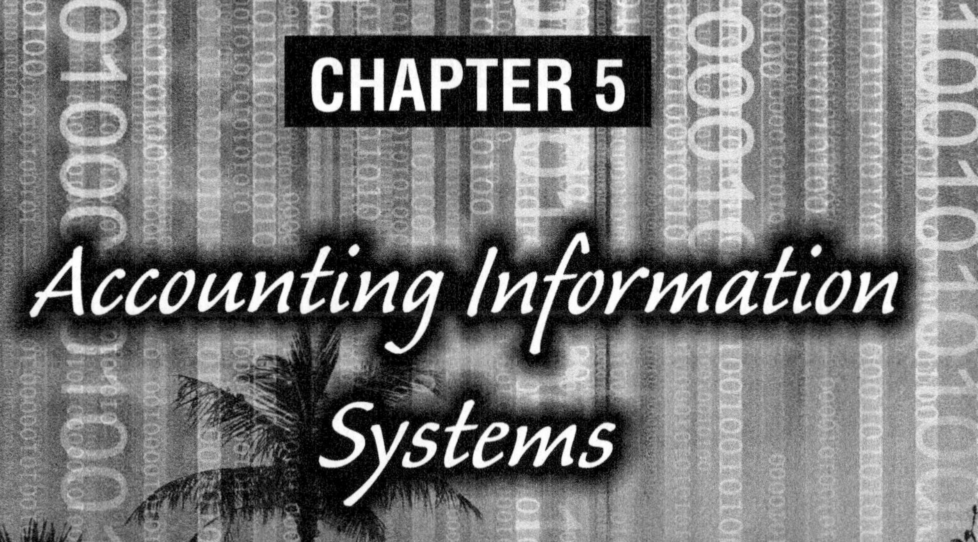

"Accounting is the language of business, and you have to learn it like a language. You can't be comfortable in the country if you aren't comfortable with the language. To be successful at business, you have to understand the underlying financial values of the business."

Warren Buffett

CHAPTER OUTLINE

INTRODUCTION

Accounting is several centuries old. Luca Paciolo, an Italian mathematician and Franciscan Friar, developed the double-entry accounting system (debits and credits) in 1494, which revolutionized business and earned him the title, "Father of Accounting." Accounting is a discipline of which all hospitality graduates, regardless of job position, should have knowledge. For example, hotel front desk supervisors use accounting skills for balancing cash accounts and ensuring that charges and payments are appropriately posted to guest accounts. General managers use past and current accounting statements to judge the success of their businesses. While managing and interpreting accounting transactions and information may not be as fun as creating new menu items or talking to customers, these skills are crucial to business success and cannot be overlooked.

Manual accounting systems (paper ledgers and journals) are error prone, labor intensive, and tedious. A transaction typically requires several manual entries. Computers have made accounting tasks easier, faster, and more accurate. The computer posts all entries correlated with a transaction. It also enables records to be found more quickly (e.g., outstanding invoices) and automatic document production (e.g., pay bills, create purchase orders, etc.).

The application of information technology to an accounting system creates an **ACCOUNTING INFORMATION SYSTEM (AIS)**, a computerized system for recording accounting transactions and information (1). Once data is entered into an AIS, it be can be used and reused in generating timely, summarized, and relevant reports that support decision making in areas such as performance evaluations, resource allocations, and borrowing.

The configuration, scope, and capabilities of an AIS primarily depends on the type and size of the hospitality organization (e.g., 1000-room, full service resort), the ownership/affiliation (e.g., corporate, independent, franchisee, management contract, etc.), the information needs of management (e.g., cash flow statement), and the regulatory requirements (e.g., income and payroll taxes). Most independent restaurant owners, for example, use Quickbooks accounting software because it is inexpensive and easy to use and navigate, has integrated help screens, and meets their information and reporting requirements (2). Many of them lack formal accounting training, like most small business owners. M3 Accounting Services has become the market leader in hotel accounting software by providing a feature-rich, cloud-based solution that eliminates up-front investments, upgrades, and system maintenance. Hospitality Specialists, a hotel management company overseeing 13 hotels, provides centralized accounting services using M3 accounting software. This results in lower administrative costs and fewer onsite accounting tasks, which may all be assigned to the general manager at a limited service hotel. Do not be surprised if a hotel general manager's job description includes accounts payable tasks, such as scanning, coding, and approving of invoices. Yet one more reason why hospitality graduates should become more adept at hospitality accounting and related business functions and processes.

The Accounting Function Important

The best way to think about accounting and reporting is like driving a car. You look at the gauges on the dashboard to determine how you are doing and adjust from what you see depending on how fast you want to go, how far, how much fuel you have. In your car you have warning lights that go off in advance of an emergency so you can take care of a problem before it occurs. Accounting and reporting functions serve as a road map to help you get where you want to go. There are far too many operators who end up closing their doors because they did not identify a problem before it was too late.

EMILY DURHAM,
"HOW TO DETERMINE THE BEST WAY TO MANAGE YOUR RESTAURANT'S ACCOUNTING FUNCTION," RESTAURANTOWNER.COM, 2012

Accounting Information System

The purpose of an **AIS** is to record all financial transactions that occur with customers, suppliers, employees, and financial institutions. It helps in managing cash flow, collecting monies owed by customers, controlling and tracking expenditures, evaluating financial status, and tracking monies owed to creditors.

This section focuses on four accounting modules found in most hospitality AISs: general ledger, accounts receivable, payroll, and accounts payable (see Chapter 3 for a discussion on inventory control and purchasing and Chapter 4 for a discussion of the PMS night audit).

General Ledger

General Ledger. The general ledger is the principal ledger. It contains all of the balance sheet and income statement accounts. Accounts receivable, payroll, and accounts payable are considered subsidiary ledgers because their end-of-the-month totals are posted to the general ledger. If the accounting system is fully integrated, subsidiary and daily report totals are posted automatically to the general ledger (see Figure 5-1 for an example of a daily

DAILY REPORT GENERAL LEDGER ENTRIES

		Beg. Balance	Today	Ending Bal.	G.L. Acct. #
Room Revenue	-				4010
Dockage	-				4051
Water	-				4052
Ice	-				4053
Food Wharf	-				4015
Food Harbour	-				4020
Island Bar	-				4030
Harb. Lounge	-				4040
Food Function	-				4015
Beverage Func.	-				4030
Gas	-				4046
Oil	-				4047
Diesel	-				4046
Tournament	-				4070
Telephone	-				4074
Gift Shop	-				4072
Rentals	-				4073
Membership	-				4071
Miscellaneous	-				4072
Room Tax	-				2090
Bed Tax	-				2100
TOTAL REVENUE AND TAX	-				* PROOF 1
Cash	+				1030
Checks	+				1033
TOTAL CASH	+				* PROOF 2
Paid out Exp.	+				9580
Comm. Expense	+				9800
Credit Card E.	+				9480
TOTAL EXPENSES	+				*PROOF 3
Guest Ledger	+/-				1080
City Ledger	+/-				1070
Advance Pay	+/-				1090
NET MOVEMENT	+/-				*PROOF 4

TOTAL PLUSES AND MINUSES. SHOULD EQUAL ZERO WHEN IN BALANCE.

FIGURE 5-1. DAILY REPORT FOR HOTEL WITH MARINA.

report document used to manually update the general ledger). The following paragraphs discuss the mechanics involved in constructing and operating a general ledger system.

Create Chart of Accounts

Step 1. Create chart of accounts. The first step in setting up the general ledger is to create the **chart of accounts** (see Figure 5-2). This is a listing of all balance sheet and income accounts. Each one is assigned a number classifying it as an asset, liability, equity, sales/income, or expense. Account numbers can range from 3 to 16 digits, depending on the general ledger software and the operation's numbering preference. The number of

CHART OF ACCOUNTS
**** THE XYZ HOTEL ****

ACCOUNT NUMBER	DESCRIPTION	TYPE
1000	ASSETS	TITLE
1010	CURRENT ASSETS	SUB-TITLE
1020	House Banks	ASSET
1030	Deposits	ASSET
1035	Time Deposits/Cert. Deposit	ASSET
1040	Accounts Rec. Guest Ledger	ASSET
1050	Acc. Rec. City Ledger	ASSET
1060	Allowance for Doubt. Acct.	ASSET
1070	Inventories	ASSET
1080	Prepaid Expenses	ASSET
1090	Other Current Assets	ASSET
1100	PROPERTY AND EQUIPMENT	SUB-TITLE
1100	Land	ASSET
1120	Buildings	ASSET
1130	Furniture and Equipment	ASSET
1140	less: Accum. Depreciation	ASSET
1200	OTHER ASSETS	SUB-TITLE
1210	Security Deposits	ASSET
1220	Deferred Expenses	ASSET
2000	LIABILITIES	TITLE
2010	CURRENT LIABILITIES	SUB-TITLE
2020	Accounts Payable	LIABILITY
2030	Accrued liabilities	LIABILITY
2040	State W/H Tax Payable	LIABILITY
2050	Fed W/H Tax Payable	LIABILITY
2060	Sales Tax Payable	LIABILITY
2070	Notes Payable	LIABILITY
2080	Current Mat. on L.T. Debt	LIABILITY
2100	LONG TERM DEBT	SUB-TITLE
2110	Long Term Debt	LIABILITY
2120	less: Current Portion L.T.D.	LIABILITY
3000	EQUITY	TITLE
3010	Retained Earnings	EQUITY
3020	Draw	EQUITY
4000	SALES	INCOME
4010	ROOM SALES	SUB-TITLE
4020	Room Revenue	INCOME
4030	Extra Room Revenue	INCOME
4040	FOOD AND BEVERAGE SALES	INCOME
4060	Food Sales	INCOME
4070	Beverage Sales	INCOME

FIGURE 5-2. A PARTIAL CHART OF ACCOUNTS LISTING.

accounts, however, primarily depends on the organization's size and the level of detail required in financial statements. In the following account numbering scheme, the first digit indicates the account type.

First: Assets = 1000 (e.g., House Banks 1020)
Second: Liabilities = 2000 (e.g., Accounts Payable 2020)
Third: Equity = 3000 (e.g., XYZ Equity 3080)
Fourth: Sales/Income = 4000 (e.g., Food Sales 4060)
Fifth: Expenses = 5000 (e.g., Wages 5040)

Because account numbers cannot be deleted without a zero balance, it is important to provide sufficient space between account numbers to allow for the insertion of new accounts.

The **Uniform System of Accounts**, devised for hotels, motels, resorts, restaurants, and clubs, is a helpful reference when creating the chart of accounts as it provides a standardized system for classifying, organizing, and presenting financial information. Since it is widely used, uniformity in the reporting of financial data allows hospitality operations to gauge their performance as compared to others.

Posting Transactions

Step 2. Posting transactions. The account number is used for posting to the general ledger. Typically, a debit is posted as a "plus" and a credit as a "minus" as shown below.

4210 = -100.00 (vending machine sales)
1030 = +100.00 (cash)

Since accounting is not a popular college subject, a posting guide is listed in Figure 5-3 for a brief refresher.

Account Type	Increase	Decrease
Assets	Debit +	Credit -
Liabilities	Credit -	Debit +
Equity	Credit -	Debit +
Sales/Income	Credit -	Debit +
Expenses	Debit +	Credit -

FIGURE 5-3. POSTING GUIDE.

Technology Tidbits

The author, before installing an accounting system for a high volume, independent restaurant, read that it had over a 50 percent food cost in a trade journal. When installing the system, the author discovered that equipment and utensil purchases were being posted as a food expense.

There are three types of general ledger entries:

- **Manual entries** can be reviewed, added, deleted, or changed before updating the general ledger. Most systems do not allow the posting of out-of-balance entries.
- **Standard entries** are created for the automatic posting of recurring monthly entries such as depreciation and amortization.
- **Interface entries** are automatic postings from the subsidiary modules.

Print a Trial Balance

Step 3. Print a trial balance. Performing a trial balance manually is an error-prone task that may take days or weeks to complete. In an automated system, a trial balance can be produced in minutes showing each account's beginning balance, transactions posted to each account during the current month, and each account's ending balance. It also automatically totals debits and credits to determine whether the system is in balance.

A trial balance does not, however, indicate whether the right amounts were posted to the correct accounts. For example, this author was hired by a private country club as a consultant to discover why its food and beverage cost percentages (cost/sales) were so high. The club's board of directors were blaming the problem on employee theft and poor cost control. The culprit was actually the club controller. Because he wanted to get rid of the general manager, he altered general ledger account entries to inflate food and beverage costs.

Print Financial Reports

Step 4. Print financial reports. In the general ledger module, a variety of financial reports with budgets, comparatives, and variances can be generated at any time, including custom-designed reports. Detailed or consolidated financial reports can be generated by department, property, or company for specific time frames (e.g., week, month, quarter, and year-to-date). These reports paint a picture of the transactions that flow through a hospitality business. Each transaction (e.g., room or meal sold), for example, contributes to the whole picture.

The following reports are commonly found in general ledger modules.

- A **balance sheet** summarizes assets, liabilities, and equity accounts (Assets = Liabilities + Equity). This shows the operation's financial condition on the last day of the accounting period and indicates whether the company has sufficient liquidity to pay its bills promptly.
- An **income statement** shows income and expenses incurred during a certain interval of time (Income – Expenses = Profit: Increase in Equity or Loss: Decrease in Equity). An income statement indicates how effectively management has optimized profit.
- A **comparative balance sheet or income statement** compares the current account balances to a previous period to highlight significant changes that have taken place. Account balances are expressed as a dollar figure and/or as a percentage of total assets for balance sheet accounts and total revenue for income statement accounts.

Comparative Income Statement Example				
	Current Period	% Of Sales	Period Last Year	% Of Sales
Labor Cost	$50,000	36	$45,000	33

Income statement comparisons also include actual versus budget and actual versus previous period versus budget. According to financial consultant David White, CPA (3):

Almost all of us regularly see and produce reports showing current period, budget, and prior period information... Although these presentations do give the "big picture" in terms of the numbers, we are usually so familiar with them that we gloss over critical relationships or focus on what upper management thinks are the most critical issues. There may very well be other relationships that, individually or collectively, have a greater impact on the business than those initially considered.

For example, your hotel's year-to-date food and beverage department operating results are below expectations. Upper management, focusing on comparative financial data, feels that the decline in profitability is a function of occupancy. Your analysis of nonfinancial data, on the other hand, indicates that occupancy is only part of the reason for the decline. While the total number of food covers is reasonable given the achieved occupancy levels and market segmentation is unchanged, the number of food covers by meal period is shifting. This might indicate that menu content or pricing needs revision, or that you need to refocus your catering sales efforts.

Information presented in graphic form brings financial data to life and illuminates facts that would otherwise be lost in a maze of seemingly unconnected numbers. Graphs can be used to illustrate financial statements, relationships, and trends. The charts used most often for communicating financial statistics include line, bar, pie, and bubble charts (see Figure 5-4). According to Edward Tufts, a professor of political science at Yale University, "Statistical graphics are the only place where art and science come together in a meaningful way."

Close out the Period

Step 5. Close out the period. The final step in the accounting process is to close out the period. By doing this all of the dollar totals for the period selected are zeroed out and transferred into historical files (e.g., quarter-to-date and year-to-date).

Technology Tidbits

A New York-based finance firm uses a program to boost its rate of collection from tardy customers. Using a variety of scientific data, the program informs the user of the most effective collection approach for a particular customer such as a phone call or sending out another bill.

FIGURE 5-4. EXAMPLE OF A BUSINESS INTELLIGENCE LINE GRAPH.

Source: M3 Acconting Services, Gainesville, GA.

Accounts Receivable

Accounts Receivable. The purpose of the accounts receivable or city ledger system is to improve cash flow by assisting in the timely collection of monies owed by customers. The following paragraphs discuss the mechanics involved in constructing and operating an accounts receivable system.

Create Customer Accounts

Step 1. Create customer accounts. Each customer account is assigned a number. Customer account information typically includes name, contact person, individual or business address, telephone number and extension, credit limit, account type (e.g., credit card, corporate, transient), tax exempt status, last payment, account balance information, sales and credit history, etc. The front office system may also automatically establish temporary city ledger accounts for any "skips" or "late charges" billed.

Create Invoices

Step 2. Create invoices. Invoices are created and printed for customers whenever needed. An invoice is a detailed list of goods and services provided, together with charges and terms.

Post Transactions and Maintain Account Balances

Step 3. Post transactions and maintain account balances. Revenue charges (plus tax and tip), payments, credit and debit memos, and finance charges are posted to customer accounts. When entering a revenue charge, the amount is distributed to a general ledger account number such as $500 to restaurant revenue (e.g., 4060) and $500 to room revenue (e.g., 4020). Payments are applied to a particular invoice or against the total account balance.

Print Reports

Step 4. Print reports. The following reports are commonly found in accounts receivable modules.

An **aging receivables report** (see Figure 5-5) displays the balance due for each customer and the age of each outstanding bill (e.g., 30 days, 60 days, 90 days, and 120 days old) based on its invoice or due date. Knowing this information enables an operation to stay on top of its receivables before they become old and difficult to collect.

- **Customer Statements** can be produced at any time showing both the previous and ending balances, the itemized and disputed charges, the debit and credit memos issued, the payments received, and the interest on late charges. Dunning letters (reminders and past due notices) may also be sent to customers with delinquent payments. Dunning letters and regularly issued statements help in collections.
- The **Sales Journal** shows all the transactions and the general ledger distributions entered during the accounting period.
- A **Cash Receipt Journal** shows payments received.

Close out the Period

Step 5. Close out the period. At the end of the accounting period, account information is automatically transferred to the general ledger in an integrated accounting system.

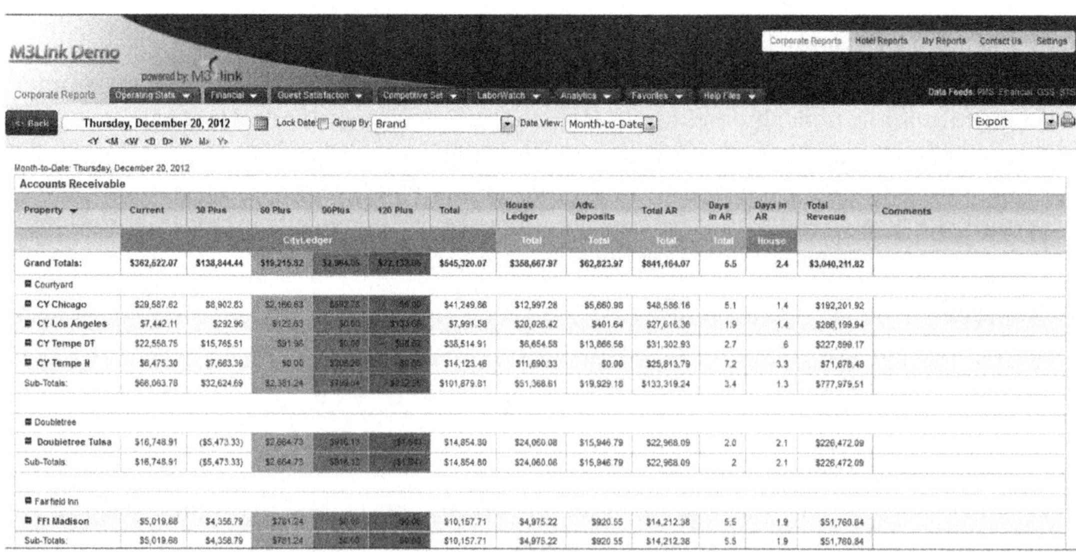

Month-to-Date: Thursday, December 20, 2012

Accounts Receivable

Property	Current	30 Plus	60 Plus	90Plus	120 Plus	Total	House Ledger	Adv. Deposits	Total AR	Days in AR	Days in AR	Total Revenue	Comments
	CityLedger						Total	Total	Total	Total	House		
Grand Totals:	$362,622.07	$138,844.44	$19,215.82	[illegible]	[illegible]	$545,320.07	$358,667.97	$62,823.97	$841,164.07	5.5	2.4	$3,040,211.82	
Courtyard													
CY Chicago	$29,587.62	$8,902.83	$2,166.63	[illegible]	[illegible]	$41,249.86	$12,997.28	$5,660.98	$48,586.16	5.1	1.4	$192,201.92	
CY Los Angeles	$7,442.11	$292.96	$122.63	$0.00	[illegible]	$7,991.58	$20,026.42	$401.64	$27,616.36	1.9	1.4	$286,199.94	
CY Tempe DT	$22,558.75	$15,765.51	$91.96	$0.00	[illegible]	$38,514.91	$6,654.58	$13,866.56	$31,302.93	2.7	6	$227,899.17	
CY Tempe N	$6,475.30	$7,663.39	$0.00	[illegible]	[illegible]	$14,123.46	$11,690.33	$0.00	$25,813.79	7.2	3.3	$71,678.48	
Sub-Totals:	$66,063.78	$32,624.69	$2,381.24	[illegible]	[illegible]	$101,879.81	$51,368.61	$19,929.18	$133,319.24	3.4	1.3	$777,979.51	
Doubletree													
Doubletree Tulsa	$16,748.91	($5,473.33)	$2,664.73	[illegible]	[illegible]	$14,854.80	$24,060.08	$15,946.79	$22,968.09	2.0	2.1	$226,472.09	
Sub-Totals	$16,748.91	($5,473.33)	[illegible]	[illegible]	[illegible]	$14,854.80	$24,060.08	$15,946.79	$22,968.09	2	2.1	$226,472.09	
Fairfield Inn													
FFI Madison	$5,019.68	$4,356.79	$781.24	[illegible]	[illegible]	$10,157.71	$4,975.22	$920.55	$14,212.38	5.5	1.9	$51,760.84	
Sub-Totals:	$5,019.68	$4,356.79	$781.24	[illegible]	[illegible]	$10,157.71	$4,975.22	$920.55	$14,212.38	5.5	1.9	$51,760.84	

FIGURE 5-5. AGING ACCOUNTS RECEIVABLE REPORT.

Source: M3 Accounting Services, Gainsville,GA.

Payroll

Payroll. A payroll module saves time by performing payroll calculations, by distributing payroll expenses among departments, and by printing checks, W-2s, 1099s, payroll and deduction registers, and quarterly tax reports. The following paragraphs discuss the mechanics involved in constructing and operating a payroll system.

Create Employee Information File

Step 1. Create employee information file. This file contains information required to calculate wages and taxes and to maintain accurate payroll records, each of which contains data about a particular employee such as name, address, social security number, wage rate, salary history, vacation and sick pay, deductions, and department. Hospitality operations cross utilizing employees require payroll systems allowing employees to be assigned multiple wage rates.

Enter and Process Employee Hours and Print Checks

Step 2. Enter and process employee hours and print checks. The payroll module provides for the entry of regular hours, overtime hours, sales, tips, and commissions. It also performs all calculations from gross to net pay. Checks are automatically printed with a check stub containing period and year-to-date totals or directly deposited into employee bank accounts. Many hospitality companies enable employees to access pay statements online, which typically include the same pay information on printed check stubs.

Payroll systems for food service operations must comply with wage and hour laws as well as the 1983 federal law concerning tax on tipped employees. The payroll system should automatically pay the minimum wage (e.g., $7.25) to employees who fail to report sufficient tips. Federal law requires the reporting of allocated tips (8 percent of server sales) on W-2 forms. Many restaurateurs expose themselves to significant liability when they do not comply with tip-credit regulations. Mario Batali, a well-known Chef and Restaurateur, settled a class action lawsuit ($5.25 million) for the mishandling of employee tips. It is important to remember that a tip is the sole property of the tipped employee and an employer may not use an employee's tips for any reason except as a credit against minimum wage. Tip allocation information, as shown in the following example, may also appear on the server's check stub.

The federal minimum wage rate is $2.13 for tipped employees, which is used in the above example. However, states are free to enact minimum wage laws that provide a higher rate mandated by federal law. In Iowa, for example, tipped employees are guaranteed at least $4.35 per hour. The $4.35 minimum wage for tipped employees plus the tips must equal the standard $7.25 per hour minimum wage, or the employer has to make up the difference by paying the tipped employee additional wages sufficient to equal $7.25 an hour.

	Current	Year-to-Date
Adj. Gross	173.68	1,313.56
Tips	240.00	680.60
Total Gross	413.68	1,994.16
Taxes	92.92	365.57
Deductions	20.78	179.56
Tips	240.00	680.60
Net Pay	59.98	768.43
Reg Hours	40.00	375.00
Ovt Hours	12.00	37.00
Sales	2,100.00	5,557.80
Allocation	–72.00	–235.98

More and more hospitality organizations are using outside payroll vendors (e.g., CompuPay) because they have the expertise and resources to complete payroll accurately, on time, and at a lower cost. In the high turnover hospitality industry, ensuring that new employees are added properly and old employees are deactivated requires constant attention. Payroll also comes with a thicket of IRS rules and regulations. According to the IRS, 40 percent of small businesses pay an average penalty of $845 per year for late or incorrect filings and payments. Most national payroll services provide a guarantee that customers will incur no penalties.

Hourly information is collected from worksheets filled out by supervisors or from a **TIME AND ATTENDANCE TERMINAL**, which automates the process of collecting, calculating, and reporting employees' time and attendance data and automatically transfers it to the payroll system when the two systems are interfaced. Time and attendance systems use various security measures to prevent unauthorized punch-ins such as password security, biometrics (e.g., face, finger, and hand reader, iris scanner, and voice verification), and RFID badges. Additional benefits include fewer paycheck challenges and the elimination of early punch-ins, of late punch-outs, of calculation errors, and of variances in the rounding of time.

A **TIME AND ATTENDANCE MOBILE SMART PHONE APPLICATION** helps managers and employees to communicate more effectively and efficiently from any location. Managers can use this application for approving employee time cards and scheduling requests, reviewing labor costs, checking posted schedules, managing late staff, and requesting shift coverage if there are call-ins. Managers can also receive alerts when employees are due for a break or approaching overtime. Employees can user their version of the application for viewing

Variable Staffing System

A variable staffing system (VSS) can allocate available labor resources according to work requirements. Allowing for employees' preferences and availability, a VSS results in improved morale, reduced training and turnover expenses, and maximum flexibility in the utilization of a hospitality firm's greatest asset—its people.

The system automatically figures out the number of hours required and how the hours should be distributed, saving valuable supervisory time. Short-term variables such as vacations, sick leave, flextime, and personal days off are all considered when using the scheduling module.

The opportunity for employee input and lack of bias in the schedule address two of the most important factors—worker empathy and management efficiency.

Scheduling can be run with such items as wage costs, seniority, proficiency, or availability as either primary or selectively weighted criteria. A VSS can exchange information with a payroll or time and attendance system and it can generate a series of management reports formatted by day, task, union contract, or other selected source.

The key to controlling labor is the development of a good forecasting system. Without it, controlling labor costs and maintaining service requirements is impossible.

A VSS system can use nonstatistical pattern technology to forecast workloads (e.g., covers, rooms, check-ins, check-outs, phone calls). By using all the conditions and variables affecting a particular business, such as weather, promotions, holidays, special events, etc., complex patterns are automatically created containing the same knowledge it would take the human forecaster months and years to gain. This tool gives managers the ability to forecast quickly and accurately.

work schedules, submitting time punches and time off requests, and swapping, dropping, or accepting shifts.

Time and attendance data can also be transferred to a labor management system to help managers analyze payroll hours and costs. Labor is often the largest operating expense, which is why work production standards must be formulated and labor productivity monitored for every facet of the business. For example, the work standard for a room attendant might be 17 minutes for a stay over and 30 minutes for a checkout. Consequently, the labor management system would determine the number of room attendants needed for a particular day based on the work standard and the forecasted room attendant work volume (checkouts and stay overs). It would then generate a report evaluating labor efficiency by comparing the target or scheduled hours (ideal staffing) to the actual hours worked for a particular time period. The weekly labor productivity report in Figure 5-6 reveals the actual work hours exceeded the target labor hours resulting in an unfavorable variance. There are a number of factors which can impede labor productivity, such as inaccurate forecasts, poor training and hiring practices, ill-conceived policies and procedures, inadequate equipment, tools, and supplies, and inefficient layouts (e.g., dining room and kitchen). For example, room attendant productivity is hindered if vacuum cleaners are shared.

Position	Actual Hours	Target Hours	Variance Hours	Variance %	Variance $	Cover/Meal Forecast FCST ACTL	Hours per Cover
Server	469.5	449.0	20.5	4.6	143.50	4102 4084	.115

FIGURE 5-6. WEEKLY LABOR PRODUCTIVITY REPORT FOR RESTAURANT SERVERS.

According to Brian Sill, principal of WA-based Deterministics, consultants to foodservice on technology-based systems:Now, thanks to amazing reductions in the cost of raw computing power, we can expect to see new management systems that provide an instantaneous and highly descriptive panorama of daily operations.

Many of these systems will critique management's performance in graphic form to provide a more compelling picture of actual operations. For example, rather than calculating a daily labor cost figure to measure the effectiveness of labor scheduling, the dining room manager may receive a graphic report of labor staffing at the end of each shift [see Figure 5-7]. The report can include both an actual account of that shift's labor use and an 'ideal' account, from which the manager can make comparisons. Given the 'time stamp' capability of the point-of-sale device, the number of guests can be recorded by the minute to reflect, when measured against a server standard, the ideal server staffing based on the actual guest traffic pattern for that day (4).

Print Payroll Reports

Step 3. Print payroll reports. The following reports are commonly found in payroll modules:

A **CHECK REGISTER** details all earnings and deductions by employees.

A **941 QUARTERLY REPORT** is required by the federal government to report tax contributions. Payroll systems also produce state quarterly tax reports.

A **HISTORICAL SUMMARY REPORT** contains quarter-to-date and year-to-date tax accumulations for each employee and must be filed with the 941 report.

A **LABOR COST ANALYSIS REPORT** compares labor hours, dollars, and statistics (e.g., average time spent per cover, room, check-in) to historical and ideal performance. This information can be broken down by department and job position.

Close out the Period

Step 4. Close out the period. At the end of the accounting period, payroll distribution totals are automatically transferred to the general ledger in an integrated accounting system.

Accounts Payable

Accounts Payable. The purpose of an accounts payable module is to:

- Provide information on what the operation owes to creditors to take advantage of discounts and to prevent double payments.

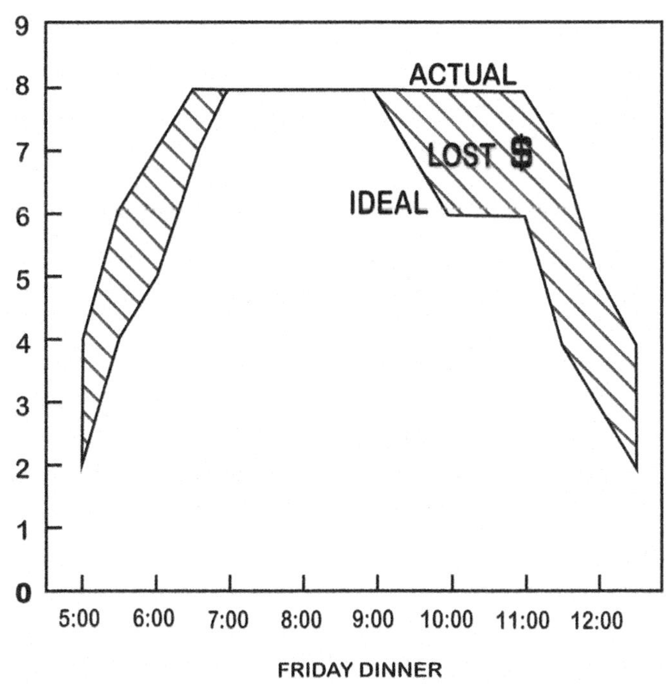

FIGURE 5-7. GRAPHIC REPORT OF STAFFING EFFICIENCY.

Source: Deterministics, Kirkland, WA.

- Facilitate timely payments to vendors to maintain an excellent credit rating and to prevent the interruption of supplies.
- Assign general ledger account numbers to invoices for classifying and controlling expenses.

The following paragraphs discuss the mechanics involved in constructing and operating an accounts payable system.

Create Vendor File

Step 1. Create vendor file. This file contains a record for each vendor and typically includes the name, address, telephone number, contact person, account type (e.g., food supplier, office supplier), current balance, and year-to-date purchases.

Post Invoices

Step 2. Post invoices. Information about each invoice is kept in an invoice file and typically includes the description, invoice number and date, payment due date, invoice amount, discount terms (e.g., 1/10 net 30 days), and general ledger account numbers for purchases on the invoice. For example, a $1000 invoice has $500 distributed to china, glassware, and silver (5050) and $500 distributed to operating supplies (5110). The general ledger distribution amounts must equal the invoice amount to complete the transaction.

Approve Invoices for Payment

Step 3. Approve invoices for payment. Invoices can be individually approved by the user or automatically approved based on such things as their due date and discount date. Approval for payment, however, is only tentative until checks are printed. Two reports that can be printed at any time to assist in invoice approval are the following:

- **Cash requirements report.** This report lists items selected for payment and denotes the cash requirement for the bank account upon which the checks will be drawn.
- **Aging payables report.** This report lists all open invoices (in voices not paid) and places them into aging columns (e.g., 30, 60, 90, and 120 days old) according to their invoice date. This enables delinquent bills to be spotted quickly and helps to prioritize invoice approvals when cash is tight. A separate column or report may also list open invoices eligible for a prompt-pay discount.

Print Checks and Check Register

Step 4. Print checks and check register. Checks are automatically printed with a list of paid invoices itemized on a check stub or voucher. Paid invoices are erased from the invoice file to prevent the possibility of double payment. Invoices are reinstated when checks are voided or cancelled.

The accounts payable system also processes handwritten checks and automatically prints travel agent checks and accounts receivable refunds when it is interfaced to the front office system. A record of all checks, including handwritten and voided, is printed on a **check register**. The accounts payable module may also provide a **check reconciliation** system to track cleared and outstanding checks.

A Global luxury hotel and resort chain streamlined their accounts payable process by replacing paper check disbursements with an automated electronic payment and reconciliation process. This reduced costs, increased security, and provided a more efficient workflow.

Print Reports

Step 5. Print reports. The following reports are commonly found in the accounts payable module:

A **vendor activity report** lists month-to-date and year-to-date purchases from each vendor. For larger organizations, this information can be used to evaluate vendors and to negotiate discounts.

A **purchase journal** lists each invoice entered, the general ledger distribution for each invoice, and the general ledger account totals used for posting to the general ledger.

Close out the Period

Step 6. Close out the period. At the end of the accounting period, account totals are automatically transferred to the general ledger in an integrated accounting system.

Information Technology Auditing and Internal Control

Information technoloy auditing assesses the computer's role in ensuring that data and information are reliable, confidential, secure, and available as needed. **Auditing**, the verification of transactions, records, accounts, and financial statements, requires the establishment of internal controls. **Internal controls** are the methods, procedures, and systems put into place to promote organizational efficiency and adherence to company policies or values. They also safeguard against fraud or unauthorized use or theft of a company's assets. Internal controls are affected by an organization's structure, work and authority flows, people, and auditing methodologies and software tools. There are two types of controls:

- *Preventative Controls*. These are designed to discourage errors or irregularities from occurring (e.g., all cash register voids performed by a supervisor).
- *Detective Controls*. These are designed to find errors or irregularities after they have occurred (e.g., reviewing departmental phone bills for personal calls).

An internal control system consists of five components: control environment, risk assessment, control activities, information and communication, and monitoring (5). Each of these is addressed in the following paragraphs using a restaurant point-of-sale (POS) system as an example for the discussion.

Control Environment

Control Environment. This establishes the tone of a company and lays the foundation for all the other internal components.

Factors that affect a company's control environment are: (a) the integrity, ethical values, and competence of the company's personnel, (b) management's philosophy and operating style, (c) management's assignment of authority and responsibility, (d) procedures for the hiring and training of personnel, and (e) oversight by the board of directors. Not using built-in POS system security features (e.g., void authorization), for example, weakens the control environment.

Risk Assessment

Risk Assessment. This involves identifying, analyzing, and managing those risks that pose a threat to the achievement of the organization's objectives. A general rule is: The more liquid an asset, the greater risk of its misappropriation.

Cash is among the assets stolen frequently from hospitality employers (6). Laube maintains that solid cash controls are imperative for restaurants and to never underestimate the lure of quick (illegal) cash and the length that some employees will go to get it (7). POS functions such as reprinting a check, removing items or orders, splitting checks, comping, and discounting can all be used by employees for pocketing cash. According to Lavery, Lindberg, and Razaki, 5 percent of employees commit fraud in any situation, 10 percent do not commit fraud regardless of circumstances, and the remaining 85 percent consider committing fraud only if not getting caught or suffering little or no repercussions if caught are possibilities (8).

The National Restaurant Association (NRA) reported that the cost of employee theft for its members totaled over $8.5 billion in 2007 or 4 percent of food sales. An older NRA study estimated the annual average theft per employee at $218 per employee (9). These are significant statistics because a restaurant's pretax profit margin typically ranges between 2 and 6 percent (10).

Control Actvities

Control Activities. These are the policies and procedures that management puts into place to address the risks identified during the risk assessment process. Examples of control activities include segregation of duties, approvals, authorizations, reconciliations, and verifications (see the following scam counteractive measures for illustrations).

The following describes cash scams noted in recent cases and the book, "How to Burn the House Down: The Infamous Waiter and Bartender's Scam Bible" by Two Bourbon Street Waiters, and examples of corresponding counteractive control activities or measures recommend by Radiant Systems for the Aloha restaurant POS system (11, 12, and 13):

- **Scam 1:** A server reprints the same check throughout a shift and uses it repeatedly for different cash-paying customers. **Counteractive Measure**: Limit the server's ability to reprint checks to a predefined number.
- **Scam 2:** A server has a tab voided by the manager under the guise that the customer walked out on the check but in reality paid with cash. **Counteractive Measure:** Check audit report for servers with a pattern of "comps."
- **Scam 3:** A server convinces cash-paying customers to order the same menu items in order to reuse checks, a slight variation of Scam 1. **Counteractive Measure:** Spot check tables and review corresponding server checks for accuracy and order time of menu items.
- **Scam 4:** A server takes and transfers another server's credit card slip, which has not been closed yet, to collect on the tip. The server must know the other server's login to perform the transfer. **Counteractive Measure:** Eliminate the ability to transfer checks.
- **Scam 5:** Having collected cash, a server persuades the manager to void an item off the check (e.g., presents a barely touched entrée) and pockets the value of the item. **Counteractive Measure:** Managers should only void off items that have not been produced. The correct process would be to "comp" the item under the appropriate reason code.
- **Scam 6:** Servers collaborate by transferring commonly ordered items to each other and reprinting checks. For example, server 1 orders a beverage on the system, prints

the check, presents the check to the customer, and then receives a cash payment. Prior to closing the check, server 1 creates a separate check by moving the beverage off the current check. Then server 1 transfers the new check with the beverage to server 2. Server 1 closes the check minus the beverage and pockets the amount of the beverage. **Counteractive Measure:** Managers must approve transfers between servers.

- **Scam 7:** A server presents a slightly higher, similar check in hope that a cash-paying customer will not closely review it**. Counteractive Measure:** Track the number of checks that have been reprinted and reopened by servers.
- **Scam 8:** A server enters an incorrect gratuity total for meal vouchers collected from customers (e.g., tour bus group). For example, a server collects 10 vouchers each with a $2.00 tip value for a total gratuity value of $20.00. The server then enters $200.00 into the system, something that could be easily explained as a benign slip of the finger. **Counteractive Measure:** Activate payment reconciliation by job code at the end of each shift to identify totals that do not match.
- **Scam 9:** For identical orders, a server enters only one item then moves it from the original check to newly created seats or checks (split checks). The checks are then reprinted for pocketing extra cash. For example, if two people at the table order the same menu item (e.g., an appetizer that the server has direct access to), the server enters only one menu item into the system, creates a second check for the second customer, transfers the menu item to that check, prints a bill for that customer, and then transfers the menu item back to the original check for the first customer. **Counteractive Measure:** Monitor check reprints and split checks by server in the audit report.
- **Scam 10:** A server collects $23.00 cash from a customer to settle a check. Before closing out the check, the server reduces the check amount to$20.00 by transferring an order item that is not fulfilled by the kitchen or bar (e.g., server pours a cup of coffee or retrieves a dessert from reach-in cooler) to a new customer ordering the same item. The server pockets the difference in check totals ($3.00). **Counteractive Measure:** Track menu items transferred between customer checks.
- **Scam 11:** A server inflates the charge tip and voids off other check items to offset it for a cash advance. **Counteractive Measure:** Check audit report for servers with a pattern of "voids."
- **Scam 12:** A server with a promotional coupon applies it after a customer has paid the full check, leaving the server with the cash incentive intended for the customer. **Counteractive Measure:** Check audit report for discount activity.

The basics input into an AIS are the financial transactions. An AIS system maintains an **AUDIT TRAIL** or transaction log, a record of user activity of applications and the financial transactions performed within the system. A good audit trails enables managers and auditors to the follow the path of the data recorded in transactions from the initial source (e.g., server opens a check and places an order via the POS system) to the final disposition of the data (e.g., server settles the check via the POS system). It provides a means of accomplishing theft-related objectives, including individual accountability and reconstruction of events or actions that happen within an AIS (14). Review of POS audit trail reports by restaurant managers, for example, is often tedious and time consuming. The sheer volume of transactions or events can make it difficult to identify actionable data or to surface suspicious events. POS systems, however, typically lack the auditing capabilities (e.g., algorithms for knowledge discovery) found in other industry auditing systems. The POS audit interface is simply a listing of transactions that can be queried for a rudimentary data analysis and extraction, such as listing the number of voids by user ID. Most POS audit events lack sufficient context and detail (e.g., time and date of activities, business volume, job classification, station location, etc.) necessary to explain what happened. Michael Fodor, vice president of marketing and sales for F&B Management, a Phoenix-based restaurant technology reseller, also maintains that many restaurant managers lack the professional training and experience necessary to connect POS data to effective decisions and actions.

A key ingredient towards the success of most organizations is the ability to leverage and create knowledge from the data according to Schmidt (15). A survey of chief internal audit executives indicated that the ability to find trends or patterns in large, complex data sets will be the most important skill for auditors in the future. However, new audit processes that use increasingly sophisticated data mining tools will be required (16). **Data mining** is the process of extracting valid, novel, and actionable patterns from large data sets by combining methods from statistics and Artificial Intelligence (AI) with database management (http://en.wikipedia.org/wiki/Data_mining). The integration of data mining tools with auditing tools is a relatively new concept making auditing faster and cheaper (17). Furthermore, many companies report that such auditing solutions detecting fraud early on pay for themselves in a few months (18).

Information and Communication

Information and Communication. Employees must understand their role in the internal control system and the roles of others. This can be achieved through policies and procedures manuals, training (e.g., Webinar), e-mails, bulletin board postings, and the company intranet. In a restaurant, policies and procedures must be carefully formulated to find the optimal balance between internal controls and service delivery. Restricting user access (e.g., only managers can perform voids) in a restaurant environment, for example, will improve accounting control but may lengthen service times with the potential of degrading customer experiences and reducing throughput or revenues. Unfortunately, maintaining desired customer service levels for various tasks have frequently resulted in compromised POS accounting controls.

Monitoring

Monitoring. Evaluation of the design and operation of internal controls should be an ongoing process. Corrective action must be taken when specific controls are not functioning or being executed properly. Auditing tools, such as Aloha Restaurant Guard (ARG), can be deployed to monitor internal control.

ARG is a unique theft deterrent application for restaurant point-of-sale (POS) systems developed by Radiant Systems (now owned by NCR), a provider of POS technology to the hospitality and retail industries. This AI application is used with the Aloha POS system (65,000 installations worldwide) and has been deployed in more than 6000 quick service and table service restaurants in the United States and the United Kingdom.

ARG, the first auditing solution of its kind for restaurant POS systems, uses an AI engine to monitor POS data and transactions and to identify fraudulent or irregular activities. If a fraudulent behavior pattern is detected, an alert is generated that includes the details of the suspicious transaction as well as a history of any similar behavior.

ARG was conceived in 2008 by the Radiant Systems Innovation Team, which consisted of senior administrators and technicians, to provide an automated auditing solution with real-time transaction intelligence and pattern and trending analytics for quickly identifying potential employee as well as manager theft. About 41 percent of employee theft perpetrators are managers according to the ACFE (19).

The ARG product development and management team, with expertise in programming, statistics, data analysis, artificial intelligence, and operations, unveiled the alpha prototype in three restaurants for testing and evaluation in early 2009. Later that year, the beta version of ARG was deployed in 3000 U.S. and U.K. restaurants. In February 2010, the official ARG launch took place.

ARG is provided as a Software-as-a-Service (SaaS) solution, which means that access to the application is on a monthly subscription basis and the subscriber does not have to install the software or acquire any additional hardware to operate the software. POS transactions, polled daily via the Internet, are analyzed by ARG, an "in-the-cloud" hosted application. Exception-based reports with employee-specific actionable data are generated weekly and accessible via a Web portal.

ARG has been helpful in identifying common scams and undesirable employee behaviors, evaluating security levels and controls, and creating an environment of accountability and fraud deterrence. For example, ARG was deployed at Nichols Restaurant, an independently owned casual dining restaurant located in Marina Del Ray, California. Owner and operator Jim Nichols was very skeptical that his servers could be stealing from him until ARG revealed widespread and ongoing theft. One year of data revealed theft by more than 40 percent of the servers. A 12-year employee had stolen as much as $10,000 per year.

Insights from an Expert

QuickBooks... Why it's the ideal accounting software for your restaurant by

JOHN NESSEL, PRESIDENT, RESTAURANT RESOURCE GROUP INC.

As a restaurant financial consultant for more than 20 years (and a restaurant owner for twenty years before that), I am regularly asked to recommend an accounting software program to independent owners and operators. In my mind there is really only one choice, and it's QuickBooks.

Aside from the fact that QuickBooks is easy to use, inexpensive, and well suited to day-to-day restaurant bookkeeping tasks; it's also the most popular accounting software program in the universe, and well known to almost every accountant and bookkeeper. Add to that both a Windows and Mac version as well as an online version, and you have a product that will suit every conceivable user.

Unlike most software applications that can be utilized as soon as the program is opened, accounting software, including QuickBooks, requires that some setup tasks be completed before you can get started. A "company file" must first be created that is specific to your restaurant. That file will include a list of all the "accounts" that you'll need to record everything from your checking account balance, accounts payable, loans, revenues, payroll, cost of goods sold and other expenses. This account list is called the "Chart of Accounts", and it provides the financial foundation for accurate accounting as well as the organization you need to produce useful financial reports on a regular basis.

The restaurant industry even has its own established chart of accounts that you can use to get up and running. It's called the Uniform System of Accounts for Restaurants and can be obtained directly from the National Restaurant Association.

Once you have created your company file you will need to enter your beginning balances. If you are starting a new restaurant that simply means entering every transaction that has occurred since you got started. If you have an existing business then you'll need to get together with your accountant to get that information.

Now it's time to enter your daily sales information and the associated cash and credit card receipts, record your payroll, enter and pay your bills and other miscellaneous day to day financial transactions that are occurring.

Sales and Deposits information will come from your POS System or Cash Register. Either one will produce a daily sales report that summarizes your sales, sales tax, discounts, complimentary food and beverage, charged tips you may owe to your servers, cash received and the various credit card receipts. A few options exist for how to enter this information into QuickBooks, but no matter which method select it's critical that you understand all this information is organized into a single balanced QuickBooks bookkeeping entry.

QuickBooks does offer a few integrated options to process your weekly or biweekly payroll but I suggest that you hire an outside payroll service. It's cost effective and easier than grasping all the issues associated with payroll on your own. The payroll service will file and pay all your federal and state payroll liabilities and its one less headache to deal with.

One more thing as it relates to payroll. Most restaurants produce monthly profit and loss statements, but process payroll either weekly or biweekly. That means that every accounting period includes 30 or 31 days of revenue and expenses, but most often only 28 days of payroll. This discrepancy will result in payroll expenses being underreported most months and over reported in others. Avoid this problem by either "accruing" payroll or create four week accounting periods (13/yr) instead of 12 monthly reports.

Most of your bookkeeping time will be spent entering and paying your vendor bills. QuickBooks is incredibly easy and efficient when it comes to your Accounts Payable tasks. Make sure that all bills are dated when the products are delivered as opposed to when the check is cut to make the payments. This is called Accrual Accounting as opposed to Cash Accounting, and all restaurants should use this accounting method.

Rome was not build in a day and getting a grip on your restaurants bookkeeping will not occur overnight. But, without accurate accounting information and the financial reports they produce, you are flying blind. The restaurant business is very unforgiving when it comes to bottom line profitability. Give yourself the chance you deserve by taking full control of your restaurants bookkeeping. Great food and service is not enough in this business. If you need help, do not be afraid to get it. Take a finance course, hire a consultant, talk to a friend but make sure to get the help you need.

Tech News

Web-based Solution Streamlines Scheduling and Reduces Labor Costs

HOSPITALITY TECHNOLOGY

King's Seafood Company has evolved through more than 60 years of family-restaurant business experience. Having turned its focus to seafood a decade ago, King's Seafood Company continues to establish seafood-inspired restaurants that are committed to providing guests with products of superior quality and freshness. King's Seafood concepts include Water Grill, Ocean Ave Seafood, 555 East, Lou & Mickey's, Fish Camp and the King's Fish House/King Crab Lounge establishments. In addition, King's Seafood Company established King's Seafood Distribution, an exclusive seafood-distribution operation catering to its growing stable of restaurants, to provide the finest seafood to Southern California.

With so many locations, scheduling and managing staff was often a Herculean task. At one point in time King's Seafood was utilizing an online scheduling product that required managers to leverage each restaurant's one connected computer in order to work on various schedules; the work could not be completed from home or elsewhere. Additionally, software files didn't always download properly, creating added delays and headaches for managers.

King's Seafood Company vice president of operations, RJ Thomas, saw the potential for improvement and decided it was time for an upgrade. HotSchedules emerged as the leading solution and as an improvement from the previous system. HotSchedules provides intuitive mobile and web-based solutions for the restaurant industry and provides a streamlined and more accurate employee-scheduling process, in-depth forecasting abilities and significantly reduced labor costs.

HotSchedules rolled out its integrated Workforce and Digital Logbook solutions at King's Seafood Company concepts in Southern California, including all 18 locations of the Water Grill, Ocean Ave Seafood, 555 East, Lou & Mickey's, Fish Camp and the King's Fish House/King Crab Lounge establishments. The King's Seafood team saw positive results within the first four weeks. When describing the implementation and training, Thomas praised the process as being thorough, complete, quick and, "In one word: seamless."

In addition to an improved level of accuracy in scheduling, creating employee schedules is also significantly faster. For King's Seafood Company, the process has dropped from an hour-long hassle to a simple 15-minute task for managers. "Using our previous system, the average manager was taking 45 minutes to an hour to create each schedule for 30-45 crew members," Thomas explains. "With HotSchedules, that's down to 15 minutes. That's time they can spend doing other, more important tasks."

Communication between King's Seafood Company staff and management has also been made easier with the elimination of paper schedules posted on bulletin boards and hard copy shift-trade books, which had a tendency to go missing. All this communication now takes place within the HotSchedules tool, which is accessible to all employees online or via smartphones.

"With HotSchedules, we aren't flying blind any longer," Thomas says. "Our schedules are absolutely more accurate now because we base our labor on precise sales forecasts from the HotSchedules system. We view the average trend over the previous six to eight weeks and can achieve accuracy down to within 30-minute increments. When you really dial into your sales, you can control your labor." Thomas reveals that labor control is where Hotschedules has had the most substantial impact. King's has enjoyed a nearly two-percent reduction in labor costs.

Going Beyond Labor Management

"We leverage HotSchedules to communicate about more than just scheduling too," Thomas says. "For example, we recently used it to send out an online survey about healthcare benefits. It's a great tool to get messages from the home office out to the field without spending a lot of time or money to get it done."

In addition to manager and staff benefits, King's Seafood Company has been able to provide an improved guest experiencesince implementing HotSchedules solutions, which has led to an increase in sales. "The biggest trick to succeeding in the restaurant industry is accurately predicting what sales are going to come in the door on any given day," Thomas says."HotSchedules gives us that knowledge with 90 percent accuracy and it's a power that makes managing my day easy."

The management team is not the only beneficiary of the HotSchedules tool. Staff members also appreciate the convenience of features such as the ability for mobile access. "Our sales are up since we implemented HotSchedules and I attribute this to how the guests perceive us," Thomas admits. "When you have the right amount of crew on the floor at the right time, restaurant operations flow more smoothly, and it makes the whole atmosphere more comfortable for the guests. Hence, sales go up."

References

1. Bagranoff, N., Simkin, M., and Norman, C., *Core Concepts of Accounting Information Systems,* Hoboken, NJ: John Wiley and Sons, 2010.
2. Nessel, J., *Restaurant Operators Complete Guide to QuickBooks*, Boston, MA: Restaurant Resource Group, 2007.
3. White, D., "Beyond Dollars and Cents," *IAHA: Bottomline*, October/November 1990, p. 15.
4. Sill, B., "Future Computer Applications," *Restaurant Business*, June 10, 1989, p.136.
5. Committee of Sponsoring Organizations of the Treadway Commision (CSOTC), *Internal Control-Integrated Framework* (COSO Report), 1992.
6. Walsh, J. A., Employee theft. *International Office of Protection Officers,* 2002. Retrieved 2011-04-15, from http://www.ifpo.org/articlebank/employee_theft.html.
7. Laube, J., Don't let theft happen in your restaurant: What every independent operator should know about internal controls. *Restaurant Startup and Growth*, 2010. Retrieved 2011-04-18, from http://www.restaurantowner.com/members/1116.cfm.
8. Lavery, C., Lindberg, D., and Razaki, K., "Fraud awareness in a small business," *The National Public Accountant, 45* (6): 40–42, 2000.
9. National Restaurant Association, "Avoiding an inside job," *Bread & Butter Newsletter*, 1999. Retrieved 2011-04-14, from http://www.restaurant.org/business/bb/1999_12.
10. National Restaurant Association and Deloltte, *Restaurant Industry Operations Report 2010 Edition*, Washington, DC: Authors, 2010.
11. Francis, P. and DeGlinkta, R. C., *How to Burn Down the House: The Infamous Waiter and Bartender's Scam Bible*, New Orleans, LA: Merry Goldentree, Publishers, 2005.
12. Radiant Systems, *The Aloha Solution to Restaurant Employee Scams*. Atlanta, GA: Author, 2006.
13. Albright, B., "Case study: How much illicit cash are your employees pocketing?," *Integrated Solutions for Retailers*, 2010. Retrieved 2011-05-22, from http://www.retailsolutionsonline.com/article.mvc/How-Much-Illicit-Cash-Are-Your-Employees-0002.
14. National Institute of Technology and Standards, *Introduction to Computer Security: The NIST handbook*, Washington, D.C.: National Institute of Standards and Technology Administration, U.S. Department of Commerce, 1995.
15. Schmidt, C, "Lessons learned in the design of an undergraduate data mining course," *Journal of Computing Sciences in Colleges 26*(5): 189–195, 2011.
16. Hunton, J. E., and Rose, J. M., "21st century auditing: Advancing decision support systems to achieve continuous audit," *Accounting Horizons 24*(2): 297–312, 2010.

17. Bagga, S., and Singh, G. N., " Comparison of data mining and audit tools," *International Journal of Computer Science and Communication 2*(1) : 275–277, 2011.

18. Burleson, D, Critical audit system features, *Burleson Consulting*, 2011. Retrieved 2011-05-26, from http://www.dba-oracle.com/t_auditing3_critical_system_events.htm.

19. Association of Certified Fraud Examiners, *Report to the Nation on National Fraud and Abuse*, 2006. Retrieved 2011-06-03, from http://www.acfe.com/documents/2006-rttn.pdf.

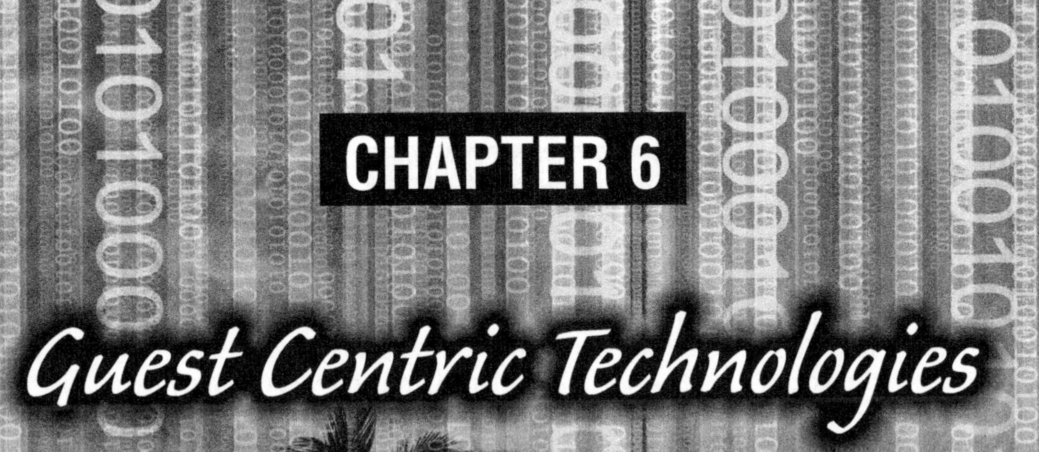

CHAPTER 6

Guest Centric Technologies

"The good news is that the PMS market has seldom seen such a variety of different approaches to solving your property's automation needs. The further good news is that the systems available have never been better for what is still the key system, the hub around which all other property systems revolve and in which you collect a huge amount of highly valuable guest data."

Jon Inge, Hotel Systems/Technology Consultant

CHAPTER OUTLINE

Technology in the Room: Historic View

"Home away from home!" This is how we would like to express what hotels mean to our guests. For this to happen, we must provide technologies that guests use in their home. Figure 6-1 shows how hotels followed the in-home technologies to create the feeling of "home" for their guests. Only after 1970s, we started to see some of the advancements in the guest room.

Of course, the main purpose of the guest room has never changed: to provide a clean, safe place to spend the night. In 1970, for the first time, hoteliers put ice cube makers and small refrigerators inside the guest room. In the beginning, not all rooms would have them. Usually, those rooms that had these special "amenities" were charged more than the other rooms. In 1972, the first models of telephone systems were introduced to the guestroom. In those days, there was only one telephone line for the entire hotel; therefore, guests sometimes waited long hours before they could place a call. In 1975, after color TV was well established in homes, hotels started to offer it. In the beginning, some of the hotels advertised that they had color TV to differentiate them from the competition and charged extra for rooms with TV. In 1980, Hotel Billing Information System (HOBIC) was introduced. In 1981, it became legal for hotels to make a profit from phone calls. This is when the use of call accounting systems exploded in the hotel industry. In 1986, electronic

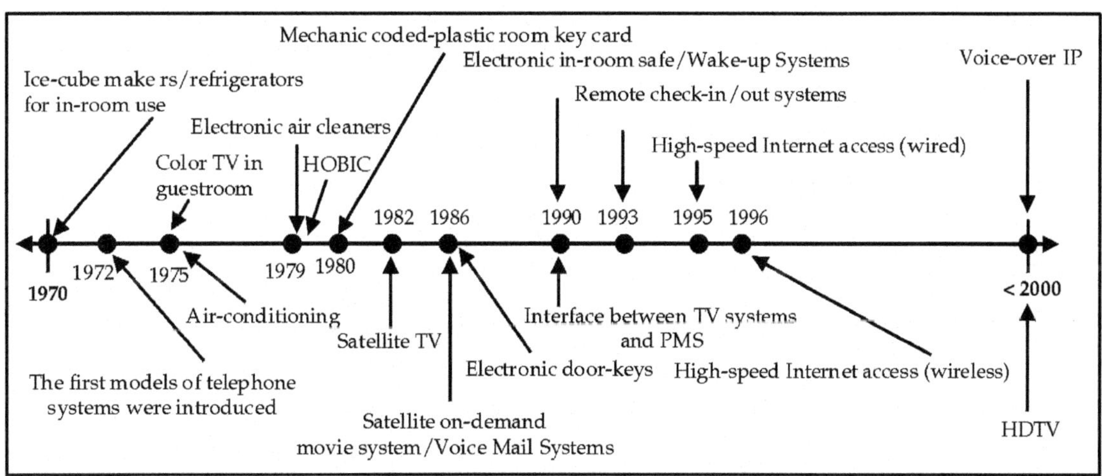

FIGURE 6-1. HOTEL GUESTROOM TECHNOLOGY BETWEEN 1970 AND 2000.

door-keys were introduced, increasing the security and the convenience of guests. In 1990, interface between TV systems and PMS was established so that the guests can see their bills through TV. With that, in 1993, guests were able to checkout from their room by using TV. In 1995, high speed Internet access was available in hotel rooms. After 2000, hotels started to use voice over Internet Protocol (IP) phoning systems, high definition TV, wireless Internet access, interactive entertainment systems, smart energy man agement systems, and many other systems that we will be addressed in this chapter.

The Big Picture

Today, technology is an indispensable part of the operations of hotels. It is almost impossible to imagine a hotel without any technology systems. On the most basic level, a hotel, even the smallest one, most likely has a property management system. Technology does not only increase the efficiency of the staff members, but also enhances the experience of the guests (in some cases it decreases). Figure 6-2 shows the typical technologies in a hotel. In a 1000-room full service hotel (i.e., Marriott Hotel), there are more than 60 different systems. In a limited service hotel (i.e., Courtyard), this number could be as many as 35. These numbers show the dependence of hotels on technology. Many of these systems become "mission critical" systems. This means that if the system does not work, the hotel cannot operate efficiently. For example, if the central reservation system or the reservation website does not work, the hotel cannot receive any reservations, which will impact the business directly. Similarly, a property management system (PMS) is also "mission-critical" software for a hotel. For a restaurant, mission-critical software is the Point of Sale System (POS). The hotel industry did not come to this point quickly.

The hospitality industry in general is maturing in its use and investment in technology. What used to be considered "technology for the sake of technology" (because hotels were

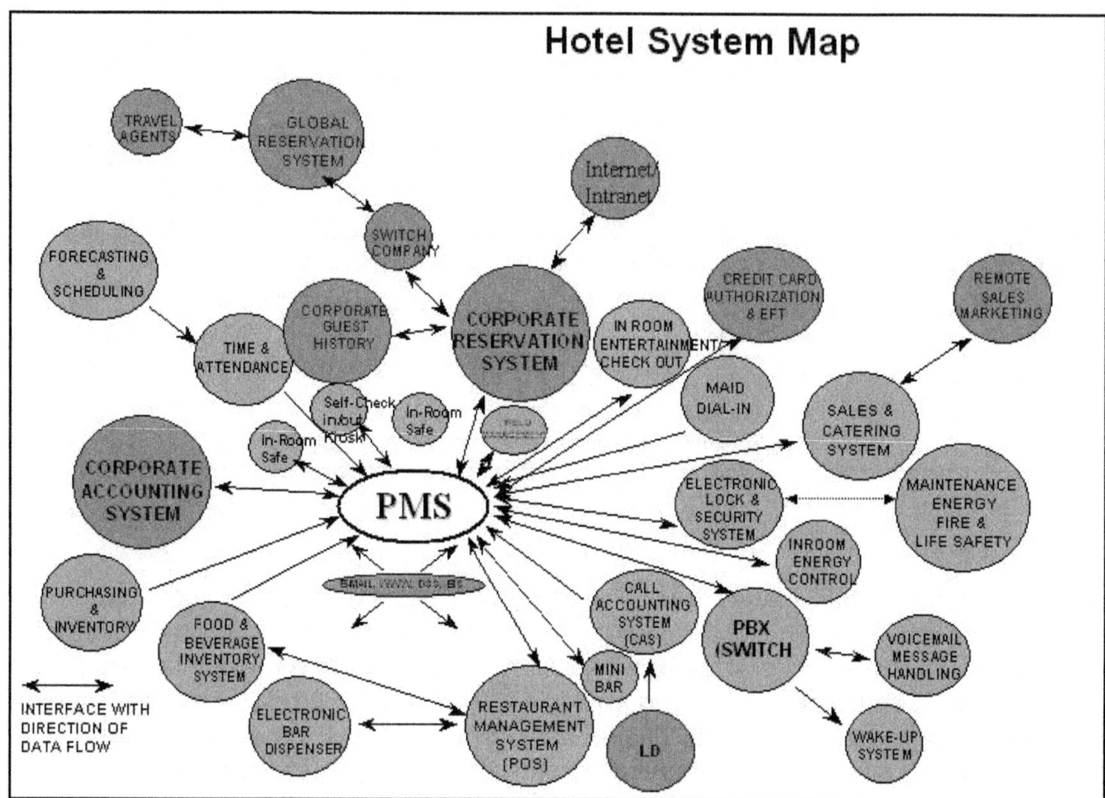

FIGURE 6-2. HOTEL SYSTEM MAP.

notorious buyers of products that either failed to work as promised or simply provided no benefit to the operation) has changed over the last decade. Many products foisted on hotels in the mid-to-late 1990s are now represented by companies that are either out of business or simply no longer support the product they once sold. Out of the 12 hospitality technology vendors that placed an ad in the first issue of Hospitality Upgrade magazine in 1992, only 3 of them are still in business today (Hospitality Upgrade, Spring 2007). As technology matures in the hospitality industry, so do the technology vendors.

Hotels are finding new ways to use technology for a strategic advantage. For example, Mandarin Oriental is keeping track of the fruits eaten by the guest. These records are kept in the guest's profile. When a fruit basket is sent the next time the guest visits the hotel, it is dominated by the fruits that guest likes. This creates a "wow" factor since it is not directly solicited, rather, quietly observed and recorded with the help of proper training and technology.

The airline industry's product is a seat, which became a commodity a long time ago. In the contemporary age, travelers do not necessarily care about which carrier will take them from point A to point B. Price seems to be the most important factor in selecting an air carrier. The Hotel industry is showing similar symptoms. As in the example of the

Mandarin Oriental, hoteliers are turning to technology to create a "*differentiation*" so that they do not become a commodity in the eyes of guests.

Advantages and Disadvantages of Technology in Hotels

In the following sections, we will look at the technologies in the guest room.

A technology system should be viewed as a tool for solving problems and effectively managing information, but, even more importantly, it will improve profitability through more effective utilization of resources. The key advantages of technology are as follows:

1. Improved labor productivity and organization efficiency
2. Enhanced decision-making capability in less time
3. Reduced operating costs
4. Increased information accuracy
5. Increased revenues
6. Greater guest satisfaction and loyalty
7. Improved controls
8. Ease of use

While technology brings great advantages to hotels, there are also some disadvantages. Some of them can be categorized as follows:

1. Security
2. Ergonomics
3. Cost
4. Upgrades and maintenance

For example, security issues can be a real disadvantage of technology. Let's take wireless Internet access at a public meeting area in a hotel. Even though wireless Internet access provides great convenience to guests and staff, it may pose a serious security risk. Therefore, before utilizing wireless Internet in a hotel environment, technology managers need to assess the risks associated with it and take precautions, such as using a wireless security protocol (i.e.,WPA; defined as a set of protocols that secures data when transmitted wirelessly) or having the guests accept a disclaimer. In terms of ergonomics, computers may pose a risk to users in terms of ergonomic structure. For example, if a user is exposed to computer monitors 8 hours a day, radiation may affect the user. The organization needs to take precautions to prevent this from happening, such as using LCD monitors instead of cathode ray tube monitors. Cost also can be a disadvantage of technology. Every day, the prices of technology decline. However, if an organization waits for the prices to drop to a lower level, it may be too late. So, even though you know that the prices will fall tomorrow, the organization may need to invest in them today. Finally, upgrades and maintenance can be a disadvantage because if systems are not regularly updated and maintained, they will be less efficient and will harm the business instead of helping it.

In Room Technologies

In today's modern hotel rooms, it is very possible to see the following technologies that make the guest stay a more comfortable one:

1. Electronic Locking System
2. Energy Management & Climate Control Systems
3. Fire Alarm & Security Systems
4. In-room Minibars
5. In-room safe boxes
6. Guest room Phone System
7. Voice-mail/Wake-up Systems
8. In-room Entertainment Systems
9. Guest room control panels
10. Self-check-in/out systems

Now, let's look at each of these systems in more detail.

Categories of Locking Systems

The first thing a hotel guest does after checking in is to unlock the room and get comfortable. To do so, the guest needs a key to enter. For many years, hotels gave traditional mechanical keys to the guest. These mechanical keys were heavy and usually were attached to a heavy metal piece to make it difficult for the guests to carry it around, therefore reminding them (or forcing) to return the key to the front desk when they leave the room. However, in 2008, a large majority of hotels have started using electronic keys that enable the guest to take the key with them when they are not in the room.

Mechanical Locks

Until 1980, hotels used mechanical keys to allow/deny access to Guest rooms. These keys are still widely used by guests in their personal lives. Figure 6-3 shows an example of what a mechanical hotel lock and key looks like. Usually, hotels attach a heavy piece to the key to make it difficult for the guest to take the key. Even though, there are hotels using mechanical keys, the majority of hotels, especially, 3-star and higher, have given up using mechanical keys.

Mechanical keys are cheaper than electronic keys. However, the disadvantages of mechanical keys are:

- heavy, difficult to carry
- inconvenient
- once lost, it is easy for others to have access to the room because the key had the hotel name and room number on it.
- once lost, the lock and the key have to be changed, therefore resulting in financial loss. The Holiday Inn hotel chain reported that mechanical lock replacement cost them at $1 million annually in the 1980s.

FIGURE 6-3. MECHANICAL LOCK AND KEY.

Source: © Devis Da Fre', 2008. Used under license from Shutterstock, Inc.

- not trackable: it is not possible to determine who accessed the room
- duplicable: guests or employees could duplicate these keys, therefore raising a significant security problem. In the 1980s, there was even a strong black market for stolen hotel keys (up to $1000 for a master key), and many hotel employees knew about it.

Non-Electronic Locking Systems

All these potential problems with mechanical keys made the vendors and hoteliers to look for alternative solutions.

In 1980, a mechanical punched-hole coded-plastic room key card was used in hotels for the first time. These were an alternative to mechanical keys. They were not unique; meaning that for each room, there was one key and the same key was used from guest to guest. However, since the key did not have the hotel location and room number, they were safer than the mechanical keys. In addition, they were plastic, therefore, did not weigh a lot, making it easy for guests to carry with them or even take it to wet areas such as the pool or beach. However, if keys were lost, key locks needed to be changed, therefore making the key replacements expensive.

Electronic Locking

The third generation guest room locks are electronic locking systems (ELS). ELS are the most used hotel keys in the world today. About 85 percent of lodging establishments in the United States have electronic locking systems installed (1).[1] There are different versions of ELS:

Hard-wired systems and microprocessor based systems.

Hard Wired Systems

Hard-wired system is an example of a first generation ELS. They operate through a centralized master code console interfaced to every single key lock. This particular fact makes it a very expensive solution even while it enhances the security features. When a guest checks in, the front desk clerk programs a new key and transmits the new code for the new guest to the key lock through wires. By the time the guest goes to his/her room, the key lock has the new unique code for the new guest. Key codes issued to previous guests became invalid at that point.

Microprocessor based ELS

These systems operate as a stand alone system. There are two kinds of microprocessor based ELS: 1) One-way communication ELS, and 2) Two-way communication ELS.

One Way Communication ELS

This system uses a microcomputer (key card console) with an electronic key encoder, a device used to encode new lock combinations on guest key cards at check-in (See Figure 6-4). When the key card is inserted into the correct door lock, which contains a battery powered microprocessor and card reader (stand-alone lock), the new combination automatically cancels the previous one. This allows the lock to be

FIGURE 6-4. AN ELECTRONIC KEY LOCK.

electronically changed with each new guest. Communication locks have several advantages over mechanical keys.

They are:

- Unique keys: For every single guest, there is a new key.
- Light plastic, magnetic stripe keys: The magnetic stripe key cards are light and easy to carry. They are not affected by water or sand, which makes it easy to carry to pool and beach areas. (See Figure 6-5)
- Security: these plastic keys do not have the hotel location and room numbers on them, making the room secure even if the key is lost.
- Replaceable: In the case the electronic key is lost; a new one can be issued immediately, cancelling the previous code immediately. The cost of a new key is very minimal (about 10 cents per key card).
- Recyclable: The used keys can be used again for different guests for different guest rooms. The cost of rekeying is nonexistent.
- Access control: These keys can be programmed to allow hotel staff members to access certain rooms. For example, a house keeper may have access to all rooms in one certain floor with only one card.
- Audit-trail capability (the date and time each lock was accessed): These key locks tracks entrants to the room. In the case of a need (such as stealing occurring in the room), the manager can download the entries to see who has entered the room.
- Privacy Feature: The guest can turn the door knob to the "lock" position. This option typically employs an indicator that displays a notice when someone tries to access the room key. Usually a signal at the door lock will let the person (i.e., housekeeping, minibar attendant) know that there is a guest inside and does not want to be disturbed.

However, the one-way communication locks have some disadvantages as well. They are:

- One key cannot be used in multiple locks.
- If the guest decides to change rooms, he/she has to go to front desk to recode the key.
- If a wrong key is inserted into a lock, it does not alert security staff.

Two-Way Communication ELS

Two-way communication keys are more expensive to install; however, they offer several security and convenience features. In the two-way communication locks, a central database communicates to locks wirelessly (or wired). This way, the guest can use his/her key for multiple locks such as pool, fitness room, parking facilities, elevator, and concierge floor. In the case that the guest decides to change rooms, the guest does not need to go back to the front desk to recode the key. The front desk staff can simply enter the new code into the lock and ask the guest to go to the new room. Similarly, if a housekeeper is now assigned a different room on a different floor, the housekeeping manager can give the housekeeper access to the room remotely. Two-way communication locks can be interfaced to other systems such as the property management system, the point of sale system, and the in-room safe system.

Key Cards

Key cards are essential components of any ELS. There are four types of key cards today in the market. They are:

- ***Magnetic stripe cards:*** The most frequently used key card. Magnetic stripe cards have three tracks (See Figure 6-5). The first track is the most utilized track by hotel ELS. Similar to bank ATM cards (in terms of how they look not what information they contain), the card carries the lock access information and expiration date. In some cases, some ELS systems allow the hotel to encode other information on other tracks. For instance, in addition to room key information, some casinos encode their slot club or frequent guest number on a separate track so the customer can use their room key in slot machines or for ratings on table games. Hotels can also encode room charge information on the keys to allow the customer easier access to room charges while in various hotel restaurants and retail outlets. Recently, there was a myth that hotel magnetic stripe key cards had guest's credit card information; however, this myth was rejected by hotel IT executives and ELS companies. The cost of a magnetic stripe card can be as low as 10 cents a card.
- ***Memory Cards:*** A memory card is equipped with a memory chip to store lock access codes and records. They can store data from 2 kilobyte (KB) (it can carry 25 different key lock codes), 8 KB (it can carry up to 125 different key lock codes), or 64 KB (it can carry up to 1350 different key lock codes). These are great for staff

FIGURE 6-5. KEY CARD.

Source: © Albert Lozano, 2008. Used under License from Shutterstock, Inc.

members or managers that have access to multiple locks. The cost of a memory card can be from $2.00 to $4.00 per card.

- ***Smart Cards:*** A smart card, chip card, or integrated circuit(s) card (ICC), is defined as any pocket-sized card with embedded integrated circuits which can process information. Smart cards can store more data than the memory cards. Smart cards can also process data, allowing it to serve as an electronic purse or ID. The cost of a smart card can be $10 per card.
- ***RFID Cards:*** See the section below.

New Generation of ELS

Biometric ELS

The first generation of biometric ELS was seen in 2004. Saflok was one of the first companies to introduce the biometric locks. Hospitality Financial and Technology Professionals revealed "Guestroom 2010" in 2006. In the "Guestroom 2010", they included an electronic biometric locking system from IBM that works with an iris scan of guests. Here is how a biometric lock works:

The guest registers his/her fingerprint, iris scan, or other biometric metric (i.e., hand scan, palm scan) at the time of check-in. Once the registration is complete, the information is wirelessly sent to the lock, authorizing the guest to enter the guest room. In addition, additional locks can also be authorized for that fingerprint such as pool door, fitness room door, and parking facilities. Even though this is a huge convenience for the guests, biometric door locks have not been widely deployed because of security and cost factors. Guests do not feel comfortable giving such sensitive information (fingerprint or iris scan) to a third party company (hotel), especially provided that even the most secure organizations such as CIA or FBI can be hacked. Several researchers demonstrated that biometric keys can be hacked and unauthorized access can be gained (2). The guests can easily replace a lost key card; however, in the case of a stolen fingerprint, it is almost impossible to replace. The vendors must show concrete security features for guests to feel comfortable using this technology or offer alternative methods of access for guests who feel uncomfortable with the biometric technology. The Boston-based Nine Zero Hotel employs an iris scanner to monitor access to its Cloud Nine suite (3). This provides the highest level of security for its exclusive suite. In addition, iris scans are used at Frankfurt Airport in Germany where the airport uses iris scanning to expedite boarding for frequent fliers (4).

Radio Frequency Identification Tag (RFID) ELS

Radio-frequency identification (RFID) is an automatic identification method, relying on storing and remotely retrieving data using devices called RFID tags or transponders. There are two main components of an RFID ELS:

- RFID Lock: This is the key lock that looks for an RFID tag to grant access. They are battery operated.

- RFID tags (keys): These are the identification codes for key locks. They can be in the shape of a plastic key card, or can be stored in different devices, such as a wristband. With this new system, an encrypted code is programmed into the RFID tag (key) making it a unique communication credential. This credential carries information to the lock "instructing" it to either allow or deny access. Each exchange of information between lock and RFID tag (key) is stored, and is available for audit inside the lock.

Some of the advantages of RFID ELS are that the RFID key lock does not have any parts that require physical contact, therefore, making it ideal for resorts and beach properties. In the regular ELS, the key has to be inserted through a slot. Over time, this slot may be filled with dust, sand, or other materials making the lock inoperable. In addition, RFID keys are convenient for guests to carry (i.e., in the shape of a wrist-band) key cards easily. RFID key locks also make it possible for handicapped guests to open the door from proximity. Another advantage of RFID keys is that with one key, multiple access points can be controlled such as the pool, minibar, fitness room, electronic safe box, and parking facilities without physical contact to the key lock. Finally, RFID keys can also be used as an electronic wallet, allowing the guest to carry "cash" on their card. They can even authorize their children to carry some electronic cash on their RFID keys to be spent in the hotel or resort's outlets.

Energy Management & Climate Control Systems

After labor, energy is the second-largest operating expense for a hotel (5). The hotel industry spends almost $5 billion a year on energy (6) according to Environmental Protection Agency. (EPA) and costs are rising. Guest room energy consumption typically accounts for 40 percent to 80 percent of a hotel's total energy cost. Energy management systems help control some of the energy consumption in the guest room. A huge savings can occur especially when the guests are not in the guest room, which is usually when the energy costs are charged at a peak rate. Most guests do not turn off the heater or air-conditioner when they leave the room for the day, and may not turn off the lights or electronic devices in the room. This causes the extra energy consumption. There are three main types of energy management systems: 1) centrally controlled systems, 2) individually controlled systems, and 3) network controlled systems. For the centrally controlled systems, there is little the guest can do to adjust the temperature in the guestroom. The temperature is adjusted by the engineering department in the hotel for the entire hotel. Even though this allows management to control the temperature, it is usually not desired by guests since it does not allow them to alter the settings. Each guest may like a different temperature, making the centrally controlled systems undesirable. The individually controlled systems give the guests the comfort of setting their own temperatures; however, controlling the costs is a challenge. Finally, network controlled systems are the most ideal systems for hoteliers and guests. While network controlled systems allow guests to alter the temperature to their likings, they also allow hotel staff to control the energy consuming devices in the room when the room is not occupied. There are 3 different types of energy management system solutions used in the hospitality industry today.

Types of Energy Management Systems

a. Electronic key card based energy management systems: This system employs a wall mounted unit that controls the electrical devices and Heating Ventilation and Air Conditioning (HVAC) devices with the help of a magnetic stripe key card. This system is an example of individually controlled energy management system.

When the guest enters the guest room, the lights and HVAC equipment will not operate unless the guest inserts the room key card into a wall mounted unit. When the guest leaves the guest room and takes the key from the wall unit, the lights and HVAC equipment stop after 1 or 2 minutes to allow the guest to leave the guest room. This system is the simplest form of energy savings in a hotel room. The most obvious advantage of this system is that when the guest is not in the guest room, lights and HVAC equipment will not work, saving the hotel money. Another advantage of this system is its cost, probably the cheapest among all energy management systems. However, this system has several disadvantages:

i. Inconvenience factor: When the guest leaves the guest room and takes the key card from the wall mounted unit, the HVAC equipment stops, making the room very hot or cold depending upon the season. When the guest returns, the room temperature might be at a very uncomfortable level, making the recovery of a desired temperature a long process.

ii. Control: The wall mounted unit requires any key card to work. Some guests ask for a second or third key and leave the extra key in the wall mounted unit at all times, causing the lights and HVAC equipment to work at all times. Some guests carry another hotel's key card, and leave this key in the unit, causing the electrical systems to work even when they are not in the guest room.

b. Body motion detector based energy management systems: A body motion detector is installed inside the guest room and in some cases in the corridors. When the body motion unit does not detect a motion, indicating that there is not a guest or an animal in the room or in the corridor, it controls the lights and HVAC equipment. The clear advantage of this system over the electronic key card based systems is that it can bring the HVAC equipment to preset levels instead of turning it off completely, making the recovery quicker. For example, HVAC equipment in the summer can be preset to 80 Fahrenheit degrees in non-occupy mode. When the guest comes back into the guest room, the system will automatically recall the last entered temperature by the guest and try to come back to whatever that level is. The biggest disadvantage of this system is that if the body motion detector is not installed in multiple locations, it may not see all angles such as corners or bathrooms, allowing a false "non-occupy" mode, and turning off the lights and HVAC equipment. Some people sleep with no motion. There are anecdotal cases of guests sleeping and not moving and the system turning off the HVAC equipment, causing the guest to be sick in the morning. In the hotel corridor installations, when the system detects a motion, it turns on the lights for the guest and when there is not any motion, turning off some of them, saving electricity costs.

c. Body heat detector based energy management systems: Similar to body motion detector based systems, this system detects body heat of a human or an animal. This system is more reliable than the body motion detector. When the system does not detect body heat, it assumes that it is non-occupy mode, and sets HVAC equipment back to preset temperature. Body heat sensors can also act as an occupancy sensor, communicating the presence of a human being or animal in the guest room to a central system.

Network controlled energy management systems have four levels of temperature setbacks:

- Sold
- Unsold
- Sold Occupied
- Sold Unoccupied

This requires that the occupancy sensors not only communicate to the energy management system, but also it requires the energy management system to communication with the property management system. This way, maximum energy saving is achieved.

Smart Systems International (http://www.2getsmart.com/) developed a new energy management system based on body motion and body heat detectors to increase reliability and accuracy of "true detection." Figure 6-6 shows an example of a body heat & body motion detector.

In addition, they have added an adaptive learning system to the energy management system which predicts the amount of time needed for the Smart System energy management system to return the temperature to the guest's set point once they walk back into the room. Recovery time (which is usually 12 minutes) is programmed into the controller when the Smart System is installed and can be changed by the facility at any time. Unlike fixed setback thermostats, drifting the temperature around the recovery time safe-

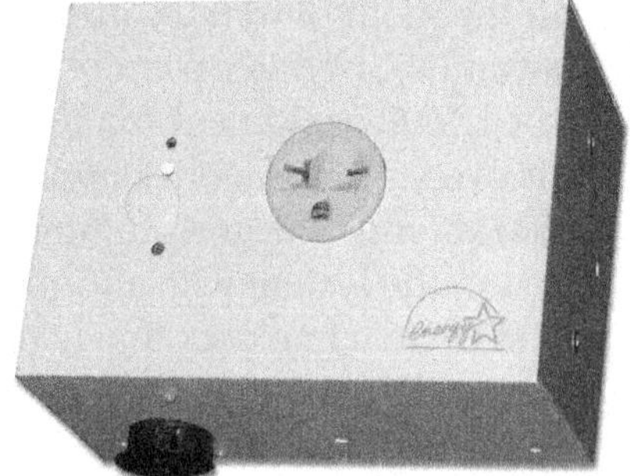

FIGURE 6-6. HAN EXAMPLE OF A BODY-HEAT AND BODY-MOTION DETECTOR WITH A DIGITAL THERMOSTAT. COURTESY OF SMART SYSTEM.

guards the guest's comfort; the temperature is always minutes away from their comfort setting.

- An integral part of energy management systems is the digital thermostat which allows the guest to control the HVAC conditions within the guest room.

Fire Alarm and Security Systems

On November 21, 1980, a fire at the MGM Grand in Las Vegas killed 85 and injured 700 (7). It was the worst hotel fire the nation had seen since an Atlanta blaze in 1946. It spawned a legacy of tighter fire regulations and broader deployment of water sprinklers in hotel rooms and common areas. Because of these tight fire regulations, there are several technologies implemented in hotels to help control fires and notify the security department immediately in the case of a fire or smoke. Almost every household in the U.S. has an independent smoke alarm. Even though these are great precautions to possible fires, in hotels, independent fire alarm systems may not be enough because hotels are composed of many rooms and large public areas where they may not be attended at all times. Therefore, this requires the need for a networked fire alarm system. An integrated fire safety system saves lives, reduces fire damage and insurance premiums, and prevents costly litigations. It requires a centralized computer or fire command console which utilizes electronic and audio control devices for fire protection, alert, and response. In addition, many hotels have installed sprinkler systems inside the guest rooms. The Hotel and Motel Fire Safety Act of 1990 (8) requires that Federal employees, when on official travel, should stay in fire-safe accommodations. For the purposes of this Act, every guest room in a hotel or motel must have an AC powered smoke alarm. These are commonly called hard-wired. The alarm must be installed in accordance with National Fire Protection Association (NFPA) Standard 72. An alarm that is solely battery-powered is not acceptable. An AC powered alarm with battery backup is desirable, but not required. If the building is more than three stories in height, it must also have a full automatic sprinkler system.

Networked Fire Alarm System: In this system, smoke detectors are networked to a central management system wirelessly (See Figure 6-7). In the case of an alarm, the smoke detector notifies the closest receiving unit which then transmits this information to a central management system. The system may even be interfaced to a paging system, therefore, notifying the security personnel on duty to go to alarm room or area immediately to check the status. If needed, the security personnel would call the emergency services to seek help. In these systems, smoke detectors should be directly wired to an energy source to eliminate the problems with battery wearouts and theft of the batteries.

In-Room Minibars

There are three different types of minibar systems. These are: 1) Traditional minibars (nonautomated), 2), Semiautomated minibars, and 3) Automated minibars (microprocessor based).

FIGURE 6-7. SMOKE DETECTOR.

Source: © Niki Crucillo, 2008. Used under License from Shutterstock, Inc.

Traditional Minibars

Traditional minibars are based on manual checking and/or honor system. After minibar staff members fill out the minibar initially, they have to check every occupied room every day to see if anything has been consumed. If yes, they refill manually and fill out a form manually to be given to the front office so that the correct charge is charged to the guest's folio. This is labor intensive. When the guest is checking out, the front desk asks the departing guest if any minibar items have been consumed within the last 24 hours. Some guests will advertently or inadvertently give wrong information, causing the hotel to lose revenue. Minibars are extremely convenient and play an important role in guests' satisfaction especially in full service hotels. Guests are often willing to pay a premium for the convenience of snacks and drinks available in the room 24 hours a day. However, maintaining minibars manually is costly and may result in revenue losses for hotels. To minimize the labor spent on checking if the minibars were used, some hotels use a "seal" that the guest must tear or break to access the minibar. The minibar staff member would peek in the minibar and see if the seal is broken. If it is, then they would physically check the minibar to refill and charge the guest. If not, they would go to the next guest room. There are still a significant number of hotels that offer traditional minibars. Some limited service hotels offer a mini refrigerator, not filled with any of the snacks or drinks, giving the guest an option to fill the refrigerator with their own snacks and/or drinks. In addition, minibar staff members disturb the guests who do not need service. In response to problems with traditional minibars, vendors offered semiautomated minibars as the second generation of minibars in hotels.

Semiautomated Minibars

Semiautomated minibar Systems are equipped with a door alert-system that reports directly to the minibar central computer system via existing telephone wiring each time the bar door is opened. This way, minibar staff members know which rooms need refilling and which rooms do not. Consequently, restocking time and guest disturbances are significantly reduced.

Automated Minibars

Automated Minibar Systems (Microprocessor based) are capable of monitoring and posting sales transactions, determining refill quantities, reminding the expiration dates of products offered, and enhancing profitability.

I was staying at the Omni in Atlanta. I had something that I needed to refrigerate. I put it in the minibar and was immediately charged for a whole bunch of stuff that I had moved around. That was a challenge to clear up with the front desk.

The automated minibar had infrared sensors that sense when a product is removed from the tray. When the automated minibar is in stalled, each tray is programmed to carry a certain item. Each system is capable of setting an "inspection time" in which the guest can take an item from the automated minibar and look before deciding to consume (purchase). This time limit can be anywhere between 10 seconds up to 1 minute. When the time limit is finished and the item is not returned to its tray, the cost of that item is automatically charged to the guest's folio. This is accomplished by an interface between the automated minibar system and property management system (PMS).

Automated minibars work on the following sequence:

1. The guest is checked into the guest room.
2. The PMS sends a signal to automated minibar management system to unlock the minibar in the guest room.
3. The guest goes to guest room.
4. The guest consumes an item from the minibar. If he/she does not return the item to its tray within the time limit, the automated minibar system sends the charge and item details (time of the purchase, the item title, cost, tray location, and time) to the guest folio in PMS.
5. The guest settles the bill at the time of check-out. If there is a dispute, the front desk agent can print a detailed minibar report that shows the consumption details (See Figure 6-8). This usually helps the guest to recall the charges.
6. The guest checks out.
7. The PMS sends a signal to automated minibar management system to lock the minibar in the guestroom.

At the same time, minibar staff member will get a daily consumption report for the entire hotel. Figure 6-9 shows an example of this report. Minibar staff member can use this report as a requisition form to obtain these items from the inventory. Because of this report, minibar staff member will take the exact amount of items consumed the previous day with him or her. Once these consumed items are obtained, another report from the

TOTAL PURCHASES
Minibar

Minibar Bill for Room: 101 **TIME: 12:54** **DATE:** SUNDAY 15 APRIL 2007

Date	*Time*	*Contents*	*Price (US $)*	*Location*
13 April 2007	11:32:45	Imported Beer	3.50	Location 11
13 April 2007	12:45:55	Tonic Water	1.50	Location 08
14 April 2007	12:55:12	Gin	4.50	Location 07
14 April 2007	12:55:10	Nuts	2.00	Location 13
15 April 2007	09:02:12	Mineral Water	1.50	Location 15
15 April 2007	09:03:01	Orange Juice	2.00	Location 17
15 April 2007	14:32:34	Domestic Beer	3.00	Location 10
		Total Purchases	**18.00 (inc tax)**	

Guest checked in 11:25 13 April 2007

***************THIS BILL FOR CHECKING PURPOSES ONLY*************

FIGURE 6-8. MINIBAR REPORT.

REFILL REQUIREMENTS REPORT
Automated Minibar System
Date: 15 April 2007

Refill Requirements report for the following rooms/groups/zones: **ALL**

Item	Unit
Spa Still Water	22
Gordons Gin	12
Canada Dry Tonic Water	14
Orange Juice	78
Vodka	45
Coca-Cola (Can)	76
Evian Water (50cl)	56
Seven-Up (Can)	14
Domestic Beer	45
Imported Beer	23

FIGURE 6-9. MINIBAR CONSUMPTION FOR ENTIRE HOTEL.

automated minibar system will help to refill the minibars. Figure 6-10 shows the detailed refill report for each room. The system is capable of reporting for each room, floor, or entire hotel. So, when the minibar staff member comes to Room 103, he/she will take 1 Spa Still Water, 1 Gordon's Gin and 1 Canada Dry Tonic Water with him/her to the room. The report will tell him/her where to put the item in the automated minibar.

In-Room Safes

A reported disadvantage of automated minibars is that when the guest would like to store his/her personal items in the minibar (i.e., milk, children's formula, or medicine), they have to take out items from the minibar (because usually the automated minibars do not have empty spaces for guest items) and put aside. Then, the guest puts the personal items into the minibar. Since the items were taken from the minibar, the system will charge the guest for the items taken out, however, in reality, the guest did not consume them. The minibar staff member will have to manually void the charges from the guest's folio. The other potential problem with automated minibars is that when the interface between the automated minibar system and PMS is not working, all charges may be lost. The hoteliers should make sure that in the case of an interface failure, the system notifies the information technology staff so that it can be fixed immediately.

REFILL REQUIREMENTS REPORT
Automated Minibar System
Date: 15 April 2007

Refill Requirements report for the following rooms/groups/zones:
FIRST FLOOR/ ROOM BY ROOM

Room: 103	**Quantity**	**Item**	**Tray #**
	1	Spa Still Water	6
	1	Gordons Gin	9
	1	Canada Dry Tonic Water	3
Room: 109	1	Orange Juice	12
	2	Vodka	14
	1	Coca-Cola (Can)	4
Room: 115	1	Evian Water (50cl)	5
	2	Seven-Up (Can)	7
	1	Domestic Beer	8
	2	Imported Beer	17

FIGURE 6-10. DETAILED REFILL REPORT FOR EACH ROOM.

More and more hotels are providing safety boxes as a way to secure guest valuables. Traditionally, hotels used to offer safe boxes in the front desk. However, in today's hotels, most rooms are equipped with modern, small, individual size safes. The safes should be small but large enough that a laptop computer and/or camcorder and camera can fit. There are three main types of in-room safety boxes:

a. **Mechanical key safes:** The first generation of in-room safety boxes. It works with a traditional, mechanical key that is obtained from the front desk. It requires the guest to carry the key at all times. In the event of loss, the hotel is required to change the lock and the guest is usually charged for the cost.
b. **Electronic in-room safes:** Since it was not very practical nor easy to carry the mechanical keys to open the in-room safes, the vendors developed electronic in-room safe boxes. There are four different kinds of electronic in-room safety boxes:

    1. **Key card safes:** Similar to mechanical key safes, key card safes work with the guest's key card.
    2. **Code-based electronic in-room safes (Digital Safes):** Digital safes are superior to mechanical key safes or key card safes because there is no secondary element (the key or the key card) to be lost. Code-based electronic safes use a code programmed by each new guest. Everyone has a few digits stored in their brains: birthdates, bank personal identification number (PIN) and so on. With a simple "code and close" safe, the guest places the secured items inside and shuts the door, enters a unique PIN code, punches the "close" button" and walks away. It is as simple as that.
    3. **Smart-card based safes:** Similar to key card systems, these safes open when the guest inserts the smart card into the safe. It is popular in resorts where the use of smart cards is popular.
    4. **Biometric safes:** Similar to biometric electronic key locking systems, these safes require each new guest to register their finger print (or other biometric information such as iris scan) with the safe. Then, the guest uses his/her fingerprint to lock or unlock the safe. This is the most convenient safe because there is no losing of the key card or forgetting of the PIN code. However, in the case of multiple guests staying in the same room, some models do not allow more than one registered "user."

Electronic safes have an override feature. Guests can conceivably forget their code combination, maybe their spouse programmed it and then left, or possibly they thought they had entered a code but pushed the wrong buttons by mistake. Should this occur, hotel management has the ability to open the safe by overriding the current combination code or key card code. Usually, such an override requires two inputs: some type of handheld unit, key, or device as well as a secure override access code. Most electronic safes maintain an override audit trail.

Even though it is not found in many hotels, some electronic safes may be hard wired to a central processing unit. This central processing unit is interfaced to PMS, allowing safe charges to be posted to the guest's folio automatically. However, hard wired safe systems are very expensive to install, therefore, most of the safe box use charges are posted to the guest's folio manually by front desk staff. Some hotels do ask the guest at the time of check-in if they would be using the safe boxes and if they do, they program the PMS to charge the fee (usually from $1 to $5 per day) automatically when the night audit is done. Some hotels charge the safe box fee whether the guest uses it or not. Of course, this approach causes some guests to complain about this charge. And a recent new trend is to charge all guests a small "resort fee" for the use of in-room safe, in-room coffee machine, and free local phone calls. Guests often have the option to reject the "resort fee." Some hotels may not charge for the safe box, offering it as a room amenity. Charging for the safe box is a way of payback for the installation cost of the safe boxes. In addition, safe boxes reduce a hotel's insurance premium. Evidence suggests that safes do reduce theft. Electronic locking systems do battle with external theft and in-room safes with internal theft. Experts say that internal theft by employees is usually an impulsive act caused by temptation (laptop computers are proving to be one of the most tempting items of all). The safe reduces the employee opportunity to steal. It also undermines guest moves to defraud the hotel or the insurance company.

Guest Room Phone Systems

For a typical U.S. hotel, the revenue derived from local and long-distance phone calls remained relatively flat from 1998 through 2000, and then declined severely from 2001 through 2004 (Mandelbaum, 2005). In 2000, U.S. hotels averaged $4.16 per occupied room in telephone revenue. This statistic fell to an estimated $2.00 in 2004, thus indicating that the magnitude of the decline in phone revenue was greater than the falloff in rooms occupied after 9/11. During the late 1990s, Telecommunications Departmental profit margins reached 50 percent, and represented about 2.5% of the hotel's revenue. However, in 2007, Telecommunications Departmental revenue was less than 1% of the total revenue. This dramatic revenue loss is attributed to two factors: 1) the significant increase in the use and ownership of cellular phones, and 2) the unfair profit margins added to telephone charges in guest rooms. Most of the people who stayed in hotels would have a horror story about the phone charges that they faced while staying in hotels.

Hoteliers are trying new models to recap the lost revenues from phones. These new models will be discussed later in the chapter.

Brief History of Hotel Telephone Service

In 1944, the Federal Communications Commission (FCC) approved a proposal that was to structure the economic relationship between the hotel industry and the telephone industry. The ruling required telephone companies to pay a 15% commission for all long-distance calls originating in hotel rooms. As expected, this rule expedited the general introduction of telephones into American hotels. On June 1, 1981, the FCC ruled that hotels could make their own surcharges on interstate calls. After this date, telephone revenue started to become a significant revenue source for hotels. Hotels made significant revenues from phone calls up to the 2000s. For the last decade, many U.S. consumers adopted cell phones, therefore, eliminating the need to use hotel guest room phones. As explained above, hotels now lost this profitable revenue source.

HOBIC: Before 1981, hotels were using Hotel Billing Information System (HOBIC) to charge for the guests who used phone services in the guest room. In hotels using HOBIC, the guest talks to a phone company operator who then connects the guest to the desired number. After the call is over, the phone company charges the hotel and the hotel charges the guest. Before 1981, hotels could not charge more than what the phone operator would charge the guest. The phone company would then pay a commission to the hotel (typically 10 to 15%). HOBIC caused hoteliers to lose revenue because:

- Guests were giving wrong room numbers
- Mispostings and late charges
- Insufficient commissions

Once it became legal for hotels to make a profit on phone calls after 1981, hotels started to use a call accounting system to keep track of calls made from the hotel. Call Accounting System (CAS) is software that tracks the extensions where the calls originated, number dialed, duration of the call, and cost of the call. CAS works with Private Branch Exchange (PBX), which is a system that manages the actual phone lines. For each call, CAS creates a "call record" in which all details of the call are recorded. CAS can stand alone or be interfaced to PMS. In most hotels, CAS is directly interfaced to the PMS, eliminating the need to post the phone charges to the guest's folio manually. In stand-alone CAS, the call records are printed via a printer. From there, the front cashier enters them into guest folios. CAS keeps track not only of guest calls but also hotel staff calls. This way, hotel management can determine the cost of staff calls and even keep track of calls made by staff members. A typical CAS will have the following features:

- Call Automatic identification of outward dialing: As soon as an external number is dialed, CAS identifies the extension from which the call is made. This way, if the call is made from a guest room, the folio may be charged at the end of the call. If the call originated from a staff extension, the cost of the call is then recorded.
- Automatic route selection: This feature is applicable to hotels where more than one carrier such as AT&T or Sprint is used. Hotel management can enter the rates charged by common carriers for different areas. CAS will choose the best carrier based on given rate information as soon as the caller dials the destination number. For example, if a guest is calling Boston from New York City, CAS will compare the rates from carriers for that distance. If the per minute cost of that call is $0.20 for AT&T and $0.15 for Sprint, the CAS will place that call over Sprint. If Sprint is not available for any reason, then the call will be placed using AT&T.
- Least cost routing: As soon as the number to be called is dialed, CAS is capable of choosing the least cost carrier to that particular destination as explained above.
- Call rating program: Once the call is finished, CAS will rate the call and send the charge to the guest's folio. CAS has the capability to rate the calls differently depending upon the time of the day, day of the week, or destination. The hotel management can enter the rating information into CAS.

INTERNET ACCESS IN HOTELS

Internet access is becoming a necessary amenity of a hotel room. There are two different business models currently: some hotels offer Internet access free of charge, in other words, they build in the Internet cost into the room rate; and some hotels charge extra for Internet access, usually a daily rate. The rates for 24-hour Internet access can change anywhere from $6.99 to $49.99 per day. There are three main types of Internet access in guest rooms:

- Dial-up access: This is the first generation of Internet access in the guest rooms. In this system, guests connect to their Internet service providers via computer modem and data port of a hotel room phone. Dial-up access is limited to 56 kilobits per second (Kbps) transmission speed, which is not acceptable for most travelers in 2010. However, there are some business travelers who would prefer dial-up access because of security concerns.
- High-Speed Internet Access-Wired: Once the dial-up access to the Internet did not satisfy guests, hotels started to offer wired high-speed Internet access. Depending on the type of the cable and bandwidth used by the hotel, the speed of the high-speed Internet connection can change from 1 Megabit per second (Mbps) to 100Mbps. Guests have an Ethernet cable inside the guest room which they attach to the network interface card of their computer, usually a portable computer. Once they are connected, most hotels would force guests to accept a liability statement even if the high-speed Internet is provided free of charge or for a fee. The setup cost of wired high-speed Internet is quite high.
- High-Speed Internet Access-Wireless: There are two main reasons why hotels started to offer wireless high speed Internet access: physical constraints (i.e., public spaces) and cost. The cost of setting up a wireless Internet system compared to wired Internet system is significantly lower. However, there are increased security concerns with wireless Internet access. Since the wireless Internet waves are usually not protected, or unsecure, the information which the guests are transferring over the air may be captured and seen by hackers. Even though the security is an issue, the use of wireless Internet access in public spaces, such as a hotel, is increasing every day. There are four main standards that wireless Internet access is provided. These are 802.11b, 802.11g, 802.11a, 802.11n. All of them are wireless Internet standards created by the Institute of Electrical and Electronics Engineers (IEEE). 802.11b is one of the first standards that transmit data up to 11Mbps. A newer standard, 802.11g and 802.11a can transmit data up to 54Mbps. The most recent 802.11n can transmit data up to 100Mbps. There are several wireless standards being developed by IEEE, such as 802.11i and 802.11r.

FUTURE OF TELEPHONES IN HOTELS

Since the phone revenue center practically died in hotels, hoteliers are looking for new ways to create revenue centers. One ways hoteliers are trying is to offer "bundles" to the guests. Wyndham International was one of the first chains that offered a bundle to their frequent guest stay program members (Wyndham by Request). Any Wyndham by Request member got free Internet access, free local and national calls. Westin Hotel at O'Hare Airport is charging $9.99 for Internet access for 24 hours. However, they also offer a "Telecom Bundle" option for $16 a day that includes:

- High Speed Internet Access
- Domestic Long Distance Calls
- Toll-free Calls
- Local Calls
- Operator Assistance

Many other hotel chains started to offer bundle rates. The reason why hotels can freely offer these bundle options where unlimited local and long distance calls are included is the birth of a new telecommunication technology: Voice over Internet Protocol or VOIP.

Voice over Internet Protocol is a technology that allows the users to make voice calls using a broadband Internet connection instead of a regular (or analog) phone line. The human voice is carried over the Internet instead of twisted-pair cables. In the early days of the VOIP technology, the sound quality of VOIP calls was less than regular analog calls. However, as the technology evolves, the quality is nearing that of traditional telephones. For a hotel to use a VOIP system, it must have a broadband, high-speed Internet connection and additional hardware, such as a digital modem or VOIP gateway, is required (See Figure 6.11C).

Hotel chains have so many locations, and those locations are typically connected via an IP network that supports the chain's data services. By utilizing that IP network to carry

FIGURE 6-11A. MODEM.

Source: © Pablo Eder, 2008. Used under License from Shutterstock, Inc.

FIGURE 6-11B. VOIP.

Source: © Rob Bouwman, 2008. Used under License from Shutterstock, Inc.

FIGURE 6-11C. VOIP GATEWAY.

Source: © Lukasz Krol, 2008. Used under License from Shutterstock, Inc.

the long-distance portion of guests' voice calls, hotels can significantly lower their telecom costs. In fact, those savings can be substantial enough to allow hotels to pass a significant percentage of those savings on to their guests and still increase their per call profits.

The hotels will most likely pay a flat monthly fee to the Internet service provider (ISP) for an unlimited number of calls. A hotel can switch its traditional phone system into VOIP by using two methods:

- Using the traditional, analog handsets: The hotels can use their existing handsets; however, they have to use an "analog adaptor" to convert the analog signals into digital signals. The average cost of an analog adaptor is $50 per telephone handset.
- Replacing the handsets with VOIP digital phones: This is the expensive option. In 2007, average cost of a VOIP handset is about $500 per unit. (See Figure 6-12) However, it offers many more options than the traditional handset. By using VOIP phones, hotels can offer more features than just the phone calls to the guest. VOIP phones become service and application delivery devices. They can offer and act as:
    - Digital voice mail
    - Alarm clock
    - Room service order device
    - Internet access
    - Gameboy
    - High speed Internet access port
    - Guest room control console (i.e., control lights, TV, DVD, temperature)
    - Digital hotel guide
    - Order hotel services (i.e., spa, massage, golf)
    - Group calling

VOIP phones are clearly the future of hotel telephony.

FIGURE 6-12. VOIP HANDSET.

Source: © Elena Elisseeva, 2008. Used under License from Shutterstock, Inc.

Voice Mail/Wake-Up Systems

Most of the hotels that have telephone in the guest room offer voicemail service. A hotel using voice mail assigns a voice mailbox to each guest upon check-in. If the voice mail system is interfaced with PMS, the voice mail talks to the guest in the guest's language (i.e., English, German, Spanish). The guests have the option to set up the voice mail or leave it as a default message. Guests can record their greeting recording or set a unique PIN code to access the voice messages. When the guest presses the button on the guest room telephone, he/she is connected to the voice mail system. Voice mail system then confirms that the mailbox corresponds to the room number. A guest may hear, for instance, "This is mailbox 1100. You have three unplayed messages. Please press 1 to hear the new messages." Once the guest listens to a new message, the voice mail system gives the guest the option to cancel, save, or forward the message to another user in the hotel. In some systems, when the guest presses the "voice mail" button on the telephone, it connects to the operator, then the operator connects the guest to the voice mail system manually. When the guest is checked out, some voice mail systems delete all messages and refresh the voice mail system for the new guest. In some voice mail systems, messages may be available for up to 24 hours after departure to accommodate guests who did not have time to pick up their messages before check-out, provided that there is no new guest checked into the same guest room.

The voice mail system has the following advantages for the guests:

i. It enables the guest to leave a personalized greeting message.
ii. It eliminates the delivery of inaccurate and incomplete messages.
iii. It enables the messages to be delivered in the guest's native language.
iv. It quickly notifies the guest that new messages are waiting.

The voice mail system has the following advantages for the hoteliers:

a. It significantly reduces the number of messages taken by the operator.
b. Voice mail can be used to broadcast wake-up calls and other announcements to groups.
c. Voice mail can improve communication among the staff members.

Voice mail systems also have automatic wake-up systems. In hotels, there are four different wake-up systems:

1. Manual wake-up system: The guest calls the operator and the operator logs the time desired on a paper. When the time comes for the guest's wake-up time, an operator calls the room phone to wake up the guest. Obviously, this system requires manual attention. In addition, in the case of multiple wake-up requests at the same time, it may take a lot of time for the operator to call the rooms manually, especially when the guest does not answer on the first or second trial. This may cause the other wake-up calls to be done later than requested.
2. Semi-automated wake-up system: In this system, the guest calls the operator with a request for a wake-up call. The operator enters this time into wake-up system manually. When the wake-up time comes, the wake up system calls the room automatically, playing a prerecorded message. The message most likely will say: "This is your wake-up call. This is your wake-up call." If the guest does not answer, the system waits 5 minutes and tries again. If the guest still does not answer, the system tries again ringing the room after 5 minutes. If the guest does not answer after the fourth trial, some systems can simply ignore the wake-up call request. Some wake-up systems may send a message to the hotel operator who can then send security personnel to the room to check on the guest. Sometimes, this happens simply because the guest wakes up before the wake-up time and leaves the guest room without cancelling the wake-up call.
3. Full-automated wake-up system: In this system, when the guest presses the wake-up call button on the guest room telephone, he/she is connected to wake-up system to enter the wake-up time. Typically, the guest hears a message like this: "Welcome to Wake-up system. Please enter your desired wake-up time by pressing the buttons. For example for 7 o'clock in the morning, please enter 0700." Once the guest enters the wake-up time, the system asks the guest to confirm. Upon confirmation, the system records the desired wake-up time and when that time comes, it calls the guest room phone automatically. Upon answering, it plays a prerecorded message.
4. Interactive TV System Wake-up System: Some interactive TV systems may also employ an interface to a wake-up system. The guest can set his/her wake-up time by using the TV remote control.

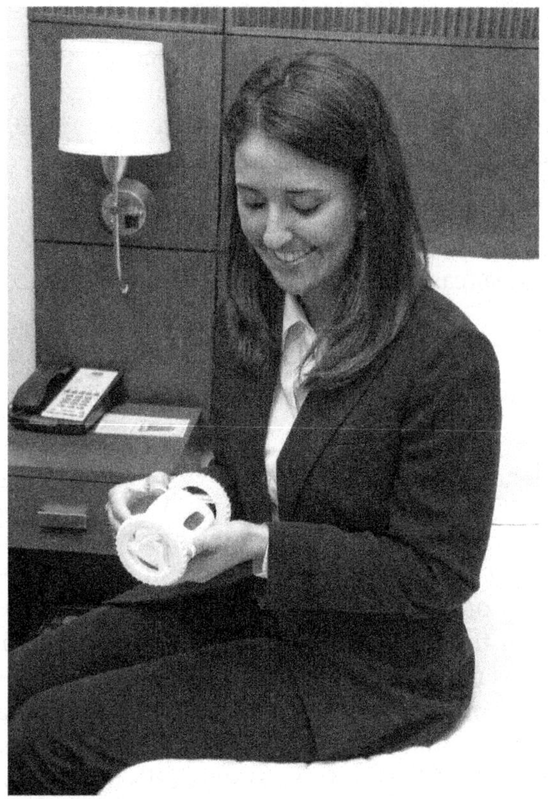

FIGURE 6-13. A GUEST SETTING CLOCKY, THE WALKING ALARM CLOCK.

In addition to wake-up systems, most hotels also provide an alarm clock in the guest room. Alarm clocks are one of the most important technology items in a business hotel (9). There are new innovative alarm clocks. For example, a walking alarm clock, Clocky in X-Room at the University of Delaware's teaching hotel, Courtyard by Marriott, has been very popular. Figure 6-13 shows a guest setting Clocky.

In-Room Entertainment Systems

In 1975, the only entertainment system some hotels offered was color TV. After 1980, even small hotels offered color TV as an amenity. Since 2007, in-room entertainment systems include much more than just a color TV. At home, at work, and even on the go, business and leisure travelers are spoiled with a myriad of multimedia and entertainment options. These days, travelers are making it known they expect a high level of entertainment choices in their hotel rooms. In-room entertainment is one of the fastest growing revenue generating opportunities in hospitality (10). Guests are showing a greater willingness to pay for movies, video-on-demand, in-room games, and high-speed Internet access. Traditionally, hoteliers have provided little to no entertainment in the guest room aside from conventional cable television. Now, the entertainment medium offers technologies, like high definition flat-panel monitors and video-on-demand equipment. This new generation of technology allows the guests to watch what they want, when they want it. In-room entertainment systems along with other interfaced systems offer:

- Personalized welcome message upon check-in: When the guest checks in, a personalized welcome message appears on the TV.
- Video on demand (pay per view): The digital videos that the guests can order and have the option to start, pause, rewind and fast forward. Not only movies are available but also shows such as Naked Chef are also available.
- High speed Internet access (with some free content such as weather or news websites)
- Wake-up call: The system can be interfaced to a wake up system.
- Order room service: An interface to a point of sale system allows the guest to order room service through the TV. This way, the guests can see the pictures of the menu items.
- Live feedback (through surveys): When the guest fills out the hotel survey and marks any of the questions very low, the system, through a paging system interface, automatically pages the manager on duty so that he/she can fix the problem before the guest leaves.
- Different languages: All interactive TV systems can be available in multiple languages, making it easy for guests to use.
- Internet Protocol based Radio: Interactive TV systems can tune into radio stations that are broadcasting over the Internet and allowing guests to listen to radio channels from all over the world. (i.e., A Turkish guest staying in a New York hotel can listen Kral FM, a popular radio channel in Turkey).
- View Bill/Self-Check-out System: Through an interface to property management system guests can view their folio and check out from the convenience of the guest room. Once they are checked out, they can leave the hotel. The invoice will follow them in the mail.
- Parental Controls: Interactive TV system allows parents to control the content of the system. For example, parents may want to block adult movies for their children's room.

In-room entertainment systems offer compatibility with the guests' own multimedia devices. Many travelers today carry their MP3 players and portable DVD players. These interactive TV systems allow guests to connect these devices to the TV, allowing the guest to watch/listen to his/her digital content on a more comfortable media. For example, TeleAdapt Company offers guest connectivity panels which allow the guest to connect any laptop, iPod, digital or video camera to the TV system in the room.

Guest Room Control Panels

There is nothing worse than finding out that you have to get out of bed to turn the lights off once you are in bed. If you are in a hotel where there is no guest room control panel, this might be what you will have to do. Some hotels may install a switch by the bedside for the guest to control the lights in the room. Even though this is a great idea, it may not give full satisfaction. In the guest room, there are many things that can be controlled

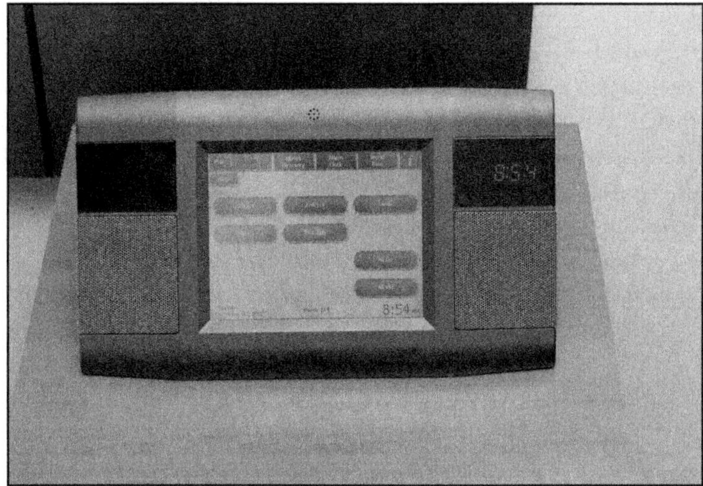

FIGURE 6-14. MEDIA HUB.

by the guest to customize the experience. These can be done by installing a guest room control panel. Figure 6-14 shows different screen shots of a guest room control panel by Inncom.

What guests can control by using a guest room control panel varies with the technology amenities that the guest room offers. However, in a typical hotel, a guest can control the following systems with a guest room control panel:

- Temperature (HVAC Equipment)
- Lights

- Curtains
- TV
- DVD player

If the guest room control panel supports it, it can also function as:

- Alarm clock (set the alarm clock or see the clock)
- Radio
- CD Player
- Digital Gameboy
- Do not disturb/make up my room device

Additionally, hotels may employ an electronic "do not disturb/ make up my room (DND/MUR)" button. This device, working with security systems, allows the guest to activate/deactivate a button by the bedside guest room control panel. Activation of DND will disable the door bell and illuminate a red light by the door alerting outsiders that the guest does not want to be disturbed. If there is an interface to the door lock, the door lock may not even open the lock unless a master key is used when DND is active. Activation of MUR alerts the housekeeping department electronically to send a housekeeper to the room immediately. The use of electronic DND/MUR buttons have clear advantages over paper/ over the doorknob DND/MUR signs. The paper signs can fall or be taken by someone, therefore allowing the guest to be disturbed.

Self Check-In/ Out Systems

High-tech or high-touch? This is the question that many hoteliers would like to answer. Even though we are in the service industry, there are cases where our guests do not want personalized service, and they just want to do the job by themselves. Checking-in and checking-out are two of them. According to BusinessWeek magazine (11), business travelers will expect self-service technologies from airlines and hotels like they expect ATMs from banks. Business travelers repeatedly indicated in surveys that they hate to wait in line when they are checking in or checking out from a hotel. Here is when the self-check-in/check-out technology comes into play. For the typical airline, kiosks process approximately 40 percent of check-ins, reducing costs approximately $32 million dollars annually on a baseline of labor costs for check-in of $118 million dollars per year (12). For the typical hotel, one study showed that self-check-in/check-out technologies can generate a savings of 15 to 20 percent on staffing as well as reduce replacement costs, which ranges from $6,000 to $11,000 per person.

- Up-selling room categories based on availability and guests' buying habits.
- Making dynamic one-to-one marketing offers—such as spa, restaurant and local attraction tie-ins—at critical guest touch point.
- Providing advertising screen real estate to local merchants. There are several ways of self-check-in:
- Kiosk-based: The hotel has a kiosk set up in lobby area where any traveler can identify themselves with the swipe of their credit card, hotel's loyalty card, or their reser-

vation confirmation number. The kiosk machine is capable of cutting an electronic key card for the guest room, printing registration information, and printing the instructions to go to the room from that particular kiosk. The kiosk must have an interface to a PMS. These kiosks can also be used for self-check-out. Embassy Suites hotels differentiate themselves by offering self-check-in service in every single Embassy Suites hotel in the world(13).

- Internet-based: Guests can check themselves in via the hotel's website up to 7 days in advance of the check-in day. Radisson Hotels and Resorts launched the first Internet based check-in service in 2004 (14). "Express Yourself" features a three-step process. First, guests reserve a room via any Radisson booking process (Web site, call center, hotel direct or through a travel agent). Then, seven days prior to their visit, they will receive an e-mail inviting them to "express" themselves by checking in at the Radisson Web site. Personal preferences might include requests for a specific room location (e.g., proximity to elevators, high or low floor), high speed Internet access, and special service requests. The last step in this process is that when the guests arrive at the hotel, they only need to identify themselves and pick up the room key and information. Some hotels also offer Internet-based check-in in smart phones or personal digital assistants such as Blackberry or Treo.
- Handheld PMS based: In addition to kiosk and Internet based check-in systems, there are also handheld PMS based check-in systems. In this system, the guest is checked in by hotel staff.

Usually cross-trained non-front desk employees such as servers or hosts/hostesses come out to the front desk to help check-in guests by using a handheld version of PMS. This system is ideal for resorts where many hotel guests check-out and check-in within the same day. The staff can check in guests on the curbs, parking areas, or in lines. The majority of the PMS vendors do offer their handheld version using a tablet PC or smaller portable computer.

There are also several ways of self-check-out:

- Kiosk based: Self check-in kiosk can also be used as self-check-out kiosks. The kiosk is capable of accepting credit card payments, printing the invoice, and accepting the used guest room key card.
- TV-based: If the TV system has an interface to PMS, the guest can check out by using the remote control and TV in the room. The guests are usually provided with a copy of their final bill in the morning of the check-out day. If the guest agrees with all the charges, he/she can simply press the "check-out" option of the TV-PMS interface. The total bill amount is credited to guest's credit card on file. If the guest does not agree with the charges, then self-check-out cannot be made at the guest room.

References

1. Elis, R. (April 2004). "Lodging has seen rapid advances in fire safety and security." *Hospitality Technology, 8* (3).
2. Shenglin Y., & Verbauwhede, I. (2005). "Automatic secure fingerprint verification system based on fuzzy vault scheme." In Acoustics, Speech, and Signal Processing, 2005. Proceedings. (ICASSP '05). IEEE International Conference on, 5 (pp. v/609–v/612 Vol. 5). doi: 10.1109/ICASSP.2005.1416377.
3. Ellis, D. (2006). "Get ready for the hotel of the future." CNNMoney. Available at http://money.cnn.com/2006/02/14/news/compa-nies/hotels_future/
4. Available at http://www.htmagazine.com/ME2/ dirmod.asp?sid=&nm=&type=MultiPublishing&mod=PublishingTitles&mid=3E19674330734FF1BBDA3D67B50C82F1&tier=4&id= 75D57CDB40E84DC59EE6C20622A66ED0
5. Whitford, M. (1998). "Technology: Energy-management systems save hoteliers money." Hotel-Online. Available at http://www.hotel-online.com/SpecialReports1998/Dec98_EnergyMgmt.html
6. Terry, L. (March 2003). "The conservative hotel." *Hospitality Technology, 7* (2).
7. Stoller, G. (November 10, 2005). "Better fire safety in hotels saves lives." USA Today. Available at http://www.usatoday.com/travel/destinations/2005-11-20-hotel-safety_x.htm
8. The Hotel and Motel Fire Safety Act of 1990. Available at http://www.usfa.dhs.gov/applications/hotel/hm-faq.cfm
9. Kistner, M., Cobanoglu, C., & Dickinson, C. (2005). "What keeps the hospitality industry from making the right technology investments—even when they are staring us in the face." International Hotel, Motel and Restaurant Show." Available at www.ahma.com/pdf/NewYorkHotelMotelShow-AHLA2005.pdf
10. In room entertainment system solutions. Available at http:// www.microsoft.com/industry/hospitality/solutions/ inroomentertainment.mspx
11. Available at www.businessweek.com/adsections/2005/pdf/ 0544_businesstravel.pdf
12. Available at http://www-03.ibm.com/industries/travel/doc/ content/solution/1353316106.html
13. Available at http://embassysuites.hilton.com/en/es/brand/ Business_Traveler.pdf;jsessionid=5I2GOSFHGM3LOCSGBIXMVC QKIYFCVUUC
14. Radisson Hotels & Resorts Initiates Online Check-in Process at all Hotels In the Americas. Available at http://www.hotel-online.com/News/PR2004_3rd/Sept04_RadissonExpress.html

CHAPTER 7

The Internet and Social Media

The Internet is becoming the town square for the global village of tomorrow.

Bill Gates

CHAPTER OUTLINE

What Is the Internet?

*The Internet is about Communication, **not** Technology*

The Internet, the world's largest collection of networks, is referred to, among other things, as cyberspace, the matrix, and the information superhighway. More accurately, it is a "global information and resources network" where people are able to share ideas and information and become acquainted (see Figure 7-1). This medium has revolutionized the way people can communicate and the ways business can be conducted. Each day, new additions are made to the existing applications and new sites are added. It covers all over the world like a blanket, and its coverage extends to the most unlikely of places. Check into an Internet discussion group on any evening and do not be surprised to see users from Hungary, Turkey, Fiji, or Brasilia.

Technically, the Internet is a conglomeration of thousands of computer networks utilizing a common set of technical protocols to create a worldwide communications medium. The Internet is a collection of networks linking millions of people throughout the world. It is the world's largest wide area network and the most complex data network existing today in the United States. There is no central computer, just a web of connections between thousands of independent systems. Technically, the Internet is an interconnected network based on the Transmission Control Protocol/Internet Protocol (TCP/IP) protocol,

FIGURE 7-1. INTERNET: A NETWORK OF NETWORKS.

Source: © Ilin Sergey, 2008. Used under license from Shutterstock, inc.

or sets of rules that govern how computers communicate on the Internet. Because the Internet uses a well-known and widely used communications protocol, a user can communicate via the Internet with about any kind of computer hardware (Dell, Apple, etc.). TCP enables two hosts to establish a connection and exchange streams of data. TCP depends on IP to move packets around the network on its behalf. Like a postal system, IP allows a user to address a package and drop it in the system. There is no direct link between the sender and the recipient. IP is referred to as a connectionless protocol because there is no continuing connection between the end points that are communicating. Each packet that travels through the Internet is treated as an independent unit of data without any relation to other units of data. IP is inherently unreliable, however. It does not guarantee to actually deliver the data to the destination undamaged or that data packets will be delivered in the order in which they were sent by the source. IP does not guarantee that only one copy of the data will be delivered to the destination. Consequently, TCP protects against data loss, data corruption, packet reordering, and data duplication by adding check sums and sequence numbers to transmitted data and, on the receiving side, sending back packets that acknowledge the receipt of data (webopedia.internet.com). IP networks refer to connectionless networks in which information and data are sent out by packets. IP networks have been expanding rapidly in the field of Internet and computer communications, where real time communications are normally not required. However, today, IP networks handle real time applications, such as Voice over IP (VoIP) (e.g., long distance phone calls, videoconferencing, video streaming, and unified messaging), with a high degree of reliability. Given the increasing demand for Internet access and a growing reliance among business users on IP networks, outfitting wireless and satellite networks with TCP/IP capabilities has become a top priority for providers. It can be likened to superhighways connecting major cities with smaller highways linking together small towns and villages where single lane residential and rural roads prevail. There are thousands of services over the Internet that provide access to electronic mail, World Wide Web (WWW) real time voice and video conversation, information storage and retrieval, document storage, social networking, Web 2.0 and 3.0 applications and chatting.

History of the Internet

History of the Internet: In the 1960s, information could be stored onto intermediate devices like tapes and disks and then transferred physically to another computer. Computer scientists began to explore ways for computers to directly communicate with each other and to connect to remote sites. This led to the development of ARPANET, a network project funded by the US Advanced Research Projects Agency. This experimental network was established to allow the military and research and educational institutions to exchange information between dissimilar hardware and operating platforms. Also, the network was designed to function when certain parts were physically damaged should the country come under nuclear attack.

In 1964, Paul Baran, a Rand Corporation research scientist, devised a computer communications network upon which messages were broken down into small packets, each with the address of the sender and the receiver. The packets were released over the network of interconnected computers and reassembled upon reaching their destination. Lost or damaged packets were resent. Baran's network allowed several users to share one communication line, eliminating the need for each computer to have its own communication line. Thus, the information superhighway was born where different types of data could travel down the same path.

The development and acceptance of **TRANSMISSION CONTROL PROTOCOL/ INTERNET PROTOCOL (TCP/IP)** as the standard communications protocol emerged in the 1970s. It allowed computers to talk to each other. Also in the 1970s, the educational community began to use the Internet. The number of users increased inspiring the development of new Internet tools such as electronic-mail, World Wide Web (WWW), file transfer protocol (FTP), Usenet, and remote log in.

By the 1980s, ARPANET had become the backbone (physical connection between major sites) of the Internet with 213 registered hosts (computers that provide services). There was a liaison of three organizations responsible for specific areas of the Internet. The National Science Foundation (NSF) provided funding for the backbone. Technical support was provided by the Internet Engineering Task Force (IETF), which included scientists, engineers, and other experts. They resolved technical and support-related issues to meet the standards set by the Internet Architecture Board (IAB). In the mid 1980s, the NSF connected educational and research facilities to various supercomputers located across the United States. In the late 1980s, a consortium of Michigan educational institutions (MERIT) was awarded a contract for the maintenance, upgrading, and administration of the network.

In the 1990s, a proposal by MERIT to allow commercial traffic was accepted. Profits generated were used to maintain and upgrade the infrastructure of the network. Commercial traffic made more people aware of the Internet. Today, a wide variety of businesses use every type of media (e.g., newspaper and television advertisements, business cards) to reference their Internet sites. Internet sites now became part of the brand and image of the company (i.e., Marriott.com, Hilton.com, and Starwood.com). New companies emerged solely on the Internet and their brand name is their website name (i.e., hotels.com, priceline.com, travelocity.com).

In April 1993, cooperative contracts were awarded for the management of the Network Information Center. Network Solutions (http://www.networksolutions.com) assigned each computer on the Internet with a unique address and handled the registration of **Domain Names** or the name of the computer connected to the network. In October 1998, the **Internet Corporation for Assigned Names and Numbers (ICANN)** was formed. ICANN is a nonprofit, private sector corporation formed by a broad coalition of the Internet's business, technical, academic, and user communities. ICANN has been recognized by the U.S. government as the global consensus entity to coordinate the technical management of the Internet's domain name system (DNS), the allocation of Internet Protocol (IP) address space, the assignment of protocol parameters, and the management of the root server system. These functions were previously performed under U.S. Government contract by Internet Assigned Numbers Authority (IANA) and other entities. The goal of ICANN's 19-member board is not to control the Internet, but to coordinate the management of specific technical, managerial, and policy development tasks that require central coordination. For example, ICANN approved 7 new top level domains in November, 2000. These new top level domains are: .biz, .info, .name, .pro, .aero, .coop, and .museum. Today, there are hundreds of sites that register domain names (i.e., register.com, directnic.com, hostito.com).

Usage and Growth

Usage and Growth. The Internet now serves approximately 2.4 billion people in more than 160 countries as of June 2012 (1). It is estimated that the net grows at a rate of 10% a month.

Asia ranks as the biggest user of the Internet (1 billion), followed by Europe region (518 million), and the United States of America and Canada (273 million). Oceania/Australia has the least population with access to the Internet (24 million). In Japan, Hong Kong, Korea, Singapore, Taiwan, India, Indonesia, and Malaysia, popularity of the Internet has risen significantly over the last decade. Even the remote Scott's Base on Antarctica is on the Internet. The number of Internet hosts in the world as of 2008 was about 541 million. This number was only 72 million in 2000 and 171 million in 2003. This dramatic increase can show the pace of the Internet adoption in the World. (2)

Who Uses the Net?

Who uses the Net? Today the answer would be anyone who has a computer and an Internet access. Before 1990, users were limited to government, educational, and research institutions. But today there are corporate and individual users online. Between 1990 and 2000, Commercial networks such as CompuServe, America Online, Prodigy, and AT&T provided their members with Internet connectivity via dial up. After 2000, a lot of Internet Service Providers (ISP) started to offer faster Internet connections to end users. These connections include Cable Modem, Integrated Services Digital Network (ISDN), Digital Subscriber Line (DSL 1.5 Mbps), and ISDN (128 kbps). In 2008, some companies such as Verizon started to offer Fiber Optic access to homes which is the fastest connection method available today.

The first hint of commercialism stirred up a storm of disapproval. Today, users are bombarded with commercials and receive "junk e-mail." Internet analysts estimate that 80 percent of the e-mails are junk e-mail (spam). The user community was once populated with scholars, researchers, and computer students who now comprise just a third of all users.

> *Give a person a fish and you feed them for a day; teach that person to use the Internet and they won't bother you for weeks.*
>
> ~Author Un-known (4).

Technology Tidbits

Just because a user deletes a message, does not mean it is gone. An able hacker or systems administrator can undelete a message.

1. **Domain Names.** A mail address is required to send e-mail. Host addresses and names are required to retrieve information, to have a conversation, or to connect to the various sites worldwide.

Each site on the Internet is identified by a unique "domain name." A domain name identifies the user name and the organizational name type. Snooty@XYZHotel.com is an example of a domain name where *Snooty* is the user name; *XYZHotel* is the organizational name, and *com* the organizational type. Listed below are original and new top level domains:

Original Top Level Domains	Used By	Access
.com	Commercial/ Business	Open to anyone
.net	Network	Open to anyone
.org	Organizations	Open to anyone
.edu	Educational Institutes	Restricted
.mil	Military	Restricted
.gov	Government	Restricted
.int	International Organizations	Restricted
New Top		
Level Domains		
.aero	Air transport industry	Restricted
.biz	Businesses	Open to anyone
.coop	Cooperatives	Restricted
.info	For anybody (Information)	Open to anyone
.museum	Museums	Restricted
.name	Individuals	Open to anyone
.pro	Professionals (Doctors, Lawyers, etc.)	Open to anyone

There are 243 country top level domain names. Each country name is somewhat associated with the country name. Here are some examples:

Country	TLD by Country
Argentina	.ar
Canada	.ca
Japan	.jp
New Zealand	.nz
Switzerland	.ch
Turkey	.tr
United States	.us

Larger organizations like Universities may have more than one Internet server requiring a subdomain. For example, Biff@math.univ.edu. Here, *Biff* is the user. *Math* is the name of the server at an educational institution. From this e-mail, we can know that Biff is a user in the math department of the University. At the University of Wisconsin, the dairy state, individual servers are named after native cheeses.

Mailing Lists

2. **Mailing Lists.** With mailing lists, messages can be sent in a flash to everyone on it. People with common interests are able to exchange information. Updates on a hotel property, good deals or new menus can be sent to regular guests. A user must subscribe to be on a mailing list. When no longer wishing to be on a list, a user must unsubscribe. Someone takes the responsibility to ensure that the content adheres to the topic on some mailing lists. This is not true of them all. In addition to the Unix-based mailing lists, there are web-based mailing lists (e.g., http://www.yahoogroups.com or http:// www.googlegroups.com) where one can create a group e-mail address and add and invite members. One of the hospitality related mailing lists is hotel-online. Hotel-online is a daily newsletter sent to subscribers via e-mail. About 20,000 hospitality professionals receive hotel-online e-mail newsletter. To subscribe, users should visit hotel-online.com website.

IRC: Internet Relay Chat

3. **IRC: Internet Relay Chat.** Internet Relay Chat (IRC) is a form of real-time Internet chat or synchronous conferencing. It is mainly designed for group (many-to-many) communication in discussion forums called channels, but also allows one-to-one communication via private message and both chat and data transfers via Direct Client-to-Client (5). The Windows version of IRC is called mIRC (http:// www.mirc.com)

Client software is necessary to connect to an IRC server. Channels are named after the topics they represent. For example, *#news* as the name suggests, is a place where news are discussed and *#chat* is simply a place to chat. Some IRCs are private. It is possible to participate only if invited by the operator or administrator.

Although IRCs seem to be chaotic recreational communication systems, they can be used for business purposes. Meetings and seminars are held on specific channels to discuss issues. Today, most users use web-based communication platforms. For example, Yahoo's Yahoo! Messenger (http://messenger.yahoo.com and Skype's instant messenger (http://www.skype.com) are used by millions of users everyday with the capability of tele- and videoconferencing.

Usenet Sites	
alt.beer	Everything you wanted to read about beer.
clari.biz.market	Commercial news articles on market trends.
misc.legal	Information on a variety of legal issues.
misc.jobs.misc	A place to start your job search.

Usenet: Internet Newsgroups

4. **Usenet: Internet Newsgroups.** Two Duke University students created Usenet, an electronic posting board to share information on the intricacies of the UNIX operating system. Today, Usenet has become a powerful communication medium on the Internet with nearly 9,000 groups enrolled. This feature can be likened to a large convention where meetings on different topics are being held in different meeting rooms where people are free to express opinions. The people in the meeting rooms are a mixture of personalities. Some are loud and vocal. A few are obnoxious characters. Others just observe.

Usenet, a worldwide distributed discussion system, consists of "newsgroups" with names classified hierarchically by subject. "Articles" or "messages" are "posted" to these newsgroups by people on computers with the appropriate software. These articles are then broadcast to other interconnected computer systems via a wide variety of networks. An article has three components: 1) a *header* tells the system where this message is to be posted, 2) the *message body* is where the user types the message, and 3) a *signature* reveals information about the author. The signature may be a creative ASCII graphic which is considered prestigious among cybernauts.

No persons or group has authority over the Usenet as a whole. No one controls who gets a news feed, who can post articles, and which articles are propagated where. Some newsgroups, however, are moderated where articles are first sent to a moderator for approval before appearing in the newsgroup. The new generation Usenet supports HTML-based messages which give the users more options in terms of how they can format their messages (e.g., color, pictures, and hotlinks). For those who have access to the Internet, but do not have access to a news server, Google Groups (http://www.googlegroups.com) allows reading and posting of text news groups via the World Wide Web.

TELNET

5. **Telnet.** Telnet (TELecommunication NETwork) allows a user to log onto a computer system on which he or she has an account from a remote computer. For example, while visiting a friend at another University and wishing to view e-mail or to send messages, a user can access his or her University's computer with the friend's computer via Telnet. It is very similar to a phone call where an extension must be dialed. All that a user needs to get there from here is an internet protocol (IP) address (e.g., telnet system name where systemname is the remote system's IP address or domain name). Once connected, a user must enter an I.D. and password to access the system. TELNET, by default, does not encrypt any data sent over the connection (including passwords), and so it is often possible to eavesdrop on the communications and use the password later for malicious purposes. Because of this weakness of TELNET, users prefer Secure Shell or SSH that is a network protocol that allows data to be exchanged using a secure channel between two computers.

Information Retrieval and Search Services

File Transfer Protocol (FTP)

1. **File Transfer Protocol (FTP).** FTP is one of the oldest yet widely used services available on the Internet. It allows users to transfer files from one computer to another. FTP was developed by computer scientists to be used by computer scientists. Thus the syntax or commands used are not very user friendly. It is, however, a very useful tool to transfer information. To retrieve a file a user must know on which computer and directory it is stored. The Internet has a large volume of data in numerous computers making the process of looking for data like finding a needle in a haystack. "Index" read-me files, found at most sites, contain information about the files stored there. Users should read these files to acquaint themselves with information available. Some of the FTP clients are: WS_FTP (http:// www.ipswitch.com/), CuteFTP (http://www.cuteftp.com/) and FileZilla (http://filezilla-project.org/). Messages can be sent to the administrator to request more information about the site. Helpful FTP Commands include:

- *ls* – List files in the current directory
- *dir* – list files with detailed information
- *cd* – changes directory
- *get file* – downloads files to your computer
- *put file* – uploads files from your computer
- *help* – displays a help message
- *binary* – Informs the FTP server that you are downloading a binary file

Search Tools

Search Tools. Search engines, which compile an index of where information is stored, have three major components:

1. Spiders
2. Indexer
3. Search engine software

1. **Spiders:** A spider, also called a crawler or robot, is a program that automatically retrieves information from Web pages. The search engine sends out a spider to retrieve as many documents from the Web as possible. The spider visits a Web page, reads it, and follows the links contained in the site that lead to other pages. It returns to the same website on a regular basis to update the content.
2. **The Indexer** is another program within the search engine that reads and organizes the data received from the spider. The indexer adds this organized data to the index. The index, or catalog, contains a copy of every Web page that the spider has visited.
3. **The search engine software** is the program that scans through all the pages listed and recorded in the index to find matches to the requested information (keyword or phrase) or query as inputted by the user. The search engine ranks the Web sites in the order it believes most closely matches the requested information.

All major search engines work in the same manner, containing spiders, indexer, and search engine software. However, it is possible to get very different results to the same query from different search engines. The reason for this is the database and algorithms they use when searching for pages. Google (http://www.google.com) is the most used search engine in the world. According to the Nielsen// NetRatings Mega View Search reporting service, Google handles 60% of the all searches (6). Search engines also allow "targeted ads" where the users can buy "keywords". For example, Hilton Philadelphia can buy "Philadelphia Hotels" or "Philadelphia Marriott" keyword from Google. When a user enters these keywords, Hilton Philadelphia's website will appear on top of the list under "Sponsored Links" section. This is one of the main sources of revenue for search engines.

Search Engine Optimization

Search Engine Optimization (SEO) is the process of affecting the visibility of a website in a search engine's search results. Typically, if a website has higher rankings on the results, the more visitors will see the website, thus the more people will actually visit the link. For instance, if a visitor searches for "New York hotel", most likely the visitor will click on the links that appear on top.

The Internet and Hospitality Business

Travel

Destination Information

1. **Destination Information.** The Internet provides a wealth of information. Travelers on the Internet do not need passports or visas to get from one part of

the world to the other. The Internet abounds with ways to promote tourism. Technologically sophisticated sites can engage people in answering questions, making choices, and exploring vivid scenarios (e.g., 3D rendering of the Grand Canyon), significantly influencing their travel decisions.

Transportation

2. **Transportation.** There are resources for transportation on the Internet. Schedules to fare charts on airlines, trains, and buses can be found. The Internet brings mixed messages for the travel industry. If the Internet brings new opportunities, it also brings some threats. In the opinion of some analysts, the Web poses a threat to travel agents. Traditionally, travelers have relied on the expertise of travel agents. Today, most information is readily available on the Internet.

All U.S. domestic and the majority of the International airlines sell tickets on the Internet. Flight schedules and airport information can be found on almost all airline Web sites. American, United, and North west airlines provide reservation capability on online services. They even allow travelers to choose a seat online. In addition, airlines offer web-based alerts (via e-mail or cell phone short message-SMS) for flight information, cancellation, and delays. Even the Official Airlines Guide (OAG) has a Web presence. In order to get customers, airlines have offered online users deep discounts. American, Southwest, and North-west Airlines now send e-mail messages to subscribers informing them of last minute discount deals, which was formerly the domain of travel agents.

For the airlines, in the era of cutthroat pricing and fierce competition, there are substantial savings not having to pay commissions to travel agents.

Rather than be overrun by the Internet, many entrepreneurs have responded to this threat. The Internet now offers online travel agencies (OTAs); Expedia offers to travelers the services of a local travel agent. Instead of calling a discount agency or a local travel person, go online and make travel plans. There are hundreds of OTAs. Some of them are: Expedia, Travelocity, Hotels.com, Cheaptickets, TravelZoo, Yahoo Travel, Qixo.com, and Hotwire. Most countries offer also local OTAs. For example, in Turkey, one of the leading OTAs is sonfiyat.com (last price). In U.K., Cheapflights.co.uk is an example of an OTA.

Innovative and creative merchandising is now seen on the Web. Cathay Pacific Airlines auctioned off business class seats at reduced prices which appealed to travelers. This ploy enabled Cathay Pacific to sell seats which would have otherwise remained empty. The success of the first promotion was followed up by an auction of all the seats on a Boeing 747 to inaugurate services from New York to Hong Kong. U.S. Airways started to sell "choice seats" online to travelers when they check-in 24 hours before the flight departure time. This allows the travelers to pay about $10 for a better seat (usually in front of the cabin).

Lodging

Lodging. In 1994, The Hotel Switch Company (THISCo), a long-standing developer and provider of central reservations technology, started the TravelWeb. Hyatt hotels were the first chain to list its hotels and resorts on it. When this service first went online, the first reservation received was from two businessmen in Korea who requested rooms on Christmas Eve at the Westin in San Francisco (4). Today, the Internet is not just the domain of large hotel companies. Independent hotels and Bed and Breakfasts have gained access to this new delivery system. The following paragraphs discuss how this technology is being utilized in the lodging industry.

Reservation Capability

1. **Reservation Capability.** A guest can go online, search for hotels, select the room type and rate, and access information about the hotel and its location. If the guest is satisfied, data is entered which would verbally have been given to an agent to complete the reservation. The system provides the guest with a confirmation number.

Apart from reservations capabilities, most Web sites offer location search capability or the ability to search for a hotel at a particular destination. A Web site can be updated more quickly than any paper directory and a new addition to a chain can be listed more quickly and at a lower cost. For hotels of every size and destination, the hotel Web site is an increasingly critical source of profits. In 2007, Web-direct bookings climbed to over 34 percent of total reservations for major hotel chains, while independent hotels achieved an annual growth of 20 percent for direct bookings. (8)

Hoteliers are excited by the prospect of this relatively low cost delivery system for reservations. Most of the savings come from a reduction in labor costs and elimination of commissions to travel agents and CRSs. There are three different ways that a hotel can receive a reservation online:

1. **Hotel's Direct Website:** Some hotels have their own website in addition to the hotel chain's website. For example, Holiday Inn Niagara Falls has a website (http://www.holidayinn niagarafalls.com/) where they accept reservations.
2. **Hotel Chain's Website:** Since this hotel is part of the Holiday Inn chain as a franchisee, they also accept reservations from Holiday Inn's corporate website (http://www.holidayinn.com). This website acts like a central reservation system (CRS). The chain usually charges a fee for this reservation. The cost of the reservation to the hotel is different depending on the source of the reservation.
3. **Online Travel Agency (OTA).** A hotel can receive a reservation from an OTA. OTAs are supported by Global Distribution Systems (GDS). The main GDSs are Sabre, Galileo, Amadeus, and Worldspan. For example, Travelocity is supported by Sabre.

There is another company that acts as a bridge between hotels and OTAs. This company is called a switch. Switch Company enables a hotel's room inventory to be interfaced to OTAs. This way, travelers can book a hotel room directly from OTAs.

Each system involved in distribution has a different cost to hotels. For example, GDSs charge approximately $4.00 per transaction, switch systems charge $0.36, and CRSs charge $2.50. (15)

Guest Relations

2. **Guest Relations.** The Internet makes it an ideal tool for communication. Valuable feedback can be received from guests. Guests have the opportunity to send e-mail to the corporation to provide feedback on the products and services. In most hotels, senior executives have little contact with guests. The Internet can break these barriers. Guests can communicate with senior management. For example, the general manager of a Holiday Inn in the Midwest started a guest forum. Guests were encouraged to e-mail any comments. The general manager personally responded to each message. Hoteliers can e-mail regular guests about promotions and special events while keeping in mind that most Internet users are bombarded with junk e-mail. Finally, customer service can be taken to new heights if Web sites are linked to guest history files. This would enable guests to review and update their guest histories and to access and transfer points earned through frequent traveler programs (e.g. Hilton.com membership program). There are hotel review sites such as TripAdvisor.Com that enable travelers to post their experiences to the web that is shared with thousands of travelers.

Public Relations

3. **Public Relations.** If handled properly, corporate information can be put online. Most sites provide information about the corporate philosophy and financial status. This can promote goodwill and attract potential investors. The Internet is also a great way to emphasize any awards and distinctions earned by the property and its staff. Favorable comments from guests who have used the facility in the past can be posted online. Sheraton Hotels started a new program called "Share Your Story" (http://www.starwoodhotels.com/sheraton/index.html), which allows the Sheraton guests to post their travel stories and pictures on the Sheraton website.

For hospitality industry executives, the Internet is a double-edged sword. Free speech still prevails and users will express their discontent. A dissatisfied customer could set up a home page ridiculing a product or send an unflattering e-mail message to millions of users. Some have already felt the heat from "flames" sent by dissatisfied guests. A lot of travelers search review websites before they make a booking, especially for hotels with which they are not familiar. On the other hand, some hotels use the reviews as a marketing tool. For example, Affinia Hotels (http://www.affinia.com/) posts a link to TripAdvisor.com website where the potential guests can view the hotel's guest reviews. This shows that Affinia Hotel is very confident that the independent guest reviews will be very good and that potential guests will book comfortably from Affinia.

Electronic Newsletters

4. **Electronic Newsletters**. Internet users can subscribe to various newsgroups. Hospitality organizations have the opportunity to invite guests to subscribe to their newsletters which can be customized to give guests relevant information.

Product Information

5. **Product information.** Guests can preview sleeping rooms as well as the lobby, restaurant, and recreational facilities. Potential guests can print maps. The Shangri-La hotel chain, for example, offers interesting facts about the various locales on their Web site. Homewood Suites by Hilton (http://homewoodsuites1.hilton.com) is the first hotel that offers an interactive tool allowing guests to view hotel floor plans and book specific suite types based on their location, photographs, and descriptions.

Competitive Advantage

6. **Competitive Advantage.** The Internet levels the playing field. It is the closest an independent property or privately owned bed and breakfast can come to a global reservation system without investing millions of dollars.

Electronic Brochures

7. **Electronic Brochures.** Electronic sales brochures can be created on the Web to provide meeting space and convention services information to meeting planners and guests. With VRML, three dimensional pictures can be easily incorporated into a Web page. Guests are able to view meeting room space and various types of room setups and layouts. Forms can be created for potential customers to request more information.

Conference Registration

8. **Conference Registration.** If guest room reservations can be taken on the Internet, then hotels can expand the use of the Web. Guests can check the web site for various conferences being held at the hotel, complete their registration online and even complete room reservations.

Event Information

9. **Event Information.** Information on conferences and various upcoming events can be displayed for meeting planners.

Food and Beverage

Food and Beverage. Food service resources are a presence on the Internet as restaurants, pubs, cafes, magazines, suppliers, institutional foodservice companies, and consultants.

Dining Guides

1. **Dining Guides.** The printed dining guides now have Internet versions which include the currently text-based *A La Carte Guide to North America* and the *Interactive City Guides*. These electronic guides give either summarized or detailed information about an eatery. Some guides have been established by big city guide developers. In smaller cities, Web site promoters offer restaurateurs the opportunity to get their restaurant online. Most sites provide menus. Most chains list daily specials and nutritional analysis. Helpful information such as the hours of operation, credit cards

accepted, reservation information, directions, and house policies are provided by most sites.

Reservations and Order Taking

2. **Reservations and Order Taking.** Some restaurants have started accepting online reservations (i.e., http://www.papajohns.com/). An easy to use form enables guests to provide the necessary information. The restaurant then calls back to confirm the reservation. New third-party online ordering companies emerged. One of the leaders is OpenTable (http://www.opentable.com/) that is a supplier of reservation, table management, and guest management software for restaurants. The system replaces pen-and-paper at the host stand. It automates the process of taking reservations and managing tables, while allowing restaurants to build robust diner databases for superior guest recognition and targeted e-mail marketing.

Guest Relations

3. **Guest Relations.** E-mail offers all restaurants an opportunity to communicate with potential and current patrons. A potential guest unfamiliar with a cuisine can get additional information. Customers can comment on their dining experiences. Not all sites offer interactivity. The operations budget may not allow for it. In that case, a restaurateur can subscribe to an online service to communicate via e-mail.

Public Relations

4. **Public Relations.** Upbeat information (e.g., restaurant reviews, testimonials, community activities, etc.) about an establishment, and its employees can be put online to promote an establishment.

Merchandising and Promotion

5. **Merchandising and Promotion.** Promotions, coupons, and contests can be put online to attract customers.

Information

6. **Information.** Restaurateurs or "Cyberateurs" can use the Internet to access recipes as well as the latest issues and regulations concerning the industry.

Technology

Technology. Most major hospitality technology vendors are online providing:

- Product updates and information.
- Help desk services.
- User Group forums. These can be archived so that users can search for solutions to problems.
- Software upgrades and demo versions of the software.

Education and Research

Education and Research. The Internet is the world's largest library. It is like one huge database, a virtual library. It has a vast amount of educational and reference material. As users browse the Internet, they will probably find something that fits right into something they are working on. It is a good place to start research. Examples of databases include:

- Legal information
- Food and nutrition
- Alcoholism
- Article databases
- The Library of Congress card catalog
- Distance learning

These databases are created and maintained by people attached to full-time Internet nodes. They were usually created with another market in mind and then added to the Internet as an afterthought.

Since people can easily contact each other, collaborative research will proliferate and speed innovations to the marketplace. Google Scholar (http://scholar.google.com) is a great example of an information resource that academics and industry professionals can access easily.

Intranets

What is an Intranet?

What is an Intranet? An Intranet is an internal network within a company (i.e., Marriott or Hilton). It communicates using Internet technology. The promise of cross platform collaborative technology was brought to the forefront by "groupware." It was believed that groupware products such as Lotus Notes and Microsoft Exchange would allow corporations to access data around the globe with ease, creating a collaborative environment. It proved, however, to be too costly and too complex. Many organizations settled for basic e-mail and meeting-scheduling software. The development of Intranets made groupware obsolete.

Why Does a Business Need an Intranet?

Why does a business need an Intranet? Most companies do so much paperwork—manuals, phone lists, human-resources documents, travel forms, countless reports, and internal memos. This information is forever changing and often out of date. With an Intranet, employees can browse the Web for current information. An Intranet, restricted mainly to employees of a corporation, sometimes may provide limited access to business partners and customers. A Silicon Valley based computer equipment manufacturer provides access to an online travel agency where employees can make travel plans.

The Intranet is easy to use and is not too costly. It runs on virtually every platform making it a popular choice in most industries.

Intranet in the Hospitality Industry

Intranet in the Hospitality Industry. To find an Intranet in a 50 room limited service hotel is unlikely. Hospitality organizations that distribute a large amount of data (such as corporate headquarters of hotel chains, large hotel properties, restaurant chains, institutional foodservice enterprises, and universities) could benefit from this technology.

E-Business Models

E-Business Models. One of the major characteristics of the Internet is that it enabled the creation of new business models. A business model is a method of doing business by which a company can generate revenue to sustain itself. Here are the some of the new business models that emerged on the Internet:

- **Name your price:** Pioneered by *Priceline.com*, this model allows a buyer to set the price he or she is willing to pay for a specific product or service. Priceline.com will try to match the customer's request with a supplier willing to sell the product or service at that price.
- **Find the best price:** According to this model, a consumer specifies his or her need and then the company locates the lowest price for that product or service. *Hotwire.com* uses this model to offer the best price to the customer. The customer has 30 minutes to accept or reject this offer. Similarly, insweb.com uses the same model for insurance services and eloan.com uses it for mortgages.
- **Affiliate marketing:** Affiliate marketing is an arrangement where a marketing partner (business, individual) has an arrangement with a company to refer consumers to the company's website so that the consumer can purchase a product or service. The marketing partner receives a predetermined commission (usually between 2 to 10 percent of the sales price) on the purchase of a product or service to which they referred. *Amazon.com* has over a half million affiliates.
- **Online auctions:** This model allows users and buyers to auction online. The most famous auction website is *ebay.com*. A commission is usually charged to the buyer and the seller.

The Future

The Internet has a history of surprises. The founders of the Web never envisioned the current usage, popularity, and growth. However, recent developments do provide some sense of where the Internet is headed. Here are some important issues to keep in mind:

Traffic

1. **Traffic.** Users often used to wait for extended periods of time to access popular sites because of the heavy traffic. In today's environment, waiting 5 seconds or more for a website to load is considered "unacceptable." People expect quicker download times every day. With the advancement of infrastructure such as fiber-optic networks, the speed that users connect to the Internet will be even faster. Verizon Company now offers fiber-optic, the fastest transmission medium, to households for affordable prices.

Broadband Service Availability

2. **Broadband Service Availability**. Broadband is a common term for technologies, such as DSL or Cable Modem offering higher speed access to the Internet in relation to dial-up service. The greater speed allows users to transfer larger data files and view streaming video faster and with fewer interruptions. Broadband speeds typically range from 128 Kbps to 30 Mbps or higher. Certain types of broadband services require a certain amount of bandwidth in order to function at an optimal level.

Current technologies include cable modem networks, DSL, fiber-optic networks, wireless cable networks, including multipoint microwave distribution system (MMDS) and local multipoint distribution service (LMDS), personal communication services (PCS) networks, and satellites. The apparent wealth of choice belies a void in broadband service availability and maturity, which could persist for many years. Business and residential users will frequently find fiber-optic broadband fiber-optic service and provider alternatives in locations outside of the top 60 U. S. metropolitan areas.

Security Issues

3. **Security Issues.** The perceived lack of security is insignificant compared to credit card fraud, paper money theft and break-ins in the real world. The notion that a hacker could steal credit card numbers, passwords, and information has many people concerned. These threats, however, have not stopped users from cybershopping. Today, almost everything can be purchased online. Users view the electronic catalogue, make a selection, and enter the required data: name, address, item quantity, and credit card number. The vendor verifies the order and calls up a credit card agent to authorize the charges.

For peace of mind, many cybershoppers want to also verify the identity of both the seller and the buyer. They do not want unauthorized people viewing transactions as they occur. They also want protection from hackers while the data is in transit or in storage. With the development of digital cash, digital counterfeiting will become a concern.

Businesses on the Web have set up firewalls to protect themselves from hackers. Others are incorporating encryption technology for sending sensitive e-mail messages and to protect transactions occurring on the Internet.

Encryption technology was developed at Stanford University in 1967. The software uses formulas to scramble data which makes it meaningless to an unauthorized user. Authorized users are provided with electronic keys to decode and unscramble the data. The system is similar to the process used with safe deposit boxes in hotels and banks. The hotel and the guest have keys, both of which must be inserted for the box to open. A variation of this technology is the usage of a digital or electronic signature. The sender digitally signs data by coding it with a private key. The receiver verifies the data with a public key to authenticate the identity of the sender and to check for any tampering in transit. Other variations being developed are digital certificates and digital cash. A digital certificate, like a driver's license, would include the name, address, public encryption key, and a digital signature. Businesses conducting online transactions can verify certificates to ensure that both parties are legitimate.

Consumer Generated Media (CGM) or Electronic Word of Mouth (eWOM)

4. **Consumer Generated Media (CGM) or Electronic Word of Mouth (eWOM).** As marketers would agree, word of mouth is one of the most effective marketing tools. Word-of-mouth referrals such as online reviews or guest blogs carry a whopping 92 percent trust rating.

There are many travel-related blog Web sites, including tripadvisor.com, travelpod.com, travelblog.org, and travellerspoint.com. According to American Management Association, there were 57 million blogs in 2006, doubling every six months. Approximately 40 percent of Internet users in the U.S. read blogs and 10 percent post blogs regularly. Considering the 92 percent trust rating placed on word-of-mouth, you can see how powerful this tool can be.

Similarly, social networking sites such as Facebook.com and MySpace.Com are becoming marketing tools for potential travelers. People read each other's experiences that include transportation, accommodations, and places to eat.

Software as a Service (SOAS)

5. **Software as a Service (SoAS).** With the advancement of Internet connection quality and speed, companies will be offering their software over the IP. SoAS is also known as Application Service Provider (ASP) or Cloud Computing. This will eliminate the need to set up expensive and time-consuming servers at properties. The software will be provided from the vendor's headquarters. Currently, only a few companies offer this because the Internet connection is not very reliable. For example, innRoad (http://www.innroad.com) is a cloud-based property management system (PMS). Literally a hotel can have a PMS in a day whereas, in the traditional server-client model, installation can take days if not weeks. SoAS or ASP is definitely a way to go in the future. The main concern with this service is that data is housed at a different location, on the vendor's servers. In the case of a dispute, organizations fear that the vendor may keep the data. This problem can be prevented with careful and thorough contacts.

Social Networks (SNW)

Social Interactions

As human beings we are social creatures, therefore, interactions with people are important parts of our daily lives. In the morning, you wake up and go to the coffee shop and interact with your barista, later you go to work and start interacting with your colleagues, you recommend a restaurant to your friend for lunch, you listen to your colleague about his or her vacation; personal interactions are everywhere. Lately, social media websites enabled *"virtual interactions"* with other people. We are not only interacting with people face to face, we are also virtually interacting with people and even with companies in front of the monitors. Conversations require people, and *social media* allows "electronic" conversations by bringing people together in a digital environment. Social media can take many different forms, including Internet forums, weblogs, blogs, picture-sharing, vlogs, wall-postings, e-mail, instant messaging, music-sharing, crowdsourcing, and voice over IP, to name a few. And they all share one common thing, they empower and enable us to reach out and connect. In the early 90s, the Internet was about "push" content, where the websites provided the content to the Internet users just like the printed media does. Over the past few years, social media websites such as Facebook, Twitter, TripAdvisor, and Yelp have revolutionized the Internet by allowing users to provide, connect, and interact with each other and also interact with businesses. Hotels, restaurants, even destinations within the hospitality industry must have a keen understanding of how to deliver their messages via social media websites if they are to compete in today's business environment. Social media changed the rules of the Internet game.

Definition of Social Media

You have heard the term social media lately everywhere but probably nobody explained to you before what social media is. Boyd and Ellison define social media websites as web-based services that allow individuals to (1) *construct a public or semi-public profile within a bounded system,* (2) *articulate a list of other users with whom they share a connection,*

SOCIAL MEDIA BECAME ONE OF THE MOST EFFECTIVE MARKETING TOOLS THAT HOSPITALITY COMPANYS USE

Source: © Artellia, 2013. Used under license form Shutterstock, Inc.

and (3) *view and traverse their list of connections and those made by others within the system*. So, they exist in online contexts, they allow users to create a profile, users may gather information from other users, and more importantly it allows users to post information and enable social interactions. Social media is one of the six crucial motivations for using the Internet. It has become a routine daily exercise for millions of users around the world. Forrester Research reported that 75% of Internet users use social media. Users of social media exercise a wide range of activities to include joining social groups, reading blogs, or contributing reviews to shopping sites.

Social media websites promote users to interact with each other. Key goals of those website users are not essentially to meet new people; instead, they are primarily communicating with *people who are already a part of their extended social network*. Therefore, social media plays an important role in word-of-mouth.

History of Social Media

Collaboration and community became the important characteristics of the Internet. These characteristics evolved the term Web 2.0. This term consists of a second genera-

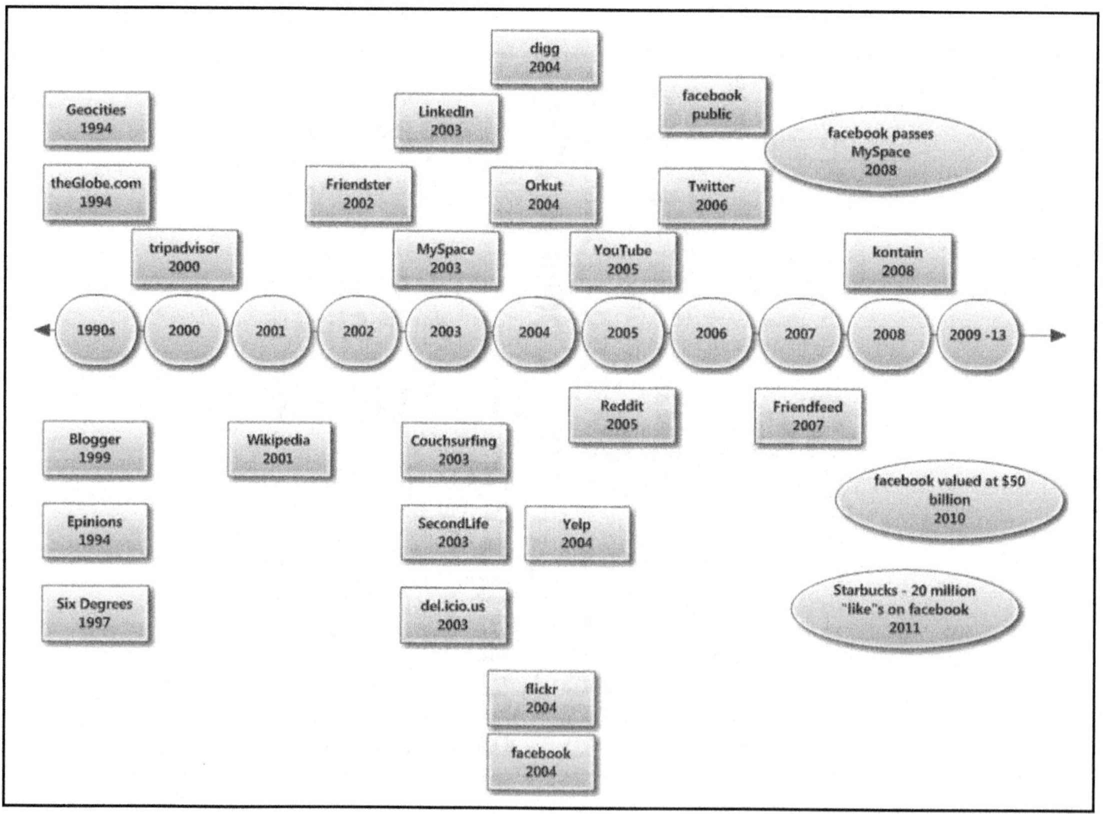

Source: Image courtesy of Anil Bilgihan.

tion of Web services that let people cooperate, collaborate, and share information online. Some of the Web 2.0 applications include social networking sites, wikis, blogs, and podcasting. Earlier social networking on the Internet started in the form of generalized online communities such as Theglobe.com (1994), and Geocities (1994). The first online communities concentrated upon gathering people to interact with each other via chat rooms. In 1995, Classmates.com took a different approach by linking people to each other via email addresses. In the late 90s, social media websites introduced user profiles as the principal feature that allows users to compile lists of friends and search for other profiles that shared similar interests. Newer social networking approaches were developed by the late 90s and social media websites initiated to expand advanced features for users to find and manage friends. This trend of social networking sites began to increase with the introduction of Friendster in 2002, and rapidly became a part of the Internet mainstream. MySpace and LinkedIn were introduced a year later. The rise of the MySpace was remarkable; by 2005, they were reported to get more page views than Google. Finally, Facebook launched in 2004, and turned out to be the largest social networking site. After the introduction of smart phones with GPS Location Based Services (LBS), consumers started to use virtual "check in" in social media websites that feeds "friends" about the location one visits and companies such as Starbucks started to use these services as a marketing tool.

Social Media Revolution

According to the Internet World Stats, the Internet usage has grown by 380% from 2000 to 2009. The Internet has changed the lifestyle of consumers dramatically. It changed the way that they shop, search, read, communicate, and so on. The foundation of these sites is maintenance of preexisting social networks such as colleagues, and alumni, on the contrary some help strangers connect based on their shared interests, friends, political views, or activities. Social media websites differ in the magnitude to which they incorporate new information and communication tools, such as mobile connectivity, blogging, microblogging, and photo/ video-sharing. Moreover, those sites developed rapidly as an information medium for hospitality product consumers and a platform for hospitality organizations to represent themselves. Web 2.0 presented new applications that changed the communication of the users in a social basis. As a result, electronic word of mouth became an uprising trend for consumers. Online communities became a common platform to broadcast e-word of mouth.

Individuals have many motivations to visit the Internet such as searching for information, communication, and shopping. Increasingly those individuals meet online to share their opinions and information, express views, and regularly update their status or post blogs and microblogs. More and more people discuss on forums and exchange information/opinions on social media websites. Even though most of these developments have been pushed by noncommercial purposes, consumers started to use these websites to review products and services, and to support or criticize organizations for the quality of their offerings. Consumers tend to trust their peers more than the marketing of organizations. Consequently these tools are turning out to be extremely significant for organizations. Travel discussion websites (such as Tripadvisor) and restaurant discussion websites (such as Yelp) are gaining popularity in terms of number of users and postings per user. From the industry perspective the trend is the same, meaning more and more organizations are using these websites as communication tools with their guests.

It is evident that people are depending on their peers' reviews before purchasing products and services. As a result, social media websites are growing both in popularity and importance for the consumers as well as corporations. They are not anymore only a platform for friends to stay connected. Those websites have advanced to a critical part of brand marketing. Unique visitors to Twitter increased around 2 percent every year. Additionally, Zimbio and Facebook had a significant growth of 240% and 228% respectively, in the last year. Facebook users can be a fan of their favorite brands and share their opinions and experiences with other fans. There is an unlimited number of opportunities that social media websites present to hospitality organizations.

Social media has become an important part of modern society. It is fascinating that there are social networking websites whose number of active users is larger than the population of most countries. Such websites have expanded with millions of users and grow daily. Social media had become an integral part of the society by the ways that people communicate, socialize, and work. Social media is not a fad, it is a fundamental shift in the way we communicate. This movement in some ways has also been dubbed as the "Social Media Revolution". There are niche sites for every special interest such as airline reviews, hotel reviews, restaurant reviews, dating services, etc. People update their Facebook status, tweet or write online anywhere, anytime thanks to new generation smart phones, and imagine what that means really for customer experiences.

Name	Focus	Number of Registered Users
Bebo	General	117,000,000
Classmates.com	School, college, work	50,000,000
CouchSurfing	Making connection between travelers and the communities they visit	2,967,421
Delicious	Social bookmarking, users can locate and save websites that match their own interest	8,822,921
devianArt	Art	22,000,000
Facebook	General	1,000,000,000
Flicker	Photo sharing	32,000,000
Foursquare	Location based, virtual check-in	20,000,000
Google+	General	400,000,000

Name	Focus	Number of Registered Users
Hospitality Club	Hospitality	328,629
Last.fm	Music	30,000,000
TravBuddy	Travel	1,588,000
Twitter	General, Microblogging	500,000,000

When you visit a hotel, you now see people using their smart phones to tweet, take a picture of the hotel and share it with their social network, or write a review. These social media messages can impact businesses significantly and as a future hospitality leader, you need to understand how social media impacts the industry. Not only are social media messages very influential when they come from friends and family members, but also they are powerful in the decision making process when they come from recommender websites.

Applications of Social Media in Hospitality Industry

Lately, social media has gained significant popularity in the hospitality industry. The impact of social media is significant for the industry. For example, contemporary consumers of hospitality services benefit from the Internet to acquire information, share their experiences/opinions/reviews for hotels, resorts, inns, vacations, restaurants, travel packages, vacation packages, and travel guides to reduce their risk before purchase. Therefore, social media plays a significant role in the process of decision making. After the introduction of Web 2.0, individuals started to build relationships with people from various destinations around the world. Additionally, through the travel phase, tourists have options to access social media websites while on the go, with smart phones that support social networking tools. Those people can share experiences, review hotels and destinations, and post photographs and videos from their trips. This applies to social media where you share the content with your friends and families (e.g., you share the photograph of your delicious entrée in Instagram), it also applies to social media where you share your opinions with people that you do not know necessarily (e.g., you share the photograph of your delicious entrée in Yelp.com and write a review about the restaurant). Travelers also use social media to depict, reconstruct, and recall their travel experiences. The impact of social media reviews is vital to hospitality industry, it is estimated that online reviews influence more than US$10 billion in online travel purchases every year.

In the hospitality industry domain, travelers gather information from popular travel website tripadvisor.com and similarly people who are looking for restaurants go to Yelp .com to read the reviews of restaurants. Therefore, social media websites present excellent opportunities for the hospitality industry to make greater contact with its customers, with the goal of building long lasting relationships with customers, and fostering brand image. Another potential advantage of social media is that guests are willing to share information about what they like and do not like. By using data-mining techniques, hoteliers and restaurateurs can get a sense of what guests want. Gathering data from social media websites with tools such as web spiders is important for hotels. Uses of these data may be more meaningful for specific properties that identify changes or for specific customer review trends. In these cases, managers and companies can find focus areas and determine how they vary with each property. By combining service scores with visualization data, an indexed service score results, which may be a more rigorous measure of the service delivered by properties and companies, because it allows for multiple measures.

Companies under the travel umbrella have their own Twitter pages and the number of companies that tweet is growing every day. Morgan Johnston, manager of corporate communications with Jet Blue explained their Twitter philosophy as "our role on Twitter is driven by the requests of our followers. Twitter is a great way to talk, but even better for listening." They defined their goal to make themselves available, help whenever possible, and to show that their brand is built by real people who care about their customers. According to Christi Day, the emerging social media specialist at Southwest Airlines, he used their Twitter page and had been blogging since he discovered Twitter in July 2007. He stated that the company is fascinated by Twitter's possibilities. Southwest Airlines uses their Twitter page to make their announcements, and they claim that they are open to ideas. Luxor Vegas explained that they are tweeting for "Customer insights, customer service knowledge & educating guests about the new Luxor and all our new offerings and/or special promotions." Hertz Official uses social media to create more community and awareness around their car rental service and sharing club. They see the service as a supportive outlet for developing relationships and building dialogue with customers.

Facebook pages of some hotels are encouraging their guests to provide online content in order to build a strong web presence. Some hotels provide an "Info" section in order to provide a lot of details about their hotels in their Facebook fan pages. Historic properties tend to share their heritage by posting old pictures of their properties. Some of the hotels are using these tools as a communication medium to announce events and then publishing photo albums of them. Very few hotels provide "insider access experience" by posting interview videos of their employees so that guests can meet the individuals behind the scenes. Again, very few hotels are engaging their followers by asking questions. Hilton Hotels' Facebook is followed by 62,213 fans, Sheraton has 61,330 fans on Facebook and Sheraton lets users to post their travel photos (currently they have 223). The phenomenon is valid in every segment, for instance Ritz-Carlton has a Facebook fan page (30,341 followers) that enables users to post their photos and videos.

Users and Statistical Data

A new, growing body of social media users are emerging and changing the ways we view our buying habits. Social media users receive and send positive and negative messages to millions of people a day about the hotels and restaurants they visit, how they were treated, how the food/room was, and if they would return again. These messages are likely to impact one's restaurant/hotel decisions and will only continue to be heavily relied upon in the future.

Social media has become the new "norm" of communication and is replacing the traditional face-to-face communications of the past. The difference now is instead of one person receiving the communication someone can send a single message to hundreds, thousands, or to millions all at once and within seconds.

More than half of consumers access social media websites both with their personal computers and mobile phones; the mobile access is on the rise (See Tables below). Around 40% of US consumers use social media to look for destination information, 35% use for restaurant information seeking, and 31% use for hotel information seeking before making purchase decisions (See Tables on following page).

TABLE 7-1. SOCIAL MEDIA WEBSITE USAGE PERCENTAGES

Social Media Website	Percentage
Facebook	97%
LinkedIn	17%
Myspace	22%
YouTube	71%
UStream	2%
Second Life	1%
Twitter	23%
Flickr	5%
Blogger	8%
Trip Advisor	10%
Other	6%

TABLE 7-2. SOCIAL MEDIA WEBSITE ACCESS WAYS

Access to SNW	Percentage
Mobile	2%
Computer	42%
Both mobile and computer	55%
Other	1%
Total	100%

TABLE 7-3. INFORMATION SHARING TRENDS (1 STRONGLY DISAGREE-7 STRONGLY AGREE)

Statement	Mean	Variance	Standard Deviation
I share information related to my hotel stays	3.45	3.51	1.87
I share information related to my airline trips	3.45	3.44	1.85
I share information related to my travel	4.45	3.69	1.92
I share information related to my dining experiences	4.23	3.54	1.88
The information I share with my network influences my decision to purchase travel related products (e.g., hotel, airline, destination, restaurant)	3.74	3.41	1.85
I share photos related to my hotel stays	4.58	3.67	1.92
I share photos related to my airline trips	4.16	3.82	1.95
I share photos related to my travel	5.45	3.09	1.76
I share photos related to my dining experiences	4.47	3.41	1.85
The photos I share with my network influence my decision to purchase travel related products (e.g., hotel, airline, destination, restaurant)	3.85	3.55	1.89

TABLE 7-4. PURCHASE DECISION THROUGH SOCIAL MEDIA WEBSITES

Statement	Percentage
I look for restaurant information	35%
I look for hotel information	31%
I look for destination information	36%
I look for bar/night information	37%
I do not use it to make decisions	45%

Statistics for Discussions

- *Travelers spend an enormous amount of time researching hotels online. On average, hotel consumers made twelve visits to an OTA's website, requested 7.5 pages per visit, and spent almost five minutes on each page before booking." (Cornell University research, April 2011)*
- *A negative review or comment on the Twitter, Facebook, or Youtube Web sites can lose companies as many as 30 customers.* (Convergys Corp)
- *"'Guest experience factors' which include past experience, reputation, recommendations, and online reviews, are critical to selecting a hotel by the majority of hotel guests. (51%)*

- *92% of internet users read product reviews and 89% of people say that reviews influence their purchasing decision.* (e-tailing group)
- *90% of consumers online trust recommendations from people they know; 70% trust opinions of unknown users. (Econsultancy)*
- *81% of respondents said they'd received advice from friends and followers relating to a product purchase through a social site; 74% of those who received such advice found it to be influential in their decision. (Click Z)*
- *64% said they use social media to make their travel plans and within the 25-34 year old participant group, the number is even higher; 76% look to popular social media sites to plan their next getaway.* (Sheraton Survey)
- *75% of people don't believe that companies tell the truth in advertisements. (Yankelovich)*
- *53% of people on Twitter recommend companies and/or products in their Tweets, with 48% of them delivering on their intention to buy the product. (ROI Research for Performance)*
- *Consumers were willing to pay up to 38% more for a 5-star rated hotel than for a 4-star rated hotel.* (comScore/Kelsey,)
- *35% of social media users changed their hotel after browsing a social platform. (World Travel Market)*
- *69% of online shoppers said they trusted the internet for advice, versus 43% for magazines and 35% for TV. (Yahoo)*
- *1 out of every 8 minutes online is spent on Facebook. (Comscore, February 2011)*
- *The average person spends 66% more time on social sites than a year ago, almost 6 hours vs. 3 hours, 31 minutes last year. (Nielsen)*
- *96% of online Americans use Facebook. (Bank Of America Merrill Lynch, May 2011)*
- *55% of Facebook users use the site to get travel advice. (Bank Of America Merrill Lynch, May 2011)*
- *64% of Facebook users have become fans of at least one company. (ExactTarget, 2011)*
- *51% of Facebook fans are more likely to buy from the brands they fan. (Imoderate Research Technologies, 2010)*
- *72% of businesses that use social media do not have a clear set of goals or a clear strategy for their social media platforms.(Mashable, 2012)*

Just sit back and think about the statistics above. How does social media impact the hospitality industry?

Current Uses, Issues, and Effects of Social Media

Many issues have risen from the expansion of social media. Some issues have been negative, while some have been a positive opportunity for restaurants, hotels, destinations, patrons, and employees alike. Social media has given a voice to everyone, which in some cases has become a public relations nightmare.

In a video posted on YouTube, a Domino's employee in Conover, N.C., prepared sandwiches for delivery by inserting cheese up his nose and applying nasal mucus on sandwiches, while a fellow employee provided a running commentary. In a couple days, thanks to the power of social media, they ended up with felony charges, millions of disgusted viewers, and a major company facing a public relations crisis.

Social media is a great tool for hospitality organizations to monitor what guests are saying about them. Sometimes, even the best companies make mistakes and irate guests sometimes air the complaint using social media channels instead of reaching out to the company directly. When such instances occur, the main goal of the customer is to get the company to respond. When managed properly, a complaint does not have to turn into a PR-nightmare come true.

Many customers expect to get a company response quickly. Further, they expect a customized response. It is important to take control of the situation by first apologizing for any issue the customer is having and letting the customer know that your intentions are there to help. Direct messages also very helpful, thus the organizations should ask for contact information so they can get the information needed to call the customer and start a longer conversation in private. Another important strategy is to thank the customer for giving you the opportunity to fix the problem and show that the issue has been satisfactorily resolved.

Various negative influences that social media have produced are complaints and criticisms that are broadcasted hundreds of thousands of times per day to others that truly hurt the companies. These negative messages are sent to family members, friends, coworkers and many others that "follow" one another daily through social media messaging, similarly, negative messages are shared with millions of people using recommender websites (e.g., restaurant reviews Yelp, hotel and destination reviews TripAdvisor, airline and airport reviews airlinequality.com). USA Today commented in a news article about couples "Twittering" while they visited a restaurant and quoted the following remark: "On your phone, you see her tweet: "I don't like the chicken I'm eating." What? Why doesn't she send it back? Suddenly, it hits you: She's telling scores of random strangers around the world that she doesn't like her meal..."

Social Media Through the Lens of Hospitality Industry Employees

Social media also plays a critical role for hospitality industry employees. Some hospitality companies such as Hyatt benefit from social media for talent acquisition. For many organizations, social media is important for sourcing and recruiting. Organizations are more than willing to throw away traditional methods in favor of more strategic, forward looking solutions. Solutions that focus on building relationships, extending the global reach, and creating a positive candidate experience. Randy Goldberg, VP of Talent Acquisition at Hyatt defines the role of social media in talent acquisition:

Blogs: Hyatt set up a Ning network (social media/blogging platform) connecting college recruits with alumni. Through this site, new recruits engage with existing employees and alumni to learn about the culture at Hyatt. This Ning site also serves as an initial onboarding tool since many of the new recruits become management trainees through the process.

Facebook: Hyatt Hotel and Resort Careers has over 28,000 fans and serves as a powerful tool for strengthening employer branding. Candidates are able to engage with recruiter, connect with peers and get questions answered quickly.

Twitter: Twitter is used to advertise jobs through tweets and engage in conversations with possible job candidates. Hyatt prioritizes the quality of conversations versus the quantity of followers.

LinkedIn: LinkedIn is used to recruit professional positions as well as create a strong alumni group. Many organizations are beginning to recognize that an alumni program will not only improve employer branding but can also serve as a recruiting tool. The catch is that employers need to create, manage, and cultivate these programs. Hyatt ensures that it has a dedicated individual, a strong communication strategy, a system to measure the progress, and of course, technology. Talent acquisition is one of the most dynamic areas of talent management and social media is continuing to evolve to meet both the internal and external pressures of today's economy.

Local chefs in the New York area are currently using Twitter and other social media sites to criticize each other, vendors, customers, and critics by venting and backlashing against comments made about their restaurants, their food, or each other. Mr. Dobias, a chef in New York states, "chefs are now going online to confront customers, bloggers, critics, rivals, and sometimes even their bosses". Dobias proceeded to write negative comments on Twitter about his fish purveyor who didn't show up on time with his deliveries. After the purveyor saw the comments he told Mr. Dubias that his business was no longer welcome and the relationship has come to a halt.

Ryan Skeen, an executive chef at Allen & Delancey, was unhappy with his employment in New York and used Twitter to be purposely fired. In November he said that he deliberately and successfully provoked the restaurant's owner, Richard Friedberg, into firing him with a series of posts on Twitter.

Social Media in Restaurants

Fadó Irish Pubs' director of marketing, John Piccirillo, states that the use of social media has been "a good extension of what we try to do in the pub". John feels that his followers give the company more attention through social media than what traditional e-mails generate. They also use Twitter as a customer service tool by answering questions or responding to complaints.

Deborah Topeik, marketing director of Z'Tejas restaurant comments that she likes Twitter because "it is a local preferred site for hotel or convention and visitor bureaus looking to follow news of local restaurants ... and it's great for me to say that we're doing an all-night long happy hour. These organizations know what we're doing. If I had to call every group, it would take too much time". Topeik also enjoys using social media to rectify a complaint before the customer leaves the restaurant.

Overall, most restaurants are using social media to get closer to their customers, use it as a marketing tool, promote their specials or, in the end, just defend themselves and their business. Whether social media induces negative or positive messages, restaurants are learning how to integrate this technology into their everyday business life practices.

Further, integration of social media with various Internet technologies is a recent trend. For example, OpenTable is an online restaurant reservation system and upscale restaurants started to integrate the OpenTable reservations with their social media websites. For example, users can go to the Facebook fan page of a restaurant and click on a link to make a reservation on OpenTable.com.

Key Social Media Terms

- *Collective intelligence*
- *Co-developers*
- *Co-creation*
- *Consumer experiences engagement*
- *Web 2.0*
- *Web 3.0*
- *Social Interaction*
- *Participation*
- *Trust economy*
- *Word of mouth*

Generation Y, Social Media, and Marketing Strategies

More than half of Generation Y members book travel arrangements online; also they spend their times on social media heavily, therefore, as future hospitality leaders you need to understand their behaviors in online contexts. Generation Y members use the Internet for social interactions and tend to share their travel and dining experiences online more often compared to other cohorts. They spend a considerable amount of time using social media for messaging, sharing information, and keeping in touch with friends. Consequently, it is critical for the hospitality industry to develop marketing strategies that help involve Generation Y customers in online social interactions and build long-term relationships.

Among the many demographic groups of consumers, Generation Y consumers represent a young and technology-savvy group. Growing up with the Internet, Generation Y consumers are heavy users of SNWs. Social media play a huge role in how they live their lives, and how they interact with their friends and family. For instance, It is also important to take note that this cohort is an economically robust cohort that comprises $200 billion annually in expenditures, which accounts for as much as "half the spending in the economy". Furthermore, this cohort is the sweet spot of the restaurant industry by spending the most money at restaurants on a per meal basis, and also having the largest party sizes resulting in a total spend per visit that is 25 percent above the average.

They are heavy users of a wide variety of social media, though the three most popular sites are Facebook, Twitter, and LinkedIn. On average, Generation Y exhibits very active information seeking and sharing behavior. This highlights the importance of social media marketing for this cohort, in the sense that hotels and restaurants must recognize and exploit the power of social media. Instead of distributing flyers and menus on the streets and mail, restaurants should build Facebook fan pages to connect with diners and post commercials or promotions on social media. If a restaurant does not offer such online interactions, it could be losing out on a vast number of potential patrons.

Chipotle's company policy mandates that someone answer every Facebook post, whether positive or negative, and typically within an hour or two. As Zagat has warned, restaurants should never underestimate how far the words "thank you" can go. Restaurants also can benefit uniquely from social media by using them as showcases for food, explaining the origins of menu items, and even showing videos of chefs in action. For example, Instragram is an excellent tool to use as showcases for food, as people enjoy looking at artful food. Further techniques involve generating new service ideas from social media. For example, Starbucks is one of the top brands in the hospitality industry using social media around the world. The company has been building their community for years; they started implementing My Starbucks Idea website in 2008 (http://mystarbucksidea.force.com), which was made as a reputation management tactic to improve Starbucks stance in the market. This website is a social media platform for Starbucks customers to share all their ideas, suggestions, and complaints. This website empowers customers to see what other customers are suggesting, vote on ideas, and check out the results. Their Motto is "Share, Vote, Discuss, See" and they have 3 main idea categories:

1. Product Ideas: Discussing new products, coffee flavors, new branches, and more.
2. Experience Ideas: atmosphere, music, payment methods, staff, and more.
3. Involvement Ideas: building and engaging community, social responsibility, and more

Starbucks is enjoying their success on all their social media; they have the most engaging content on the web and the most loyal and dedicated fans.

Hospitality organizations can also use social media as public relations tools, by posting press information. These efforts all should help organizations drive traffic to their websites. Because social media is about making connections, and considering the importance of Generation Y, hospitality organizations should connect with Generation Yers through social media.

Travel Industry in Information Age

Over the last 15 years the Internet has completely transformed how travel products are bought and sold. With the advancements of the Internet technologies, increasing numbers of travelers are using the Internet to seek destination information and to conduct transactions online. According to the Travel Industry Association of America, 67% of US travelers have used the Internet to search for information on destinations or check prices or schedules. In addition, 41% of US travelers have booked at least some aspects of their trips via the medium. However, the emphasis in the online experience began to shift from selling, searching, and consuming to creating, connecting, and exchanging. Throughout the last few years, the overall trend in travel businesses worldwide has been the adoption of new e-marketing strategies that utilize the ever-advancing Internet technology applications available today. One of the foremost technology applications used in travel business promotion has been the use of social media.

Almost 90% of leisure travelers reported being influenced by online travel reviews. Travel review readers seek information from virtual travel communities, travel guidebook sites, and travel distribution sites. The growth and impact of the social media on travel cannot be underestimated. In order to defend the online reputations, consumer reviews in social media context should be monitored regularly. Social media help travel businesses to create, to learn about competitors, and to intercept potential prospects.

Most Popular Online Social Networks

The top five social media websites in travel are: Tripadvisor, Virtualtourist, Igougo, Mytravel, and Yelp. But not all of social media websites or blogs specialize in travel; some present social discussions and postings about travel experiences by all types of travelers including businesses, families, and groups. This section will focus on leading social network technologies that have been used in travel: Facebook, Twitter, Myspace, Flickr, TripAdvisor, and Instragram.

1. *Facebook*
   Facebook was created in early 2004 by Mark Zuckerberg, Dustin Moskovitz, Chris Hughes, and Eduardo Saverin. Facebook is considered the largest social network with over 350 million users. The median age of a Facebook user is twenty-six. For the week ending January 30, 2010, visits to Facebook accounted for 49.23% of the overall number of visits to all of the top twenty social media websites combined. The Trips application, a social travel application built on Facebook Platform, enables Facebook users to share their travel plans and to make new friends while travelling. Trips application is a powerful tool that helps users to plan trips and share travel experiences. Users can search for other users who have similar travel interests and discover who will be travelling or has travelled to the destination of their interest.
2. *Twitter*
   Twitter is among the most recent social media websites that has evolved in a short amount of time. Twitter, founded on March 21, 2006, is a form of micro-blogging that limits users to posts with 140 characters or less. The median age of a user of this social network is 31 years old. In February 2009, it was ranked as the third most popular social network site in terms of the number of users, with 55 million visitors generated by 6 million visitors. Twitter has become a popular method for tracking and directing the consumer's attention to travel related products and services.
3. *Myspace*
   MySpace was launched in mid 2003 in Santa Monica, California by Tom Anderson. A recent study by Experian Hitwise stated that Myspace earned 16.36% of the overall visits to social networking sites. Young users (in their teens and 20s) are most prevalent on MySpace
4. *Flickr*
   Flickr can also be categorized as a content community in which users do not have to create a profile to view content. Flickr was developed by Ludicorp in 2004 and later purchased by Yahoo in 2005. Flickr emerged as a rich media sharing site

allowing millions of travelers to share their travel experiences through pictures. Flickr has over two billion pictures stored and over forty million visitors each month (Flickr.com).

5. *TripAdvisor*
   TripAdvisor was established in 2000 and since then has become a major travel information site. TripAdvisor has over twenty million unique visitors each month. TripAdvisor features more than 10,000,000 traveler reviews which have been used by members to plan nearly 17,000,000 trips within one week. Looking at other tourists' comments and travel blogs is the most popular online activity on TripAdvisor. Collaborative projects are the creation of many end-users who can add, remove, and change content. Travel businesses should be aware of the impact that collaborative projects can have on their businesses because of the increasing trend toward becoming a main source of information for end-users. TripAdvisor is the world's largest travel information and advice site with over five million unbiased reviews covering 220,000 hotels and attractions worldwide.
6. *Instagram*
   Instagram is a mobile-based photo-sharing social media tool with more than 100 million registered mobile users. These profiles allow brands to seamlessly connect their online and mobile efforts, exchanging content and engagement in one application (instead of fragmented between networks like Facebook and Twitter). On the web, a brand can showcase all of its photos in one place and connect to the brand's big picture, whether it is women's health and fitness like Lululemon or a heart-warming coffee from Starbucks. While uploading the photos is still limited to the mobile app, brands can gain followers, likes, and comments from the web-based profile. This means you not only are increasing exposure to a much wider audience on Instagram, but also growing your overall social community and brand engagement (e.g., http://instagram.com/whotels).

Social Media and Word of Mouth

Word of mouth (WOM) communication is perceived to be reliable, creditable, and trustworthy. Marketers spend billions of dollars in WOM initiatives. WOM in the context of social media and travel is of interest to hospitality industry practitioners because of the extraordinary growth, popularity, and influence of such networks. Firms are intentionally pushing for consumer-to-consumer communications through WOM communications. Users of social media interact for information related to travel and dining, and thus those applications are essential to spread positive WOM. People trust unbiased views from users outside their immediate social network, such as online reviews in TripAdvisor and Yelp. Web 2.0 presented new applications changing the users' communication on a social basis. As a result, electronic word of mouth (eWOM) became an uprising trend for consumers. In some instances, eWOM is a way of sharing insider information before deciding to engage in business with a firm. It is important to note that 19% of the postings on Twitter contain a brand name for a product or service. Of these postings, more than half of them were positive; however, 33% were unfavorable to the company, or product. Therefore, as a future manager in the hospitality industry, you need to keep an eye on reviews and act accordingly.

Strategies for Social Media

DON'Ts

- Don't get started if you have significant product weaknesses or customer support issues. Engaging in social media makes good products more successful, and bad products ... dead
- Overtly market or sell
- Don't *"set it and forget it."* This makes you look worse than not showing up at all.
- Don't overwhelm your followers with too much information, or too frequently.

DOs

- Educate, enlighten, inform, and entertain your audience.
- Define your target audience. Detail how you intend to create value for them.
- Conversation builds trust. Join guests/customers.
- Monitor or "listen in" on conversations about your company, your competitors, and the best practices in the industry.
- Learn from your audience. Be prepared to rapidly evolve your products and services to meet their needs. They'll suggest valuable ideas you never thought of.

The Impact of Social Media on Financial Performance of Lodging Organizations

Social media also has the potential to move markets by driving consumers' purchasing patterns and influencing lodging performance. A recent study of Cornell's Center for Hospitality Research combines data from ReviewPro, STR, Travelocity, comScore and TripAdvisor in order to determine the ROI for social-media efforts. The report states: (http://www.hotelschool.cornell.edu/chr/pdf/showpdf/2283/chr/research/andersonsocialmedia.pdf?t=CHR&id=2283&my_path_info=chr/research/andersonsocialmedia.pdf)

- The percentage of consumers consulting reviews at TripAdvisor prior to booking a hotel room has steadily increased over time, as has the number of reviews they are reading prior to making their hotel choice.
- Transactional data from Travelocity illustrate that if a hotel increases its review scores by 1 point on a 5-point scale (e.g., from 3.3 to 4.3), the hotel can increase its price by 11.2 percent and still maintain the same occupancy or market share.
- A 1-percent increase in a hotel's online reputation score leads up to a 0.89-percent increase in price as measured by the hotel's average daily rate (ADR).
- A 1-percent increase in reputation also leads to an occupancy increase of up to 0.54 percent.
- A 1-percent reputation improvement leads up to a 1.42-percent increase in revenue per available room (RevPAR).

Web 3.0

The Web 3.0 is the next paradigm shift of the internet taking the best of Web 2.0, including rich Internet applications and social media, and bringing them ***to mobile devices.*** Information is searched for, filtered, personalized, and delivered to end users based on preferences, biofeedback, and location. Web access by consumers using mobile devices is likely to increase dramatically within the Web 3.0 environment. More and more people use smart phones and can access the Internet anytime, anywhere. Mobile booking is a recent trend as more people started using their smart phones to book their hotels. Thus, hospitality, travel, and tourism organizations need to consider how the evolving mobile Internet can be used to deliver greater value and convenience to their customers.

In the last few years, the use of social media over the smartphones has increased dramatically. The number of unique visitors to the Facebook mobile site increased from 5 million per month in January 2008 to 25 million in February 2009. The growing popularity of smart phones also reflects the trends in using mobile applications for travel experiences. According to TripAdvisor, over 40% of travelers use their smart phones to plan a trip and over 46% use their smart phones to enhance their trip while traveling.

Social Media Targeting Features

Social media websites enhance their features constantly, and one of the newer features is the "targeting features" which allows brands to target specific demographics within their fan base. Brands like seeing increased engagement in social media which means that their posts are reaching the right people and not falling on deaf ears. For instance, Facebook uses an algorithm to pinpoint which fans see the company's posts in their newsfeed. The less a fan is engaging with the brand on Facebook, the fewer of the posts will show up in the feed. More engagement means more exposure. Entire social media campaigns can now be focused more directly on a target demographic. Brands can aggregate their promotions to one page, but not overload their fans with irrelevant or redundant information. They can even cross-promote to different demographics in the same area.

Example Scenario:

A hotel brand is trying to promote a points-based credit card to international business travelers. Since members of this audience travel frequently for one or two nights at a time, they require a very different targeting strategy than the families planning a single weeklong vacation for their families. The brand chooses to schedule a series of posts targeted to fans who have earned degrees in international business, international law, and international studies. They also include a targeting option to a few specific companies they know specialize in international business.

Glossary

Address	Identification assigned to a computer.
.aero	One of the top-level domains. Stands for air transport industry.

Algorithm	A mathematical equation, formula, and/or set of rules and instructions used to solve a problem. Search engines use various algorithms and logic when conducting searches.
Archie	An Internet search tool used to locate files available by anonymous FTP.
Backbone	High speed connection within a network that connects the major Internet computer sites.
BAUD/BPS	Unit of measure of data transmission speed; usually bits/second.
.biz	One of the top-level domains. Stands for businesses.
Browser	A type of software program that enables the user to "navigate" or get around in the World Wide Web.
Client	The user of a network service.
.com	One of the top-level domains. Stands for commercial.
.coop	One of the top-level domains. Stands for cooperatives.
Dial-up	A connection between machines through a phone line.
Domain	The name of the computer that is connected to the Internet.
Download	Retrieve files from a computer.
.edu	One of the top-level domains. Stands for educational.
FAQ	(Frequently Asked Questions) A file that contains questions and answers about specific topics.
Finger	A search tool designed to assist in finding an address when you know the location of an individual.
Flame	Abusive hate mail, usually containing insulting, coarse language.
FTP	File transfer protocol; you use FTP to transfer files over the network.
.gov	One of the top-level domains. Stands for government.
Hits	The retrieval of any item, such as a page or graphic from a Web server.
http	(Hypertext transfer protocol) The language of moving information between networks, especially in the World Wide Web. (http://)
HTML	(Hypertext Mark-up Language) The standard for mat for documents on the World Wide Web.
Hypertext	A system where documents scattered across many sites are directly linked.
Home Page	A location on the World Wide Web that identifies an individual or an organization.
ICANN	Internet Corporation for Assigned Names and Numbers. The non-profit corporation formed to coordinate the technical management of the Internet's Domain Name System (DNS), allocation of IP address space, assignment of protocol param eters, and management of the root server system.

.info	One of the top-level domains. Stands for informa tional websites.
Internet	An interconnected collection of networks.
Mailing List	A collection of people with common interests.
Metacrawlers	Web sites that allow a single query to be sent to multiple search engines in one entry.
.mil	One of the top-level domains. Designates military.
Modem	A device that transfers data through telephone lines.
.museum	One of the top-level domains. Stands for museums.
.name	One of the top-level domains. Stands for individuals.
.net	One of the top-level domains. Stands for free net.
.org	One of the top-level domains. Encompasses non profit organizations.
Packet	A unit of data sent across a packet-switching network.
.pro	One of the top-level domains. Stands for professionals.
Protocol	A set of rules governing communication between computers on the Internet.
Service Provider	A company or person that provides connections to the Internet.
Signature or .sig	A personalized address at the bottom of a message often containing contact information and a short commercial description.
SLIP/PPP	Two types of direct connections available to access the Internet.
Spam	Posting or mailing unwanted material to many recipients. A flagrant violation of netiquette.
TELNET	A public-packet-switched network operated by GTE. It is also the Internet standard protocol for remote terminal connection service.
TCP/IP	(Transmission Control Protocol/Internet Protocol) The standardized set of computer guidelines that allows different machines to talk to each other on the Internet.
Upload	Send a file from your computer to another.
URL	(Uniform Resource Locator) A type of address that points to a specific document or site on the World Wide Web.
Usenet	A collection of discussion areas (bulletin boards) known as newsgroups on the Internet.
WAIS	A database search tool that looks inside documents for words and content.
World Wide Web	A browsing tool for the Internet that is text rather than menu driven.

References

1. http://www.internetworldstats.com/stats.htm
2. http://www.isc.org/index.pl?/ops/ds/host-count-history.php
3. http://www.nua.com/surveys/how_many_online/
4. http://www.itu.int/ITU-D/ict/statistics/at_glance/Internet02.pdf
5. Hahn, Harley, & Stout, Rick. *Internet the Complete Reference*, McGrawHill.
6. Cronin, Mary J. *Doing Business on the Internet*, Mary J., VNR.
7. Clark, Don, (June 17, 1996). "Virtual Safety," Technology Supplement, *Wall Street Journal.*
8. McCartney, Scott, (June 17, 1996). "Poised for a Takeoff," Technology Supplement, *Wall Street Journal.*
9. Ziegler, Bart, (August 23, 1996). "Slow Crawl on the Internet," *Wall Street Journal.*
10. Kehoe, Brendan P, (1992). *Zen and the Art of the Internet: A Beginner's Guide*, Prentice Hall.
11. Quarterman, John, (1990). *The Matrix: Computer Networks and Conferencing Systems Worldwide*, Bedford, MA: Digital Press.
12. Elmer-DeWitt, Philip, (July 25, 1994). "Battle for the Soul of the Internet," *Time 144* (4).
13. Elmer-DeWitt, Philip, (Spring 1995). "Welcome to Cyberspace," *Time (Special Issue) 145* (12).
14. http://www.quotegarden.com/internet.html
15. http://www.aromajet.com/intro.htm
16. Farrell, Scott, (February 19, 2008). Web-direct bookings: The top five mistakes hotels make. *Hotel & Motel Management Magazine.* Available online at http://www.travelclick .net/press/news/ index.cfm?arId=AR_20080320072225298100
17. Kent, S. E., & Fraser, C, (2000). *Internet Lodging: Bits Plus Beds Equal Bucks*, New York City: Goldman Sachs Investment Co.
18. http://www.tripadvisor.com/pages/about_us.html

CHAPTER 8

Strategic Use of Technology in the Hospitality Industry

"Leadership requires setting the right tone in making full use of technology."

Jon Inge

CHAPTER OUTLINE

Information systems allow managers to take a much more analytical view of their business than before.

Introduction

The ever-changing technological advancements have made technology a major strategic factor for many hospitality firms. Some firms respond to the use of technology defensively, showing resistance to change and seeing technology as a problem and burden, while others through strategic use of technology gain competitive advantage. Whether firms accept it or not, IT is a key resource for any type of business, let it be an independently owned small shop or an international corporation. In contemporary markets, it is hard to imagine how any business, especially hospitality businesses, could operate without the support of IT. As a matter of fact, hospitality organizations became IT-dependent; it would be extremely hard to compete in the hospitality industry without the support of IT. From a strategic point of view, ITs have changed the whole hospitality industry. For instance, Global Distribution System (GDS) has altered the way that the reservations work in the lodging industry.

Similarly, Point of Sale (POS) systems have changed the restaurant industry. This chapter discusses the strategic use and value of technology in the hospitality industry.

Strategic Value of Technology

The most accepted theories regarding strategic use and value of technology comes from the Harvard Business School, which is dominated by the works of Michael Porter. Almost thirty years ago, Michael Porter acknowledged the potential and value of IT for driving competitive positioning. He supports the view that technological change is among the most prominent forces driving competition. Today, firms are competing in a knowledge-based economy; therefore IT plays an important role. Similarly hospitality industry managers also realized the importance of technologies in competitive positioning.

Investing in technology simply to manage a hotel is no longer sufficient. Managers are advised to use technology strategically. We are now at a point where information becomes the catalyst for competitive advantage. While location and physical assets are still very important for the competitiveness of the firm, they are simply not enough. Hospitality firms must seek to deploy technologies that will help their employees learn faster and know more than anyone else about their business, customers, and competition, and then use this information to compete more effectively and more aggressively than their competitors – and in ways that create customized and personalized services and experiences that cannot be duplicated easily.

Strategic Enablers

Some technologies are required to survive and to keep the doors of the business open. In other words, some technologies are used to meet the basic needs of a business. On the other hand, some businesses use technology as strategic enablers. For example, Property Management System (PMS) is a support tool for a hotel; hotels need to have PMS in order to function. However, a Customer Relationship Management (CRM) may help a hotel to achieve competitive advantage because when used properly, it will result in customized and personalized services. Mandarin Oriental hotels are using CRM as a strategic competitive weapon. The Hong Kong based luxury chain attaches so much importance to personalized service that individual properties have built their own extensive databases of their guests' histories and preferences.

You might find a fruit basket in your guest room upon your check-in full of different types of fruits (see Figure 8-1). And let's say you decided to eat strawberries because you love them, and once the housekeeping department cleans your room, they take note of your fruit selection which is stored in the database. The next time you visit a Mandarin Oriental Hotel, it is likely that you will find a basket full of strawberries. Similarly, you may ask for your favorite newspaper and hotel staff enters this information to CRM; thus next time you visit their properties you will find your favorite newspaper. Good businesses are aware that good information about the customer is fundamental to good customer service. By using a sophisticated database management system, the Mandarin

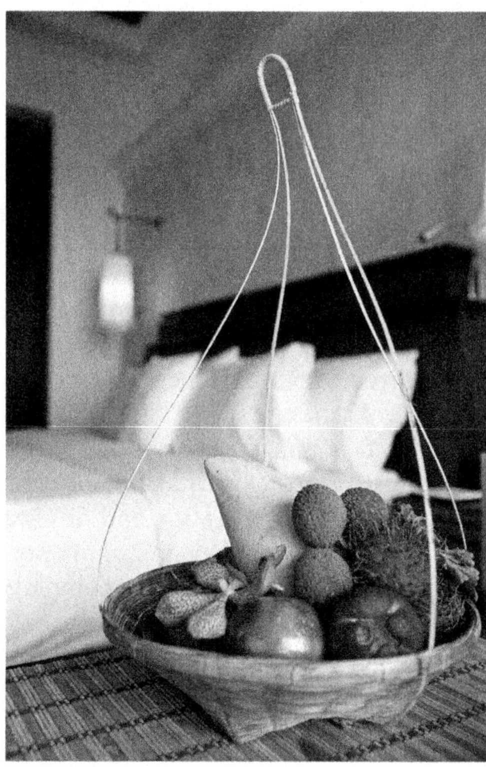

FIGURE 8-1. MANDARIN ORIENTAL USES TECHNOLOGY TO KEEP GUEST PREFERENCES OF FRUITS SO THAT WHEN THEY COME NEXT TIME, THE FRUIT BASKETS WILL BE DOMINATED BASED ON WHAT THEY LIKE.

Source: © Gh19, 2013. Used under license from Shutterstock, Inc.

Oriental is able to track guest preferences and their behavior as well as the frequency of stay, spending patterns, and multiple property usages.(1) This is an example of strategic technology usage.

Successful managers are aware that IT should not be used for the sake of technology itself, or just because it is the latest and greatest, or just because your competitors use it. Instead, IT should be used purposefully with the end business goals in mind and strategically aligned with the company's mission and vision. It should be used to solve business problems. If not used correctly, IT can become nothing more than an unwanted expense, a source of frustration, an inhibitor to change, but when used correctly, many exciting possibilities can result – from service enhancements and product differentiation to new revenue streams. Moving forward, hospitality executives must continually look towards the strategic opportunities technology offers and use technology as a competitive method – or a tool – to differentiate and create competitive advantage. Remember, today's world is all about doing things better, faster, cheaper, and differently than anyone else and technology could enable companies to achieve such goals.

In order to use technology as a competitive weapon, IT applications must be viewed holistically and be a topic of discussion in nearly every business decision, particularly those involving business strategy, marketing and distribution, operations, and future growth planning. Technologies should be viewed as tools to increase productivity and efficiency of operations, thus enhancing business management of the organization. The creation of competitive advantage must involve multiple aspects of the firm coming together (see Figure 8-2).

Examples of technologies that created competitive advantage include:

- *American Airlines → SABRE*
- *Harrah's → Total Rewards + CRM to personalize services and promotions*
- *FedEx → Shipping and package tracking*
- *Hertz → Mobile car returns*
- *McDonald's → Kitchen production systems*
- *Wal-Mart → Supply chain*
- *Marriott → Reservations and revenue management systems to achieve rate premiums and higher occupancy rates than industry averages*
- *Mandarin Oriental → In-room guest technology to create memorable guest experiences*
- *Southwest Airlines → Ding! Last minute special promotions/inventory*
- *InterContinental → Mobile technologies to enable and support guest services for people on the move.(2)*

FIGURE 8-2. HARRAH HOTEL AND CASINO IN LAS VEGAS USES TECHNOLOGY TO CUSTOMIZE THE GUESTS' EXPERIENCE DURING THEIR STAY.

Source: © Ritu Manoj Jethani, 2013. Used under license from Shutterstock, Inc.

The magnitude of the above initiatives suggests the need for a great deal of vision, competencies, and capital resources to make things happen through IT.

The challenge is to find new opportunities in which IT can be used to solve business problems, create better service experiences, provide cost and/or informational advantages, and create distinction in the market place.

Ultimately technology should be used to lower cost structure, increase revenues and market share, provide exceptional customer service, create unique value propositions for guests, and generate unprecedented returns for investors or shareholders. Creating competitive advantage requires creative, out-of-the-box thinking (see Figure 8-3).

Information Revolution

Information revolution is changing the way hospitality firms do their business. Most executives are aware that the technology can no longer be the exclusive territory of IT departments. Instead, technology should be viewed more holistically.

FIGURE 8-3. INTERNET CHANGED THE WAY TRAVELERS BOOK.

Source: © Shawn Hempel, 2013. Used under license from Shutterstock, Inc.

The information revolution affects competition in three vital ways:(3)

1. ***It changes industry structure and, in so doing, alters the rules of competition.***
   Think about how GDS altered the rules of competition in the lodging industry.
2. ***It creates a competitive advantage by giving companies new ways to outperform their rivals.***
   When American Airlines introduced SABRE, it was the best reservation system and it enabled American Airlines to outperform their rivals.
3. ***It spawns whole new businesses, often from within a company's existing operations.***
   Airbnb created a community marketplace for people to list, discover, and book unique accommodations around the world online. Whether an apartment for a night, a castle for a week, or a villa for a month, Airbnb connects people to unique travel experiences, at any price point, in more than 33,000 cities and 192 countries.(4)

Competitive Advantage

In simplistic terms, competitive advantage (CA) is derived from one or more unique capabilities of the firm and brings value to the firm (see Figure 8-4). These capabilities set one firm apart from other within the industry and within its competitive set. In other words, it requires making things different from others competing in the same place. Competitive advantage results from doing things faster, better, cheaper, or different than anyone else. It can be measured in many ways; for example, in terms of product or service quality, customer satisfaction, market share, brand recognition, customer loyalty, employee loyalty, profitability, and cost structure.

To achieve sustainable CA, industry leaders agree that a firm must continuously invest in its resources and capabilities, especially technologies to build core competencies and a culture that encourages learning, innovation, and risk taking so that new advantages can be created.

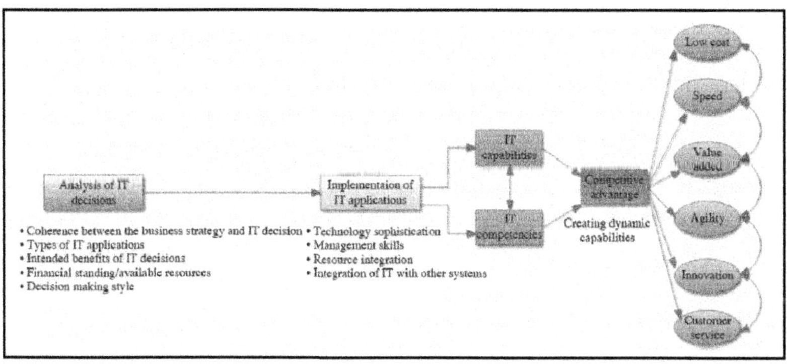

FIGURE 8-4. IT AND COMPETITIVE ADVANTAGE.

Efficient and timely deployment of new IT applications may offer opportunities for enhanced guest services to meet ever increasing customer expectations, improved cost control, more effective marketing strategies, and expanded opportunities for hotels.

Carefully selected IT investments will increase hotels' productivity, reduce costs, and at the same time add value to the services and products offered to their customers. Therefore, investments into IT applications in hotels have increased over the past decades.

Within low value-added lodging sectors (i.e., budget, economy, and midscale), hotels are likely to pursue information technologies that increase operating efficiency; whereas within high value-added lodging sectors (i.e., upscale and luxury), hotels are likely to initiate technological improvements that increase the quality of service delivery to the guest; the key is to define business strategy and choose IT investments accordingly.

IT Capabilities and IT Competencies

Deployment of technology applications can help organizations create IT capabilities and IT competencies. IT capabilities mainly focus on ***internal efficiency*** and ***reducing cost*** and they may lead to transforming key business processes and practices into IT capabilities that significantly streamline and integrate the value chain, and eliminate or reduce redundant or non-valued processes. On the other hand, IT competencies have an external focus and represent the collective learning of an IT organization. IT competencies and IT capabilities significantly affect competitive advantage of a firm.

There are three different views on creating competitive advantage, which are:

1. the positioning view,
2. the resource based view, and
3. the dynamic capabilities view.

Positioning View

The **positioning view** supports the view that companies should choose one of the three competitive positions in the marketplace if they want to achieve and maintain competitive advantage.

The first position is *cost leadership* where a firm aims to achieve competitive advantage by achieving a cost leadership position in the market.

The *differentiation* position implies that a company must offer something unique and rare.

The *focus* strategy has two options: focus differentiation and focus cost leadership. The former one aims to achieve differentiation by offering a superior and unique product or service to a niche segment. The focus cost leadership strategy aims to achieve cost leadership position by targeting a niche segment in a specific geographical area.

Resource Based View

According to the **resource based view**, it is essential to look at the company's resources when evaluating competitive advantage of a company. In this view, if resources and capabilities are to create competitive advantage, they should be 'valuable', 'rare', 'inimitable', and 'unsubstitutable'. In terms of value, resources should contribute to the performance of an organization whereas being rare refers to being owned by very few companies. In addition, it is suggested that those resources and competencies should not be easily imitated and substituted by competitors.

Dynamic Capabilities View

The **dynamic capabilities view** builds both on the positioning view and the resource based view. This view suggests that companies should have the capacity to renew competencies to achieve congruence with the changing business environment, innovative, fast, and timely responses are required and critical. Dynamic capabilities are defined as a "firm's ability to integrate, build, and reconfigure internal and external competences to address rapidly changing environments." Thus, the dynamic capabilities view suggests that companies have to develop dynamic capabilities to be able to offer superior products and services in the fastest and most efficient way in response to the developments and changes in the marketplace. Of each of the above three views, competitive advantage provides specific propositions regarding the creation and maintenance of competitive advantage. However, there is one commonality among these views, which is that in order to create competitive advantage, companies should find a way to differentiate themselves from their competitors. Technology can help hospitality companies to differentiate from competitors, thus a carefully selected and implemented technology project will bring competitive advantage to the hotels. This can be achieved either through *positioning your company* (the positioning view) (e.g., Scandinavian Hotel Chain Omena Hotels (5) differentiate themselves by offering cheap rooms using technology –guests have to check themselves in using the remote check-in terminals), *offering unique products and services* (resource based view) (e.g., Hyatt Hotels offering in-room fitness package, Westin Hotels offering Nintendo Wii in guestrooms), or c*reating unique and complementary dynamic and timely capabilities to respond to fast changing market conditions* (the dynamic capabilities view).

Omena Hotels offer a fresh and unique approach to hotel accommodation with online booking and an unprecedented value-for-money philosophy by using technology. Omena Hotels are able to offer high quality accommodation at a very low price.

They can do this by keeping things simple with online booking, SMS key codes and self-service check-in and checkout.

1. *Guests book and pay online, as they would do at any hotel or airline website.*
2. *Guests get your receipt and key code by mail and SMS.*
3. *Guests access the hotel and your room with the key code provided.*

IT investments can lead to developing IT capabilities and dynamic IT competencies, which can lead to achieving the following six closely interrelated outcomes: (6)

1. Low cost
2. Value added
3. Speed
4. Agility
5. Innovation
6. Customer service

1. Low Cost

Low cost refers to providing products/services at the lowest costs. Various technologies can help hotel companies to offer services at a lower cost ratio. For example, Vintage Inns installed an enterprise system that would allow the hotel to sell benefits to guests and combine the separate guest histories from their four properties into one database in order to increase booking efficiency. The system allowed the hotel company to manage the properties centrally and reservation staff had the ability to book rooms for any property from any of their hotels. Hotel staff only needed to learn one product, one screen, and one process; further, they can see where guests have stayed in the past and track the experience they had with them. The system has increased the staff efficiency by 15% and improved data accuracy by at least 50% with the elimination of rekeying guest information between the systems; moreover, the system decreased the training time of the employees significantly. Another example is that Morrissey Hospitality installed a yield management system at two of its luxury properties. Just two months after installation, RevPAR increased significantly and according to Smith Travel Research, their occupancy beat their competitors by 30 percent. Lately, the new trend "green technologies" also yields to cost savings in hotels by cutting down on operating costs.

2. Value Added

Value added refers to offering products and services which are highly desirable and have distinct features/functionalities. Creative and innovative use of technology that enhances the value of offered services will be the means by which hotels differentiate themselves from their competitors. IT could be a primary catalyst that helps hotels innovate their service offers and add value to what they offer to their internal and external customers. For example, guest room technologies, such as electronic ordering system, TV checkout, and electronic and video entertainment services can be value-adding services. IT has not only improved in-room services, but has also increased choices in entertainment. City center hotels, whose clientele are primarily business travelers, are more likely to equip their rooms with advanced in-room technologies as opposed to hotels in more remote or resort locations.

3. Speed

Speed refers to systems and processes that offer faster and superior services and products. For instance, hotels can increase the speed of housekeeping departments with guest room status indicators. Once a guest asks for his/her room to be cleaned, he/she can choose the room and a message will be delivered to the hotel staff. Guests can also use self-check-out through their television to facilitate and speed up the checkout process. Back office IT solutions provide numerous ways to speed up various departments; Hyatt Hotels & Resorts announced a migration to Microsoft's cloud-based Business Productivity Online Suite to provide unique e-mail addresses for 17,000 tethered employees, and purchased licenses to provide e-mail to an additional 40,000 "deskless" associates. This cloud computing initiative provided significant functionality in HR systems such as providing employee schedules via e-mail. RFID minibars that report inventory immediately are another example that could increase the speed of folio posting in hotels.

4. Agility

Agility refers to the ability to manage change faster than competitors. IT driven agility could be achieved via Decision Support Systems (DSS) in hotels. Business Intelligence (BI) is one of the latest developments of DSS (see Figure 8-5). It offers imperative tools for analyzing and presenting data to hotel managers such as trend analysis so they can make more informed decisions. Hotels store massive amounts of operational data, generated by daily transactions, in operational databases. These databases contain detailed information whereas managers need aggregate, summary information in the decision making process. By utilizing BI, the data from separate source systems is loaded into a data warehouse through a process of extraction, transformation, and loading. The data is then transformed into useful information and knowledge that enables agility in hotels.

5. Innovation

Innovation refers to the continuous flow of new products and services, which are valued by the customer. Managers are seeking to incorporate IT innovations as a means of attaining competitive advantage, specifically through improved guest services, increased employee productivity, and enhanced revenue generation. For instance, technological innovations designed to improve employee productivity included voice mail and interactive guides that allow automation of the service delivery system, thus reducing the guest communications workload of the front office and concierge staff and allowing time for a greater focus on other guest services. In order to achieve innovation through an IT project, hotel managers should continually seek new technologies. X-Room, short for "Experimental Guest room," is located in a Marriott hotel and includes innovative technologies that are valued by the guest, such as a Nintendo Wii gaming console. Hotels could also generate revenue with such innovative technologies by charging the guest for the used amenities or services. GUEST ROOM 20X is another example that demonstrates innovative technologies for hoteliers. The room represents HFTP's vision as the information source for the lodging industry by exhibiting how future guest rooms can mix high-tech touches with a soft-touch delivery to make a guest's stay the ultimate experience. The room includes innovations from high-definition artwork that changes to match a guest's mood to the more practical self-cleaning shower.

6. Customer Service

Customer Service refers to a superior responsiveness to customer needs. For example, Marriott's reservation system manages the booking of more than 355,000 hotel rooms globally. This system delivers Marriott a priceless opportunity to gather information about the characteristics, habits, and preferences of their guests. As a matter of fact, the 12 million customer profiles stored in Marriott's frequent-lodger program establish the largest such database in the lodging industry. This information allows Marriott to cross-reference the personal profiles of customers with product preferences. By doing this, Marriott is able to target incentives and promotions with unprecedented precision and offers distinctive customer service. Trump SoHo implemented Cisco solutions for the hotel network, pervasive wireless access, and unified communications in order to provide highly personalized guest experience. Hotel employees wear a wireless IP voice badge that operates over the same Cisco Unified Communications system used for typical voice calls. When the bellhop asks the guest's name at the door, the check-in staff hears so that a moment later they can greet the guest by name. When guests arrive in their room, the color display on the IP phone shows a personalized welcome message. Furthermore, guests can use the IP phone's touch screen for voice mail, weather by zip code, airport information, and e-mail. Employees can also use the in-room phones in order to confirm that a room is ready for the next guest. The room attendant enters a code on the phone which updates the property management system. Finding out right away that a room is ready helps the hotel to accommodate guests who would like to check in early, thus improving customer

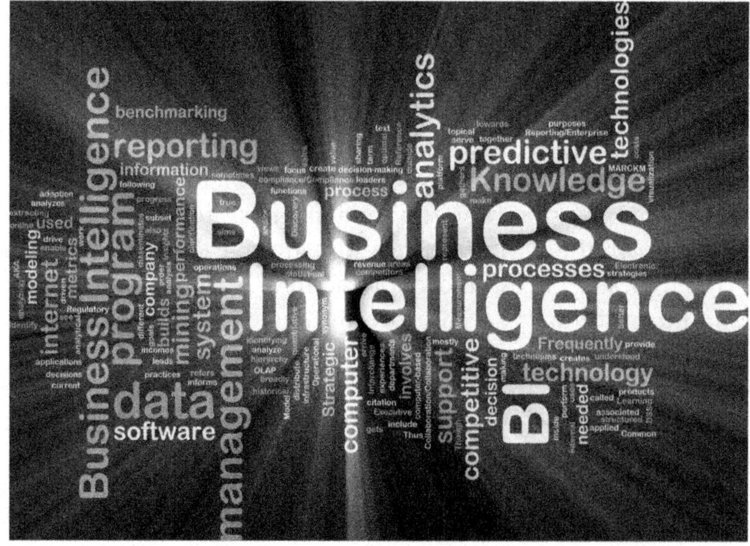

FIGURE 8-5. BUSINESS INTELLIGENCE (BI) SOLUTIONS ARE BENEFICIAL TIME MANAGEMENT TOOLS AND ALLOW MANAGERS TO MAKE NECESSARY ADJUSTMENTS AT ANY TIME AS INFORMATION BECOMES MORE READILY AVAILABLE.

Source: © Kheng Guan Toh, 2013. Used under license from Shutterstock, Inc.

service. The above six areas are closely related, as one positive outcome in one area may positively impact others. In fact, IT can increase staff efficiency by providing the ability to communicate and collaborate from anywhere on the property and empower staff members to create personalized guest experiences. For instance, an employee who directs a guest to the spa can alert the spa that the guest is on the way and greet him/her by name, thus improving the guest's overall experience.

Business Intelligence (BI) solutions are beneficial time management tools and allow managers to make necessary adjustments at any time as information becomes more readily available. BI tools will help hotel managers access instant reports instead of waiting until the end of the period. They can optimize usage and schedule resources, adjust labor schedules and supply orders, maximize the hotel's profitability, increase customer profitability and RevPAR. Managers can also pinpoint and give priority to the most profitable guests by knowing and predicting guest trends, profitability, and preferences.

Sustaining Competitiveness

Creating competitive advantage requires managers to see things that others cannot see and then act on these opportunities to make them happen. But it does not stop there, it is just the beginning of the journey as the challenge shifts to sustaining that competitive advantage or distorting it and either reinventing it or replacing with something else before anyone else has time to copy it and catch up to their lead. This is called sustainable competitive advantage.

Technology's Impact in the Hotel Industry

Research indicates that companies that effectively use technology will have the highest impact on customer satisfaction. Siguaw and Enz(7)discussed three hotels that were awarded best practices in the industry for their IT innovations. These programs included The Balsams Grand Resort Hotel, Ritz-Carlton Chicago, and Fairmont Copley Plaza.

Balsams Grand Resort Hotel uses technology to develop guest history logs. The hotel uses the guest history logs to capture customized information on the guests that had already made a reservation at the hotel. The hotel deploys an expert system model to gauge the wants and needs of its guests. The system uses special algorithms to generate information based on hotel inquiries, rooms, room types, special requests, times of year visits, etc. The system can anticipate almost any guest request, thus implementation of the system resulted in 85% repeat business for the hotel; furthermore, new business has been generated from positive word-of-mouth.

Ritz-Carlton Chicago witnessed an increase in demand of technical help with computers in the rooms. In response, the hotel management offered technical help to the guests that resulted in high customer satisfaction.

Fairmont Copley Plaza's PMS was adopted and incorporated to expedite the concierge services at the hotel. PMS enabled to get guest information such as newspaper preference, wake-up time, overnight laundry service, as well as many other options, resulting in 90% customer satisfaction.

Technology's Impact in the Restaurant Industry

In the past decade, there has been a steady increase in restaurants realizing the importance of increasing their level of technology to become more competitive in managing the business. The technological transition phase has seen restaurants shift from cash registers to today's POS systems, online reservation systems, and kitchen management systems. The previous chapters discussed the advantages of some of the restaurant technologies. This chapter will look at the restaurant technologies from a strategic perspective. As you have read previously, POS was a revolutionary technology for the restaurant industry. POS automates the jobs of the service and kitchen staff by eliminating handwritten orders and POS saves time and is a more efficient way to operate a restaurant. Today, POS systems are also useful from a managerial perspective. New generation POS systems support management decision-making. For instance Avero(8), a New York City based software company, helps restaurants to analyze POS data and support managerial decision-making. Such systems can help managers to increase the revenue per available table and help reduce waste in the restaurant (e.g., as a manager you will know the exact estimate of a specific ingredient consumption in any given week).

Avero's cloud-based, SaaS analytics platform is designed specifically for the hospitality industry. The company takes massive amounts of data and turns them into insights that lead to more profitable business decisions within a single outlet and across multiple locations.

In 2011, Romano's Macaroni Grill launched an initiative to provide guests with a superior Italian dining experience. As part of its brand renewal, the restaurant revamped every element of the concept from fork to Facebook and launched a national campaign publicizing its emphasis on the renewed guest experience. In order to deliver on what it promised, CEO of Macaroni Grill and Avero introduced a global, holistic plan to support constituents at all levels of the Macaroni Grill organization in rolling out the new brand experience.

In just over six months, Macaroni Grill saw a positive return on its investment in Avero Single Server Mentoring™, and significant benefits were seen across the organization:

- *Increased Sales and Tips: Macaroni Grill expects to see a 100 basis point improvement in same-store-sales and 5% increase in the average server tip.*
- *Lower Staff Turnover: The company has seen an annual decrease in server turnover of nearly 600 basis points due to its work with Avero.*
- *Improved Guest Satisfaction: Macaroni Grill saw a 400 basis point improvement in Net Promoter Score against the control group.*
- *Consistent Brand Experience: Macaroni Grill has found that Avero Single Server Mentoring™ has helped them better introduce new initiatives and menu items to their service team.*

IT undermines traditional forms of competition, strategic management, organizational structure, governance, and economic policy making. Conventional thinking suggested that services were less technologically advanced than their manufacturing counterparts. Under this traditional paradigm, IT was viewed as a support tool. Over the years, this thinking influenced IT spending, investment, and usage throughout the industry, placing the primary emphasis on tactical systems with calculable ROIs.

IT Investment Philosophies

Six prevailing philosophies regarding IT investment within the hospitality industry:

1. *Projects that were essential to survival*
2. *Project requiring act of faith (or gut feeling) that an investment will provide beneficial to the firm over the long term*
3. *Projects with an intuitive appeal and seemingly obvious outcomes*
4. *Projects that were required or mandated either by law, by regulation, or by top management*
5. *Projects in response to moves by competitors to achieve parity or project market share*
6. *Projects that had to undergo intense scrutiny and analysis due to the high degrees of uncertainty and risk (9)*

Industry Specific Technologies

Many hospitality ITs were adopted from other industries; they were considered inadequate or clumsy because of their poor fit and their inability to address hospitality industry-specific needs. Research investigated how information was being utilized by large hotel firms in the industry. In a study, it was found that only 2 of the 12 largest hotel firms in the industry had successfully developed and implemented their own data warehouses. Most of the hotels in the study were using information for support of strategic market analysis, including targeting new customers, fine tuning loyalty programs, sales analysis, and conducting trend analysis. The hotels' ability to collect, process, and access large amounts of data can help companies build a competitive advantage.

Hotel managers understand the importance and the power of information. Using information to identify the possible trends in the industry will help hotels gain competitive advantage.

Strategic Analysis

Strategic analysis is a dynamic process that requires examining both environmental and firm environments.

Co-alignment Model

The co-alignment model states that if a firm can uncover the opportunities that exist within the environmental forces driving change and select the appropriate competitive method to apply, while also maintaining a firm structure that allows it to easily create this advantage, then that firm has the greatest chance of achieving the financial performance desired. Olsen (10) created this concept of fit among four key factors:

1. environmental events,
2. strategic choice,
3. firm structure, and
4. firm performance.

Environmental Events

Environmental events are the environmental forces evoking change in an industry. While these do present threats to a firm (e.g., raising gas prices), they also present opportunities (e.g., certain trends) for which firms take advantage. In order to take advantage of these environmental forces, firms should scan their environments. Research has found that the more a firm scans its environment the more likely it is to be a high performing firm. ITs can help companies to scan their environments.

Strategic Choice

After the firm sees the opportunities and threats in the environment, next step is to choose a strategy and put the firm's selection of competitive methods that it will utilize in competing in the industry. Competitive methods are the products and services a firm employs to compete in a specific industry sector. This is the primary reason that your guest will choose to stay in your hotel or eat in your restaurant.

Firm Structure

A firm's structure is the final piece that needs to be aligned before achieving the desired financial performance. The firm structure will determine how easily the selected competitive methods can be converted into competitive advantages. This could include such things as corporate/unit level structure, financial resources available, accounting methods utilized, and so on and so forth.

Firm Performance

As long as the environment events align with the strategic choice and firm structure, firm performance will align with firm objectives. Several research studies have shown that a significant level of variance in a firm's performance is due to those key factors.

Restaurant Example

In 2003 McDonald's had posted its first ever quarterly loss. In an effort to rectify this, McDonald's began to apply a co-alignment model to their turnaround strategy. In examining the environment they noticed some key environmental events: a tired brand, the emergence of luxury coffee, and consumers' concern for their health. McDonald's decided that it would retool and begin taking advantage of these events. The first step McDonald's took was to create the firm structure that would allow for easy facilitation of change by bringing back Mr. Cantalupo, the former President of McDonald's International from 1987 to 1997. In continuing its efforts to take back some of the breakfast business sector from Starbucks, McDonald's began installing McCafes at each franchise which would offer reasonably priced, high quality espresso and other coffee style beverages. In an effort to create value while also introducing healthier options, McDonald's introduced the dollar menu, apple slices, and salads to their consumers. In the process McDonald's retrained its entire staff and introduced technology advancements that sped up the time it took for consumers to receive their food. Retraining alone took up 5% of McDonald's expenditures ($93 million), highlighting the financial investment, or commitment, it takes to instill competitive methods and foster core competencies. McDonald's was able to align environmental events, with strategy choice, firm structure, and financial performance. Consequently, McDonald's was back in the black by the third quarter of 2004.

Importance of Environment in Strategic Management

The theory of open systems introduced the term "*environment*" to the strategic management field. Firms need to consider environmental factors before making financial decisions. Olsen and his colleagues applied this theory to strategic hospitality management by stating that firms under the umbrella of the hospitality industry have to scan their environment, identify the trends, and invest in value adding competitive methods in order to achieve above average performance and named it the co-alignment model (See Figure 8-6).

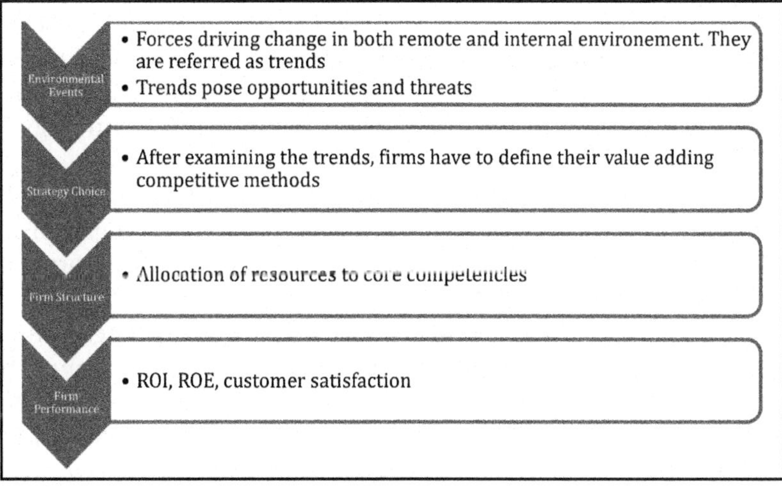

FIGURE 8-6. CO-ALIGNMENT MODEL.

The effects of technology are extremely important to consider before strategy choices as new technologies might reduce the time for food preparation, (e.g., handheld POS devices that directly prins out the order in the kitchen, kitchen display systems, e-procurement systems, table management systems). For instance, restaurants that implemented OpenTable (11) *table management and reservation system indicated that they have been performing better.*

Synergy between Higher Management and IT Engineering

The IT department typically contains the bulk of the firm's technological expertise, yet engineers and engineering managers are seldom directly involved in strategic analysis. Strategy typically trickles down to engineering in the form of technological problems demanding solutions. This weak linkage between engineering activities and strategic thinking is far from optimal, and in the current turbulent technological environment it can even endanger the firm's survival.

In order to achieve competitive advantage, the linkage should be strengthened, however this philosophy requires behavioral and managerial changes at the top of the firm and at the engineering level. First, both levels must understand the concepts of strategic management and commit to implementing them. Then the strategic nature of technology must be understood, including the limitations and potential traps of technology-based strategies. Finally, creative opportunities for considering technology strategically must be made available at the engineering level, and both design engineers and engineering managers must be rewarded for their strategic contributions.

As you have read above, ITs help hotels increase competitiveness. However, it is not the IT itself that offers the competitive advantage to a hotel company, but rather, how that IT is selected and used by the hotel company, and what IT can present in the future that makes a difference for competitive advantage. Therefore, the link between management and IT departments is very important. Technologies should be integrated into corporate strategy in order to achieve utmost outcomes. Choosing the right technology and strategic alignment and implementing it properly is the key.

Briefly, competitive advantage is possible when hotels choose to invest in technologies with higher management skills and integrate all the possible technologies in the organization with a harmony that creates synergy. It is no secret that contemporary hospitality firms strongly rely on technology applications to boost the core business and become more attractive within the market competition. Therefore, hospitality management needs to understand the challenges and the advantages of new technologies and must be able to discover their synergies with existing solutions. Indeed, the IT landscape has to be carefully planned by knowledgeable experts, with a clear vision and understanding of technology opportunities and business needs, in order to gain IT induced competitive advantage and assure a valuable return on investment.

An IT manager, director, or CTO/CIO must be forward thinking in creating an IT infrastructure that improves processes, productivity, and creates cost savings. Technologies implemented must help management to take action on the fly instead of waiting for reporting at the middle of the following month when the water has already run below the bridge and proactive steps are not implemented in a timely manner.

In the hospitality world, competitive advantage is usually driven by refined and distinctive services that can be offered to the guests. Such services often require a combination of different software applications and communications protocols, but at the same time they must provide user solutions that are attractive and easy to use. In this horizon, technology sophistication becomes unavoidable and essential. The guest exclusive experience must be sustained by a complex back-end system capable of managing several applications and hardware in a completely transparent and user-friendly manner.

Resources Integration

Resource integration becomes a must in strategic technology management. On the customer's side, resource integration enhances the guest experience, as one easy-to-use device can be used for different services (like turning on the TV, setting the lights, and managing the curtains). On the hotel side, resource integration can facilitate system support and maintenance as the same network or hardware device can be used as a platform to deliver different services provided by different applications. Technologies that both enable firms to generate revenue and significantly enhance the guest experience yield IT induced competitive advantage. The integration of the technologies was critical for hotels to gain IT induced competitive advantage. It is also important to note that IT integration is one of the biggest challenges of the industry.

Analysis of IT Decisions in Hotels

There are five closely related areas when analyzing IT decisions in hotels, which are:

1. *Coherence between the business strategy and IT decision*
2. *Types of IT applications*
3. *Intended benefits of IT decisions*
4. *Financial standing of the company and available financial resources*
5. *Decision-making style*

It is expected that there should be coherence between the business strategy and functional strategies of a hotel company. Managers should therefore justify and illustrate how their IT investments will support the hotel company's overall business strategy or the hotel units' competitive strategies.

Otherwise, such IT proposals/projects may not be fully supported by the hotel's owners and the management team. Hotels are likely to focus on a select set of technology initiatives that are tied to a specific strategy.

The second area is determining the type of IT applications in which the hotel company will invest. Hotels may invest in IT applications purely for front of the house, back of the house, or both. Some IT applications may be used by customers, managers, and employees whereas some IT applications may be for special functional areas such as human resources management, finance and accounting, and sales and marketing. For example, customers not only want IT applications faster, but they also want better value and higher quality. Customers are well informed, empowered, and capable of using self-service IT capabilities. Thus, hotel companies are now forced to use IT to reinvent their operations and maximize customer value; self-check-in kiosks are examples of such matters. The shifting business paradigm needs hotels to be more customer oriented, responsive, flexible, quick, innovative, and collaborative. For instance, in 2008, Sheraton

Hotels & Resorts and Microsoft introduced a new hotel guest experience with Microsoft Surface, which was Microsoft's first commercial surface computer. Surface units are placed in the lobbies of select Sheraton hotels aiming to offer an experience that would bring interaction, connectivity, and a social setting to the lobby, providing guests with an entirely new way to explore local highlights and enhance their hotel stay.

Customers may also have different IT needs and expectations. For instance, business travelers may expect hotels and airlines to provide online check-in. On the other hand, leisure travelers may request more in-room entertainment amenities. Meeting and incentive travelers may require specific IT applications for their meetings and conventions. Put simply, each customer segment may need and request different types of IT applications. Therefore, identifying your target market and understanding its wants and needs is very important.

The most important technologies to customers are Wi-Fi hotspots, in-room entertainment systems, and kiosks for airline check-in/boarding passes, respectively. Research reveals that the most important in-room technologies for male travelers are express check-in/check-out, high-speed internet access, and easily accessible electrical outlets, whereas easily accessible electrical outlets, guest control panels, and high-speed internet access were identified as the most important in-room technologies for female travelers, respectively.

Hospitality-linked ITs can be broadly categorized under back-office operations and front-office requirements. Back-office technologies include software solutions for inventory management, financial reporting, menu management, security management, green technologies, labor management, data management, etc. Front-office technologies mainly revolve around the point of sale and property management system (PMS).

Another important area is identifying the cost of the IT project and its intended outcomes from IT. Certainly, the cost of each IT project and its projected return on investment are carefully assessed. The major factors driving technological implementations in hotels are increased transaction volumes through consolidations, complex reporting requirements, and international communication needs. Advances in the areas of guest services, reservations, food and beverage management, sales, food service catering, maintenance, security, and hospitality accounting have required the utilization of computer systems technology in every aspect of lodging operations.

Executives should evaluate the influence of investment on the firm's current operational and strategic performances and also the impact on the bottom line. Alongside the former, they must evaluate the outcomes of falling behind a competitor or misplacing a competitive position and not making investments in a timely fashion. IT investment decisions made in a timely manner improve a company's competitive position and when postponed, make the firm weaker to competitive forces.

IT investments improve performance through greater operational efficiency, cost reduction, and increased sales and revenue that contribute to cash flows. Managers are usually conscious of these benefits and take them into account in their IT investment decisions. However, also remember that the technology itself may be easy to acquire by competitors, therefore, it is not necessarily a source of competitive advantage.

Numerous companies spend on IT inefficiently. Firms are susceptible to under-invest in some areas, particularly in weak financial periods, missing opportunities to increase productivity, reduce costs, offer greater customer service, or achieve competitive advantage. Conversely, firms usually overspend in financially strong periods; frequently buying into hype that promised huge returns from investments in trendy hardware/software solutions, sometimes just copying their competitors, often resulting in disappointment and disillusionment. It is not the IT itself that offers the competitive advantage to a company, but rather, how that IT is selected, used, what it provides to the company, and what IT can present in the future that makes a difference for competitive advantage.

Technology Induced Competitive Advantage Stages

Depending on the company's resources, management skills, integration of the technology, and the sophistication of the deployed technology determine the results of the technology. The diagonal line in below figure 8-7 represents the technology induced competitive advantage as it yields better results (basic to advanced), which require high resource integration, management skills, critical resources, and technology sophistication.

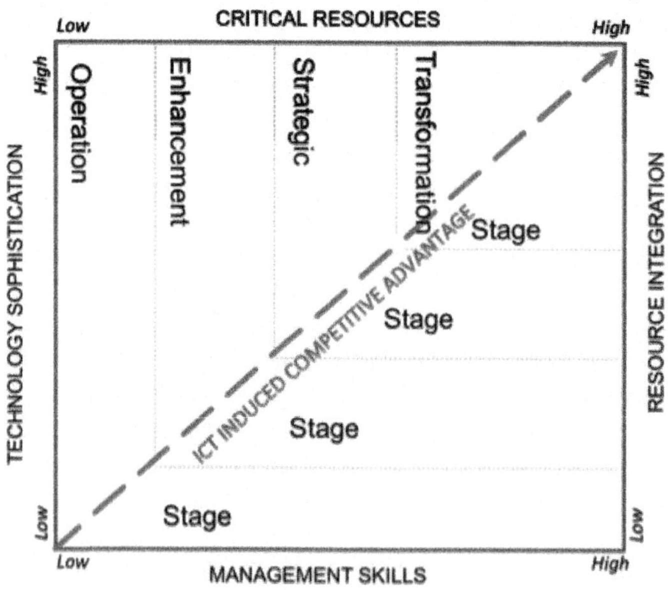

Stage	Technology Applications
Operation	Word Processing Software, E-mail, security systems, Electronic Locking Systems, In-room TV systems, Call Accounting Systems, PBX, Cost Control Systems, Internet/Website
Enhancement	YMS (Yield Management Systems), Energy Management Systems, PMS, POS, Biometric Systems, RFID, Self-Service Kiosks, Social Networking Websites
Strategic	XML based schema for interoperability, supply chain technologies
Transformation	DSS, CRM, Business Intelligence, Data Mining, Customer Equity Modeling

FIGURE 8-7. INDUCED COMPETITIVE ADVANTAGES BASED ON THE LEVEL OF THE FIRM'S TECHNOLOGY SOPHISTICATION AND MANAGEMENT SKILLS.

Operation Stage

Technologies that manage daily operations are defined as the operation stage. The goal of the operation stage is to keep the business running and going. In other words, technologies are used to meet the basic needs of a business. For instance, e-mail communication and property websites are classified in the operation stage. This stage only requires basic knowledge and does not offer significant competitive advantage. The productivity impact of those technologies is zero or minimal. In this stage, competitive advantage is derived by lowering the cost of routine transactions, usually by replacing humans with machines. The technologies in this stage do not offer competitive advantage and companies should move forward to higher stages.

Enhancement Stage

In the enhancement stage, technologies are used mainly to increase productivity and efficiency of operation, thus enhancing business management of the organization. Technologies used at this stage increase and enhance the overall value to the hospitality organization. The value of the technology increases in the organization. As a result, this stage requires higher management skills compared to the operation stage. Basic technologies that are used in the operation stage improve in this stage. For instance, PMS and POS are classified under the enhancement stage umbrella. In this stage, organizations get familiar with the ITs that they are using. In order to gain competitive advantage from mid-sophisticated technologies, hotels should be able to manage the systems; consequently this stage requires relatively higher management skills. The enhancement stage improves business operations. Additionally, it increases the organizational effectiveness obtained by using the IT application. This stage improves the reservations process that leads to additional basic strategic advantages. Improvements in distributed computing architecture along with organizational reactions against local, costly, frequently inefficient microcomputer-based initiatives, helped firms to organize according to markets, product lines, or geographic areas. In this stage firms also combine network and software economies that create opportunities for value creation.

Strategic Stage

In the strategic stage, organizations achieve strategic competitiveness with aligning their technologies with overall organizational goals to set apart themselves from competitors. Technologies used at this stage strategically improve intra-organization and inter-organizational business processes in addition to enhancing productivity and efficiency at the enhancement stage. Additionally, technologies used at this stage are helping hospitality organizations to achieve strategic goals, such as reducing costs, improving customer service, and adding more value to the organization through improved decision making processes. Customer Relationships Management (CRM), Computer Reservations Systems (CRS), and Global Distribution Systems (GDS) are some tools used in the tourism industry in the strategic stage. The tools in the strategic stage could be used as a competitive weapon; however, they are such technologies that they could be duplicated by the competitors. Technologies in this stage both enhance the number of intra-organizational and inter-organizational processes. Competitive advantage depends on the creation of knowledge with the intention of providing added value to customers. Customers are becoming more knowledgeable, demanding, and are asking for more personalized products and services. Hotels should gather and use guest information in order to provide more personalized services, which could be managed by using CRM tools that are under this stage.

Transformation Stage

At the transformation stage, technologies are used in an integrative and synergistic manner in order to achieve ultimate competitive advantage. At this stage, integration and coordination of various technology applications/systems with maximum synergy are achieved so that business processes and procedures are transformed in a way that long-term competitive advantage can be achieved. The stage requires higher management skills. The resource integration is at the maximum level, while at the same time maximum critical resources and technology sophistication are needed. Strategic alignment with the selected ITs is accomplished. Organizations' mission, vision, and goals perfectly match with the ITs. Moreover, these technologies are integrated with each other which enable such a variety of different approaches to solving organizations' needs. It enables organizations to collect a large amount of highly valuable guest data. PMS in a hotel that consists of different hardware and software all connected with both intra-organization and inter-organization ITs is an example of the transformation stage. For instance, hotels having their F&B technologies integrated with their PMS had significantly higher hotel property operational productivity. ITs in this stage have evolved from simple interrelated components working together to collect, process, store, and disseminate information in order to support decision making, coordination, control, analysis, and visualization in an organization, to dynamic, interoperable mechanisms of collecting, processing, and disseminating intelligence within organizations and in their extensive environment. Additionally shifting to embedded systems and individualized systems are key characteristics of this stage. Integrated systems, shared databases, and systematically working technologies that work together to create synergy are required to reach that level. It should be noted that very few companies reach that level. Another perceived trend in transformation stage is that ITs act as a strategic tool for hospitality managers. Decision Support Systems (DSS), Business Intelligence (BI), and data mining are some of the transformation stage technologies.

Integration of software is one of the challenges and integration of data and business process orchestration is vital for managers. Some of the vendors offer technology solutions that manage all aspects of hospitality operations, including property management, point-of-sale, inventory and procurement, spa, golf, document management, and so on. However, currently in the hotel industry there are only a few truly integrated systems used owing to the fact that numerous heterogeneous systems already exist and scalability, maintenance, price, and security issues then become difficult to overcome.

Barriers to Technology Projects in the Hospitality Industry

Hospitality companies, their employees, and especially their managers are faced with the enormous practical and conceptual challenge of transforming today's organizations into automated enterprises. There are lots of barriers to the implementation of technologies such as high costs, lack of skills and resources, time limitation, priority of other businesses, technical difficulties, internal politics, commitment to the current practices, and strong organizational culture. As future managers, you need to be aware

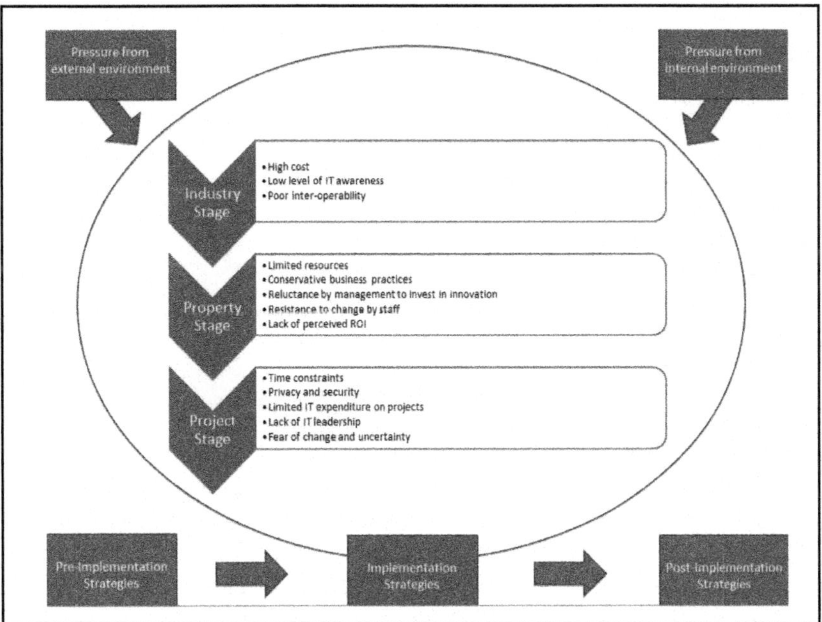

FIGURE 8-8. EXTERNAL PRESSURES IMPACT IT DECISIONS.

of the potential barriers and strategies to overcome such barriers. This is very important, because failure of overcoming IT implementation barriers will result in failure of organizations.

Figure above highlights that firms have pressure from the external environment. For example, if you are operating a restaurant, your customers may ask for an online reservation system, or if you are a hotel, your guests may ask for high speed Internet in the guest rooms. Such pressures from the external environment push companies to invest in some technologies. Similarly, there are push factors from the internal environment; for instance, Marriott may require all of their hotels to have a touch screen concierge in the lobby areas. Once companies decide to implement a technology, there are barriers that managers need to overcome. Firstly, there are industry stage barriers, such as a low level of IT awareness. Sometimes, managers are not aware of potential technologies, therefore, it is important for managers to go to industry specific shows such as HITEC and subscribe to industry specific magazines. Secondly, there are property level barriers such as resistance to change by staff. Your employees have their own ways of doing things. Some people do not want to change; they do not want their "cheese" moved. The fear of change and resistance are the big barriers to moving hotels forward. If hotels add the dynamic of people, this will break the inertia to IT implementation. Finally, there are project specific barriers, such as time constraints.

Technology Barriers

Cost of Implementation
Return on Investment
Leap of Faith
Resistance from Owners
System Integration/Interoperability
Outsourcing communication problems
Contract management
Guests' perception
Resistance to change
Training issues
Pace of technology
Time

Market Oriented Strategic IT Investment Planning

Market oriented strategic planning is the managerial process of developing and maintaining a feasible fit between the organization's objectives, skills, and resources and its changing market opportunities. Managers need to consider the objectives of the organization before investing in any technology. There should be a fit between the selected technology and the organization's objectives. For example, if you are operating a fast food restaurant you may decide to invest in kitchen management systems and kitchen production systems to speed up the food preparation process, however, you might not necessarily want to invest in CRM software. Similarly, if you provide excellent service as a luxury hotel, personal interactions would be important for your business, therefore, investing in a self check-in kiosk might not be a good idea for your hotel.

References

1. http://photos.mandarinoriental.com/is/content/MandarinOriental/corporate-jul11businessprofile-1
2. Nyheim, P. D., McFadden, F. M., & Connolly, D. J. (2004). *Technology strategies for the hospitality industry*. <Location>: Prentice-Hall, Inc.
3. Porter, M. E., & Millar, V. E. (1985). How information gives you competitive advantage. <Location>: *Harvard Business Review*, Reprint Service<page(s)-?>.
4. https://www.airbnb.com/about
5. http://www.omenahotels.com/about-omena/
6. Bilgihan, A., Okumus, F., Nusair, K., & Kwun, D. J.-W. (2011). Information technology applications and competitive advantage in hotel companies. *Journal of Hospitality and Tourism Technology*, *2*(2), 139–153.
7. Siguaw, J. A., & Enz, C. A. (1999). Best practices in information technology. *Cornell Hotel and Restaurant Administration Quarterly*, *40*(5), 58–71.
8. http://www.averoinc.com
9. Lee, S., & Connolly, D. J. (2010). The impact of IT news on hospitality firm value using cumulative abnormal returns (CARs). *International Journal of Hospitality Management*, *29*(3), 354–362.
10. Olsen, M. D., & Roper, A. (1998). Research in strategic management in the hospitality industry. *International Journal of Hospitality Management*, *17*(2), 111–124.
11. http://www.opentable.com/info/aboutus.aspx

CHAPTER 9

Data Mining in Hospitality

"The journey of a thousand miles begins with a single step."

Old Chinese Proverb

CHAPTER OUTLINE

INTRODUCTION

Have you ever wondered why you were called by the credit company the very next day after you charged to your credit card $100 in Toronto, bought $30 gas in Niagara, and then paid a dinner bill for $50 in Pittsburg within two days? Because this was very different from your regular pattern if you live in Dallas, Texas and never traveled to Toronto and north New York. This automated pattern finding process, which is called data mining, alerted the staff at the credit card company that there might be fraudulent activity in your credit card account and wanted to verify with you if you actually made these charges. Or think about car insurance companies! Why do you think that the car insurance costs $1000 more for a 23 year-old driver who drives a red sports car and has three recent speeding tickets than a 35 year-old who drives a minivan with no speeding ticket history? It is all about mining the data for the hidden patterns and eventually making decisions based on these patterns. After the tragic events of 9/11, we started to hear the term "data mining" more often. Visual data mining, profiling, mass data ware houses, and classifications were some of the terms used by news reporters in reports of preventing future terrorist events. Even though an old quote, below is a 2002 article from ComputerWorld Magazine that shows the importance of data mining in national security:

"Legislation that Congress failed to adopt two years ago would have created an interagency data-mining capability that could have detected and helped prevent last September's terrorist attacks," a senior Republican congressman asserted last week.

Speaking near his home district at the Information Sharing & Home land Security conference here, Rep. Curt Weldon (R-Pa.) lambasted the federal government, including

Congress, for failing to act on critical data-mining and intelligence integration proposals that he and others authored years before the terrorist attacks.

"There are 33 classified agency systems in the federal government, but none of them link their raw data together," said Weldon, chairman of the House Subcommittee on Military Research and Development. "We could have and should have had a better data-fusion capability on and before 9-11." (1)

We don't know if the proposed legislation could have prevented the events of 9/11 but we know that data mining would have helped find hidden patterns in data that we wouldn't have seen otherwise.

This chapter addresses data warehousing and mining fundamentals. As the quotation in the beginning of this section puts it, the process of data mining involves vast challenges of putting very small pieces together to be able to get the big picture. In other words, this chapter will tell you the process of transforming "data" into "knowledge" that managers use. The following chapters will explain the pieces of the puzzle not only in a general business environment but also in the hospitality industry environment.

Data Warehousing

A data warehouse is a copy of transaction data specifically structured for querying, analysis, and reporting (2). According to Agosta, data warehousing is an architecture that aims to align business imperatives, such as customer knowledge and brand development, with the system structures representing the business questions and issues about customers, products, services, and markets, and making possible applications that transform inarticulate, dumb data into useful business knowledge (See Figure 9-1) (3). A data warehouse is a database system which is not only capable of storing large quantities of data, but capable of performing detailed, complex operations on extremely large amounts of data. Because of the often massive size of these data base structures, a traditional database would not be capable of performing all of the necessary operations. In other words, a traditional database may track the sales at a hotel one day or even one transaction at a time. A data warehouse, on the other hand, would be capable of examining the sales data of an entire chain of hotels for an entire year or more and would not typically be used to handle day-to-day transactions. Instead, large numbers of transactions would be executed in batches to the warehouse at some predetermined interval. Data ware houses are often created using standard databases which handle everyday transactions as sources.

Data warehouses are sourced from three main kinds of transactional systems: legacy systems (i.e., Marriott's Marsha; Holiday Inn's Holidex), Enterprise Resource Planning (ERP) (i.e., Micros/Fidelio's Opera Hotel System), and electronic commerce systems (i.e., Internet-based Centralized Reservation System) (4).

The goals of data warehousing and data mining overlap. The difference between them is that data warehousing is architecture; whereas data mining is best described as an application. In other words, the data warehouse provides the cleansed, consistent,

	Data	Functions	Connectivity	Presentation	Events	Business Drivers
Score	Relations between fundamental entities	Business intelligence	Metadata	Online Analytic Processing (OLAP)	Time horizon of forecasting	Knowledge of the customer, market, product; brand development
Concept	Structures	Decision support	Library science	Cubes	Time series	Decision making
Logical	Data definition language	Data transformation	Navigation	Canonical aggregates	Irreversibility	Coordination of commitments
Physical	Containers	Data scrubbing	Repository	"Reach through"	Scheduling	Value added business goals
Build	Consistent dimensions, relevant facts	Aggregation	Indexing and retrieval	OLAP server engine	Three to five years of data	Visibility: market share, profitability, product performance
Deploy	Star schema join	Information supply chain	Systemic interoperability	"Invisible" interface, transparent access	Speed, accuracy of decision making	Customer service, demand planning, cross selling, warranty program, profitability

FIGURE 9-1. DATA WAREHOUSE ARCHITECTURE. (3)

1. Recognize that the job is probably harder than you expect
2. Understand the data in your existing systems
3. Be sure to recognize equivalent entities
4. Use metadata to support data quality
5. Select the right data transformation tools
6. Take advantage of external resources
7. Utilize new information distribution methods
8. Focus on higher payback marketing applications
9. Emphasize early wins to build support throughout the organization
10. Don't underestimate hardware requirements
11. Consider outsourcing your data warehouse development and maintenance

FIGURE 9-2 ELEVEN STEPS TO SUCCESS IN DATA WAREHOUSING. (5)

quality-conformed, accurate data for the data mining process (application). In addition, data warehousing provides context and background for a meaningful interpretation of the data. Sanjay Raizada, Vice President of Strategic Solutions of Syntel, summarizes the eleven steps to success in Data Warehousing (See Figure 9-2) (5). Now, let's see the data mining process: (6).

Data Mining

Simply put, data mining is the process of finding trends and patterns in data. The objective of this process is to sort through large quantities of data and discover new information. Data mining has also been referred to as Knowledge Discovery in Databases (KDD) (7). In the hospitality business, there are clear reasons for investing in data mining. If data mining can provide actionable results that improve business processes, then data mining is a competitive weapon. For example, Table 9-1 examines the three clear cases where data mining can directly affect a hotel's profitability.

Data Mining Process

Data mining is a process which includes a systematic way of using business and information technology tools. This process can be summarized in the following 7 steps (See Figure 9-3):

1. Problem Definition
2. Identifying source data
3. Discovery
4. Solution Formulation
5. Implementation (Action)
6. Monitoring the Results
7. Process Redesign

Problem definition is perhaps the most important step of the data mining process. As seen in Table 9-1, a clear problem definition is needed to be able to seek the solution and

TABLE 9-1. THREE CASES ON HOW DATA MINING CAN AFFECT A HOTEL'S PROFITABILITY.

Data Mining in Hotels	
Business Problem 1	Increase response rates on direct-mail campaigns
Solution	Through data mining, hotel marketing staff build predictive models that indicate who will most likely respond to a direct-mail campaign
Benefit	Increase revenues by targeting campaigns to the right audience
Business Problem 2	Improve ability to predict the likely fluctuations in the occupancy rate
Solution	Through data mining, hotel marketing staff build predictive models that identify patterns that have historically caused market fluctuations
Benefit	Increase revenues by adjusting room rates more intelligently (yield management)
Business Problem 3	Improve ability to predict the likelihood of success rate of a prospective employee
Solution	Through data mining, hotel human resources staff build predictive models that predict the success chance of a potential employee based on criteria (i.e., references, behavior tests results, past employment history)
Benefit	Decrease turnover rate by hiring most qualified candidates

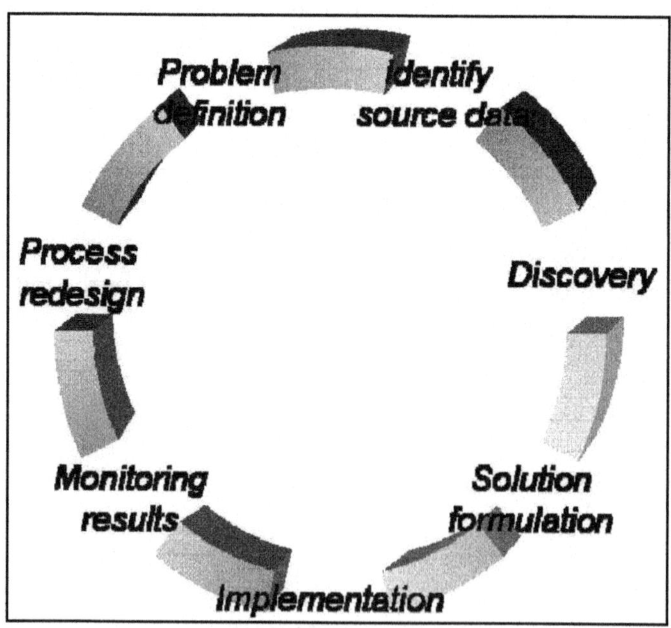

FIGURE 9-3 DATA MINING PROCESS: A CYCLICAL APPROACH.

employ the right tools. The next step, *identifying source data*, is critical because without clean, focused, and correct data, any data mining tool will give results that will not do any good to solve the business problem identified in the previous section. To be able to provide quality data, the organization should have a data warehouse strategy and architecture that brings all company data into one single depository for future use. After the data that will be used is identified, the next step is *discovery* in which data mining analysis begins. The next step after discovery is *solution formulation*, which lists the set of solutions based on the results of the discovery step. After the solution(s) has been operationalized, the *implementation* is the next logical step. After some actions have been taken, the results should be monitored in the *monitoring the results* step to be able to see the immediate effects of the actions taken in the previous step. The final step is *process redesign*, which is a critical analysis of the whole process and feeds the results into the future analyses to solve other business problems.

Data Mining Strategies

These strategies can be broadly classified as either supervised or unsupervised (8). Supervised learning builds models by using input variables to predict output variable values. Many supervised data mining algorithms only permit a single output variable. Output attributes are also known as dependent variables as their outcome depends on the values of one or multiple input variables, which are also referred to as independent variables. In the case of unsupervised learning, there is no dependent variable (output variable). All variables used in unsupervised learning are independent variables.

Data mining goals

According to Elmasri, et al., the goals of data mining can generally be categorized into one of the following groups (9):

Prediction

1. *Prediction.* Often referred to as *predictive data mining*, mining goals in this category are usually based on predicting the result of some event. For companies involved in sales, this is a way to predict the possible results of a new sales drive, product, or discount. Credit card companies may use this form of data mining to try to predict the reaction of potential card holders to a new benefit or lower interest rate on a credit card. Hospitality data miners can use prediction to predict future business or the effect of a marketing promotion to certain groups of guests. Goals of this category are very popular for many different applications.

Identification

2. *Identification.* The goals which fall into this category include those which hope to identify the existence of something through the discovery of hidden patterns. Data miners use these patterns to create rules about whether or not something exists. An Internet-based Centralized Reservation System (CRS) computer security staff

may use patterns in system logs to determine if a user has managed to hack into the system. The same system may be used to identify website users who visit the reservation page but leave without making a reservation. Though not as commonly used as the ones described in the previous section, the methods used to accomplish identification can be very useful and effective.

Classification

3. *Classification.* Goals in this category involve the division and organization of data into classes. These classes are often created and adjusted according to a set of parameters or combinations of them. Hospitality companies could use classification methods to determine the types of guests they have. For example, guests could be classed according to how frequently they visit a brand or store. Occasional guests are leisure travelers and those who stay less than 10 nights a year. Normal guests are those who stay between 10 and 30 nights in a year. Frequent guests are business travelers and those who stay more than 30 nights a year in a hotel.

Optimization

4. *Optimization.* The goals of optimization include the discovery of ways to balance the use of resources against each other. For example, an organization could use these methods to optimize a large project. Optimization techniques could be used to create multiple designs for a project, perhaps one which costs the least, one which can be completed the fastest, and one which is the most flexible in its use of resources. As a relatively new data mining goal, optimization is still developing and not yet as popular as many of the older categories. Improvements in technology, such as processing speed, storage size, and new mining techniques, will help to unleash the power of this category in the future.

These four categories are by no means comprehensive and not every goal in the field of data mining can fall directly into a single category. Some simply do not fit in a category, while others fit in many different ones. Because new and different goals can be developed for potentially every data mining system, the above categories can only be used as a general guide.

Data Mining Techniques

A data mining technique is used to apply a data mining strategy to a set of data. A specific data mining technique is defined by an algorithm and an associated knowledge structure, such as a tree or a set of rules. There are many available techniques used to mine data. Some are the traditional, standard techniques, whereas some of them are relatively new and have only become possible because of today's more developed and more capable technology. This section discusses some of those techniques.

Basic Descriptive Analysis

Basic Descriptive Analysis. This technique is usually the first one applied to a set of data. Though it is often not thought of as mining, many questions about what data should be mined can be answered by simply finding the maximum and minimum rates of important variables. A restaurant might want to know, for example, during which month the highest number sales for a particular menu item were made or, more specifically, on which day(s). While many factors have influenced this figure, no effort is made to eliminate external or other influences. The technique is intentionally implemented this way to provide a general picture of how the company has performed. Information gathered with this technique is often used to help determine what other mining techniques should be applied to the data. There are many other names for this standard "opening" technique, but all result in the same overall picture and the results are often displayed in a graph format.

Classification (Supervised Learning)

Classification (Supervised Learning). The human mind naturally segments things into distinctive groups(i.e., babies, children, teenagers, adults, and elderly). It involves breaking groups of data into like categories, then modeling that data into a conceptual hierarchy based on the characteristics of each group. Hotel companies may use classification technique to classify current customers on how they pay their bills. For example, hotel guests could be classified into three groups: those who pay their entire bill at the time of check-out, those who generally do not pay at the time of check-out (i.e., Corporate accounts) but pay after in a predetermined period of time, and those who are delinquent and have not paid the balance for the most recent invoice. Based on this information, a further model can be established to identify the pattern between good guests and risky guests.

Clustering (Unsupervised Learning)

Clustering (Unsupervised Learning). Clustering, or segmentation, is a method of grouping rows of data that share similar trends and patterns (14). Clusters of data are formed when a group of data all shares some common feature. The feature which they share could be some attribute (such as date) or a complex combination of attributes or relationships (such as date, type, and number of relations to another cluster). These clusters can then be compared and contrasted in many ways including through multidimensional modeling or graphing. The resulting infor mation can then be summarized and used for the decision making process. Clustering technique has no dependent variable. An example of clustering technique in hospitality business might be used if a hotel manager would like to segment its customer base; the manager can cluster the data by employing cluster analysis technique to create distinctive groups from each other but very similar within the clusters. Figure 9-4 shows the result of such a cluster analysis. When we look at the graph, we see that there are distinctive groups:

Cluster 1 (circles)
Income: High
Education: High
Number of nights spent: High

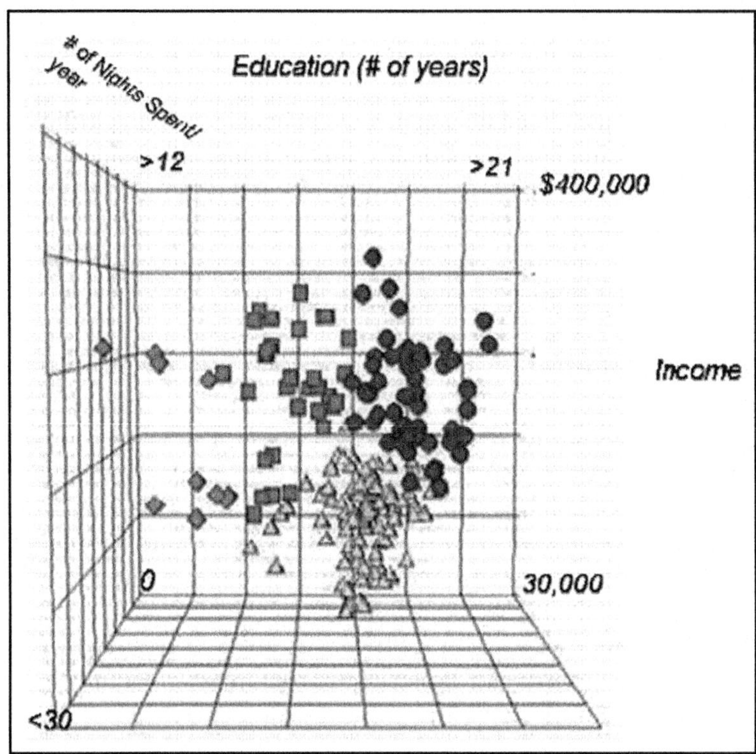

FIGURE 9-4. AN EXAMPLE OF A CLUSTER ANALYSIS RESULT.

Cluster 2 (squares)
Income: High
Education: Average
Number of nights spent: High

Cluster 3 (diamonds)
Income: Low
Education: Low
Number of nights spent: Low

Cluster 4 (triangles)
Income: Low
Education: Average
Number of nights spent: High

Dependency Modeling

Dependency Modeling. This technique attempts to describe the dependencies between variables in the data. (11) It can also be adapted into a graphical form and usually results in information about the data from two distinct aspects. The first aspect, often called the structural level, defines how variables depend on each other and which are involved in such dependencies. The second aspect, called the quantitative level, provides a method for determining the strength of a specific dependency or group of dependencies.

Summarization & Association Rules

Summarization & Association Rules. The summarization technique provides a method of examining a subset of data, mining that subset, and arriving at a group of specific conclusions about that data. Association rules correlate the presence of a set of items with another range of values for another set of variables (12). In other words, association rules attempt to identify and predict patterns of events based on otherwise unrelated data. After the development of such a rule, a database operator may "drill-down" such rules, trying to find the most essential parts of a specific relationship. This technique is also called Market Analysis (15).

Sequential Patterning

Sequential Patterning. Using this patterning method, sequences of events can lead to valuable information on which to base predictions of future events. Such sequences are found and identified, and predictions are made about what events might follow. According to Elmasri, et al., this method is common in the medical field where predicting patient reactions to certain medical conditions and practices can assist in the recovery of the patient (13). However, a sufficiently large history of cases like the one in question is necessary in order to make valid predictions.

Data Mining Algorithms

Data Mining Algorithms. The purpose of a data mining algorithm is to discover and represent the between-variable relationships. The following paragraphs discuss some of the most widely used data mining algorithms:

1. Decision Trees
2. Neural Networks
3. Bayesian Belief Networks
4. Statistics
5. Web Mining

Decision Trees

Decision Trees. Decision trees are tree-shaped structures that represent sets of decisions. Decision trees start with broad characteristics and progressively narrow the focus onto specific independent variables that relate to the target. The tree starts with a single "parent" node which then gives rise to several "children" nodes at the second layer of the tree. Each of these children nodes then gives rise to its own children at the third layer of the tree, and so on, as indicated in Figure 9-5. Decision trees are used in data mining to create segments which are homogeneous as possible with respect to some

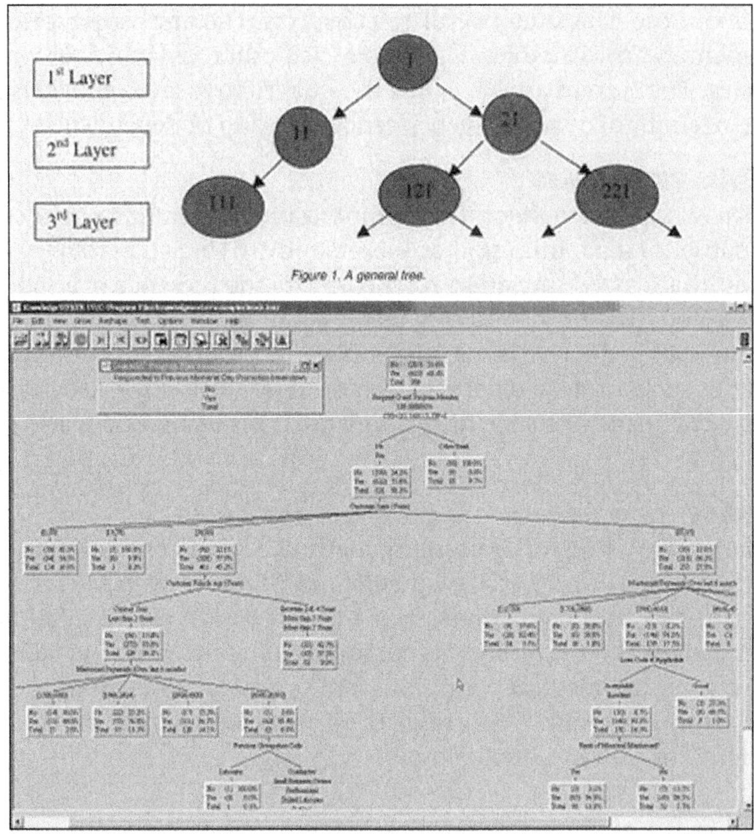

FIGURE 9-5. A DECISION TREE EXAMPLE (SOURCE: KNOWLEDGESEEKER).

dependent variable. Each successive layer in the tree represents a partitioning of the population into subgroups based on the different values of some independent variable. Decision trees are used in risk analysis to make optimal decisions in the presence of uncertainty and in financial analysis (e.g., evaluating how a stock's price changes over time). In both these applications, each successive layer in the tree represents different possible states of the world at successive points in time. Also, decision trees are used in marketing to specify how customer satisfaction at an overall level relates to customer satisfaction at more specific levels. Figure 9-5 shows an example of a decision tree result which is obtained with a software called KnowledgeSeeker from ANGOSS Software Corporation. In this example, the parent node is "Responded to Memorial Day Promotion." The tree is structured based on this question (yes or no). The strongest relationship is formed and then the sub-leaves are formed based on the level of the relationship. Decision trees are also called Chi Square Automatic Interaction Detection because they use Chi-Square as a statistical tool to develop the tree.

NEURAL NETWORKS

Neural Networks. Neural networks are defined as information processing systems inspired by the structure or architecture of the brain (16). Rather than using a digital model, in which all computations manipulate zeros and ones, a neural network works by creating connections between processing elements, the computer equivalent of neurons (17). The organization and weights of the connections determine the output. Neural networks are particularly effective for predicting events when the networks have a large database of prior examples on which to draw. They are constructed from interconnecting processing elements which are analogous to neurons (See Figure 9-6). Neural networks can also be applied in supervised and unsupervised learning methods. Supervised learning starts with the process of training the neural network to recognize different classes of data. This is accomplished by exposing it to a series of examples. The next step is to test how well it has learned from these examples by supplying it with a previously unseen set of data. Unsupervised learning (which is a form of cluster analysis) is so called as the neural network requires no initial information regarding the correct classification of the data with which it is presented. The neural network employing unsupervised learning is able to analyze a multidimensional dataset in order to discover the natural clusters and subclusters which exist within data.

BAYESIAN BELIEF NETWORKS

Bayesian Belief Networks. Bayesian Belief Networks (BBN) are not as commonly used in the data mining community as decision trees and neural networks. Belief networks are used to model uncertainty in a domain. The term "belief networks" encompasses a whole range of different but related techniques which deal with reasoning under uncertainty. Both quantitative (mainly using Bayesian probabilistic methods) and qualitative techniques are used. Increasingly, belief network techniques are being employed to deliver advanced knowledge based systems to solve real-world problems. A Bayesian network is commonly represented as a graph, which is a set of vertices and edges (See Figure 9-7). The vertices,

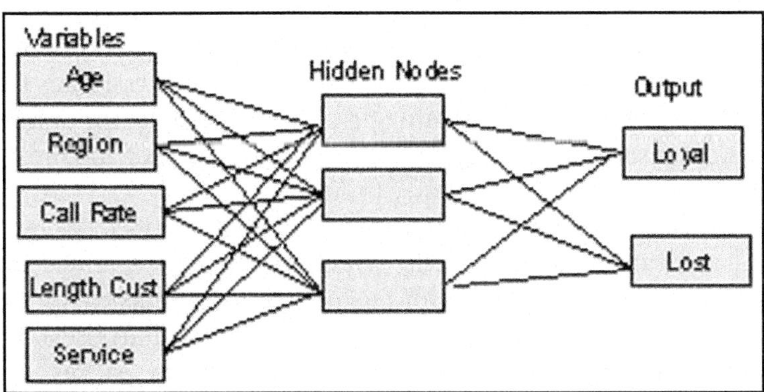

FIGURE 9-6. A NEURAL NETWORK EXAMPLE.

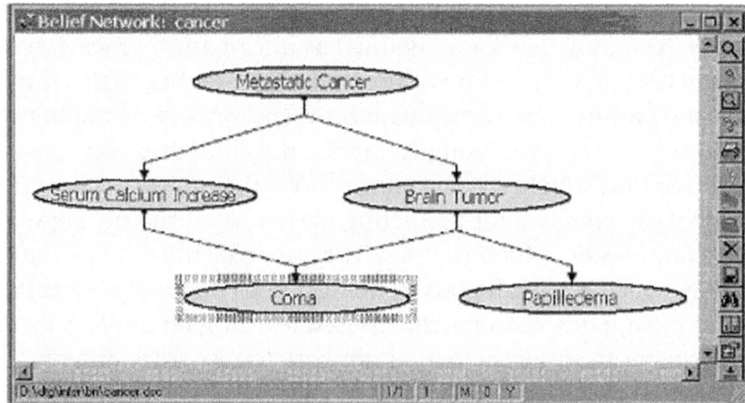

FIGURE 9-7. AN EXAMPLE OF A BAYESIAN BELIEF NETWORK SETUP IN MICROSOFT'S BAYESIAN NETWORK. EDITOR.

or nodes, represent the variables and the edges, or arcs, represent the conditional dependencies in the model. The absence of an arc between two variables indicates conditional independence; that is, there are no situations in which the probability of one of the variables depends directly upon the state of the other. Belief networks are particularly useful for diagnostic applications and have been used in many deployed systems.

Statistics

Statistics. Statistics have been used for many years to create a model of data sets. Two of the most used statistics in data mining are regression and discriminant analysis. A regression equation is one that estimates a dependent variable using a set of independent variables and a set of constants (18). Regression techniques can be used to perform prediction when techniques of conditional probability are introduced. One type of regression model is the logit model, which is a model where all independent variables are categorical. A logistic regression model is similar to the logit model, but has continuous variables as well. There are many types of regression models. For situations where no linear functions easily fit with data, there are nonlinear regressions and nonlinear multiple regression models. A regression model is popular for business professionals to predict variables such as occupancy rates, loyalty rate of a customer, risk factor of a customer, or likelihood of customer satisfaction. Regression is probably one of the most used data mining techniques used within the hospitality industry.

Discriminant analysis is the study of finding a set of coefficients or weights that describe a Linear Classification Function (LCF) which maximally separates groups of variables. Discriminant analysis is popular for business professionals to find common groupings of variables (i.e., segmenting customers for marketing purposes).

Statistics can be calculated with the help of computer software packages such as SPSS, SAS, or Minitab.

TEXT MINING

Text mining is one of the data mining techniques that works with large volumes of textual information in order to discover underlying patterns in the studied text. Text mining has the same objectives and relies on similar processes as data mining, however, it works with unstructured data such as word documents, pdf files and other types of textual information. Applications of text mining include some of the processes that are common for data mining, such as summarization, classification, and clustering. Some other applications, such as question answering and text link analysis, are specific to text mining.

The use of text mining provides the most benefits to the fields that need to process large volumes of textual information such as academic research, law, and marketing (19). Marketing area is one of the key areas of text mining applications for the hospitality industry. The industry generates large volumes of customer reviews that are available to the managers via the comment cards, online surveys, or customer postings on the review websites. Monitoring the customer reviews and understanding the key patterns has become very important for the hotel industry, since hotels have to operate in a competitive, rapidly-changing environment. Increasing commoditization of the hotel product has amplified the competitive nature of the business. It has become very important to understand what makes customers return, or not to return; what makes them recommend a hotel or discourage friends and relatives from visiting; what items, services, and features create value for customers; and it is important to create and communicate a clear brand image. Text mining is a valuable tool to answer questions like this.

The applications of the text mining to the analysis of hotel online reviews may be demonstrated in a research study conducted by a team of university researchers (20). The main purpose of the study was to analyze online hotel reviews and identify what makes satisfied customers happy, and what can lead to unhappy customers. For the purpose of this study all reviews for one of the resort destinations in the U.S. were collected from the Tripadvisor.com. The information was collected using an online robot developed for the purposes of this research. A total of 2,511 reviews were recorded. The file contained all standard data fields that appear on tripadvisor.com: hotel name, guest name, trip type, comment, and rating scores for value, rooms, location, cleanliness, service, and sleep quality. Next, all reviews were divided into two categories based on the guest's indicated intention to recommend or not recommend this hotel to others. The reviews were analyzed using PASW Modeler, one of the text mining packages.

The first analysis that was applied to the document is word categorization. The main purpose of this type of analysis is to compare and contrast the main topics in the reviews of happy and unhappy customers. The top most frequently used word categories in positive reviews were: place of business (in this case, it was the word "hotel"), rooms, and staff. The top three categories discussed in negative reviews were place of business ("hotel"), rooms, and furniture. The software package output for the word categorization problem is presented in a Figure 9-8 below. For every word category the figure reports the usage frequency and the number of documents (in this case reviews) where the word was mentioned.

Category	Bar	Selection %	Docs
place of business		99.7	997
health spa		3.8	38
hotel		90.3	903
office		1.0	10
restaurants		35.8	358
outlets		17.8	178
club		12.2	122
room		74.0	740
members		63.5	635
staffing		63.1	631
hotel personnel		17.3	173
housekeeper		6.3	63
clerk		0.8	8
waiter		7.7	77
tiki staff		0.7	7
attentive staff		0.2	2
pool staff		0.8	8
nice staff		0.2	2
boss		0.2	2
lovely staff		0.2	2
lobby staff		0.2	2
friendly staff		2.4	24
bar staff		0.4	4
sports		53.5	535
home equipment		48.3	483
beach		43.1	431
food & table		36.4	364
architecture		36.2	362
food		34.6	346
family structure		28.5	285
human resources		27.1	271
beverages		26.6	266
finance		25.5	255
traveller		23.8	238
place		23.4	234
view		23.3	233
lodging		23.3	233

FIGURE 9-8. WORD CATEGORIZATION FOR POSITIVE REVIEWS.

It' is logical for hotel reviews to contain words referring to the hotel itself and its rooms as the core lodging product. However, we already start seeing differences at the third category. Happy customers switch to intangible components (e.g., staff), while unhappy customers keep talking about the tangible aspects of hotel operations (e.g., furniture). Also, the results showed that the financial category was more dominant in negative reviews. This category included such words as cost, discount, and credit card. This suggests that unhappy customers more are concerned about financial issues (such as the price they paid for their perceived poor experience) than are happy customers (indicating that guests will be less concerned with price if they were satisfied).

The study also included text link analysis, which looks at pairs of words frequently used together. In this study, the word chosen for evaluation was "no". This means that the software looked for all combinations that include "no + any other word". Essentially, a word combination like this would mean a lack or absence of something. Again the comparison for the positive and negative categories was performed. The results found the following pairs of words in positive reviews: no wait, no minutes, no complaint, no noise, no questions, no issue, etc. (Figure 9-9) Despite the use of the word "no," these combinations actually have a positive meaning. On the other hand, the negative reviews for "no" often contained the following word pairs: no room, no balcony, no breakfast, no refund, no

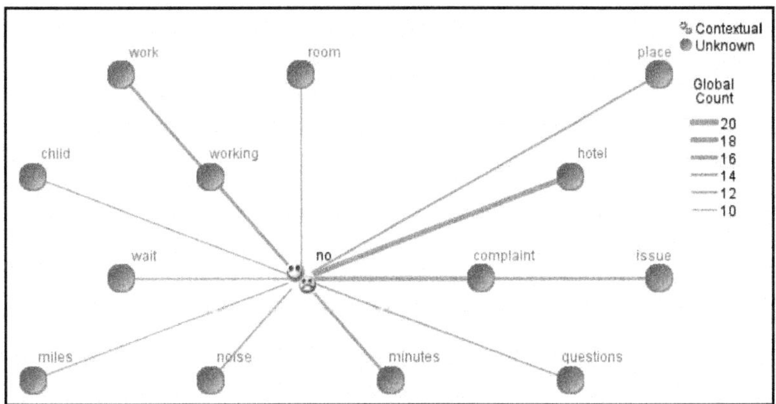

FIGURE 9-9. TEXT LINK ANALYSIS FOR POSITIVE REVIEWS.

care, no return, etc. These word pairs, found as an outcome of the text mining analysis, identified several categories of guest complaints that might require managers' attention.

Text mining may be a useful tool for hotel managers to keep an eye on the reviews of their own, and even competing, properties. Even though technology cannot perform the entire analysis for managers, it can provide a fairly accurate synopsis of what' is going on in a hotel.

Web mining

Web Mining. Although web mining is not a stand-alone data mining technique, it may be considered as a separate technique because of its data source. Web mining is commonly used to refer to three different activities: 1) mining structure, 2) mining usage, and 3) mining content (21). ***Structure mining*** is the process of extracting information from the topology of the Web. It answers questions like "Which pages are the targets of links from many others?" and "Which pages point to many others?" ***Usage mining*** is the process of extracting information on how people navigate these links. It attempts to find relationships among which pages people visit, how long they stay in each page, and the final outcome (i.e., if they book a room). ***Content mining*** is the process of extracting useful information from the text, images and pictures, and other forms that make up the pages. Content mining is very familiar in the form of search engines (i.e., google.com, yahoo.com)

The data source for each of the web mining components is different. For structure mining, the data source comes from the scanning of the web in general to create the networks of links among websites. The data source for the usage mining is the local website clickstream which can be found in web logs. The data source for content mining is the web spiders and search engines.

The Uses of Data Mining in the Hospitality Industry

This section will give examples of data mining in use in the hospitality industry context. Lau, et al. (22) proposed a method for using the web to establish direct marketing channels between tourism bureaus and potential travelers through content mining tools. Their model included analyzing the information on the potential traveler's site and identifying his/her interests and sending marketing e-mails based on these findings.

A survey by Two Crows Corporation (23) found these applications of data mining in the hospitality industry:

- Ad revenue forecasting
- Churn (turnover) management
- Credit risk analysis
- Cross-marketing
- Customer profiling
- Customer retention
- Exception reports
- Food-service menu analysis
- Hiring profiles
- Market basket analysis
- Member enrollment
- Student recruiting and retention
- Targeted marketing

Applebee's, a nationwide chain of 1,300 restaurants, uses a Teradata enterprise data warehouse to forecast demand in the fickle and promotion-driven casual dining market (24). Until mid-1999, Applebee's worked from spreadsheets and gut instinct to plot demand and distribution, service campaigns, and allocate products and labor to its far-flung chain. After creating a data warehouse and implementing data mining techniques, Applebee's has a much better grip on forecasting by combining historical store and product performance with distribution and logistics, and ties the whole chain to the purchasing department. This helps the company optimize menus, plan campaigns, drive customer frequency, and even predict staffing requirements. In addition, the company executives can predict customer sensitivity to price increases of each individual menu item. The company uses Citrix to collect its data and employs SQL Server to track it.

Finagle a Bagel, a sandwich chain with 11 units in the greater Boston metropolitan area, tied its Point of Sales System (POS) with its Customer Relationship Management (CRM) program to be able to track what its customers buy. They, then, create associations between their customer demographics and their purchasing habits. Based on the results of the associations, the company sends customized promotions to its customers. After implementing the data mining tools on the data collected from CRM and POS, the company experienced a 25 percent improvement in the average guest check (25).

Louise's Trattoria, a 13-unit Italian dinner-house in the Los Angeles area, analyzed credit card transactions and customer-purchase data through Gazelle System's (*www.gaz.com*) GAZ Reports to obtain actionable information (26). After mining the data, the chain realized an association between its customer base and the food type they like.

They, then, customized their menu and delivery options based on that data and increased their sales significantly.

AFC Enterprises, operator and franchiser of more than 3300 Church's, Popeye's Chicken and Biscuits, and Seattle Coffee Company, collects customer purchase data by item/item combination (market basket analysis), day, day part, and unit (27). Information is stored in a data warehouse and then mined using AIX RICS 6000 (*www.rs6000.ibm.com*) hardware and Informix software (*www.informix.com*). The company used multiple regression analysis to predict if a particular customer will respond to a promotion or not. Through market basket analysis, they found the best pair of foods (i.e., coffee and cheesecake) and trained their servers to upsell towards those pairs.

Harrah's Entertainment Inc. created a patented CRM program called "Total Gold" to collect data from its customers who stay, play, or eat in one of their 18 hotels, casinos, and restaurants. The company used cluster analysis to profile its customers (See Figure 9-10), offer those appropriate incentives and promotions, and then use regression analysis to predict the risk factor of each guest.

Data mining techniques are also used in tourism research. One researcher profiled the domestic tourists of a city to provide suggestions for relevant tourism enterprises such as foreign tourism investors, tour operators, travel agents, and hotels [(28). The profiling task was accomplished according to the segments based on accommodation preferences.

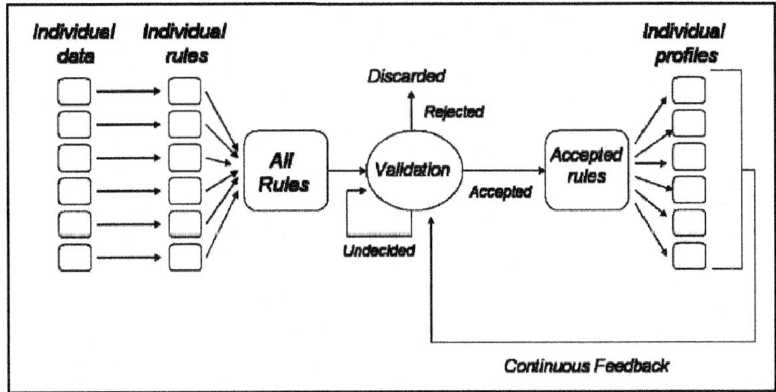

FIGURE 9-10. HARRAH'S GUEST PROFILING METHOD.

This way, they could segment outgoing tourists of this domestic tourism market which consists of various groups with different profiles. The use of data mining techniques in these kinds of research provides critical information for targeted direct marketing efforts that are "who to target" (i.e., which customer segment or segments) with "what offer" (i.e., which hotel or holiday village service attributes such as animation) using "what action" (i.e., which media and rewards)[26].

REFERENCES

1. Verton, Dan. (August 26, 2002) "Congressman says data mining could have prevented 9-11," *ComputerWorld*, [Available Online]. http://www.computerworld.com/governmenttopics/government/ policy/story/0,10801,73773,00.html Retrieved on May 4, 2003.
2. Marakas, G. (2003). *"Modern data warehousing, mining, and visualization,"* Upper Saddle River, NJ: Prentice Hall, p. 4-5.
3. Agosta, L.(1999). *"The essential guide to data warehousing,"* Upper Saddle River, NJ: Prentice Hall, p. 460.
4. *Ibid*, p.38.
5. Raizada, S, "White paper: Eleven steps to success in data ware-housing," [Available] http://www.itpapers.com/cgi/PSummaryIT.pl?paperid=33201&scid=252 Retrieved on May 8, 2003.
6. *Ibid*, p. 406-407.
7. *Ibid*, p. 4.
8. Roiger, R., & Geatz, M. (2003). *"Data mining: A tutorial-based primer,"* Boston, MA: Addison Wesley, p. 34-36.
9. Elmasri, R., & Navathe, S. (2000). *Fundamentals of Database Systems*, Addison-Wesley.
10. Wang, X. Z. (1999). *Data Mining and Knowledge Discovery for Process Monitoring and Control*, Springer-Verlag London Limited.
11. *Ibid*, p.20.
12. *Ibid*, p.859.
13. *Ibid*, p. 859.
14. Groth, R. (2000). "Data Mining: Building Competitive Advantage," Upper Saddle River, NJ: Prentice Hall, p. 23-24.
15. *Ibid*, p. 28.
16. Caudill, M., & Butler, C. (1990). Naturally intelligent systems, Cambridge, MA: MIT Press.
17. http://www.pcwebopedia.com/TERM/n/neural_network.html
18. *Ibid*, p.83.
19. Turban, E., Sharda, R., & Delen, D. (2011). Decision support and business intelligence systems (9th ed.). Prentice Hall: Upper Saddle River, NJ.
20. http://hospitalitytechnology.edgl.com/cihan-cobanoglu/Analyze-Online-Reviews-for-Clues-to-Customer-Satisfaction78506.
21. Linoff, G, & Berry, M. (2001). "Mining the web." New York, NY: Wiley.

22. Lau, Kin-Nam, Lee, Kam-Hon, Lam, Pong-Yuen, & Ho, Ying, "Website Marketing for the Travel and Tourism Industry," Cornell Hotel and Restaurant Administration *Quarterly*, *42*, (6), p. 55-62.

23. http://www.twocrows.com/applics.htm (Retrieved on May 11, 2003).

24. http://www.line56.com/articles/default.asp?ArticleID=3057 (Retrieved on May 11, 2003).

25. *Ibid*, p. 18.

26. Liddle, A. (October 30, 2000). "Casual-dining chain's mining of customer data spurs change, management indicates," Nation's Restaurant News, 34(44), p. 52.

27. "Mining the data of dining." (May 22, 2002). Nation's Restaurant News, 34(21), p. 22-24.

28. Emel, G. G., Taskin, Ç., & Akat, O. (2007). Profiling a domestic tourism market by means of association rule mining. Anatolia, 18(2), 335-343. doi: Article.

CHAPTER 10

Project Management

Some projects never seem to terminate.."rather, they become like Moses, condemned to wander till the end of their days without seeing the promised land."

Stephen P. Keider (1974) (1)

CHAPTER OUTLINE

Chances are good that you are not married; however, you have probably witnessed somebody like a family member or friend getting married. There are many tasks to be accomplished by many different people before the magic "wedding" date.

Everything is timed out, and they all should be accomplished so that finally the "marriage" can happen. This is a great example of project management. The people involved in this process may not formally recognize it as a "project," since it is a personal matter. Actually, project management was not accepted as a formal area of study until the last two decades. Our lives include tasks that require planning, execution, and control.

Project management has been part of our lives for ages. The fall of Constantinople, the Great Pyramids of Cheops, and the magnificent Blue Mosque in Istanbul are just some examples of great project management products. So, there was project management 5000 years ago, and there is project management today. However, the difference is how we manage projects. Technology is one change that helps us manage projects. First, let's define what project management is.

Project Management is the discipline of planning, organizing, and managing resources to bring about the successful completion of specific project goals and objectives (1). These goals and objectives could be professional or personal, like in the example given above. A project is a finite endeavor that means that it will have specific start and completion dates. A project is undertaken to create a unique product or service which brings about beneficial change or added value to the person(s) or the organization. According to Computerworld Magazine survey, the following are the most important skills that CIOs and IT executives will be looking for when they hire new people (2):

- Programming/application development
- Project management
- IT/business analysis
- Security
- Help desk/technical support

Clearly, project management skills are among the most important skills. The primary challenge of project management is to achieve all of the project goals and objectives while adhering to classic project constraints—usually scope, quality, time, and budget.

The secondary challenge is to optimize the allocation and integration of inputs necessary to meet predefined objectives. A project is a carefully defined set of activities that use resources (money, people, materials, energy, space, provisions, communication, motivation, etc.) to achieve the project goals and objectives. As project management advanced, different methods and tools were developed to manage small or big projects.

An IT department at a hotel, restaurant, or any other hospitality organization involves a lot of projects that need to be undertaken with time and budget constraints. Some of the IT projects that a hospitality organization may undertake are:

- A hotel is looking at replacing its legacy Property Management System (PMS). What system is the best (functionality, interfaceability, support, user friendliness, etc.) for this hotel?
- A restaurant is planning to comply with Payment Card Industry Data Security Standards (PCI DSS). How to achieve PCI DSS?
- A hotel will be implementing a customer relationship management program so that it can keep track of its guests' needs and wants better to customize the experience for them.
- A restaurant chain is implementing a wide area network so that the menu changes can be pushed electronically from the corporate to stores.
- A hotel wants to design a computer-based learning tool for its Point of Sale (POS) systems so that staff members can develop their POS skills during off-peak times.

These are all projects that require careful planning, budgeting, selection techniques and tools, implementation strategies, and controlling. Project management brings a systematic approach to managing these projects. IT project teams are increasingly dispersed across large areas, sometimes spanning the globe, and involved in more partnerships with managed service providers and outsourcers. Now, let's look at the reality. What percentages of the projects that are started in companies are successfully finished? Before this question can be answered, we need to define what "successful" is. "Successful" is finishing the project on time and budget for a project manager. "Successful" is generating profit at the finish of the project for the investor. According to a survey conducted by the Technology Executives Club (3):

- In the past twelve months, 49 percent of participants have experienced at least one project failure.
- In this same period, only two percent of organizations achieved targeted benefits all the time.
- Eighty-six percent of organizations lost up to 25 percent of target benefits across their entire project portfolio.
- To the detriment of stakeholders, organizations are making commitments, but not always delivering on outcomes.
- While organizations are getting some value from their IT project investment, the survey results show clearly that most cannot determine exactly how much.

- Many do not even try to measure the value. So what does this mean? To us it means that significant value is being lost since many organizations either do not, or are incapable of, adequately assessing the degree of commitments kept.

A computer world magazine survey gives the clues as to why a significant portion of projects fail (4). The most significant problems revealed a lack of:

- A project office or a clearly defined project organization (42 percent)
- Integrated methods (41 percent)
- Training and mentoring (38 percent)
- Policies and procedures (35 percent)
- Implementation plans (23 percent)
- Executive support (22 percent)

The hospitality industry is spending millions of dollars for Information Technology investments. IT is mission-critical for them. For this reason, it is important to manage the IT projects efficiently so that the outcome would be positive for all stakeholders. The following section will explain the proper steps of project management.

Project Management Phases

The following will describe the eight phases of project management (5). It is important to note that some of these steps of IT project management can be linear and parallel. In other words, some of these steps will be undertaken simultaneously and some of them are dependent on the previous steps.

Project Concept/Scope

This phase involves the strategic alignment principal. This principal requires that all projects must support the company mission, which is defined as the strategic direction of the company. In other words, the project outcome is expected to impact the company goals positively. This outcome is not necessarily measured with monetary units. They can be strategic measures. For example, if a quick-service restaurant chain's mission is to be the choice of fast, healthy, and clean, then the selection and implementation of a self-service drive thru system maybe a good strategic project to undertake because the system may increase the speed of service by five seconds per guest. This may increase the number of guests served during a day, which will impact the bottom-line directly. So, with any project initiation, the strategic impact of the project must be clearly identified with quantitative and qualitative measures. The following questions should be answered in this phase: What is it you are supposed to accomplish by managing this project? What is the project objective? In addition, the scope should be defined. This means that all definitions must be clearly set so that there are no confusions in the future.

Project Design/Assemble Project Team

Once the project is identified as "strategically aligned," the next step involves defining and designing the project. The people who will play roles in the project are identified, integrated schedules will be determined, and the development cost baseline will be calculated. With this step, a tentative release/finish date is set for the project. In this step, the roles are clearly identified. The leaders and key players in the project have been notified. Figure 10-1 shows a project management mind map with work flow.

In this phase, Work Breakdown Structure (WBS) is defined. WBS is one of the most important project management tools (6). With a WBS, the project manager can develop every other tool needed to manage the project successfully. WBS is the basis for planning, scheduling, budgeting, and controlling the project. WBS is a structured way of breaking the project into various components such as software, hardware, communications network, services, documentation, labor, testing, implementation, installation, and maintenance. In other words, WBS is a systematic way of breaking a big project into smaller, manageable pieces. Figure 10-2 shows an example of Work Breakdown Structure for a banquet at a restaurant.

In this phase, Gantt Charts are also used to show planned and actual progress for a number of tasks displayed against a horizontal time scale (7). This type of information display is one of the most effective and useful tools of project management. Even with a quick look, the overall process of the project can be observed. Figure 10-3 shows an example Gantt Chart for a new property management system selection and implementation project for a hotel.

Project Development

This phase focuses on developing a project that satisfies the requirements created in the Project Design phase (i.e., Design Document, Project requirements document). Information technology department develops or manages the project and verifies that it works. As they complete their verification, they pass the project to the Quality Assurance

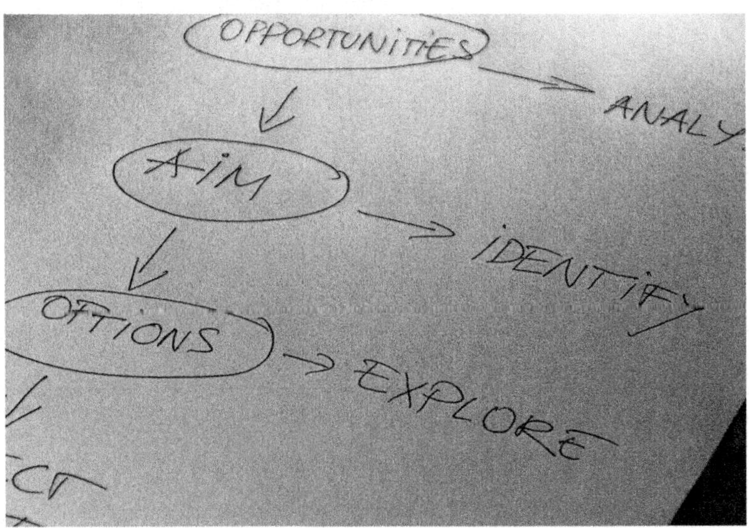

FIGURE 10-1. PROJECT MANAGEMENT MIND MAP WITH WORK FLOW.

Source: Image Copyright Maigi, 2008. Used Under License from Shutterstock, Inc.

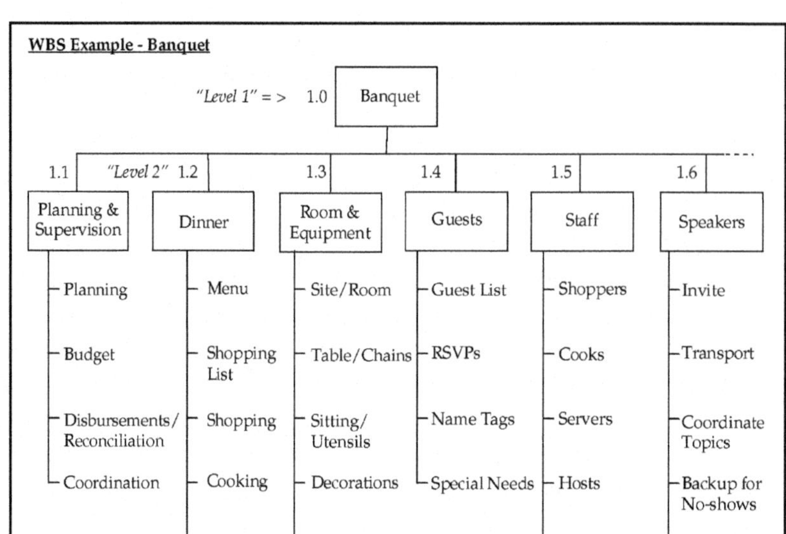

FIGURE 10-2. AN EXAMPLE OF WORK BREAKDOWN STRUCTURE FOR A BANQUET AT A RESTAURANT.

Source: http://www.hyperthot.com/pm_wbs.htm.

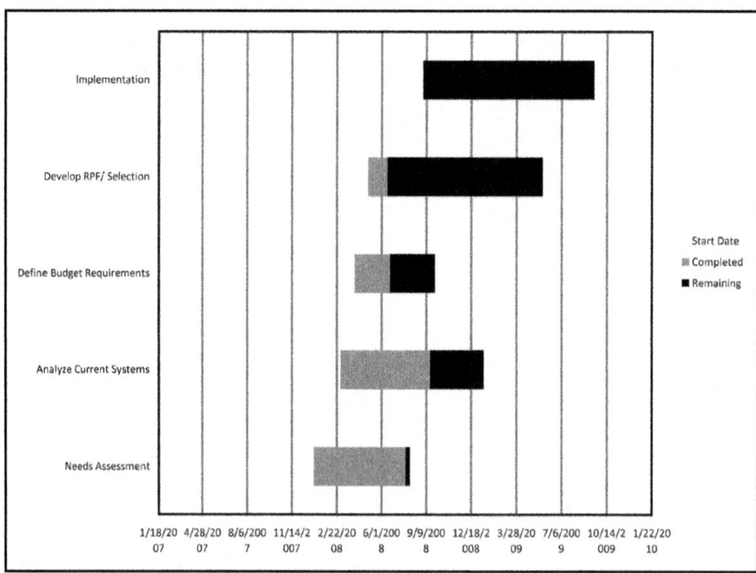

FIGURE 10-3. A SCREEN SHOT FROM A PROJECT MANAGEMENT SOFTWARE'S REPORT.

(QA) group so that QA can start testing the project to assure it meets company quality guidelines. The IT department also passes the project to Documentation so that they can start working on creating user manuals and help files that will support the project. Figure 10-4 shows a project management software's report.

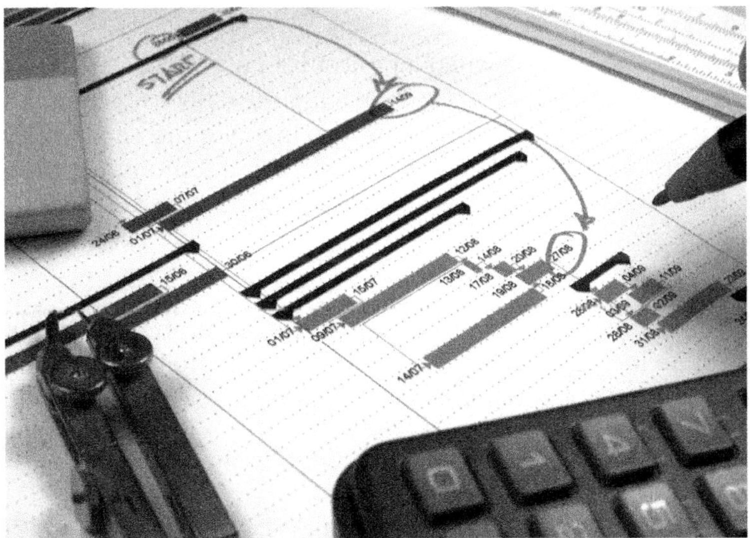

FIGURE 10-4. REPORT ANALYSIS.

Source: Image Copyright Fernando Blanco Calzada, 2008. Used Under License from Shutterstock, Inc.

Quality Assurance

Quality assurance (QA) checks to see if the current project status is in line with the initial goals and objectives of the project. QA tests the project and reads the support documentation. If there is anything that does not meet the Design Document specifications, the Documentation Plan, and the Project Requirements Document, the proper team member(s) will be notified and asked to revise. QA also prepares a Project Launch plan which will include due dates, release dates, a marketing plan, and a public relations and press release tour schedule.

Beta

Beta testing takes place after the Quality Assurance group agrees that the project, user manuals, and help files are functional and they meet the Design Document and the Documentation Plan specifications. The project is sent to pilot testers who test the project in a real environment and report the bugs to the Quality Assurance group.

Release

After the beta sites are finished with testing the project, the team starts releasing the project to users. The team monitors closely the launch, user manuals, and help documentations to ensure that all are in good order. This phase represents the time that takes for the project to be staged and sent to users. This phase could be as simple as providing a URL (web site address) for the project (i.e., new web-based purchase order system for a restaurant) or very complex where new servers, workstations, routers, or cabling may be installed and configured (i.e., wide area network for a hotel).

General Availability

General availability is the phase when a project is in use. Help Desk is assisting end users, end users are being trained, and IT is managing the daily use of the project and fixing any bugs as they are reported. This phase also involves the review of the project on an annual basis. In this phase, the help desk answers user questions, end-user training is available, scheduled hardware/software upgrades take place, bugs are fixed on a rolling basis, and patches are provided.

End of Life

This is the last phase in project management where the team decides that the project is now obsolete and no longer is useful. With any thing, all projects have a life span. This phase may be the beginning of a new project.

References

1. Lientz, B. P., & Rea, K. P. (2000). *Project Management.* New York, NY: Harcourt Professional Publishing.
2. http://www.yourdonreport.com/index.php/2007/01/06/ computerworlds-survey-of-hot-it-skills-for-2007/
3. Rosen, A. (2004). *Effective IT Project Management.* New York, NY: AMACOM.
4. Zarrella, E. (2006). Global IT Management Survey. Available online at http://www.technologyexecutivesclub.com/PDFs/ArticlePDFS/pmsurvey.pdf
5. Taylor, J. (2004). *Managing Information Technology Projects.* New York, NY: AMACOM.
6. Keil, M. (1995). "Pulling the Plug: Software Project Management and the Problem of Project Escalation." *MIS Quarterly, 19*(4), 421-447.

CHAPTER 11

Selecting and Implementing Hospitality Information Systems

"Without a blueprint or plan for the future, picking technology is almost a shot in the dark."

Peter O'Dell, *The Computer Networking Book*

CHAPTER OUTLINE

Steps in System Selection

Herodotus, the father of recorded history, wrote the first good-news/bad-news story. It involved King Xerxes, who had embarked on a Phoenician ship at Eion for passage across the Aegean sea to Persia. The ship encountered a severe storm halfway through their journey. King Xerxes, in fear of his life, asked the captain if anything could be done to lessen the danger. The captain suggested reducing the ship's weight. King Xerxes turned to his aides for help. All thirty of the men accompanying the king on the journey jumped overboard at his request. King Xerxes gave the captain his gold crown for safely guiding the ship to its destination but, because his most trusted aides died, he also had him beheaded.

Likewise, computers and information systems offer some good news and some bad news. According to George Hall, "The good news is that the potential for the strategic use of information systems has been barely tapped. The bad news is that many attempts to do so have failed" (1).

Why? Because many operations have purchased hardware and software without an information plan. This can be compared to building houses without blueprints or the services of a contractor.

An **Information Plan** includes the following steps: 1) reviewing organizational needs, 2) evaluating current systems, 3) defining budget requirements, 4) developing a request for proposal (RFP), and 5) system evaluation and selection. Such a plan provides management with a conceptual framework for making methodical and pragmatic technology selections.

> *Asking questions is how we create and evaluate ideas that can be transformed into products and applications. For example, Akio Morita of Sony Corporation wanted a pocketable radio. This well-chosen word created an inspired image that led to the development of the Sony Walkman. The word 'pocketable' not only gave designers a clear picture of Morita's vision but it captured the public's imagination.* (2)

Reviewing Organizational Needs

The first step in creating an information plan requires an understanding of the organization's mission, goals, and structure.

Understanding the essence of a business stimulates possibility thinking and a sense of priority when investigating potential computer applications. Key questions that relate business strategy to technology selection include:

What is the Mission or Purpose of an Organization?

1. *What is the mission or purpose of an organization?* A quick service operation's primary mission is to provide inexpensive, tasty food quickly. This defines the product and service strategy. Every procedure, system, and apparatus should support the mission statement.

What are the Organizational Goals or Objectives?

2. *What are the organizational goals or objectives?* To survive, an organization must meet sales goals, control expenses, and have satisfied customers. It must have the capability to quickly isolate factors negatively affecting profitability and to make the necessary adjust ments and adaptations to reach desired outcomes.

What is the Organizational Structure?

3. *What is the organizational structure?* Employees at every level of the organization should have the information and tools to do their jobs efficiently and effectively. Current systems should be capable of handling the organization's growth rate. Selecting a system that only handles current needs is eventually disruptive and expensive in a growing organization. It is important to remember that information rises exponentially with a small increase in business.

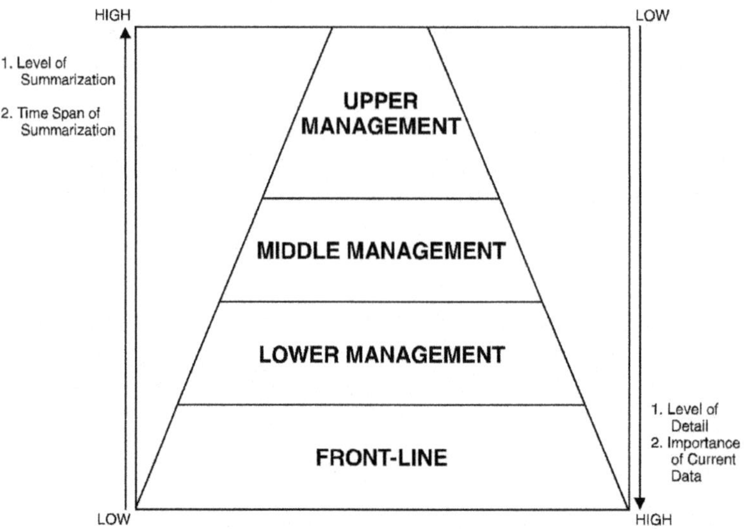

FIGURE 11-1. INFORMATIONAL PYRAMID.

Hospitality organizations typically have four levels of activity: Front-line level, lower management, middle management, and upper management (refer to Figure 11-1). Information needs vary from level to level.

Front-line Employees

a. *Front-line employees* require tools (e.g., guest history) for handling repetitive transactions expeditiously and servicing customer needs. At the front-line level, data is processed and used by the other three levels for decision-making.

Lower Management

b. *Lower Management* requires detailed daily reports to make operational decisions (e.g., labor scheduling, food and beverage purchasing).

Middle Management

c. *Middle Management* requires summarized reports of day-to-day operations for management control (e.g., labor cost, sales). This information is used to make tactical decisions (e.g., closing out a discount room rate) that support strategic objectives.

Upper Management

d. *Upper Management* requires summarized information for policy making and strategic planning. Upper management is interested primarily in reports that depict "what if" scenarios and isolate long-term trends affecting profitability and market position.

What is the Role of Technology in Service Improvement?

4. *What is the role of technology in service improvement?* According to Leonard Berry, the noted author of *On Great Service*: "In developing a technology strategy to support service strategy, managers should be clear on the specific roles of a given technology.

Integrating appropriate technologies into a cohesive strategy partially depends upon the awareness of technology service-improvement roles."(3) He contends the most important roles are:

Multiplying Knowledge

a. *Multiplying knowledge.* Service providers unaided by information technology are limited in the service they can provide by their personal knowledge. Information technology provides a vast amount of intelligence to the front-line employees, enabling them to answer questions, approve exceptions, solve problems, and evaluate guest needs. Guest history is a good example of an application with embedded intelligence. Technology also allows customers to easily access a wide range of property-specific information via desktops and mobile devices (e.g., concierge iPad mounted in the lobby).

Streamlining and Personalizing Service

b. *Streamlining and personalizing service.* Many experts predict that U.S. workers will spend more time on the job and become more sensitive to bureaucratic delays and snafus that steal away their limited vacation time or make them less productive while traveling on business. Consequently, hotels in the twenty-first century will increasingly rely on information technology for providing high-quality personalized services and time-saving devices to satisfy time-constrained guests. It is becoming a competitive necessity, for example, to provide the necessary infrastructure and bandwidth that enable hotel guests to access what they want when they want it using mobile devices. At the SLS Hotel South Beach in Miami, guests find an iPad in every room next to their bed. They can access a variety of services, such as purchasing a bottle of wine, making reservations at The Bazaar restaurant, requesting their car from the valet, and printing their boarding pass at the front desk.

Increasing Reliability

c. *Increasing reliability.* Unreliable service is often caused by an employee who does not have the knowledge or skill to carry out a particular task. Delivering dependable, accurate service requires well-selected and carefully trained employees equipped with the right tools to do their jobs. Information technology applications, such as internal/external databases, expert systems, and Web-based self-training and self-service systems, can strengthen the performance of service providers. Electronic selection systems can be used to ascertain a prospective employee's abilities and skills to interface with the public. For example, one system has the individual being tested view realistic vignettes of various job-related situations and respond to multiple-choice questions about how he or she would handle particular situations. Studies suggest that electronic selection systems can be highly effective in selecting high-aptitude employees.

Facilitating Communications

d. *Facilitating communications.* Communication between hospitality organizations and customers is vital to quality service. The potential for hospitality companies to improve communications with customers through technology is remarkable. Communications technologies can be used to expand access to needed information, provide more relevant information, reduce the time and effort necessary to obtain the information, and deliver information in a more pleasing form. Two Mixx restaurants located in Kansas City, Missouri feature healthy fast food. Customers are queried via Facebook and Twitter (e.g., t@MissMixxKC Cream of Mushroom is my vote!") about which soup to add the daily lineup. The Soup of the Day is then posted online (e.g., "MissMixxKC Homemade soups 2day are Tom Veggie & Pumpkin Bisque at Plaza location. Beer Chz and Italian Sausage and Veggie dwntwn. 11:51 AM August 24th via TweetDeck") as well as in the stores under the heading of "Mixx Fans Heard." The owner, Marie Scalgia, cites a 50 percent increase in soup orders (4).

There are a growing number of customers expecting organizations to keep historical records of their personal transactions with Internet access. This requires the integration of functional databases across a hospitality organization. The lack of an accessible complete customer history may create an information gap or a difference between what information customers expect and what information the hospitality organization can deliver. For example, customers might expect a hotel Web site to have a detailed record of their past reservations so they can book future reservations more quickly. If, for instance, loyalty rewards points are not available online, then the level of customer service may not meet a customer's expectations.

Evaluating the Current System

The second step is a summary of how information is processed, organized, and distributed throughout the organization. The existing systems may be computer-based, manual, or a combination of both. Before selecting or enhancing a system, a good grasp of work and information flows is necessary. This can be depicted in a flowchart.

The second purpose of a systems evaluation is to identify problematic areas, such as inaccurate data (e.g., poor forecasting); duplicated work efforts (e.g., reservation system not connected to a multichannel distribution system); inadequate equipment (e.g., clerks must wait in line to check-in/out guests since there is only one front desk computer); inefficiencies in information flow (e.g., late charges); poor customer interaction (e.g., front desk clerk spends too much time looking at computer monitor); outdated equipment (e.g., in-room TV system does not allow guests to stream movies from their Netflix accounts); procedural bottlenecks (e.g., check-out process is too long); discontented workers (e.g., computer program not "user friendly").

The third purpose of a systems evaluation is to determine whether current systems address an organization's most vital areas. For example, should an international hotel use key resources updating reservation distribution channels manually or invest in new technology where room pricing decisions are largely automated and free up these resources to focus on strategic performance issues? The hospitality industry is constantly changing and existing systems may not be able to accommodate new and unique situations (5).

Finally, after a thorough systems evaluation, information system objectives are formulated, which may include adding new computer applications, upgrading or refining current systems, integrating systems, and/or re-engineering information and work flows.

U.S. businesses increased productivity by about 2 percent each year from 1995 to 2000, and one-third of that increase was attributable to technology, according to consulting firm McKinsey & Co. Retailers Wervices companies, for instance, were able to increase productivity through the use of technology more than were hotels and hospitals. McKinsey analysts say businesses that re-engineered their operations to make use of technology benefited the most (www.siliconvalley.com/mld/ siliconvalley/4559923.htm).

Defining Budget Requirements

Many organizations want to spend the smallest possible amount and reap the most benefits. This short-sighted philosophy often paralyzes organizations. One world-class hotel's guest history resides in the head of an elderly employee which, one day, will die with her. Will a computerized reservation system with guest history be purchased before the property reaches the meltdown stage?

The problem with investment evaluation is that a capital resource always has alternative uses. A quantitative evaluation of the economic gains and/or losses of different alternatives help permit the decision maker to select the use which most closely conforms with organizational objectives.

Determining whether an information system purchase is worthwhile requires the identification of investment costs and annual savings. Typically, investment costs include hardware, software, training, and installation. Annual savings typically include reduced operating expenses, increased revenues, and improved cash flow less annual operating expenses (supplies, system maintenance, customer support, personnel, administrative, etc.). While there are various investment evaluation techniques, a popular and easy to understand method is payback. Payback determines the length of time required for a new system to generate enough savings to recoup the investment outlay. Generally, if the payback is five years or less, the organization should proceed with the investment. If it is estimated that a hotel would save $13,689.03 per year by implementing a Web-based application that costs $45,000, for example, the payback period would be calculated by dividing the investment by the annual savings:

$$\text{Payback} = \frac{\text{Investment}}{\text{Annual Savings}}$$

$$= \frac{\$45,000.00}{\$13,689.03}$$

$$= 3.29 \text{ years}$$

If an operation lacks the financial resources to purchase a system, leasing one may be a consideration. Two types of lease plans offered by hospitality vendors are:

Five-Year Lease Options		
	Open Lease	Financial Lease
Amount leased:	$65,669	$65,669
Financing rate:	12.10%	13.75%
Monthly rate:	$ 1,465	$ 1,517
Annual cost:	$17,580	$18,204
Total cost:	$87,900	$91,020

An Open Lease

An OPEN LEASE provides the lessee with the option to purchase the equipment at fair market value at the end of the term. Although typically it is relatively expensive, it may provide advantages such as: 1) protection against equipment obsolescence, 2) reduced business risk and income taxes, and 3) increased borrowing capacity. With a **FINANCIAL LEASE**, the financing rate is higher because the lessee owns the equipment and retains depreciation. At the end of a five-year period, the equipment is completely depreciated and the liability is paid off.

Software can also be leased (or subscribed to) through an application service provider (ASP). An ASP is a service firm or outsource information technology (IT) company that manages, deploys, and remotely hosts software or cloud-based applications through centralized servers. Only "thin-client" or "low-cost" workstations and a robust and reliable Internet connection with a backup option (e.g., cable modem) are required at the property level. Consequently, onsite hardware, support, and maintenance costs are significantly reduced. The lease or subscription pricing plan is usually per transaction or flat monthly fee. "Using an ASP is not, however, simply a matter of outsourcing your IT as a whole. You have to determine which applications you may want to lease through an ASP. These might be old legacy systems which you do not want to maintain anymore, or they may be new applications which you do not have the resources to maintain."

(*www.itforhousing.co.uk/Technical%20Tim/TTArticle1/ TechnicalTim_article1.htm*).

Developing a Request for Proposal

The remainder of this chapter discusses the selection and implementation of a **Property Management System** (PMS). A PMS normally performs both back and front office functions. It also supports a variety of other functions, such as housekeeping, energy management, and call accounting (6).

To understand which PMS will be best suited for a particular property, it is essential to specify system requirements and parameters. To make these specifications, a PMS committee comprised of representatives from the various departments targeted to be computerized should be formed. The findings should be incorporated into a report called a property profile to be distributed to vendors. This will enable the property to clearly define what it desires in a PMS as well as to communicate its needs to vendors.

A problem that often arises is unrealistic expectations concerning the capabilities of a PMS. Many people feel that a computer can do everything. To ensure a pragmatic approach in the development of system requirements, the PMS committee needs to become familiar with products that are currently available on the market by obtaining relevant product literature and information. The easiest way to secure sales literature and product information is from vendor Web sites, which may also provide sample screens, demonstration videos, tutorials, live one-on-one demonstrations, and downloadable evaluation copies. Other sources of information include industry trade shows, paper and online trade journals (e.g., hospitalityupgrade.com), and trade associations such as the American Hotel and Lodging Association (AHLA) and the Hospitality Financial and Technology Professionals (HFTP).

Property Profile Report

A **Property Profile Report** covers a number of details relating to the computing needs of the property. Its development begins with the specification of required reports that are of high value and improve operational performance and decision-making capability. Committee members then vote on the retention and modification of old reports and the creation of new ones. Sample reports showing the required information and desired format should be included in the property profile.

Management should list specific tasks that it would like the PMS to perform. A detailed checklist of desired functions should be devised for each affected work area. There should be a description of staffing levels and business volumes for each area under consideration. This aids in the assessment of hardware and software requirements and pinpoints opportunities for improvement in labor productivity and guest service.

The report should familiarize the vendor with the products and services offered. This educates the vendor as to the desired service levels and the types of service that appeal to the property's clientele.

The report should describe the layout of the facility, showing where hardware will be located to assist the vendor in determining the hardware configuration.

Finally, the report should briefly review the level of job knowledge, experience with computers, typing skills, and attitudes toward automation of all employees to help the vendors assess the training needs (see Figure 11-2).

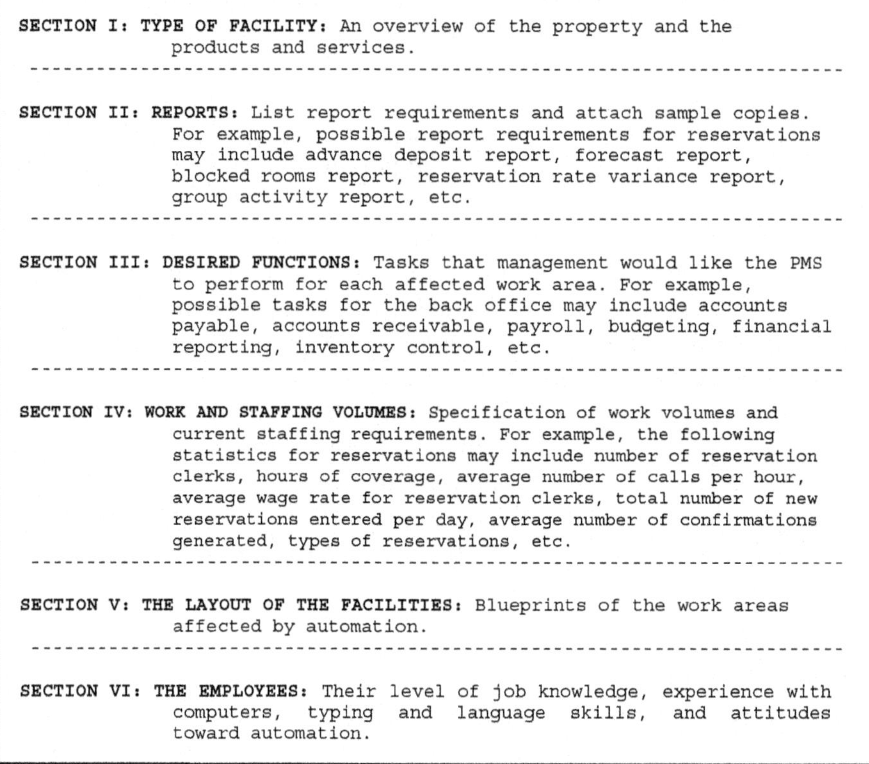

SECTION I: TYPE OF FACILITY: An overview of the property and the products and services.

SECTION II: REPORTS: List report requirements and attach sample copies. For example, possible report requirements for reservations may include advance deposit report, forecast report, blocked rooms report, reservation rate variance report, group activity report, etc.

SECTION III: DESIRED FUNCTIONS: Tasks that management would like the PMS to perform for each affected work area. For example, possible tasks for the back office may include accounts payable, accounts receivable, payroll, budgeting, financial reporting, inventory control, etc.

SECTION IV: WORK AND STAFFING VOLUMES: Specification of work volumes and current staffing requirements. For example, the following statistics for reservations may include number of reservation clerks, hours of coverage, average number of calls per hour, average wage rate for reservation clerks, total number of new reservations entered per day, average number of confirmations generated, types of reservations, etc.

SECTION V: THE LAYOUT OF THE FACILITIES: Blueprints of the work areas affected by automation.

SECTION VI: THE EMPLOYEES: Their level of job knowledge, experience with computers, typing and language skills, and attitudes toward automation.

FIGURE 11-2. PROPERTY PROFILE DESCRIPTION.

Constructing the RFP. Once management has completed the fact-finding mission, the results should be incorporated into a report, referred to as a **REQUEST FOR PROPOSAL** (RFP). This report should contain the following sections:

- *Property Profile.* A description of the property and its computing needs.
- *Solicitation Instructions and Conditions.* A guideline for submission of vendor proposals and a description of how vendor responses will be evaluated. Figure 11-3 provides three approaches to appraising vendor answers.
- *System Specifications.* A detailed description of desired features and requirements for each of the following areas: software and hardware performance, customer support, vendor reputation, and training and installation.

These requirements should be presented in questionnaire format as illustrated in Figure 11-5.

The primary benefit of the RFP is that a vendor must respond to a standardized format. This eases the evaluation process when comparing the suitability of different property management systems.

It is mandatory that the RFP include guidelines for submission. To protect the property's interest, all bids must be in writing. For promises relating to the price and performance of a PMS to be legally binding, they must be included in a written contract. Therefore, it would be prudent to include the following conditions in the RFP:

- Vendor's responses to RFP questions shall be included in and incorporated into any sales contract which may result.
- Vendor statements and claims within or appended to the RFP regarding product performance and capabilities shall be considered part of the proposal and therefore part of any sales contract which may result.
- The proposed prices, terms, and conditions shall remain valid for a certain number of days following submission.

The RFP should specify how the proposal will be evaluated. Three rating approaches include simple ranking, rating scale, and weighted average.

SIMPLE RANKING

1. *Simple Ranking.* This method assigns a score of 1 for "yes" or 0 for "no" for each system requirement. The proposal with the highest collective score is considered the best.

RATING SCALE

2. *Rating Scale.* This method allows more flexibility in response where a range of numerical values are used to indicate the degree of acceptability. Figure 11-3 provides three rating scale examples.

COLLINS RATING SCALE

4 = Satisfies system requirement
3 = Satisfies system requirement with minor modifications.
2 = Satisfies system requirement with major modifications.
1 = Does not satisfy system requirement.

LONAM RATING SCALE

4 (YES) = Meets the system requirement.
3 (YES-BUT) = Meets the system requirement partially or in a manner different than stated.
2 (NO-BUT) = Does not meet the system requirement, but development is planned or can be custom programmed.
1 (NO) = Does not meet the system requirement.

BUCHHOLZ RATING SCALE

1 = More than meets the requirement - above average.
2 = Meets the requirements - average.
3 = Does not meet the requirements - below average.

FIGURE 11-3. RATING SCALE EXAMPLES.

STEP 1: Identify system requirements.

1) Software Performance
2) Hardware Performance
3) Customer Support
4) Training and Installation

STEP 2: Prioritize system requirements through assignment of weights.

System Requirements	Assigned Weight
Software Performance	.30 (Most Important Requirement)
Training and Installation	.25
Customer Support	.25
Hardware Performance	.20 (Least Important Requirement)
	1.00

STEP 3: Define rating scale.

4 = Satisfies system requirement
3 = Satisfies system requirement with minor modifications
2 = Satisfies system requirement with major modifications
1 = Does not satisfy system requirement

STEP 4: Compute the average score for each system requirement. Each system requirement can be graded on various criteria as illustrated in the table below.

	Average Score		
System Requirements	Vendor 1	Vendor 2	Vendor 3
Software Performance	3.5	3.0	3.8
Training and Installation	3.8	4.0	3.0
Customer Support	3.0	3.2	3.0
Hardware Performance	3.5	4.0	4.0

STEP 5: Calculate the final score by multiplying the average score by the assigned weight and adding up the weighted averages.

	Final Score		
System Requirements	Vendor 1	Vendor 2	Vendor 3
Software Performance	3.5 X .30 = 1.05	3.0 X .30 = .90	3.8 X .30 = 1.14
Training & Install.	3.8 X .25 = .95	4.0 X .25 = 1.00	3.0 X .25 = .75
Customer Support	3.0 X .25 = .75	3.2 X .25 = .80	3.0 X .25 = .75
Hardware Performance	3.5 X .20 = .70	4.0 X .20 = .80	4.0 X .20 = .80
FINAL SCORE	3.45	3.50 (BEST CHOICE)	3.44

FIGURE 11-4. WEIGHTED AVERAGE APPROACH TO SCORING VENDOR EVALUATIONS.

Weighted Average

3. *Weighted Average.* This method assigns an additional value to the rating scale to account for the relative importance of certain requirements. The process of assigning weights can be a tedious and subjective process. Figure 11-4 describes the mechanics entailed in this scoring approach. Perhaps an easier way of assessing the importance of a function is to categorize it as essential or nonessential. An essential requirement could be assigned a weight of 1 and a nonessential requirement a weight of .50. For example, an essential function receiving a score of 4 would have a weighted average of 4 (4 X 1.0), as compared to a weighted average of 2 (4 X .50) for a nonessential function. Another approach is to keep separate score sheets for essential and nonessential requirements.

The evaluation process requires the translation of system requirements into precisely worded questions accurately describing the desired features. An ambiguous and superficial questionnaire results in vague vendor responses. For example, the question "How does your system handle travel agent commissions?" can lead to a multitude of answers, whereas a series of focused and in-depth questions, as shown in Figure 11-5, identify specific performance capabilities. A well-designed questionnaire elicits exact and relevant answers, facilitating a judicious assessment of vendor proposals.

Many organizations use automated RFP selection tools to expedite the evaluation process. This type of software not only provides pre-loaded questions, which can be prioritized and modified, it also automatically evaluates responses from vendors in detailed reports and graphs.

In the Figure 11-5 questionnaire example, the vendor is responsible for placing a checkmark next to the choice which most closely indicates the degree to which their product satisfies that particular requirement.

In evaluating property management systems, many operators get carried away with options, forget about essential system requirements, and lose sight of budgetary constraints. The purpose of putting together an RFP is to ensure that the selection criteria are firmly intact during the tough decision-making process.

Author and philosopher Henry Thoreau wrote about a traveler on horseback at the edge of a bog. He asked a local boy whom he encountered whether the bog had a firm bottom. The youth replied confidently that it did. The traveler proceeded across the bog and began to sink.

"I thought you said that this bog had a firm bottom," the traveler shouted to the boy.

"So it has," replied the youth, "but you are not yet halfway there."

Asking the right questions is critical to sound decision-making. One person should be chosen to deal with vendors. This prevents vendor confusion when seeking clarification on RFP details but, more importantly, eases the negotiation process. Many hospitality operations have been duped because the expertise of the designated representative was deficient. This person must be prepared to handle a variety of questions in a competent manner. Knowledge of the topic can be strengthened through formal classroom

I. TRAVEL AGENT COMMISSIONS	4 YES	3 YES WITH MINOR MOD.	2 YES WITH MAJOR MOD.	1 NO
A. Online access to all travel information.	...	....	....	...
B. Allows the user to cross-reference reservation information with the travel agent file.	...	....	....	...
C. Computes travel agent's commission and has the following commission structures:				
1. fixed percentage of room revenue by guest type.	...	....	....	...
2. fixed amount per guest.	...	....	....	...
3. fixed amount per reservation.	...	....	....	...
4. fixed amount per room night.	...	....	....	...
5. percentage of total revenue.	...	....	....	...
6. percentage of total room revenue.	...	....	....	...
D. Automatically prints commission checks with check reconciliation capability.	...	....	....	...
E. Handles prepaid commissions.	...	....	....	...
F. Has the ability to keep track of commissions due to travel agents and sales agents.	...	....	....	...
G. Provides monthly and yearly statistics which show for each travel agent:				
1. number of no shows and cancellations.	...	....	....	...
	...	....	....	...
2. number of room nights.	...	....	....	...
3. number of reservations.	...	....	....	...
4. total sales revenue.	...	....	....	...
5. total room revenue.	...	....	....	...
6. total commission paid.	...	....	....	...
7. total commissions due.	...	....	....	...

FIGURE 11-5. QUESTIONNAIRE EXAMPLE: SOFTWARE SPECIFICATIONS FOR TRAVEL AGENT COMMISSIONS.

instruction, attendance at seminars and trade shows, or home instruction courses provided by the Educational Institute of the AHLA.

Intelligent decision-making capability is always based upon knowledge, and a lack of it will leave the property in a weaker negotiating posture and vulnerable to the whims of a salesperson.

Software Evaluation

It has been incorrectly assumed that Property Management Systems are all alike. There are numerous products on the market varying significantly in capability and performance. The PMS committee should identify four or five packages that satisfy basic requirements. This may be accomplished by having vendors complete a **pre-screening survey**, a short questionnaire that identifies the availability of key system features.

When evaluating software packages, four basic questions must be answered:

- Does it satisfy system requirements?
- Does it have the ability to interface with existing systems (such as point-of-sale, room key, back office accounting, and CRS/GDS) as well as future systems planned (e.g., mobile apps) for installation?
- Is it easy to operate?
- Does it have software bugs or logic flaws?

Properties have been stuck on occasion with unsatisfactory property management systems. A resort hotel located in New England, for example, purchased a PMS that did not handle meal and package plans which they needed to have. Management was extremely dissatisfied and removed the system. Who was at fault? In this case, the property had failed to stipulate this requirement to the vendor. Management must adhere to the maxim, "Do not expect, but inspect."

A typical property (e.g., resort, business) serves as the standard in the development of most software programs. Consequently, the likelihood of identifying an ideal PMS is slim, although more and more packages are being designed to allow users to quickly modify databases, menus, reports, and routines to meet their specific needs. Most software packages, however, assume a "one-size-fits-all" approach where unique requirements can be negotiated with the vendor. Modifications to the program normally increase the product cost and, in some instances, delay its implementation. To protect the property's interest, include any revisions to the software and the required completion dates in the sales agreement.

A product feature of a PMS that has been frequently misrepresented is its capability to interface with other programs and hardware devices. An intelligent, integrated software package will make provisions for numerous interfaces. The primary benefit of system interfaces is the automation of workflows, which improves labor productivity, enhances guest service, and maximizes revenues by making the sale of hospitality products easier and more efficient. A point-of-sale interface, for example, allows restaurant charges to be posted directly to the guest folio without human intervention. Other popular interfaces include credit card, in-room movie system, guest information services, distribution channels (e.g., Travelocity), electronic locking systems, energy management systems, call accounting, sales and marketing, and minibar systems.

Disillusioned operators stuck with a software product that will not communicate with other systems have discovered the importance of investigating interface options, as the number of cost effective applications could be severely restricted, forcing the operator to begrudgingly live with the system, discard the system, or invest in the costly development of interfacing capabilities. "Hold vendors accountable for promised interface work. Mohonk Mountain House, a 256-room Victorian Mansion in New Paltz, N.Y, required that one of its tech vendors pay its transaction fees for a year, until a promised payment gateway was delivered" (http://hospitalitytechnology.edgl.com).

A "user-friendly" software package allows the user to easily move through the program without encountering frustrating obstacles. To assess the human/computer interface, allow employees to view and to interact with systems under consideration and then ask for their perceptions of program effectiveness (refer to Figure 11-6 for sample employee survey).

Programs that require users to memorize abstract abbreviations, codes, and information to carry out standard routines should be avoided. Poorly designed software forces users to frequently reference documentation to operate it, sacrificing valuable guest contact time as well as hindering worker productivity. A well-conceived software program provides self-explanatory choices, painlessly guiding the user through the successful completion of tasks.

The format of the screen display can aid the execution of tasks. Information should be presented in an organized fashion so that the user can quickly spot the appropriate command or choice. It should not overwhelm the user with too much information. A nicely formatted screen display resembles a restaurant menu and cleverly utilizes such things as color, icons, underlining, and highlighting to enhance the user's comprehension rate. The ideal user interface is both intuitive and logical enabling employees to navigate through various processes (e.g., check-in) with ease.

The user's response, whatever it may be, should not cause the program to abort. This intimidates the learning process if the user cannot correct mistakes without starting over. It should include an on-screen help to help users complete tasks when they get stuck. This improves labor productivity and reduces training time.

To ensure that a program runs properly, it should be thoroughly tested to uncover logic flaws. The risk of discovering bugs or logic flaws becomes less as the product ages and is subjected to rigorous industrial use. Customer-oriented vendors have established user advisory groups who help in product refinement.

TECHNOLOGY TIDBITS

Timing is everything. One restaurant chain delayed the signing of a purchase agreement due to an internal paperwork bottleneck, during which time the vendor declared bankruptcy. The company had failed to assess the vendor's financial strength.

System Evaluation

Rate the following statements from 1 to 5 where
1 = not satisfactory
2 = minimally satisfactory
3 = satisfactory
4 = good
5 = excellent

	(circle your choice)				
1) Do you understand the task descriptions?	1	2	3	4	5
2) Are tasks/functions logically grouped?	1	2	3	4	5
3) Are the screen layouts easy to understand?	1	2	3	4	5
4) Do you like the color selection?	1	2	3	4	5
5) How would you rate the demonstration?	1	2	3	4	5
6) Does the system provide you with the necessary functions/tasks to do your job?	1	2	3	4	5
7) Do you feel that this system would improve productivity?	1	2	3	4	5
8) Do you feel that this system would enhance guest satisfaction?	1	2	3	4	5
9) Overall, how would you rate this system?	1	2	3	4	5

Comments: ____________________

____

____

____

____

10) Have you ever worked with this system? Describe your experience.

____

____

____

FIGURE 11-6. EMPLOYEE SURVEY.

Evaluation of Customer Support and Vendor Reputation

Hospitality vendors have been plagued with financial problems, which have led to tech-firm mergers and a high attrition rate. Purchasing a PMS from a firm that later declares bankruptcy could leave a property without any software support and, consequently, a worthless investment. It is important to select a PMS from a vendor with enough financial strength to last five more years or with enough value (large client base) to exist within another entity. Characteristic warnings of a financially troubled vendor are poor customer support, lack of parts, premature invoices for maintenance contracts, high employee turnover, declining stock price, management restructuring, company for sale, etc. To evaluate a vendor's financial health and ability to provide customer support, the following questions must be included in the RFP:

- How long have you been in business? How does this compare to your competitors? Who do you feel are your four best competitors?
- How many properties have you installed?
- What is your financial status? May I see your financial reports?
- What has been your average growth in sales? What are your sales projections for the next five years?
- Describe management. Who are your key personnel? What has been their length of employment?
- Who are your references?

The sales representative plays a critical role in the selection process. A competent sales representative should thoroughly understand hospitality operations and automation. He or she must have the ability to translate the computing needs of an operation into system specifications. Many products have been misrepresented because the sales representative was misinformed and unqualified. A prudent step would be to scrutinize the sales representative's credentials.

Be wary of vendors who are more interested in closing a sale than satisfying a customer. To validate performance capabilities, check references carefully, do an on-site inspection of a property already using the system being considered, ask other vendors, and/or visit the vendor's headquarters.

In a hospitality environment, system downtime can be costly and aggravating and will happen periodically, even with the most reliable systems. Therefore, it is mandatory that a hospitality operation purchase a maintenance agreement covering both hardware and software. This can be provided through the vendor or a third-party service organization, which usually just performs on-site hardware support. References should be checked to evaluate the friendliness of the customer support staff and to determine whether downtime has been a problem.

In most cases, PMS vendors are unable to deliver local service and primarily rely on a telephone hotline service to solve software problems. Many vendors can diagnose and correct problems over an Internet connection. This allows a technician to gain access to the program from a remote location, enabling a more rapid diagnosis and system recovery.

When a PMS is rendered inoperable, the vendor should provide an alternative way of functioning until the system can be restored. The staff should be fully trained in emergency backup procedures or the property could suffer a disastrous collapse. Unprepared properties may find themselves with no means of generating a guest folio or tracking financial transactions.

Software and hardware may be provided by different vendors, or one vendor may provide both. There must be a decision made to go with a multi-vendor (best-of -breed solution) or single-vendor (integrated solution). Both options have advantages and disadvantages.

Vendors who provide both hardware and software market their product as a "**Turnkey System**." The primary advantage of a turnkey system is having only one vendor to contact to resolve all problems. In a multi-vendor environment, resolving problems spawns conflict and finger-pointing. Avoiding this dilemma requires the development of clear, acceptable guidelines for communication between vendors (5).

It would be much easier to purchase the entire PMS from one vendor. However, a PMS vendor may not supply a particular component for an application; another may provide a more appropriate software application; or equipment from one vendor may cost less than the same item offered by another vendor. The bottom line is that the entire system should smoothly function when all the parts are assembled.

The annual cost of customer support ranges from 5 to 15 percent of the total PMS purchase price (software, hardware, and training). For point-of-sale (POS) systems, the annual cost may vary from 3 to 15 percent of the hardware price. Since POS systems may use specialized hardware, several customer support options may be provided by the POS vendor:

Spare Parts

1. **Spare parts** which replace failed devices that are repaired and returned within a certain time period. This is the most expensive option, but minimizes downtime. This is also an appealing option for restaurants where restaurant on-site service cannot be obtained within 24 hours.

On-Site Service

2. **On-site service** within X hours, depending on the distance between the restaurant and service center. This middle-priced option is better suited for restaurants which can obtain same-day service.

Repair of Failed Devices

3. **Repair of failed devices** within X hours of receipt. This is the most inexpensive option, but the restaurant may have to wait two to four days for repaired devices.

A POS vendor may also offer a maintenance contract with a low flat fee where the vendor and the restaurant split the cost of service calls and repairs. The annual cost may only be 3 to 5 percent of the hardware price when equipment failures are low. The maintenance contract should provide a ceiling on service fees to protect against costly system failures. The maximum annual cost should not exceed 15 percent of the hardware price.

The following questions should be included in the RFP to assist in the evaluation of customer support:

- Can routine maintenance be easily done by employees or must the computer vendor perform this task?
- How often is there computer downtime?
- What is the average time that the computer is down?
- Does the vendor respond promptly when there is a problem?
- Does the equipment need a regulated environment?
- Are there built-in precautions to safeguard the system from power fluctuations? Is the system equipped with a battery pack to compensate for interruptions (e.g., blackouts and brownouts) in the power supply?
- Does a local computer organization service the equipment?
- Do you provide a hardware maintenance contract? How much does it cost and what does it cover?
- Do you provide telephone and online customer support, including the evening shift (4 p.m. to midnight) and the night audit (midnight to 8 a.m.)?
- Do you provide a software maintenance contract? How much does it cost and what does it cover?
- Is system documentation provided? Is it easily understood?
- What measures have been taken to safeguard the database? Is the POS/PMS database stored on a dedicated server? Do you have a standard operating procedure that outlines the dumping of critical information to hard copy or printed paper? Are there provisions for easily backing up information to another storage medium (e.g., Flash drive, magnetic tape, remote data center) on a daily basis? Does the program provide security access codes and other security measures to prevent unauthorized use? Does the program alert management to possible tampering and security violations? Is it PCI compliant? Are proper measures (e.g., commercial router with firewall protection) taken to prevent attacks via an Internet connection? Will each workstation have reliable, up-to-date antivirus and Internet security software installed? Do you provide a data breach insurance policy?
- Can the software be upgraded? What will be the cost for software updates? Are there any plans for software enhancements? Do you have a user advisory group to assist in the formulation and refinement of products and services?

- Will you provide a warranty guaranteeing software support for 10 years? In the event of bankruptcy, will the source code and documentation be put into an escrow account?
- What are the guarantees? Vendors provide widely varying guarantees. Some provide parts and labor for one year, while others include free phone support for that first year, as well.

Evaluation of Training and Installation

A successful installation is the by-product of a structured and well organized training program. This is clearly illustrated by the recent experience of a major hotel chain, which would have selected a different PMS vendor if training requirements had been included as part of the RFP selection criteria. A detailed training plan should be developed by the PMS vendor answering the following questions:

When Should the Training Take Place?

1. **When should the training take place?** Training begins before the installation of the computer system and continues through the various stages of implementation. By extending training sessions over a greater time period, the learning process is eased, alleviating employee anxiety; introducing a new system during a tense seasonal rush can block normal learning behaviors.

What Employees will be Trained?

2. **What employees will be trained?** To develop training schedules, a list of employees must be obtained by the vendor. An employee profile should be developed specifying the following information: job title, job knowledge, length of employment, typing ability, computer literacy, and work schedule. This information determines the content and format of the training sessions. The intensity of these sessions depends on the quality of the existing work force.

It is not the responsibility of the vendor, however, to teach typing or basic job knowledge such as reservations, registration, and guest accounting terminology. The vendor's role is to identify employee deficiencies that would impede the normal learning of the computer system. The responsibility of the property is to correct cited deficiencies by engaging in pre-installation training programs that provide the skills needed to successfully operate the computer. For example, an employee evaluation of a large Caribbean property pinpointed weak typing skills. Consequently, typing classes were begun to strengthen this skill, which ultimately led to a successful installation.

Never underestimate the degree of anxiety that can be instigated by computerization or learning a new system. Employees may perceive it as a threat to job security. This is especially true of older, longer-serving employees who have mastered the existing system. Others may resist learning a new system for fear of losing control and influence. Creating positive feelings requires a communication plan which emphasizes the benefits of the new system, periodically provides updates on its progress, and informs staff of potential problems during implementation. However, the most important thing to remember is that patient and sensitive training can overcome feelings of inadequacy, enabling all employees to gain a good command of the new system.

Management must also be trained to use the new system. Without management participation, the system will probably be poorly utilized. Educating managers does present some interesting challenges. Some managers may feel uncomfortable being in the same training classroom with subordinates. It may provoke feelings of insecurity and embarrassment as their employees watch them struggle to learn the program. Overcoming feelings of inadequacy may be accomplished through individualized instruction or "manager only" training sessions.

A PMS Coordinator or representative should be trained as a systems troubleshooter. The PMS coordinator will receive specialized training on every aspect of hardware and software operations. This will enable the PMS coordinator to handle minor problems and to serve as a liaison between the property and the vendor in solving major problems. The best candidate for this position would be one already familiar with hospitality information systems who has a basic understanding of the areas affected by automation or the new system.

What Should be Covered in the Training Program?

3. **What should be covered in the training program?** The training program should take an employee through four basic learning phases: learning the user interface (e.g., program navigation and input), learning the format and organization of the program, learning to carry out job responsibilities utilizing the computer, and utilizing the computer to perform job responsibilities in the actual work environment.

Training should also cover standard operating procedures for tasks for which the handling of information will change. Adding a PMS credit card interface, for example, will eliminate the need for stand-alone terminals and change how payment information is inputted, processed, stored, and reconciled.

Effective standard operating procedures also optimize guest contact time. Procedures that require extensive use of the computer when carrying out guest-related routines force the user to eye the screen rather than the guest and to increase the time requirements to complete the task. A customer-friendly system should not require a guest to watch a clerk laboriously input information into the computer. This time should be profitably spent tending to the needs of guests. Servicing the guests takes top priority, requiring that clerks be trained to efficiently use their time during slow periods to do clerical work. The policies, procedures, and methods should all say to the guest, "This apparatus is here to meet your needs" (7).

An easy-to-use PMS is easy to learn if there is an appropriate training program designed especially for the naive user. An effective training program repeats information and uses more than one channel of communication. Each training session should include three basic steps:

Instruct the Trainee about What to do and How to do it

- *Step 1. Instruct the trainee about what to do and how to do it.* For example, the trainer describes step by step how to cancel a reservation through lecture, written materials, pictures, video, and performing this task on the PMS. Avoid training programs which rely too heavily on the lecture method in communicating information. Information that is presented in an unprovocative and abstract way provides trainees with little insight as they tackle the nuances of the system. An effective training program uses a variety of tools including "hands-on techniques" to stimulate learning.

Directly Involve the Trainee in Performing the Task in a Simulated Environment

- *Step 2. Directly involve the trainee in performing the task in a simulated environment.* The trainee, under supervision, carries out the task using a "dummy" database (simulation). A training program that provides trainees with the opportunity to experiment with a "dummy" database, where realistic work situations are simulated, accelerates their progress and reduces "computer-phobia." Every PMS should include a permanent training option allowing trainees to make transactions without disturbing the "live" database.

Review the Information Presented in the Training Sessions and Test Trainees

- *Step 3. Review the information presented in the training sessions and test trainees.* To reinforce learning, give trainees plenty of practice time and hypothetical work assignments. Before performing actual work tasks utilizing the new system, trainees must have a good grasp of the system. Tests should be administered to pinpoint areas where further training is needed. Prepared employees will approach the PMS with more confidence and less anxiety.

Although a PMS vendor may offer a superior training package, an instructor plays a critical role in its success. Therefore, it is important to evaluate an instructor's qualifications. Competent instructors have training experience and possess extensive experience with both the computer and the software they are teaching. Furthermore, employees are more receptive to training sessions conducted in the morning in a pleasant environment where the student-to-teacher ratio is no more than four students per instructor, two people per computer, or 16 people per seminar (8).

The final phase of training occurs after the system has been fully installed and is operational. A trainer will assist the user, if needed, while performing actual work tasks utilizing the new system. This step takes on added importance when it involves guest contact positions. The presence of the trainer to gently remind front desk clerks how to check-in a guest prevents them from becoming frazzled during heavy business periods. Stressful situations may impair memory recall, causing an employee to self-destruct. Employees have been known to walk away in tears screaming that the system is incomprehensible.

The best insurance against this frightening possibility is a solid training program. Unfortunately, some people who do not understand the significance of training try to minimize this cost. A major hotel chain discontinued PMS test sites because the operations vice president was upset with the increase in labor costs due to training.

This short-sighted, frugal view of training has led corporate America into the doldrums. According to Tom Peters, the noted co-author of *In Search of Excellence and A Passion for Excellence*, a lack of training is the primary culprit in the demise of American corporate supremacy. Peters stated that the Japanese invest 350 percent more in the training of their employees (9).

Although employees may participate in a comprehensive training program when the computer is first installed, future employees will need training too. With the traditionally high turnover rate in the hospitality industry, a property could quickly find itself with an untrained work force. Furthermore, employees have been known to blackmail employers for higher wages because they alone could operate the system. Therefore, it is important to select systems with a short learning curve and an effective instructional system for new hires. Instructional systems commonly used include:

User-Manual

- **User-manual.** Training manuals and user-documentation should be laid out in a step-by-step fashion and customized to reflect the system that employees will be using. Instructional manuals are good indicators of how easy it will be to operate the system. However, most operations cannot solely rely on user-manuals for conveying information. It should be used in conjunction with other instructional methods. Steve Corum, Director of Strategic Business Development, AMTEC Information services, states it well (10):

"Paper. For all of its versatility and abundance, paper is a "dumb" medium for transmitting information. Paper doesn't know what's printed on it, it can't tell the reader if the desired information is on the page being looked at, and paper just sits there waiting to be manipulated by the reader. Paper just isn't an adequate medium for conveying information quickly and effectively."

On-The-Job Training

- **On-the-job Training.** Due to the high turnover rate in the hospitality industry, training is continuous and makes additional vendor training economically infeasible and in-house training laborious and tedious. Consequently, most training happens on-the-job, where information is handed down from one employee generation to another in an unstructured, ad hoc manner. This dilutes knowledge of the system over time, diminishing system utilization and acceptance.

Hospitality vendors have been exploring various ways to improve in-house training. The focus has been on computer-based training (CBT).

Computer-Based Training

- **Computer-based Training.** CBT allows the viewer to interact with the computer, reducing the need for personalized instruction and allowing each trainee to go at his or her own pace in a nonthreatening work environment. Thus, the computer becomes an on-demand learning device.

Early attempts at CBT were not particularly successful. CBT information was typically stored on multiple floppies or CDs due to storage limitations, which properties had a propensity to lose, damage, and misfile. Furthermore, CBT content was poor and presented in a manner inconsistent with sound learning principles. However, a few vendors are approaching the task with a deeper understanding and utilizing multimedia technologies to develop self-training systems which are enjoyable, "idiot proof," easy to use, and effective.

Web-Based Training

- **Web-based Training (WBT) or E-Learning**. Apple Computer began converting training courses to CD-ROM due to a shrinking budget. This approach was designed to accommodate needs of an accelerating number of employees throughout the world. The program was discontinued when it became too costly to keep current. Consequently, Apple Computer and other organizations explored the option of WBT, a type of CBT or multimedia training that is delivered over the Internet or over an Intranet.

WBT is accessed using a Web browser, such as Internet Explorer. According to Hall (11), training over the World Wide Web specifically refers to the readily available, interactive, multimedia nature of Web browsers and associated plug-ins. Web-based training can be delivered to any type of computer accessing the Internet or a company Intranet. These devices include personal computers used at work or at home as well as notebooks and laptops used on the road. In order to have training available to others, a Web server is required. A corporate department, vendor, or public Internet service provider (ISP) can maintain the server. WBT courses can be created using e-learning authoring systems such as Blackboard, Authorware, Quest, and ToolBook.

WBT is a breakthrough for the companies that have struggled with various training methods over the years because it can be delivered nationwide or worldwide 24 hours a day to a large audience (12). Lower training costs result from the reduction in time and of resources for delivery and the updating of online materials.

> *Computer-based instruction produces at least 30% more learning in 40% less time at 30% less cost, compared with traditional classroom teaching.*
>
> Lewis Perelman, Director of Project Learning 2001
> At the Hudson Institute in Alexandria, VA

Advancements in network and bandwidth capabilities enable the creation of WBT multimedia training applications. The advantages of MULTIMEDIA (presentation of information using audio, graphics, animation, text, video, etc.) self-training systems include (13):

- The ability to combine audiovisual elements into a presentation that captures the viewer's attention and is consistent with sound learning principles: Tell, Show, Do, Test, and Review.
- The reduction of personalized instruction because it effectively responds to individual learning styles. Training presentations can be viewed as many times as needed where the employee controls the pace of instruction.
- The quality of training never varies because new users are exposed to the same instructional presentation. Consequently, a computer system will experience a higher acceptance and utilization rate and enable all users to gain a good command of the system.

Looking for training tools to combat the deterioration of computer knowledge and acceptance that accompanies high employee turnover should be a high priority for all hospitality operators who have automated their properties. Choice Hotels International, for example, provides interactive multimedia WBT modules for the Choice Advantage PMS. Among users of this cloud-based solution, the company reports satisfaction ratings of about 90%.

Hardware Evaluation

The hardware component of the PMS has a pervasive impact on software performance. Failure to select the right type of computer and the appropriate hardware configuration can create system entropy. Hardware that is slow to respond to user requests, is difficult to operate, or frequently malfunctions hinders the ability of employees to get work done. To determine optimal hardware requirements, the following questions must be answered:

Which Comes First, Selection of Software or Hardware?

1. **Which should come first, selection of the software, hardware, or operating system?** A property owner bought hardware from an in-law and later discovered that no suitable software packages would operate on it. A restaurant company selected Linux, a free operating system similar to Unix, because the software license fees and the computing costs were lower than other operating systems. However, it took five years to find a suitable Linux point-of- sale solution, a key application in any restaurant operation. Therefore, the answer is first to select software (based on business requirements and needs) before choosing the hardware, operating system, and network platform.

What Type of Computer Should be Purchased?

2. **What type of computer system should be purchased?** An important factor in computer selection is the speed at which the system processes information. The speed in which tasks are carried out primarily depends on the number of users, the

size of the property (volume of transactions),the number of applications, and the type of hardware (refer to Chapter 2 for a discussion of factors affecting processing speed) and network (client/ server, workstations connected to remote server via Internet connection, etc). For example, if a LAN database server has an undersized CPU, the response time will be slow, resulting in bottlenecks where speed is essential in handling guests. It can also create a backlog of administrative work.

Typically, a database server is dedicated to the PMS because larger applications running on the same server may compromise overall system performance. Depending on the property size, multiple servers may be required. For example, A PMS with an Internet reservation module may require an additional server to manage concurrent reservations made directly by guests through the property Web site, which are then stored on the PMS database server. To find a system that satisfies a property's requirements, visit similar properties with the proposed computer system to observe response time at the front desk, in reservations, and in accounting.

A computer must provide adequate storage capacity. Early microcomputer systems would only allow the storage of 20 million bytes of information. Most of the storage space would be monopolized by one or two software applications. Foreseeable space shortages would trigger frequent visual warnings commanding the deletion of outdated information to prevent the "freezing up of the system." Unfortunately, this old, useless data was often guest history information which, if kept, could have been profitably used in marketing and sales applications. It is important to select hardware which allows for growth in use and new applications.

Strategic questions must be answered: "Can the system be expanded?" Is the technology upgradeable? New demands on the system may create the need for more storage space (e.g., catering program); the need to interface with other devices (e.g., energy management program); the need to handle more users (e.g., property plans to add 200 more rooms); the need to enhance guest services (e.g., self-checkout); the need to improve guest security (e.g., electronic locking system); the need to increase room revenue (e.g., revenue management); the need to reduce late food and beverage charges (e.g., POS interface). A well-designed system will allow for the existing hardware to be modified or expanded to accommodate more processing capabilities, greater data storage, and more operations.

What Should the Hardware Configuration Be?

3. **What should the hardware configuration be?** The design of the computer system should be based on the physical layout of the property and the projected workloads. The heart of the system, housed in a protected, isolated area, can support workstations strategically located throughout the property. Users interface with the system through these workstations, which are part of the communications network.

Vendors have the sales-driven tendency to recommend more equipment than is actually needed. To avoid paying for unused computer capacity, an operator must closely analyze each work area and identify the users and the amount of computer time each user needs. For guest contact positions, it is important to provide the capability (measured in workstations) to accommodate peak business periods. Equipment costs can be saved through sharing resources. Workstations can be used by different users. Printers can be set up to support more than one workstation. For example, although a printer can be conveniently located between two front desk workstations, a vendor may argue that trying to be frugal may backfire, adversely affecting the operation. A cost-effective approach to this scenario would be to install the necessary communication cables and equipment allowing for a future workstation, if needed, to be quickly brought on-line.

The vendor must conduct a site inspection to accurately assess the equipment needs and architectural considerations. The technician must map out a strategy for installing communication and electrical cables and wired and wireless communication equipment. Areas, such as the front desk, may have to be redesigned to accommodate computer equipment. Poor site preparation can lead to grave problems. Failure to conduct electrical testing can result in the irreparable damage of computer equipment. Communication cables, haphazardly installed, can repeatedly cause system crashes. A conscientious vendor has a pre-installation checklist covering these factors.

Human/Computer Interface

> *In the past, PMS vendors paid little attention to the human/computer interface and were more concerned with hardware reliability and functionality. War stories were circulated about unsuccessful installations where equipment constantly malfunctioned or critical information was destroyed. But today there are many good systems which have been subjected to rigorous industrial use. In the next decade, product differentiation will focus on the human element. It has been widely recognized that the ease and effectiveness of human interaction with computers depends on how well the interface reflects human needs.*
>
> Galen Collins

Does the Vendor Understand Hardware Ergonomics?

4. **Does the vendor understand hardware Ergonomics**? A well designed facility is essential in an environment where people and computers work together. Poor lighting, glare, noisy printers, cramped work space, heat and ventilation problems are all factors that can hinder the quality of the work environment. An experienced vendor understands how to adapt the equipment and environments to human skills and physiological requirements (14).

Reducing Eye Fatigue

- *Reducing Eye Fatigue.* Many users complain about eye strain. A contributing factor is glare from incident light sources such as over head lights, white walls, and sunlight. To reduce glare, position the monitor to minimize incident light reflections and select a tiltable, nonglare monitor. Indirect lighting should not exceed 300 lux for back ground lighting. The legibility of screen characters also has an impact on eye comfort. Select a high resolution monitor where characters are legible at a viewing distance of 28 inches. Frequently referenced written materials should be located at the same distance with a clip-type holder. Constantly viewing objects at difference distances can tire the eyes by forcing them to continuously refocus.

Avoiding Unnatural Body Positions

- Avoiding Unnatural Body Positions. Physical stress can be the result of awkward body positions due to the design and placement of equipment and furniture. A comfortable workstation will prevent muscle tension and restricted blood flow, making for a better work environment.

Select detachable, adjustable keyboards where the table height places it in a natural position for the user's hands. It should have a maximum pitch of 11 degrees to minimize the fatigue that often occurs when hands are constantly elevated.

Select an adjustable monitor to alleviate neck fatigue and place it at a height which allows the screen to be viewed 10 to 20 degrees below the user's line of vision.

Purchase chairs that provide adequate back support and distribute weight through the buttocks, not the thighs. The seat length and width should accommodate tall, short, and heavyset people. The ideal chair can be adjusted for seat height, back height, and back inclination. It is important that an operator's feet touch the floor since this relieves back stress. If this is not accomplished through chair adjustment, install a foot rest. For workstations that require standing, the keyboard and monitor should be placed at a height that prevents users from stooping over and assuming unnatural body positions.

Creating a Productive Work Environment

- Creating a Productive Work Environment. There is no harsh noise in a pleasant work environment. It is maintained at a comfortable temperature and humidity level and it has an efficient work layout.

Equipment noise annoys and distracts employees when it exceeds a sound level of 40 decibels. Printers, keyboard beeps, and disk drives are the primary sources of workstation cacophony. To reduce noise, isolate equipment when possible and use acoustical hoods and sound-absorbent materials. Choose software programs that intelligently use sound without high-pitched, intermittent beeps. Disruptive noise should be replaced with pleasant background music, which has a positive impact on a worker's psyche.

Computer equipment gives off heat and may affect the surrounding air temperature and humidity level. In order to maintain a healthy, attentive staff as well as an environment free of static electricity, keep the temperature and relative humidity at the appropriate level. Controlling atmospheric conditions may require air conditioning, a higher ventilation rate, or humidifying equipment.

The design of a computer workstation should allow users to complete tasks with a minimum number of movements. A front desk workstation should have frequently used equipment and supplies, such as the folio printer and registration cards, located within an arm's length of the computer operator. Movements going beyond this parameter disrupt the work flow, creating additional work and reducing guest contact time. However, this requires adequate work surface and shelving space and may require architectural modifications (15).

Top 10 Mistakes to Avoid When Selecting Computer Systems

Mistake #1: Not using a structured process.
Mistake #2: Not defining needs beforehand.
Mistake #3: Hiring a consultant with bias.
Mistake #4: Paying too much attention to bells and whistles.
Mistake #5: Not including key users in selection process.
Mistake #6: Buying more than you need.
Mistake #7: Allowing vendors to drive the process.
Mistake #8: Allowing the "powers that be" to choose the system.
Mistake #9: Confusing the salesperson with the product.
Mistake #10: Not using an RFP process.

It Selection Strategies, June 2001

Systems Selection

Cost should not be the first consideration. This may prejudice the selection process. Instead, PMS systems should be rated on hardware and software performance, customer support, vendor reputation, and training and installation, followed by a determination of the cost of hardware, software, a software license, training and installation, a yearly support contract, and annual operating supplies. The final step is to compare cost to performance to determine the best value. Following these steps helps keep a perspective on the investment.

In business, you don't get what you deserve, you get what you negotiate.

Dr. Chester L. Karrass, Management Consultant

Closely scrutinize the vendor's standard form contract before signing it. An attorney should review the contract to protect the property's interests. Changes may be negotiated. Important questions to ask, according to Thomas Semdinghoff, JD, and James Stoller, JD, include (16):

- Does the vendor's contract satisfy your requirements, guarantee the results you want, and accept the responsibility for failure to perform?
- What is the legal effect of the various clauses commonly found in computer contracts?
- Who is responsible if a system fails to work properly?
- Does the contract provide for an acceptance test, the successful completion of which is a condition of payment of the final portion of the purchase price?

Refer to Figure 11-7 for a listing of common contract terms and conditions.

There is nothing permanent except change.

HERACLITUS (540–475 B.C.)

System Use—Explains that no other hotel can use the system.
System delivery date—Explains that the vendor is responsible for equipment until delivery to property.
Training—Identifies the cost of any additional training.
Travel Expenses—Specifies who is responsible for paying for travel, meal and lodging expenses incurred by the vendor's training and installation staff.
Software Enhancements and Updates—Specifies the charges for program enhancements and updates and the user's obligation to use program enhacements and updates.
Maintenance—Defines who is responsible for hardware and software support, what it includes, and payment terms.
Warranty—Defines contract guarantees.
Customer Obligations—Defines customer's responsibilties such as ensuring the integrity of data being input into the system.
System Prices—Defines the price of hardware, software and license, training, and the number of days the quoted prices are valid.
Termination—Defines the events that will allow either party to terminate the agreement and what the customer's obligations are if a termination should result.
Software Modification—Defines cost, completion date, and the vendor's responsibility to correct software errors due to its implementation.
Implementation Delays—Defines events that are beyond the vendor's control such as acts of God.
Force Majeure—Nonperformance of a contract due to acts of God relieves either party of contract obligations.
Hiring of Vendor Personnel—Defines compensation due to the vendor if the customer hires vendor personnel.

FIGURE 11-7. COMMON CONTRACT TERMS.

System Implementation

Implementation is a stressful event that requires a detailed plan and a well-coordinated effort between the vendor and property person nel for a successful conversion. An implementation plan will specify the dates for carrying out the following activities: hardware delivery and installation, building and loading of the database, site preparation, employee training, ordering of supplies, and system conversion.

Implementation Steps

Step 1. Contract signed. Conversion dates are usually established three to five months in advance. Interface vendors (e.g., call accounting) and employees are informed of installation date. An employee is selected to be the PMS coordinator to serve as a liaison between the property and vendor. An installation team may also be established.

Step 2. Order forms and supplies (e.g., computer paper, registration cards, folios, coupons, tickets, etc.) *two to three months* before installation.

Step 3. Prepare for hardware installation two to three months in advance. Confirm hardware delivery dates. Schedule the installation of communication cables, electrical lines, and fire equipment (e.g., smoke/heat detectors and halon fire extinguishers). Establish dates for completing construction activities (e.g., redesigning front desk) and installing the necessary communication lines (Internet connection, telephone line) for customer support activities.

Step 4. Hotel personnel provides vendor with the necessary information to build the database (e.g., room rates, codes, features, rates, descriptions, reports) *one to two months* prior to installation. Staff training at the vendor's headquarters may also be conducted during this time period.

Step 5. Verify conversion date and make final arrangements for equipment installation *one month* in advance.

Step 6. Two to four weeks before the installation date:

- Equipment arrives. Compare shipment to contract specifications.
- Forms and supplies are received. Check accuracy of shipment.
- Set up training room. Make sure that this room is free of noise and has sufficient lighting, power, outlets, and work space for computer workstations. The room should have proper temperature control and be equipped with necessary teaching aides (e.g., video projector and screen).
- Install and test hardware and cables.

Step 7. Two weeks prior to installation, a training schedule should be completed identifying the courses of study required for each employee interacting with the system and the necessary training materials. Carol Lund, former vice president of technical support for EECO, recommends the following guidelines when scheduling (17):

- Schedule reservations personnel during the first few days, since they will begin entering the backlog of reservation data on the "live" system.
- Do not schedule personnel for more than four hours per day to avoid overloading.
- Schedule around employee shifts.
- Schedule by department whenever possible because this allows for the discussion of common procedures and applications.
- Schedule simulation training right before conversion.
- Have as many employees receive training as close to the conversion date as possible. Employees may forget the training material if there is a delay of more than two days between the end of training and the conversion date.
- Prepare a master training schedule to be distributed to each department. Management must establish a strict attendance policy.
- Periodic breaks should be scheduled. Management should also attend training sessions to answer questions about standard operating procedures.

Step 8. Week of installation training begins. A session should also be scheduled to prepare employees for what can be expected during the first three months after the new system is installed.

Step 9. After night audit is completed, guest folio and city ledger balances are transferred to new system. System goes "live." The next morning the new system generates folios.

Step 10. Vendor trainers monitor system and assist employees in using the system in a "live environment."

Step 11. Vendor representative counsels PMS coordinator on implementation problems until acceptance criteria are satisfied.

Conversion Strategies

Conversion Strategies. There are several conversion methods. The conversion method depends primarily on the application, perceived risks, and management's prerogative. The alternatives include:

Direct Cutover

1. **Direct cutover.** This involves the simultaneous discontinuation of the old system and start-up of the new one at a predetermined date.

This approach, which is commonly used for front office and POS conversions, causes problems if implementation planning was shoddy.

The primary advantages of this approach include:

- Minimizes transitional costs because the old system is no longer maintained after the new system is installed.

- Forces everybody to use the new system.
- Is the most convenient way to solve a problem or to bring new capabilities on-line.

Parallel Cutover

2. **Parallel cutover.** Both systems operate concurrently for a specified period of time. This approach, which is commonly used for accounting conversions, allows an operation to function smoothly if the new system experiences problems. However, it increases transitional costs where the results of each system are periodically compared.

For a parallel cutover approach to be successful, employees must shift their loyalties to the new system and use it.

A critical question that must be asked is, "To what extent should the operation be computerized?" The areas that usually receive initial consideration are the front and back office functions. Some operators purchase comprehensive systems, while others elect to computerize only a specific function such as reservations or inventory control. Each computer application must be cost justified. A dollar value must be assigned to the projected benefits and compared to the costs that would be incurred. This approach will result in smarter choices that provide a faster return on investment.

Some managers decide to implement a new system one function at a time. This is an effective strategy for implementing change, particularly in operations where there is strong resistance to new methods, procedures, and ways of processing information. One operation began with a simple application to show employees in a small way how the system can help. After confidence is built, the system can be expanded to other areas.

Insights from an Expert

Breaking the Spreadsheet Habit

Bill Scwhartz, CHTP
CEO, Systems Concepts, Inc.

Traditional food and beverage control, at least for the past 30 years, has been comprised of three elements:

1. Profit and Loss Statements
2. MBWA (Management By Walking Around)
3. Miscellaneous spreadsheets

The introduction of food and beverage management software makes the P&L Statement less critical, gives managers some specific things to look for while walking around, and typically replaces the spreadsheet component almost entirely.

Why is it, then, that spreadsheets appear to be a hard tool to replace for many in the foodservice industry? Today's F&B management systems produce most, if not all of the reports food service operators generate with spreadsheets. Perhaps managers and purchasers don't understand the capabilities available to them through these systems. Perhaps they feel these systems will take more of their time. Perhaps they simply fear change. Even worse, perhaps they are stealing, and fear they may be caught by the new system!

When it comes to inventory control, perhaps the most widely-used spreadsheet is the inventory form. Food and beverage systems replace these inventory spreadsheets with customized inventory forms and inventory extension reports. Inventory forms are automatically generated by the system in a wide variety of sorted orders and sequences. Forms can be produced alphabetically by location, in shelf order, or a combination of both. Additionally, hand-held mobile devices eliminate the forms altogether and allow operators to scan and instantly count items are they are encountered. Once counted, the data is already in the system, eliminating any need for further data entry.

Another popular type of spreadsheet is used for ordering. Sometimes the same form is used for receiving as well. Inventory systems have specific functions for forecasting orders, building shopping lists of all items required, and then automatically distributing those items to individual vendor purchase orders. In many cases, these purchase orders can be transmitted directly to the distributor to be filled. Specific receiving forms can be produced from the purchase orders, and invoices can be reconciled easily against the purchase orders and receiving forms. In addition, items can be printed in the same order as the distributor's invoices, as well as by group, or other convenient method.

Still more spreadsheets are used to build reports for accounting and management. In all cases, specific data must be placed on the forms in order to develop the report desired. Some operations use literally dozens of spreadsheets to collect data and produce the necessary reports. Because F&B management systems use a database approach to building reports and forms, data is never entered more than once or transferred from one place to another. Information is available on request, and multiple approaches to report sorting, summarization, date ranges, item selection and a variety of other reporting options are typical with these systems. This type of functionality would be unlikely in most spreadsheet applications.

So what keeps restaurant operators from simply chucking the spreadsheets and moving to a comprehensive, automated system? The answer varies from operator to operator, but the list of reasons is still small:

1. Familiarity with current approach – comfortable
2. Unfamiliarity with new approaches – uncomfortable
3. Unwilling to invest in new systems – too expensive
4. Unwilling to learn new systems – scary and time consuming
5. Invested significant time and effort in current system – pride
6. Unwilling to spend the time required to implement new system – no extra work
7. New system could point out problems – job security

Interestingly, these seven reasons for maintaining the status quo are typical of almost any new undertaking involving new systems and technologies. They can all be traced back to fear associated with lack of knowledge. Regardless of the reason for putting off a decision to change, continuing to use the existing spreadsheet approach as opposed to today's better, faster, stronger inventory control systems keep labor and food costs higher than they need to be. Unfortunately, they don't have rehab programs for breaking the spreadsheet habit. Perhaps working together in groups to get the answers and calm the fear would work. After all, when rehab is unavailable, group therapy can be a good alternative!

Tech news

Integrated or Best-of-Breed Systems: Maybe we should be asking different questions when choosing systems

JON INGE

The argument over whether integrated hospitality management systems are superior to a combination of best-of-breed alternatives has been going on for years. It used to be argued that integrated systems lacked functionality compared to more specialized offerings, and weren't as complete as their proponents would have you believe. On the other hand, despite the best-of-breed systems' often-superior functionality the lack of decent links between them has often led to cumbersome operations based on inaccurate and incomplete data. Things have changed on both fronts, but real-world situations often demand compromises, and three other questions are actually becoming more important.

INTEGRATED SYSTEMS

It's no secret that I'm generally in favor of minimizing the number of different systems that hotels have to deal with on property. Any time that data has to be transferred from one to another there's some potential for inaccuracy, given that the two systems' designers may not have meant quite the same thing by data elements with the same name. Further, despite the interface flexibility provided by HTNG and other Web-services approaches, staff needing to use multiple systems also have to deal with multiple user interfaces, often with very different look and feel characteristics. They often also have to research guest data in multiple systems to see the full picture.

An all-in-one integrated system that provides the right level of functionality across the board for a property's needs therefore has two major advantages. The users will see it as a seamless, uniform tool for all of their needs and will have confidence in the completeness of the data they see, leading to better guest service. Further, management will have access, in real time, to accurate data from all parts of the operation in a single database, with all that this implies in terms of effective marketing and efficient management.

The fully integrated single-vendor system is no longer a myth. Several applications that integrate multiple traditionally separate areas (typically guest management, sales & catering, room reservations and activity bookings, sometimes also POS) have been around for many years but have always been partial solutions. However, there are now some that also include financial accounting, labor management and payroll to tie all these inputs into a complete hospitality ERP system providing real-time business intelligence.? These include Cenium and IDS NEXT and Prologic First. Both IDS NEXT and Prologic First were developed in India and both have a sizable customer bases in Asia, Europe and Africa. Cenium was developed in Iceland and Norway and is now gaining steady acceptance in the United States and international markets.

Best-of-Breed Systems

On the other hand, best of breed systems have continued to expand specialized functionalities and integrations between them has improved tremendously. Some of this has been through efforts such as HTNG's interface workgroups, which promote very clear understandings of which data elements mean what, and which are exchanged under well-described circumstances. The single guest itinerary is probably the best-known example, whereby spa, golf and other activity bookings are linked to a guest's room reservation, so that each system is made aware of changes in the others' bookings and all the details are collected into a single itinerary attached to the guest stay record. However, bookings in each system are still done using each application's user interface.

New specialized systems have achieved good success in recent years, especially when remotely hosted so that they can be configured and put into productive use very quickly. MTech's HotSOS and Libra On Demand's CRM suite are good examples that combine very useful functionality with ease of implementation. However, while both help their immediate users become much more effective in their own sphere of operations, both also require tight integration with GMSs if their accumulated guest profile and history data is to be put to best use as part of the complete picture.

The Real World Interferes

It's been said that to optimize the whole you must sub-optimize the parts. The whole in this case is the complete operational scenari the user experience, the consolidated data used by management to maximize the effectiveness of its operations and marketing, and the ability to keep it all running with minimal effort. Given that, choosing the best possible point solution for a single department will always introduce compromises somewhere else, and in an ideal world each property would implement a complete, fully functional ERP from a single vendor: one user interface, one database, one support number to call.

But the real world always interferes. For an existing property, replacing all of its systems in one massive upgrade takes a great deal of courage, project management and change management skill. Implementing one module at a time is usually far easier to get approved and financed, and so an integrated system stands a better chance of being sold if it can also operate in modular form. However, this always carries the need to develop new (and temporary) ways of data transfer between the old and new components until the transformation is complete, and inevitably adds many support complications and user challenges. It takes great leadership to keep such a project moving steadily to a successful, fully-integrated completion.

Even when a new property implements a complete ERP system from the start, things never stay the same. The hotel may be sold later to a new owner with several other properties all using a standard but different accounting or procurement system. For the sake of optimizing the new whole – the multi-property operation – the ERP modules may have to be replaced with the new owner's standard applications. As a result, in the real world even the most capable ERP system must be modular and must be capable of working effectively with other vendors' systems, and of course then we're back in the multi-vendor, multi-system world.

Instead of making a utopian choice between integrated systems and best-of-breed combinations, perhaps we should be asking:

1. Given the functionality needed, which system or combination of systems provides the most seamless user interface, the most complete data consolidation and the most usable business intelligence?
2. Which allows for the later addition or substitution of components in the most seamless way, both to the users and to the operation?
3. Which vendor will take first-line support responsibility for my complete set of technology, now and as the mix of systems may change in the future?

Some vendors already offer first-line support of other applications used by their clients. Multi-Systems Inc. (MSI) provides a complete IT help desk for La Quinta and Extended Stay America, covering hardware and network issues as well as managing the resolution of problems with other vendors' software. It will also be interesting to see how the current move toward service-oriented architecture (SOA) plays out with vendors such as Infor Hospitality (formerly SoftBrands) and PAR Springer-Miller. SOA makes it easier to plug multiple vendors' products or modules into a core system, but will they also be incorporated into the core system's UI? Will support for all of them be centralized?

Playing well with others has never been more necessary, but hoteliers are still looking for the most seamless solution available.

Cloud Helps Porter Apple to Avoid Capital Outlay

LeAnn Robbins, Controller, Porter Apple Company

Already four upgrades behind in its accounting software, and with server speeds so slow that "you could read a novel" between transactions, Porter Apple Company found itself in a dilemma – make a significant investment in hardware and software or continue to try to compensate using human resources and manual processes. That's when the company found a better alternative in the cloud.

The Sioux Falls, S.D.-based company owns nine Applebee's restaurants and operates three Carino's and a Chevys. Continued growth in business and ongoing upgrades in its DacEasy accounting software had put the company in a position where it could no longer move forward in the adoption of new technology without the purchase of a new server, along with the need to find a reliable IT person to install, maintain and manage it – which came with its own set of costs.

The Answer in the Cloud

Fortunately, one of the company's existing software providers, Decision Logic, had developed a Managed Private Cloud Solution in response to a similar need among many of its restaurant clients to lower the cost of technology. By moving to the cloud, restaurant groups can take advantage of the efficiencies, enhanced performance, automated back-up and scalability of the virtual environment, in a managed setting that ensured security of their data and applications for a manageable monthly fee.

Decision Logic is more widely known for its enterprise level Web-based back office solution that delivers in-depth reporting on sales, costs, and menu mix trends for multi-unit and multi concept restaurant operations. However, the Managed Private Cloud can be used to host any business applications clients use –even third-party providers.

The move to the Decision Logic Managed Cloud began with the accounting system, with took just days to implement. Personnel from Decision Logic led Porter Apple through the entire process. This included contacting the software tech from other software providers and walking through the upload together over the phone. In fact, from the first conversation to implementation, the process took less than two weeks.

Saving Time and Money

Today, Porter Apple Company is experiencing greater efficiency in its operations with dramatically faster speeds that eliminate wait times. The company's small administrative staff is able to be more efficient now that the software runs more quickly.

Cost savings were also significant. Instead of a huge capital investment, the company pays a monthly fee that covers storage, backup and software. Software is upgraded automatically, without incremental expense. And unlimited scalability allows memory and storage to be added as needed.

Work is underway to migrate the full line of business for the Applebee's stores to the Decision Logic Managed Private Cloud Solution to take advantage of the IPSec configuration. The move will increase the security of customer credit data and keep Porter Apple PCI compliant. The benefits extend to the store level, where it will help lock-down the computers and prevent viruses.

References

1. Hall, George, *Strategy, Systems, and Integration*, Blue Ridge Summit, PA: Tab Books, 1991, pp. 230–231.
2. Penzias, Arno, *Ideas and Information*, New York, NY: Touchstone, 1990, p. 167.
3. Berry, Leonard, *On Great Service: A Framework for Action,* New York, NY: The Free Press, 1995, pp. 155–165.
4. Meyer, D.L., "New and Innovative Ways of Developing and Maintaining Customer Relationships." *Restaurant Startup and Growth*, 2010, pp. 26–31.
5. Kohlmayr, Klaus, "Why Investing in Hospitality Technology is Investing in Good Business." *Hotel Business Review.* Retrieved 2013-01-02, from hotelexecutive.com/business_review/2161/test-february-why-investing-in-hospitality-technology-is-investing-in-good-business.
6. Collins, Galen, "Evaluating and Selecting a Property Management System," *FIU Hospitality Review*, Fall 1988, pp. 64–82. (Most of this chapter is based on the contents of this article.)
7. Zemke, Ron, and Albrecht, Karl, *Service America!* Homewood, IL: Dow Jones-Irwin, 1985, p. 39.
8. Umbaugh, Robert, *The Handbook of MIS Management*, New Jersey: Auerbach, 1985, pp. 257–270.
9. CNN, testimony given before a congressional committee on the state of American Corporations. Tom Peters, November 1987.
10. Umbaugh, *op. cit.*, pp. 257–270.
11. all, Brandon, *Web-based Training Cookbook*. New York, NY: John Wiley & Sons, Inc., 1997, pp. 103–104.
12. Whalen, Tammy and Wright, David, *The Business Case for Web-based Training*, Boston, MA: Artech House, 2000, p. 28.
13. Gantz, John, "Web-based training can help IT organizations," *Computerworld,* March 21, 1997, p. 37.
14. Seidman, Arthur, and Flores, Ivan, eds, *The Handbook of Computers and Computing*, New York, NY: Van Nostrand Reinhold Company, Inc., 1979, pp. 782–783.
15. Kazarian, Edward, *Work Analysis and Design for Hotels, Restaurants, and Institutions*, Westport, CT: AVI Publishing Company, Inc., 1979, pp. 79–83.
16. Smedinghoff, Thomas, and Stoller, James, "Some Thoughts on Negotiating a Computer Contract," *IAHA: Bottomline*, August 1987, pp. 12–14.
17. Merrick, Bill, *Property Management Systems: A Guide to Implementation and Staff Training*, Madison, WI: Magna Publications, 1989, p. 47.

Index

Note: Page numbers followed by f, or t indicate material in figures, or tables, respectively.

D

E

N

O

P

Q

R

S

CPSIA information can be obtained at www.ICGtesting.com
Printed in the USA
LVOW02s0711260815

R9940600001B/R99406PG450951LVX7B/1/P